From Sodomy Laws to Same-Sex Marriage

Also available from Bloomsbury

Published:
Russian Homophobia from Stalin to Sochi, Dan Healey
Fighting Proud: The Untold Story of the Gay Men Who Served in Two World Wars, Stephen Bourne
Controlling Sex in Captivity: POWs and Sexual Desire in the United States during the Second World War, Matthias Reiss

Forthcoming:
Writing Queer History, Matt Cook
The International LGBT Rights Movement: A History, Laura A. Belmonte

From Sodomy Laws to Same-Sex Marriage

International Perspectives since 1789

Edited by
Sean Brady and
Mark Seymour

BLOOMSBURY ACADEMIC
LONDON • NEW YORK • OXFORD • NEW DELHI • SYDNEY

BLOOMSBURY ACADEMIC
Bloomsbury Publishing Plc
50 Bedford Square, London, WC1B 3DP, UK
1385 Broadway, New York, NY 10018, USA
29 Earlsfort Terrace, Dublin 2, Ireland

BLOOMSBURY, BLOOMSBURY ACADEMIC and the Diana
logo are trademarks of Bloomsbury Publishing Plc

First published in Great Britain 2019
Reprinted 2019 (twice)
This paperback edition published in 2021

Copyright © Sean Brady and Mark Seymour, 2019

Sean Brady and Mark Seymour have asserted their right under the Copyright,
Designs and Patents Act, 1988, to be identified as Editors of this work.

For legal purposes the Acknowledgments on p. viii and p. 80 constitute
an extension of this copyright page.

Cover image: *Medallion (YouWe)*, 1936 (oil on canvas), Gluck, (Hannah Gluckstein)
(1895–1978). Private Collection. (© Christie's Images / Bridgeman Images)

All rights reserved. No part of this publication may be reproduced or transmitted
in any form or by any means, electronic or mechanical, including photocopying,
recording, or any information storage or retrieval system, without prior
permission in writing from the publishers.

Bloomsbury Publishing Plc does not have any control over, or responsibility for,
any third-party websites referred to or in this book. All internet addresses given
in this book were correct at the time of going to press. The author and publisher
regret any inconvenience caused if addresses have changed or sites have ceased
to exist, but can accept no responsibility for any such changes.

A catalogue record for this book is available from the British Library.

A catalog record for this book is available from the Library of Congress.

ISBN: HB: 978-1-3500-2392-5
       PB: 978-1-3501-9611-7
       ePDF: 978-1-3500-2390-1
       eBook: 978-1-3500-2391-8

Typeset by Integra Software Services Pvt. Ltd.

To find out more about our authors and books visit www.bloomsbury.com
and sign up for our newsletters.

Contents

List of Figures vii
Acknowledgments viii
Notes on Contributors ix
Foreword xii

1 From Sodomy Laws to Same-Sex Marriage: Historical Transformations *Sean Brady and Mark Seymour* 1
2 Same-Sex Sexual Relations and the French Revolution: The Decriminalization of Sodomy in 1791 *Bryant T. Ragan, Jr.* 15
3 Arguing against Intolerance: Louisiana and Britain in the Early Nineteenth Century *Charles Upchurch* 31
4 Regarding Pratt and Smith, the Last Couple of Sodomites to be Hanged in Britain *Dominic Janes* 43
5 Defining "Unnatural Crime": Sex and the English Convict System, 1850–1900 *Ben Bethell* 57
6 "It Is My Husband Who Has Such Weaknesses": A Mid-Nineteenth-Century Peruvian Divorce Case *Magally Alegre Henderson* 71
7 Flappers and Felons: Rethinking the Criminal Law and Homosex in Interwar Australia, 1920–1939 *Yorick Smaal and Mark Finnane* 83
8 Spain from Franco's Repressive Regime to Same-Sex Marriage *Geoffroy Huard* 95
9 Affecting Legal Change: Law and Same-Sex Feelings in West Germany since the 1950s *Benno Gammerl* 109
10 The Sexual (Geo)Politics of Loyalty: Homosexuality and Emotion in Cold War Security Policy *Kate Davison* 123
11 Homosexual Politics in the British World: Toward a Transnational Understanding *Graham Willett* 141
12 Gender and the Politics of Marriage in Postwar Australia and Britain *Rebecca Jennings* 155
13 From Giarre to Civil Unions: The "Long March" for Same-Sex Relationships in Italy *Yuri Guaiana and Mark Seymour* 167

14 "It's Poppycock to Say Homosexuals Can Be Excused": Rethinking the Gay and Lesbian Movement in the Republic of Ireland, 1970s–1990s *Patrick McDonagh* 183

15 " ... Do You Want More?": A Brief History of Same-Sex Partnerships, Family Formations, and Marriage in Twentieth-Century United States *Marcia M. Gallo* 201

16 Gay Marriage in England: After the Party *Daniel Monk* 213

17 Same-Sex Unions: In Retrospect and Prospect *Robert Aldrich* 227

Index 237

List of Figures

4.1 *The Arse Bishop Josilin g a Soldier—or—Do as I Say Not as I Do*, published by H. Fores, July 1822, 24.8 x 33.9 cm, Courtesy of the Trustees of the British Museum, London © (1868,0808.8554)   44

4.2 *Confirmation or the Bishop and the Soldier*, frontispiece, J. L. Marks, *A Correct Account of the Horrible Occurrence which Took Place at a Public-House in St. James's Market* (London: J. L. Marks, 1822), hand-colored etching, © The British Library Board (cup.363.gg.31, image C13670-78)   45

4.3 Detail, wood engraving, from *Particulars of the Execution of James Pratt and John Smith* (London: Thomas Birt, 1835), Harvard Law School Library, http://nrs.harvard.edu/urn-3:HLS.Libr:1087981   49

4.4 George Cruikshank, *Fagin in the Condemned Cell*, published in Charles Dickens, *Oliver Twist, or the Parish Boy's Progress* (London: Richard Bentley, 1838), volume 3, after p. 296   53

4.5 George Cruikshank, detail of sketch for *Fagin in the Condemned Cell*, pencil, pen and ink (1830s), Courtesy of the Victoria and Albert Museum, London © (9995J)   54

Acknowledgments

The editors wish to acknowledge the Birkbeck Institute for the Humanities, the Department of History, Classics and Archaeology at Birkbeck College, University of London, and the University of Otago for funding, and Birkbeck College, University of London, for providing space for the conference on which this volume is based. We thank Dr. Mark Stocker, Curator Historical International Art, Te Papa Museum of New Zealand, for suggesting the cover image, and the Gluck Estate for generous permission to reproduce Gluck's 1937 painting, *Medallion*, on the cover.

Notes on Contributors

Robert Aldrich is Professor of European History at the University of Sydney. A prolific author across a wide range of themes, his books on homosexuality include *Cultural Encounters and Homoeroticism in Sri Lanka* (Routledge, 2014), *Gay Life Stories* (Thames and Hudson, 2012), *Colonialism and Homosexuality* (Routledge, 2003), and *The Seduction of the Mediterranean* (Routledge, 1993).

Sean Brady is Lecturer in History at Birkbeck, University of London, with research interests in Irish and British masculinity and sexuality. His monograph, *Masculinity and Male Homosexuality in Britain, 1861–1913*, was published in 2005 by Palgrave (paperback 2009). He has coedited *Ireland and Masculinities in History* (Palgrave, 2019), *The Palgrave Handbook of Masculinity and Political Culture in Europe* (2018), *John Addington Symonds and Homosexuality* (Palgrave, 2012), and *What Is Masculinity? Historical Dynamics from Antiquity to the Contemporary World* (Palgrave, 2011).

Ben Bethell recently submitted his PhD on the "star class," "contamination," and classification in English convict prisons before 1930, at Birkbeck, University of London.

Kate Davison is a PhD candidate in History at the University of Melbourne. Her research is on constructions of the homosexual during the Cold War.

Mark Finnane is Professor of History at Griffith University, where he directs the Prosecution Project, a historical database of criminal prosecutions in Australian higher courts in the nineteenth and twentieth centuries. He has published widely on the history of criminal justice, policing, punishment, and criminal law in both Australia and Ireland.

Benno Gammerl is Lecturer in History at Goldsmiths, University of London. He is researching the interplay between migratory dynamics and sexual attitudes and practices in Europe from the late nineteenth century and he published *Subjects, Citizens and Others: Administering Ethnic Heterogeneity in the British and Habsburg Empires, 1867–1918*, with Berghahn in 2018.

Marcia Gallo is Associate Professor of History at the University of Nevada, Las Vegas. Her research lies in the areas of feminism, progressive queer politics, and oral history methodology, and she has written two monographs: *Different Daughters: A History of the Daughters of Bilitis and the Rise of the Lesbian Rights Movements* (Carroll & Graf, 2006) and *"No One Helped": Kitty Genovese, New York City, and the Myth of Urban Apathy* (Cornell, 2015).

Yuri Guaiana is on the executive board of ILGA-Europe and holds a PhD in contemporary history from the University of Milan. An activist as well as a scholar, he has published a range of essays and articles, as well as an edited collection titled *Dal cuore delle coppie al cuore del diritto* (Viterbo: Stampa Alternativa, 2011).

Magally Allegre Henderson holds a PhD in Latin American History from the State University of New York at Stony Brook. She teaches at the Pontifical Catholic University of Peru, where she also holds an administrative appointment as Officer for Research Advancement and Gender Equality.

Geoffroy Huard has a PhD in contemporary Spanish History from the University of Cádiz in *cotutelle* with the University of Amiens. He is a lecturer in history at the Université de Cergy-Pontoise, where he researches the repression of homosexuality under Franco. He is the author of *Los antisociales. Historia de la homosexualidad en Barcelona y París, 1945–1975* (Marcial Pons, 2014) and *Les gays sous le franquisme. Discours, subcultures et revendications à Barcelone, 1939–1977* (Orbis Tertius, 2016).

Dominic Janes is Professor of History at the University of Keele. His research field is visual culture, with particular interest in histories of gender, sexuality, and religion. Recent book publications include *Oscar Wilde Prefigured: Queer Fashioning and British Caricature, 1750–1900* (Chicago, 2016), *Picturing the Closet: Male Secrecy and Homosexual Visibility in Britain* (Oxford, 2015), and *Visions of Queer Martyrdom from John Henry Newman to Derek Jarman* (Chicago, 2015).

Rebecca Jennings is Lecturer in History at University College London, which she joined in 2018 after a research fellowship at Macquarie University, Sydney. Her research focuses on twentieth-century British and Australian lesbian history, and she is the author of *Tomboys and Bachelor Girls: A Lesbian History of Post-War Britain* (2007); *A Lesbian History of Britain: Love and Sex between Women since 1500* (2007); and *Unnamed Desires: A Sydney Lesbian History* (2015).

The Hon. Michael Kirby AC CMG was Justice of the High Court of Australia (1996–2009); President of the International Commission of Jurists (1995–8); Chair of the United Nations Commission of Inquiry on the Democratic People's Republic of Korea (2013–14); and is Co-Chair of the International Bar Association's Human Rights Institute (2018–). Kirby lives in Sydney with his partner Johan van Vloten, whom he married in February 2019, on the fiftieth anniversary of their first meeting.

Patrick McDonagh submitted his PhD thesis exploring the history of gay and lesbian activism in the Republic of Ireland, 1973–1993, to the European University Institute in late 2018.

Daniel Monk is Professor of Law at Birkbeck, University of London, where his research explores a wide range of issues relating to families, children, education, and sexuality. As well as a wide range of articles and chapters, he cowrote *The Family, Law and Society* (6th edition, Oxford, 2008) and coedited *From Civil Partnership to Same-Sex Marriage, 2004–2014* (Routledge, 2015).

Bryant ("Tip") Ragan is Professor of History at Colorado College, where he teaches the history of Europe from the Renaissance to the French Revolution. He has coedited *Homosexuality in Early Modern France: A Documentary Collection* (Oxford, 2001) and *Homosexuality in Modern France* (Oxford, 1996).

Mark Seymour is Associate Professor of History at the University of Otago, New Zealand. A historian of modern Italy, he has published *Debating Divorce in Italy* (Palgrave, 2006), and coedited *Politica ed emozioni* (2012), on the relationship between politics and emotions in Italy, as well as a range of scholarly articles and chapters. He is coeditor of the journal *Modern Italy*.

Yorick Smaal is Senior Lecturer in History at Griffith University. He is author of *Sex, Soldiers and the South Pacific, 1939–45* (Palgrave, 2015), and has published on the entwined histories of sexualities, intimate lives and institutions, criminal prosecutions and ordinary lives, and the relationship between genders, war, and identities.

Charles Upchurch is Associate Professor of History at Florida State University. His main research interest is nineteenth-century British gender and social history, and his monograph, *Before Wilde: Sex between Men in Britain's Age of Reform*, was published by California University Press in 2009.

Graham Willett is an honorary fellow in the School of Historical and Philosophical Studies, University of Melbourne. He researches Australian and international gay and lesbian studies, with a particular focus on the homosexual politics of the "British world." He is the author of many articles and book chapters and coedited *Intimacy, Violence and Activism: Gay and Lesbian Perspectives on Australian History and Society* (Melbourne, 2013).

Foreword

The Hon. Michael Kirby AC CMG

Years ago, I served the cause of human rights in Cambodia.[1] The country was devastated by a genocide perpetrated by the Khmer Rouge. Whenever, in Australia, North America, and Europe, I would talk about my work and findings I would be confronted with a well-meaning question. Was I not trying to impose Western values on the Khmer people? Was the United Nations not pursuing the hopeless dream of the universality of human rights?

The same questions have recurred more recently following further work for the United Nations on human rights in the Democratic People's Republic of Korea (North Korea).[2] In lecture halls and in private conversation, questioners would tax me with the same doubts. Why not leave people from completely different historical and cultural traditions alone? If their traditions were autocratic, patriarchal, and oppressive to European ideas of justice and freedom, what was so wrong with the North Korean UN Ambassador's demand before the Human Rights Council: that the UN should "mind its own business"?

When talking with people about the cruelties of Cambodia and North Korea, I would sometimes present the same questions to the victims. They would look at me in astonishment. They would demand exactly the same human rights as were expected in my own country. They would state that they never had any doubt that what had happened to them was fundamentally wrong. They just did not have the power to do anything about it. But they could dream of a time, yet to come when their fundamental human rights would be respected and upheld. Arguments based on cultural relativism do not tend to go down well with the victims of injustice and oppression.

So it is with the SOGIE minorities in our world.[3] There is no land on Earth where LGBTIQ[4] minorities enjoy the exact same rights and freedoms, in law and social attitudes, as their heterosexual brothers and sisters. If they are not downtrodden by criminal laws, civil discrimination, religious hostility, and antagonistic schooling, the general attitudes in society are unfriendly. This is the burden that almost every minority has to face, simply because to the majority, they are the "other." They don't quite fit.

Because social and cultural attitudes preexist, explain, and reinforce legal and religious prescriptions, many of the books on LGBTIQ equality are written by and for theologians and lawyers. In recent years there has been a steady rise in the number of such works. Now, there is a virtual tidal wave of writing on the topic, especially by lawyers. I am familiar with such texts. I have contributed to more than a few of them.

However, this book is different. Although there may be a lawyer or two among the contributors, basically they are historians. While they derive their conclusions, findings, lessons, and prescriptions from their studies, their object is basically to record and interpret what has happened in human history so far as the SOGIE minority have been concerned. History is important in the case of this minority. Only by knowing and understanding history's developments can we perceive the commonalities and differences in the global treatment of sexual minorities. Only then can we understand the very large (but not unique) role that religion and the law have played, over the centuries, in oppressing this portion of humanity.

The wide-ranging character of this book can be seen in the introductory chapter written by the editors, Sean Brady and Mark Seymour. In effect, by their survey of the individual contributions they demonstrate the particular features of SOGIE injustice and oppression in many different countries. Reading that introduction, one can begin to understand the forces, deeper than sexuality, that have resulted in a kind of global uprising against oppression and inequality that has so marked the past fifty years.

Contemplating the collection of chapters in this book as a unity, one can perceive the interconnections with other global movements that have marked the past century of human history. The movement against patriarchy and for the equality of women. The movement against racism and colonialism. The movement to recognize and respect the outcast indigenous peoples on every continent. The movement for equality in the treatment of religious minorities and also unbelievers. The demand for equality and justice for the SOGIE minorities can be fully understood only in this broader historical setting.

Several chapters explain how, following France in 1791, a number of European states (and their colonies) threw off the criminal laws that targeted sexual minorities. Those laws originated in religious texts. They were enforced and supported by theological scholars. The special cruelty meted out to gay men under the laws of England mattered more because those laws were exported to the four corners of the Earth and every land where the Union Jack had ever flown. A number of chapters describe this particular oppression. It is continuing to the present time. In the Commonwealth of Nations, which is successor to the British Empire, thirty-five of the fifty-three member states still criminalize same-sex sexual activity today. While such criminal laws exist, the notion of marriage and relationship recognition is fanciful. The criminal law reinforces prejudice. It is an obstacle difficult to remove, especially because of its religious supporters. Where God has spoken, man's duty is simply to obey.

Several chapters review developments in the law and social attitudes in continental European countries. Most of them followed the French repeal of criminal prohibitions. But that did not stop social and cultural hostility emerging later, as the chapters on Germany, Spain, Italy, and elsewhere demonstrate.

When the book turns to the reforms in England, North America, and Australasia, history reveals the slow and often reluctant changes in the law, commonly lagging decades behind shifts in social attitudes. A study of the history recounted in these chapters does not, however, fully explain why so many countries moved ahead with repeal of criminal statutes and the enactment of same-sex marriage while other jurisdictions (like Ireland, parts of the United States and continental Australia) dawdled behind, limping.

Yet by the end of the book we can surely perceive the remarkable revolution in attitudes, judicial decisions, and parliamentary enactments that have come upon this field of human activity in Europe and in the countries of "white" settlement in what is little more than half a century. Truly, as the editors state in Chapter 1, the changes constitute "one of the most remarkable transformations of official attitudes in modern history." And not only in "official attitudes." Reliable opinion polls show strong and consistent changes and improvements in majority popular attitudes. Especially among educated people who are informed on the discoveries of science and the realities of our world.

At the end of their survey of the contents of this book, the editors offer a sobering conclusion. They state that there is "little sign that social or cultural acceptance, let alone positive legal change, are emerging in areas that are home to vast proportions of the global population, stretching from Africa up to Russia and across all of Asia." They ask a haunting question, not dissimilar to the one posed to me concerning my work on human rights in Cambodia and North Korea. Will the changes witnessed in Europe and its "white" colonies ever spread to the rest of the world? Or will those changes "yet turn out to be merely a high water mark of postwar liberal-democratic values"?

Some historical attitudes would certainly give a measure of support to this hesitancy to declare that the SOGIE revolution is over and that the angels have won.

The very reluctance of such a hard core of members of the Commonwealth of Nations to repeal and replace the hostile legal impediments shows how difficult it has been in many lands to gather legislative support to repeal the criminal oppression of LGBTIQ people, let alone to provide for marriage and other relationship recognition and broader equal rights. Enactment by the Russian Federation, followed by many of its old Soviet neighbors, of laws purportedly to defend "traditional values" and to silence their critics demonstrates the still existing widespread hostility. That hostility is not only visible in Russia and the Arab and Islamic countries. It is actually on the increase as reports of violence from Bangladesh to Iran and from Afghanistan to Egypt clearly show. Even Indonesia, a country traditionally tolerant of the SOGIE minorities, has lately witnessed unprecedented violence. This is although the Netherlands left them without criminal provisions with which to oppress the minority.

When the UN Human Rights Council created a mandate of the independent expert on SOGIE violence and discrimination, the rage and opposition in the Council and later in the General Assembly of the United Nations almost killed the mandate at birth.[5] By a whisker, it survived. But the hostility of so many countries was a shock to those who felt the battle was almost over.

Yet, just when these developments give rise to the pessimism and foreboding about the future hinted at by the editors in Chapter 1, wonderful developments occur and are celebrated. In increasing number, courts in many lands are standing up for the equal rights of LGBTIQ citizens under their national constitutional provisions. This has happened in Fiji, Belize, the Philippines, Hong Kong, and elsewhere. In the face of populist legislation, courts are upholding and insisting on marriage equality, as in Bermuda. In India, the Supreme Court has taken a second look at the colonial law that penalizes sexual minorities.[6] It has expressed itself critically about the reasoning of an earlier case[7] that had overturned a decision that had struck down that law.[8] It has insisted that the earlier judicial statements, hostile to gays, should be reconsidered by the Supreme Court. So indeed, it now has been.[9]

In argument in the follow-up to the earlier Indian decision, it was pointed out that the Irish Prime Minister, who is openly gay, was "partly Indian." When one of the judges acknowledged this fact stating that the Irish leader was a "Maharashtrian," the courtroom reportedly erupted in laughter. When people laugh at a foolish law, its future begins to look doubtful. And the Government of India itself disclaimed support for the colonial criminal law. It left the survival of s 377 IPC "to the wisdom of this honourable court"[10] and in September 2018, the Supreme Court of India administered the constitutional quietus to the application of s 377 IPC to the private, consensual, sexual acts of persons of the same sex.

It is true that much remains to be done to rid the world of the punitive criminal laws. And to let the sunshine in with full relationship recognition. However, there is nothing so powerful as an idea whose time has come. This book is a chronicle of one such idea that is now upon us.

When *Weibo* reverses its ban on gay websites; when Pope Francis asks, "Who am I to judge?" the sexual orientation of gay believers; and when brave Russians at the Winter Olympics and World Cup stand up for equality, the long-term future looks promising. Science supports an end to hostility and injustice. Rationality supports change. Familiarity with members of the minority supports change. Celebrities come out everywhere and support change. The internet is full of it. The writing is on the wall.

A reflection on the histories recounted in this book, and on the histories of other continents and regions yet to be told, shows that the times are changing. Past history is turning into contemporaneous actuality. The prospects are promising. Everywhere.

Michael Kirby

Sydney

September 14, 2018

Notes

1. As Special Representative of the Secretary-General of the United Nations for Human Rights in Cambodia (1993–6).
2. As chair of the United Nations Human Rights Council's Commission of Inquiry on Human Rights in the Democratic People's Republic of Korea (A/HRC/25/CRP.1) (February 7, 2014).
3. SOGIE is Sexual Orientation and Gender Identity and Expression.
4. LGBTIQ is Lesbian, Gay, Bisexual, Transgender, Intersex, and Queer.
5. M.D. Kirby, "A Close and Curious Vote Upholds the New UN Mandate on Sexual Orientation and Gender Identity" [2017] *European Human Rights Law Review* (EHRLR), 37.
6. The *Indian Penal Code* 1860, s 377.
7. *Naz Foundation v Government of NCT of Delhi* [2009] 4LRC 828 (2009) DLT 277. Overruled by *Koushal v Naz Foundation,* (2014) 1SCC 1; [2014] 2LRC 555.
8. *Puttaswamy v Union of India*, WP(C) 494/2002.
9. Section 377 case, http://www.livelaw.in/section-377-day-1-session-2-right-to-choose-a-partner (July 10, 2018).
10. *Johar and Ors v Union of India*, WP(CRL) 76/2016; *Keshav Suri v Union of India*, WP (CRL) 88/2018 4.

1

From Sodomy Laws to Same-Sex Marriage: Historical Transformations

Sean Brady and Mark Seymour

The idea that sexual acts between members of the same sex were "unnatural" goes back to Antiquity and by the Middle Ages had been formalized in the European world through Christian doctrine and canon law. It was absorbed into the laws of a number of modern European states, and exported legislatively to much of the world through colonial expansion. Looking back from 2019, the shift from severe punitive measures for sex "against nature" to the recent introduction of same-sex marriage laws in at least twenty-five nations across five continents must rank as one of the most remarkable transformations of official attitudes in modern history. It is a change that begs many broad questions. This volume presents fresh, historically informed, international perspectives on same-sex relationships as a phenomenon poised between "nature," religion, and state regulation, seeking to answer at least some of those questions.

Questions of "nature," or what is unnatural, have held a consistent place in debates on sex, coupling, and marriage, even as authority in such matters has shifted from religious doctrine to medicine to social science and the law of human rights. Yet, as the same-sex marriage legislations underline, matrimony is an entirely social construct, an expression not of "nature" but of historical vicissitudes. Does legislation on same-sex marriage indicate a revolution in the sexual categories considered "natural"? Are official views on what is "natural" now finally being set aside by fundamental alterations to the concept of marriage, leaving more space for individuals to decide their own matrimonial destinies? Or, as neoliberal policies prioritize the individual over social bonds, is same-sex marriage a counter-measure, seeking to attract wayward couplers back into wider, more subtle structures of normativity? Finally, does Western legal emphasis on coupling, irrespective of the partners' sex, now cast multi-partner relationships as the new "unnatural"?

From Sodomy Laws to Same-Sex Marriage: International Perspectives since 1789 brings together groundbreaking scholarly research around questions of same-sex coupling and relationships in history. Inspired by recent adoptions of same-sex marriage internationally, the volume provides global perspectives on the legal and social history of same-sex relationships between the late eighteenth century and the present. From Sodom and Gomorrah to Britain's sodomy laws, from a love that "dare not speak its name" to continental Europe's abhorrence of sexual acts "against nature," the history of same-sex love traditionally ranged from fire and brimstone maledictions to secrecy and scandal. From the late nineteenth century the advance of scientific understandings of sexuality shifted attitudes away from religious foundations, but laid the groundwork for polarization and contest over same-sex relationships for much of the twentieth century.

Until very recently, legal positions across the Western world reflected the legacies of the British and French empires, as well as Christianity, particularly Catholicism. With the adoption of same-sex marriage across most of Continental Europe, Great Britain (excluding Northern Ireland), the Republic of Ireland, much of South and all of North America, and Australia and New Zealand, many of the global historic differences have now collapsed. But although the legal destination may have been the same, each polity took distinctive and far from linear historical paths to that point. With an emphasis on the areas where the impetus for change has been most noticeable—Europe, the Americas, and Australasia—this is the first volume to present a collection of essays that focus on the relationship between the legal and social position of same-sex relationships in jurisdictions that have moved from the abolition of sodomy laws to the adoption of same-sex marriage.

The historiography of homosexuality now has a long and highly respected scholarly history of its own, largely, but not exclusively, in the Anglophone world. Beginning in the 1970s and stimulated by the rise of radical gay and lesbian identity politics and activism in this period, debates raged among scholars about whether gay and lesbian identities, historically and contemporaneously, were social constructs, or "essential nature." The social constructionist argument and approach was seen as highly controversial at the time, and highly problematic to gay and lesbian activists. A key element in identity politics in the 1970s and 1980s in the "British World" and the United States was the realization that homosexuality itself had a history. The identity politics of the period rationalized what appeared at first sight to be evidence of homosexuals in history, and the radically differing attitudes toward same-sex sexualized relations in cultures and contexts as diverse as Ancient Greece, Tokugawa Japan, or Victorian Britain. If homosexuality had a long history, the arguments went, how could it be either criminal or vilified by society and governments in the present? Many activists were "outraged" by the foundational work of scholars, such as Jeffrey Weeks, who appeared to deny "their history," and "essentialist" historians sought alternative interpretations "based on fixity and permanence across time of homosexual identities."[1]

Radical scholarly developments in recent decades have expanded these debates considerably. The concept that sexuality between men and between women is indeed socially constructed and different, with profoundly different meanings ascribed to sex acts and emotional relationships between members of the same sex in different cultures and societies, historically and contemporaneously, forms the basis of most scholarship today. Few historians now accept that there is a fixed homosexual identity discernible throughout history. This "queering" of gay and lesbian politics has had a further profound effect upon the ways historians and other scholars have approached questions of sexuality in history, especially since the 1990s. Queer theorists realized in the 1990s that "homosexual identity" in the present was no more fixed than it had been in the past. "Out" gay men, for example, did not represent the full spectrum of sexual experience between men in modern Western societies, as "out" gay men tended to be metropolitan, white, and middle class. The disaster of the HIV/AIDS pandemic of the 1980s and 1990s forced political activists and theorists to realize that, for example, the transmission of the HIV virus among men who had sex with other men had a much broader epidemiology than among gay men who had an "out" identity. Men from Latino and African American heritage, who predominantly or exclusively had sex with other men but eschewed with abhorrence any kind of politicized sexual identity, seemed to have no place in the quest to seek out homosexual identity in history.

The realization that the margins of sexuality and the liminal world of same-sex relations beyond groups and individuals with "out," proud, and assertive public identities were even more revealing about the spectrum of sex and relationships between members of the same sex broadened out the scope of the historiography of homosexuality. Questions of gender, masculinities, and also full recognition of phenomena such as transsexuality and transgenderism, have in recent years given historians a seemingly limitless spectrum of possibilities to analyze in the past. Far from being a fixed binary, sexualities are fluid and mutable. Today, in the era of same-sex marriage, societies are no longer divided between vilified homosexuals and normative heterosexuals. If anything, the campaign for marriage equality, which began among religious LGBT campaigners in the 1990s in the United States, has created a new binary: hetero- and homo-normativity, centered on coupling, marriage, and ostensibly monogamy; and those who refuse, whether heterosexually or homosexually orientated in their desires, to conform to the normative married couple.

Current debates among theorists emphasize these dramatic shifts in thinking about queerness in recent decades. "Queer worlds" have moved from multiform kinds of intimacy "that bear no necessary relation to domestic space, to kinship, to the couple form, to property, or to the nation,"[2] to "the couple form" moving from the "periphery to the center of queer politics, becoming the major vehicle ... [for] ... access to cultural and legal institutions as well as broader acceptance."[3] In historical research, this also has created a paradigm shift. Queer identities in the past have been analyzed through the stresses of the public space, or in recognizably queer spaces in the public sphere. Recent scholarship, such as Matt Cook's *Queer Domesticities: Homosexuality and Home Life in Twentieth-Century London* (2014), analyzes instead "queer at home" and the formation of queer coupling and domestic space, in short the creation of queer "family life." Cook demonstrates that far from "pretend" or non-existent, evidence of queer coupling and domesticity indeed has a history. It is the tensions between the public and legal ideologies and opprobrium of queer, the politics and culture of undomesticated queer public worlds, and the historicity of the queer couple, queer families, and the development of the institutions of same-sex marriage and civil partnership across the world that underpin the focus of this volume.

Many societies today have moved on from religious and moral objections to the existence of queer lives and accepted marriage equality readily. After all, marriage, whether it is between a man and a woman, or between members of the same sex, is a more conservative and capitalist aspiration than it is a radical one. In June 2018 in the UK, for example, opposite-sex couples won the right to civil partnerships, hitherto only available to same-sex couples. This striking development in equalities reflects a rejection of the institution of marriage by opposite-sex couples—but not rejection of the couple, or its protection in law. Indeed, the quest for marriage equality among LGBT activists around the world flies in the face of decades of feminist critiques of the institution of marriage. Marriage equality is, in its essence, a far cry from the radically experimental ideas on sexuality and sexual relations between members of the same sex as espoused by, for example, the US Gay Liberation Front of the early 1970s.

The acceptance of marriage equality around the world is indeed a revolution in social attitudes. Historians today examine same-sex relationships and queer lives firmly in their historical contexts, and focus upon queer domesticities, as well as queer coteries, communities, and same-sex phenomena where they can be found in the historical past. In many respects, the history of homosexuality has moved beyond "queers in the dock" or under the microscope of the medicalized sexologist. The chapters in this volume explore the changing boundaries between law and same-sex relationships in timely, original, and innovative ways. The very question of marriage and the quest for marriage equality around the world has stimulated the editors and authors in this volume to question the historical significance of the legal frameworks in countries and regions around the world as they shifted from sodomy laws to same-sex marriage.

The volume opens more than two centuries before such questions could have been imagined. Bryant Ragan's chapter provides a foundation for the volume, analyzing and explaining the first modern example of the "decriminalization" of sodomy, in the wake of the French Revolution of 1789. Although a familiar fact, little is known about the reasoning of the committee that drafted France's postrevolutionary penal code, which effectively decriminalized sodomy merely by ceasing to mention it. Part of the problem is that there are no historical records of any discussions about this decision (if indeed such discussions took place). Ragan's chapter explains the shift with reference to the legal background of sodomy as a crime "against nature" between the high Middle Ages and the Early Modern period. It may be difficult to pin down exactly why the revolutionary penal code decriminalized sodomy, but it was not likely a result of absentmindedness on the part of the legislators. Instead, weighing the evidence carefully, Ragan argues that even if Enlightenment "savants" did not address the question of sodomy directly, they would have viewed proscriptions against it as typifying the old regime's superstitions and tendency to barbarous punishments, even of actions that were not directly harmful to society.

The French 1791 decriminalization signaled a new climate of opinion on the role of the state and criminal law. On the other hand, Ragan cautions that it would be anachronistic to explain the decriminalization as an expression of particular concern for individual rights or privacy. History had a long way to run before those attracted to their own sex were to be thought of as a class, let alone one that might warrant protection or rights. For this reason, decriminalization did not mean an immediate end to discrimination, in either France or other places, such as Italy. However, in retrospect, France's 1791 penal code was a first step toward the emergence of two distinct legal traditions in the Western world—those that abolished sodomy laws relatively early in the modern period and those that abolished them only well into the twentieth century.

This dissonance in legal cultures is explored in Charles Upchurch's chapter. The clash between English and French legal traditions, and also differences in attitudes toward legislation, questions of morality, and the rights of individual male citizens, are highlighted through Upchurch's fascinating examination of resistance to the imposition of sodomy laws in the state of Louisiana in 1814–1815. When Louisiana became a territory of the United States in 1805, new crimes appeared due to the imposition of the traditions of English common law, prevalent throughout the United States. The imposition of these new criminal statutes was condemned in a provision in the 1812 Louisiana constitution. Imposing the sodomy law, along with laws against blasphemy, Sunday trading, and other kinds of moral legislation, proceeded in other states, and was part of an evangelical-led movement after the American War of Independence to suppress the permissiveness that had been tacitly tolerated in previous generations.

In the crucible of the Battle of New Orleans, General Andrew Jackson had insisted that the Louisiana Legislature adjourn, which the Legislature refused to do until Jackson imposed martial law. This provoked a huge outcry from the Legislature's members, who objected to the imposition of measures that would impede the rights of Louisiana's male citizens, including the insistence that laws regarding morality be applied. The stout rhetoric of resistance to this by the Legislature was based upon defense of cherished freedoms against "fanatics" imposing new standards, which according to enlightened inhabitants of Louisiana were "ignorant, prejudiced, cold-blooded, false and cruel." Rather than shrinking from discussion of the "unspeakable" crime of sodomy, the Louisiana elites resisted imposition of a sodomy law in a very public and articulate way. The principle upon which the refusal was based was central to their identity as independent men.

Upchurch compares the resistance in Louisiana to a small, but significant, move by some anonymous early nineteenth-century parliamentarians to refute the sodomy law in Britain. Through examination of the anonymous round-robin poem "Don Leon," which was targeted at parliamentarians, rationalist arguments were made to convince the legislators quietly to remove the death penalty for acts of sodomy. The poem also reveals individual self-awakening where one man's story is recounted through sexual self-awareness at university, through personal and sexual fulfillment experienced through his travels in the Eastern Mediterranean. Upchurch analyzes the ideas inherent in the poem, and thereby the small group of men that constructed its arguments, as being in the same logic as the resistance by the elite men of Louisiana to the imposition of the sodomy law. In the British case, clandestine men who did identify strongly with same-sex desire, and in the Louisiana case, men who likely did not identify with same-sex desire, based their arguments upon deeply held convictions over the nature of justice in general to defend same-sex desire and acts specifically. Upchurch argues that these early rationalist rights-based struggles against the sodomy laws place these developments in conversation with the processes that led to same-sex marriage within the United States in the early twenty-first century.

Dominic Janes' chapter examines the full brutality of England's sodomy laws through interpretation of the representations and meanings of the hanging of John Pratt and James Smith, who were the last couple of sodomites to be hanged in Britain in 1835. Janes investigates the relationship between such illegal sexual coupling and the degree to which sodomitical pairs were thought of as couples. From the point of view of the law what mattered was the precise sexual act that had been committed. Reform in the application of the law and punishments changed not through greater tolerance toward the sexual acts in question or the individual men who perpetrated them, but through "sentiment" and increasing squeamishness on the part of observers of public executions. However, from the point of view of reformers, both past and present, it has frequently been important to think about the nature of the relationships between men drawn to such forms of sexual behavior and thus punished.

Janes' review of the sporadic nineteenth-century calls for penal reform of legislation in this area allows the case of Pratt and Smith to be contextualized against a wider landscape of attitudes toward the physical expression of male same-sex desire. In particular a surviving petition to the home secretary in this case is compared with the unpublished writings of Jeremy Bentham and with other materials such as Charles Dickens' account of seeing these men in prison. The justifications, constructions, and evasions offered in these materials make for a fascinating comparison with those produced by modern gay-rights campaigners, who have either argued for the importance of connecting physical with affective coupling, or have, conversely, advocated the potential of decoupling these two elements.

Moving from capital punishment to confinement, Ben Bethell investigates official attitudes to sex between men in nineteenth-century England by using one of the few historical sources that document lengthy deliberations, if not soul-searching, on the matter: the records of those who administered the English prison system. At a time when official, legal, and scientific discourses were largely silent on the question of sex between men, prison administrators were forced to grapple with it, for fear that if the matter were ignored, some men would "taint" others, and sex among prisoners would become rife. Bethell charts the development of policies whose aim was to prevent this. His research reveals that before the emergence of modern concepts of sex and sexuality, those involved in the discussion struggled for the lack of established concepts and language to discuss the issue and classify prisoners. His chapter thus shows how prison administration was a key site for the emergence of a set of modern English discourses about sexual acts among men that paved the way not only for prison policies, but also for official attitudes in broader society that were to endure well into the twentieth century.

A very different perspective is provided by Magally Alegre Henderson's chapter on mid-nineteenth-century Peru. Making use of a very unusual set of records created by a plea presented to the ecclesiastical court of Lima in 1846, Alegre Henderson's chapter examines the "divorce" case of an opposite-sex couple, one of whom accused the other of maintaining a same-sex relationship: the woman who sought legal separation from her husband wished to do so not because he kept a mistress, but a young male lover. The woman and her husband had been married for about thirty years and had children, but at the time of the plea, the husband had allegedly been in a relationship with the younger man for several years. The ecclesiastical court's requirement for evidence to be collected before it granted any sort of marital separation resulted in the generation of an unusual array of historical witness statements.

Alegre Henderson makes fascinating use of these accounts to discern nineteenth-century Peruvian social attitudes to the same-sex relationship in question, including those of family members and the neighboring community. Additionally, the chapter notes the reluctance of both ecclesiastical and civil authorities to prosecute either of the men involved in the relationship, even though several witness statements left little doubt as to its physical nature. Framing this interesting relationship within an established, but waning, Latin American tradition of visible "maricones," Alegre Henderson illuminates an interesting aspect of nineteenth-century Peruvian history as the jurisdiction over matters of sexuality and intimacy transitioned away from ecclesiastical to secular authorities.

Remaining in the southern hemisphere, but shifting from the former Spanish empire to the former British, Yorick Smaal and Mark Finnane's chapter analyzes the criminal law and "homosex" in New South Wales and Queensland in the interwar period. As a British penal outpost, Australia regulated and punished homosex from its earliest beginnings as a colony. "Unnatural" sexual behaviors had particular resonance in a convict society and fragile settler state where men overwhelmingly outnumbered women. "Unnatural" sex and the men who practiced it became crucial counterpoints to hegemonic masculinities and the long arm of the law intersected with queer Australian lives for the next 150 years. But what do we actually know about policing and prosecution patterns of homosex and what can they tell us about sexual norms and social attitudes? Who exactly was coming before the courts and in what circumstances? How did cases come to notice and with what consequences? Did particular "unnatural" behaviors draw special attention at certain moments, and, if so, why? Despite a century and a half of shifting definitions and legislative changes, the extent and limits of the law and its intersection with queer lives are not well understood.

Smaal and Finnane use large-scale prosecution data from New South Wales and Queensland between 1920 and 1939 to answer these kinds of questions. In doing so, the authors reveal sporadic and inconsistent policies in regard to the prosecution of homosex, with patterns in prosecutions and attitudes emerging particularly where the cases of situational sex between men involved minors. Smaal and Finnane interpret the prosecution data with attendant concern to the criminal law as institution and practice as well as shifting social and political attitudes toward threats posed by certain kinds of "unnaturalness." Indeed, their meticulous close reading and nuanced interpretation and contextualization of these records provide methodological inspiration to scholars about the ways in which data of this kind need to be examined in historical questions of queer identities.

Geoffroy Huard's chapter shifts the focus from colonial and settler societies back to continental Europe, with an examination of attitudes to same-sex sexuality in twentieth-century Spain during Franco's regime (1939–1975). From 1931 Spain had a progressive republican government that introduced an advanced divorce law and women's suffrage, ceased censorship, and permitted discussion of contraception and other matters that had been subject to Catholic taboos. While homosexual acts were still technically criminal, the republic's interest in detaching Spain's morality from the Catholic faith suggests that decriminalization might have followed if the republic had survived. However, Franco represented a reaction to the republic, and, after emerging victorious in 1939 from the three-year civil war sparked by his coup, his government explicitly set about re-moralizing Spanish society along traditional Catholic lines, "purifying" and restoring "virility" to the nation.

Using prosecution records for Barcelona (the only records currently accessible), Huard explores how these ideological aspirations played out at the quotidian level, charting the regime's persecution of men who flouted the dictatorship's gender norms. From 1954 the police made wide use of a law against "vagrants and miscreants," a net whose victims were exclusively working class. In the region administered from Barcelona alone, well over 1000 men were prosecuted, and the total figures for Spain in its entirety, if they were available, would be much greater. By way of conclusion, Huard's analysis also looks at post-Franco Spain, suggesting that the economic and tourism boom from the 1960s had already begun a process of social transformation well before Franco died in 1975. This helps to explain Spain's rapid social and political transformation from the 1980s, but the fact that in 2005 it became the first Catholic nation to introduce equal marriage regardless of gender remains impressive. Still on the political agenda in contemporary Spain is the question of compensation for those prosecuted under the Franco regime.

Just as contemporary Spanish attitudes to same-sex relationships cannot be understood without framing them historically against the Franco dictatorship, the subject in postwar West Germany was shadowed by the continued existence of "paragraph 175" of the criminal code, made infamous by Nazi persecution of homosexuals. And while the original Prussian criminal code's paragraph 175 and the efflorescence of gay culture in the Weimar period may have become more familiar than Spain's progressive 1930s republic or even Franco's repression, themes of liberal individualism versus collective "national virility" can all too easily dominate in both national narratives. In West Germany, paragraph 175 was subject to reform in 1969 and 1973, and was abolished altogether in 1994 after unification with the Democratic Republic (East Germany). But the process was not as ineluctable or linear as it might appear—as suggested by the challenges encountered in the German drive to introduce equal marriage, which achieved its aims only relatively late, in 2017.

Benno Gammerl's contribution to this volume seeks to complicate the linear narrative of "liberalization" in West Germany from the 1950s by exploring the nexus between emotions and legal change in the context of same-sex relationships. Revealing a history rich with emotional ambiguities and ambivalences, Gammerl examines the two-way interaction between the legal sphere and human feelings. To do so he augments traditional sources with advice books aimed at a mainstream readership, and oral history interviews with same-sex-attracted men and women who lived through an epoch of significant legal transformation. Among other things Gammerl shows the surprising legacy of the Nazi persecution in determining both sexual behavior and governing inner feelings. This helps to explain why in the 1960s the German homophile movement stressed the purity of same-sex love and the enduring nature of its relationships. Arguments employed gradually changed from the 1970s, but the oral history sources bear witness to notable generation gaps among same-sex-attracted individuals, testifying to the existence, at least in some quarters, of a complex layer of melancholia and even grief over past injustices.

The complex relationship between the personal and the political remains in view in the next chapter, by Kate Davison, which examines an unusual aspect of the way homosexuality became a key concern in national security policy across several countries in the early phases of the Cold War, especially during the late 1950s and early 1960s. In Australia, the UK, Canada, and the United States especially, homosexuality was seen to constitute a "security risk." Strong links were drawn between sexual conformity and emotional concepts like loyalty and trust. Davison's chapter compares the differences in attitudes toward male homosexuals and homosexuality in security and intelligence agencies in Australia and East Germany in the late 1950s and early 1960s, showing how homosexuality as a Cold War issue extended beyond the Anglophone world and across the iron curtain.

Davison argues that because the "homosexual" seemed to fit unnoticed into society more easily than other "deviants," the issue of invisibility was of direct concern to security agencies—indeed, the entire spying apparatus was built upon disguise, deception, and the ability to assimilate unnoticed. Measures were introduced to establish a method of detection of homosexuals either to prevent or to encourage their recruitment. Security and intelligence agencies, including those in Australia and East Germany, sought expert advice, at first from psychiatrists and medical professionals, but later, perhaps influenced by behaviorism, advice based on firsthand observation of homosexuals' emotional behavior and motivations. Using insights from the history of emotions, Davison addresses the construction of emotional "types" within international diplomacy and intelligence in relation to sexual orientation, through close reading and interpretation of two expert briefing papers.

The transnational approach continues with Graham Willett's chapter, a study of the criminality of sex between men, the origins and diffusion of homosexual politics, and the reception of the Wolfenden Report of 1957 throughout the "British World." That it should not be a criminal offence for men to have sex with each other is now, for hundreds of millions of people around the world, a relatively uncontroversial idea. Willett argues that this is a more remarkable state of affairs than it might seem. In the middle of the twentieth century, while there were countries in Europe that had removed homosexual acts from their law codes, in those places where the law still criminalized such acts, there was no reason to think that anything might change in the near future.

And then in the early 1950s debate erupted in the UK over the legal status of homosexual acts and the social standing of those who practiced them. In 1957, a British government inquiry headed by John Wolfenden recommended that homosexual acts between consenting adults in private ought to be legal, and while it took a decade to bring this recommendation onto the statute books in England and Wales, others were watching and in the British World, Canada followed England and Wales in 1969. In Australia, the state of South Australia started the process of decriminalization in 1972. New Zealand, South Africa, Ireland, Scotland, and Northern Ireland all had followed England and Wales by the mid-1990s. Willett argues and demonstrates that scholars require a concept and framework of the British World as a transnational entity through which "homosexual politics" and ideas on legal reform were developed and diffused.

In stark contrast to the "British World" is Italy, where same-sex sexual acts were effectively decriminalized in 1890. Yet, as Yuri Guaiana and Mark Seymour's chapter demonstrates, this did not mean that there was no struggle for recognition of same-sex relationships in Italy after they started to become more visible from the early 1980s. Italy had been unified more than a century earlier (1861), and, although the nation's first unified criminal code, introduced in 1890, deleted all previous mention of crimes "against nature," Italy's culture remained broadly hostile to the notion of same-sex sexuality. The hostility reached a peak under Mussolini's fascist regime, which found indirect ways to persecute and ostracize men who seemed to fall short of fascist gender norms. During the postwar period overt official hostility declined into a culture of "don't ask don't tell," but Italy was a notable latecomer to gay liberation. Although liberationist groups, inspired by efforts in the United States, the UK, and France, began to organize from the early 1970s, their efforts emerged into the public sphere only after a tragic murder–suicide of two young male lovers in Sicily in November 1980 as the subject of national headlines.

In the wake of this event nascent organizations began to coalesce, most visibly in the form of an organization known as Arcigay, which became Italy's most influential and enduring gay-rights association. While Italy's gay culture gradually became more visible and commercial during the 1980s and 1990s, so too did political organization become bolder and better coordinated. The influence of the Catholic Church in Italian politics and the relationship between Catholicism and the nation's culture gave the struggle a particularly arduous and sometimes bitterly divisive quality. Nevertheless, as Guaiana and Seymour show, a combination of courageous individual acts and concerted campaigns, gradual shifts of attitude influenced by events elsewhere, and the influence of the European Court of Human Rights (ECHR) finally resulted in Italy's parliament granting recognition to same-sex relationships with May 2016's law on civil unions. The law stopped short of granting second-parent adoption rights, but it is a step that many Italians in same-sex relationships hope will result in equal marriage legislation.

Much of the contemporary debate around same-sex marriage has been framed in legal terms. Rebecca Jennings argues in her chapter on lesbian marriages in Britain and Australia that campaigners and lobbying groups for same-sex marriage have inevitably focused on the issue of legal equality, while historians have located recent changes in the context of a more gradual progression from legal oppression to equality over the course of the nineteenth and twentieth centuries. Marriage equality from this perspective is therefore framed as the ultimate and final signifier of a successful battle against legal discrimination and for the social acceptance of homosexuality. Amid this optimistic rhetoric, a less vocal, but equally powerful, critique has been articulated by queer scholars, such as Lisa Duggan and Judith Butler, questioning the representation of marriage as an ideal or universal model for same-sex relationships and arguing that it reinforces a process of depoliticization and "homonormativity."

While these two broad arguments have dominated liberal academic debate about same-sex marriage, Jennings argues that both have, in different ways, obscured questions of gender. In focusing on marriage equality as a final stage in a teleology of homosexual law reform, campaigners and commentators have drawn on a broadly masculine framework that moves from nineteenth-century legislation against sodomy to mid-twentieth-century male homosexual law reform and culminates in same-sex marriage. Given the relative infrequency with which Western legal frameworks explicitly prohibited lesbian sexuality, this model is less helpful in considering marriage between women, and tends to obscure the different social and cultural forms of oppression faced by lesbians. Similarly, less attention is paid to the internal power dynamics within relationships and the ways in which gendered inequalities existing in wider society can be reproduced and maintained through the institution of marriage.

Drawing on oral history interviews and archival research conducted for a project that explores shifting lesbian relationship models in Australia and Britain since 1945, Jennings considers whether marriage, as it has been constructed by female same-sex couples in the postwar period, offers any scope for alternative conceptions of intimacy and partnership. Focusing on personal accounts by women in both heterosexual and same-sex marriages or committed relationships, the chapter explores how women envisage and present lesbian partnerships differently from heterosexual ones and poses questions about how this can inform our understanding of what "marriage" means.

Patrick McDonagh's chapter discusses the legal battle to decriminalize sexual activity between males in the Republic of Ireland between 1980 and 1993. McDonagh challenges the assumption that decriminalization of sex between men was entirely the result of David Norris' historic legal victory in 1988 at the ECHR and analyzes the significance of the first wave of lesbian and gay activism in the Republic of Ireland between the 1970s and early 1990s. Far from being a lone voice, Norris' two court cases in Ireland and his victory at the ECHR were underpinned by action and collectivity that gave Irish LGBT people the confidence to speak out about their sexuality.

Focusing on LGBT activist groups across the Republic of Ireland, McDonagh sheds light on the dramatic shift that took place within Irish society concerning what constituted legitimate sexual relations. During the 1980s, Irish governments argued that the 1861 Offences against the Person Act and the 1885 Criminal Law Amendment Act should be maintained to protect the moral fiber of Irish society. Was this defense a reflection of Irish society's desire to maintain the laws, or an example of a government out of touch with its electorate? Does the widespread media interest generated by the court cases suggest a general concern in Irish society around the issue of homosexuality? McDonagh argues that throughout the 1980s Irish society was decidedly more tolerant toward its homosexual citizens than Irish governments acknowledged. Television and newspapers reflected not only the actions and aims of activists, but also charted gradual changes in attitudes within Irish society toward same-sex relationships and LGBT lives. Moreover, Ireland's desire to remain a part of the Council of Europe was the key factor in forcing Irish legislators to amend the relevant laws. McDonagh's chapter is among the first scholarship to provide historical contextualization for the remarkable changes in social attitudes in the Republic of Ireland since the 1970s, and underpins the historical significance of the remarkable achievement of marriage equality there by referendum in 2015.

Like Ireland, the United States also adopted marriage equality in 2015. Marcia M. Gallo's chapter traces some of the intense debates about same-sex partnerships, family formations, and marriage among activists in the mid- to late twentieth-century United States. It touches on the arguments of activists on all sides of the issues, from the earliest proponents of lesbian and gay couples creating alternative celebrations of their relationships, to the development and acceptance of municipal- and state-level civil unions and domestic partnerships, to the ultimate triumph of those seeking marriage equality for gay people in 2015. Throughout, the chapter focuses on the ways in which the debates often have been contained within an American rights-based framework, a model that has attained a great deal of national and international publicity and significant legal successes in the second half of the twentieth century for racial, ethnic, and sexual minorities. What Urvashi Vaid and others argue, however, is that reliance on such a model does not provide for a radical reconfiguration of social norms.

In 2013, American activist and attorney Urvashi Vaid published an analysis of the US Supreme Court's 2012 ruling in *Hollingsworth v. Perry*. *Perry* mounted a significant challenge to lower-court decisions regarding California's same-sex marriage law. It paved the way for SCOTUS' 2015 decision in *Obergefell v. Hodges* and three related cases, which affirmed the constitutional right to same-sex marriage in America. To frame her assessment, Vaid used the words of legendary reggae artist and activist Bob Marley—"Now you get what you want, do you want more?"—as she argued that the marriage equality movement in the United States had seen both positive, but mostly negative, results: "On the one hand, the movement has enlisted a large circle of non-gay allies. On the other hand, the movement has narrowed its aspirations." Gallo traces the developments and tensions within LGBT lives and activism in regard to the quest for marriage equality with these tensions in mind.[4]

Civil partnerships and marriage are contracts, but the implications of the contents of the contract are rarely considered in detail by the parties. In Daniel Monk's chapter, the ways in which the courts in England and Wales have resolved disputes on the death of a partner or divorce (or dissolution of a civil partnership) are examined. The new institutions represented by equal marriage and civil partnership are gender-neutral and uphold an emerging view of these institutions involving equals. In reality, the partnership and marriage breakups examined point to considerable inequalities between same-sex partners. Marriage equality, argues Monk, is a beginning point rather than an end point in the exploration of sexuality, given the varying ways in which gay men and lesbians approach and interpret marriage and civil partnership. Monk also examines the ways in which the media has reported these stories and contrasts these approaches with the legal narratives. A key argument in the chapter is that these stories and cases represent a useful perspective for thinking about some of the causal claims made about same-sex relationship recognition and for thinking critically about the purpose and function of marriage as a state institution.

The concluding chapter, by Robert Aldrich, is both a thought-provoking reflection on the intensely variegated history of same-sex relationships represented by this volume's chapters and a prospective consideration of the global future of those who are drawn into non-normative relationships—or might like to be. While the result of long and arduous political processes, the recognition won for same-sex relationships in much of the Western world from the early twenty-first century still appears astonishing in the light of their absolute proscription up to the late eighteenth century and in most cases well beyond. On the other hand, there is little sign that social or cultural acceptance, let alone positive legal change, is emerging in areas that are home to vast proportions of the global population, stretching from Africa up to Russia and across all of Asia. And even in the West, the apparent triumph of same-sex marriage over the old sodomy laws might yet turn out to be merely the high watermark of postwar liberal-democratic values. Aldrich's afterword reminds us that the achievements of "gay liberation" are fragile, contingent, and by no means universal.

The scholarship and discussion in this volume were brought together at a groundbreaking international conference held at Birkbeck College, University of London, in 2015, funded by the Birkbeck Institute for the Humanities; the Department of History, Classics and Archaeology at Birkbeck College; University of London; and the University of Otago, New Zealand. The authors in this volume collectively and individually bring together for the first time new research and scholarly discussion of the remarkable phenomenon of shifts in attitudes toward men and women who desired sexual and emotional relationships with their own sex. The modern era has witnessed the dismantling of sodomy laws around the world, and the creation of marriage (and civil unions) for same-sex couples. Undoubtedly, these developments have profound implications for human rights and equalities, to the point that marriage equality has redefined what equality means in many societies today.

Notes

1 Jeffrey Weeks, *What Is Sexual History?* (Cambridge: Polity Press, 2016), 12.
2 Lauren Berlant and Michael Warner, "Sex in Public," *Critical Inquiry* 24, no. 2 (1998): 558.
3 Symposium, "The Ontology of the Couple," 2016, https://www.ici-berlin.org/events/the-ontology-of-the-couple/.
4 Urvashi Vaid, "Now You Get What You Want, Do You Want More?" *N. Y. U. Review of Law & Social Change* 37 (2013): 101–111.

Select Bibliography

Aldrich, Robert, *Colonialism and Homosexuality* (London: Routledge, 2003).
Cook, Matt, *Queer Domesticities: Homosexuality and Home Life in Twentieth-Century London* (Basingstoke: Palgrave Macmillan, 2014).
Crompton, Louis, *Homosexuality and Civilisation* (Cambridge, MA: Belknap Press, 2003).
Doan, Laura, *Fashioning Sapphism: The Origins of a Modern English Lesbian Culture* (New York: Columbia University Press, 2001).
Duberman, Martin, Martha Vicinus and George Chauncey (eds.), *Hidden from History: Reclaiming the Gay and Lesbian Past* (New York: New American Library, 1989).
Duggan, Lisa, *Sapphic Slashers: Sex, Violence and American Modernity* (Durham N. C.: Duke University Press, 2001).
Dynes, Wayne and Stephen Donaldson (eds.), *History of Homosexuality in Europe and America* (New York: Garland, 1992).
Faderman, Lillian, *Surpassing the Love of Men: Romantic Friendship and Love between Women from the Renaissance to the Present* (New York: Morrow, 1981).

Halberstam, Judith, *Female Masculinity* (London: Duke University Press, 1998).
Greenberg, David, *The Construction of Homosexuality* (Chicago: University of Chicago Press, 1988).
Houlbrook, Matt and H. G. Cocks (eds.), *The Modern History of Sexuality* (Basingstoke: Palgrave Macmillan, 2005).
Jeffreys, Sheila, *The Spinster and Her Enemies: Feminism and Sexuality 1880–1930* (London: Pandora, 1980).
Jennings, Rebecca, *A Lesbian History of Britain: Love and Sex between Women since 1500* (Oxford: Greenwood World, 2008).
Tamagne, Florence, *A History of Homosexuality in Europe: Volume 1: Berlin, London, Paris, 1919–1939* (New York: Algora, 2004).
Vicinus, Martha, *Intimate Friends: Women Who Loved Women, 1778–1928* (Chicago: University of Chicago Press, 2004).
Weeks, Jeffrey, *Sex, Politics and Society: The Regulation of Sexuality since 1800* (London: Longman, 1981).
Weeks, Jeffrey, *What Is Sexual History?* (Cambridge: Polity Press, 2016)

2

Same-Sex Sexual Relations and the French Revolution: The Decriminalization of Sodomy in 1791

Bryant T. Ragan, Jr.

Historians might well argue that September 25, 1791, proved a milestone in the history of same-sex relationships. For the first time since the fall of Rome, a European state decriminalized sodomy. This important, albeit unanticipated, development took place in France, during the "liberal phase" of the great Revolution. Just days before dissolving itself under the provisions of the recently adopted constitution to make way for a new legislative body, the Constituent Assembly approved a legal code for the entire country. Promulgated from September 26 to October 6, the Penal Code of 1791 made no reference to sodomy, a term that had been used for centuries in canon, customary, and Roman statutory law in France, and indeed throughout Europe, to refer to a range of illicit sexual practices. By simply leaving it out of the new code, the revolutionaries effectively decriminalized sodomy. Although the Napoleonic regime revised this penal code in 1810, reinstating some of the prerevolutionary laws that had been eliminated, it chose not to recriminalize sodomy, and sexual relations between members of the same sex have remained legal per se in France ever since.

The decriminalization of sodomy may have marked a radical departure from Old Regime jurisprudence, but it has attracted scant attention from scholars, let alone the public at large. Histories of the French Revolution, for instance, often highlight such legal achievements as the granting of civil rights to Protestants and Jews and the abolition of slavery, but they rarely even mention the word "sodomy."[1] Similarly, histories of sexuality dedicate at most a sentence or two to the decriminalization of 1791. Even Flora Leroy-Forgeot's *Histoire juridique de l'homosexualité en Europe*, a wide-ranging study published in 1994 of the legal history of same-sex sexual relations on the continent from Antiquity to the late twentieth century, contains only one sentence on the topic; in her interpretation, the impact of France's legal reform on

---

I am very grateful to Ben Bernard, Suzanne Desan, Lynn Hunt, Jeffrey Merrick, Kathryn Norberg, Dennis McEnnerney, Michael Sibalis, and Michael Sorensen for their helpful suggestions and critiques of previous drafts of this chapter.

other countries in Europe is what really matters.[2] This first case of decriminalization has attracted more attention from scholars interested specifically in the LGBTQ history of France. Michel Duchein, writing in 1961 under the pseudonym Marc Daniel, for example, published a path-breaking essay, "Histoire de la législation pénale française concernant l'homosexualité," in the early homophile journal *Arcadie*.[3] More recently, Thierry Pastorello has examined decriminalization in light of the theoretical studies on identity that have captivated scholars in queer studies.[4] For the most part, however, scholars have discussed this juridical shift within works dealing with other aspects of queer French history.[5]

The relatively small number of studies should not be terribly surprising. There are no existing primary sources that can shed direct light on the motivations leading revolutionary legislators to decriminalize sodomy. We do not have, for instance, any minutes or notes from the meetings of the Committee on Criminal Legislation, the body entrusted with the responsibility of drafting the new penal code. In fact, we do not know if sodomy was ever discussed at any of the committee's meetings. Similarly, there are no surviving transcriptions of discussions on the floor of the Constituent Assembly, thus we cannot know whether sodomy even crossed the minds of legislators as they voted for the new code. Finally, because no public debate took place over the legal status of sodomy, it is next to impossible to gauge popular opinion on the matter.

Did the national representatives simply forget to include sodomy in the penal code? Despite the absence of legislative records, it is hard to believe that they would have been unaware of such a consequential and momentous departure from tradition, especially since other crimes such as prostitution and incest were also left out without leaving any trace of documentary evidence.[6] It is important to remember that many representatives were lawyers and magistrates whose professional expertise focused on Old Regime jurisprudence, and they knew full well that sodomy had heretofore been classified as a capital crime. They may very well have felt obliged to act in silence, deeming it wiser to legislate by omission, but their decision could hardly have been accidental.

How, then, can we explain a non-event that was in fact quite significant? How can we examine the origins of something that is shrouded in such obscurity? In this chapter, I hope to identify and analyze a range of sources that help account for the historical roots of decriminalization. We will first explore the complex legal history of anti-sodomitical jurisprudence of early modern France. The authors of the Penal Code of 1791 were effectively responding to long-held assumptions embedded in both law and legal commentary about the relationship between sodomy, on the one hand, and religion, natural law, and human history, on the other. Following this overview, we will consider some of the arguments advanced by savants during the Enlightenment that helped erode the philosophical bases for anti-sodomy laws and that at the same time provided suggestions for alternative, non-legalistic ways of suppressing behavior of which they did not approve.

Although some philosophical considerations problematized interdictions against sodomy in law, it was only in France (and then in some of the territories conquered by the revolutionary armies) that sodomy was decriminalized. We must therefore explore, as best we can, how the French Revolution served as a kind of catalyst for this change. References to sodomy in contemporary texts grant us some access into the complicated ways that sodomy and revolutionary political culture were seen to relate to one another. Finally, we must underscore that in the wake of decriminalization, homosexuals in France were never again rendered criminal simply on the basis of their sexual behavior. The discourse of human rights, however, did not significantly contribute to the decriminalization of sodomy, and the Revolution left prejudice against sexual minorities largely intact. Throughout the nineteenth and twentieth centuries, they continued to face persecution in many other ways, not only by the police, but also by psychiatrists, medical doctors, teachers, and others.

The legal background

The significance of decriminalization can be evaluated only by situating it within the more general context of Old Regime jurisprudence. Unfortunately, there are few comprehensive surveys of the legal history of sodomy, whether for Europe in general, or for France in particular, so information must be gleaned from other sources. James Brundage's *Law, Sex, and Christian Society in Medieval Europe* remains the best study of secular and canonical legal codes regarding sexual behavior across the continent, but it is not focused on sodomy as such, and the modern period lies outside its scope.[7] Flora Leroy-Forgeot's *Histoire juridique* offers a useful analysis of normative texts dealing with homosexual acts into the modern period; however, this short book, focusing on Europe and beyond from biblical times to the end of the twentieth century, covers too much territory to be useful for specific cases.[8] Sociologist David Greenberg's more substantial *The Construction of Homosexuality* includes helpful discussions of anti-sodomy laws throughout Europe over the long term.[9] And for the French case, Maurice Lever's classic, albeit somewhat dated, *Les Bûchers de Sodome* gives a good historical overview.[10] In the more recent "Male Homosexuality in the Age of Enlightenment and Revolution, 1680–1850," Michael Sibalis provides an excellent analysis of the legal, political, and social history of homosexuality in Europe before and after the French Revolution.[11] Finally, a number of the most important primary sources, many of which are utilized in the present chapter, are to be found in *Homosexuality in Early Modern France*, edited by Jeffrey Merrick and myself.[12]

Scholars interested in the legal history of sodomy must bear several important considerations in mind. First, although both "sodomy" and "homosexuality" connote same-sex sexual behavior, they are not exactly the same thing.[13] A person engaged in sodomy was traditionally seen as someone who had an inclination—which could in some cases manifest itself as an exclusive preference—for sexual behaviors deemed sinful by the church and criminal by the law. In the modern West, in contrast, homosexuality came to be seen as an existential category of being. Psychologists, medical doctors, and criminologists first defined homosexuals as individuals whose exclusive attraction to members of their own sex rendered them pathological and perverse. Over time, many men and women contested the negative characteristics attributed to homosexuals, while maintaining that heterosexuals and homosexuals were mutually exclusive forms of identity. But even leaving the distinction between sodomy and homosexuality aside, defining "sodomy" in its own right is challenging, whether we are talking about the twenty-first century or the eighteenth. Early modern jurisprudence usually offered a broad definition, which could comprise a veritable laundry list of proscribed sexual acts: homosexual sex, non-procreative heterosexual sex, bestiality, and masturbation. At times, however, sodomy was defined more narrowly: it might mention heterosexual acts only in passing, for example, or separate masturbation out as a distinct category. Given the inconsistent definitions of sodomy, it really does seem, as Michel Foucault so aptly proclaimed, "an utterly confused category."[14]

It is difficult, moreover, to make broad generalizations about the legal history of sodomy before the French Revolution, largely because the evidence is so sparse. In the early Middle Ages, both statutory and customary law remained generally silent on sodomy, leaving it to the church to regulate. During the high Middle Ages, scholastic polemicists such as Thomas Aquinas railed against sodomy, and in the thirteenth century, for the first time, some of the customary legal codes in northern France made it a capital crime.[15] In particular, the Customs of Touraine and Anjou (1246); Paris, commonly referred to as the Établissements de Saint Louis (1272–3); and Beauvais (1280s) all mandated death by fire for sodomites.[16] The Customs of Orléans (c. 1260) differed somewhat by setting out increasingly harsh punishments for repeat offenders.[17] In the case of a guilty man, he was to lose his testicles for the first offence, his penis for the second, and his life, by burning, for the third. Similarly, a guilty woman was to lose a "member," that is, a breast, for each of the first two offences and be burned to death for the third. From the fourteenth through the eighteenth centuries, laws regarding sodomy in France did not appreciably change, although the application of these penalties was neither uniform nor consistent.

Throughout the early modern period, French laws and legal commentators offered three major justifications for criminalizing sodomy. First, they emphasized that God abominates this sin, which consequently deserves the worst of punishments. They frequently evoked to this effect the etymological origins of "sodomy." In the early eighteenth century, for instance, Antoine Bruneau asserted, "There is no one, however poorly versed in sacred history, who does not know where the word sodomy comes from." He took the opportunity, nonetheless, to spell it out: "It is the name of one of the two cities, which Genesis 19 speaks of, overthrown and reduced to ashes by fire from heaven because of the execrable vices, prostitution, and great lewdness of this city's inhabitants, who brought God's justice down on themselves."[18] The story of Sodom and Gomorrah, along with other injunctions found primarily in the Old Testament, reinforced the central message that sodomy was an execrable sin against God.

Secondly, jurists maintained that sodomy violated Natural Law; it was particularly grievous because it was a non-procreative sexual act. In his tellingly named essay, "Sodomy and the Sin Against Nature," Claude Lebrun de la Rochette claimed, "And in truth, it [sodomy] is rightly called the sin against nature, considering that other iniquities, such as fornication, adultery, [and] rape are either in conformity with nature or derived from natural (albeit contrary to reason) instinct. But this one, trampling the laws of nature underfoot, going madly beyond its bounds, attacks it, confounds it, and violates it completely."[19] This "unnatural" crime, more heinous than rape in that it could not lead to issue, merited the strongest penalty possible. Doubtless speaking for many other legal theorists, Antoine Bruneau reached a similar conclusion: "The penalty for sodomy could not be strong enough to expiate a crime that makes nature blush, to put the active one and the passive one to death by fire that consumes them and have the ashes thrown to the wind."[20]

Finally, commentators used examples drawn from history to show how sodomites had universally been condemned by law. However, the repertoire of precedents was actually quite limited, and writers alluded to the same examples over and over again. Daniel Jousse's exegesis on criminal justice, *Treatise on the Criminal Justice of France* (1771), is particularly instructive. Citing numerous texts, such as the Scantinian law, Cicero's letters and orations, and the law "Cum vir" in the Julian code on adultery, Jousse argued that Roman law proscribed sodomitical behavior. He also claimed, much more tersely and much less convincingly, that "in Athens this crime was punished by death."[21] Such commentators also pointed to more recent examples drawn from early modern history to highlight the centuries-old imperative to criminalize sodomy in France. Jousse, for instance, referenced cases from Amiens (1519), Montault (1557), Paris (1584), Issoudun (1598), and again in Paris (1677, 1671, 1726, and 1750) of sodomites who were executed for having committed this crime.[22] These theorists intended for such evidence, drawn from pre-Christian and Christian societies alike, to strengthen the rationale of anti-sodomitical law.

France may not have had a unified legal code under the Old Regime, but a strong consensus had nevertheless emerged, one which saw sodomy as an unspeakably monstrous crime, akin to heresy, witchcraft, and lèse-majesté. It offended God, it violated the laws of Nature, and it warranted the contempt of History. In the eighteenth century, however, this consensus began to break down. It is now time to turn our attention to the Enlightenment, which not only provided the underlying rationales for the decriminalization of sodomy, but also effectively created a blueprint on how to do so.

Enlightenment challenges

In the eighteenth century, many savants disdained the seemingly sterile and pointless studies of academic philosophers. They advocated the practical use of reason to improve the world, whether economically, socially, politically, or morally. These "philosophes" did not speak with one voice; indeed, they seemed to agree on remarkably little. Many heated debates focused on the question of rights. Should women have access to the same opportunities afforded to men? Should religious minorities be recognized by law? Should the institution of slavery be maintained, phased out, or simply abolished?

When it came to sodomy, however, philosophes generally spoke with an uncharacteristically unified voice. They avoided addressing the subject directly, but when they did, they portrayed it as a disgusting and contemptible vice. It would never have occurred to them to apply the language of rights—whether in favor or in opposition—to sodomites, as they did in the cases of women, Protestants, Jews, and slaves. After all, society did not recognize sodomites as constituting a clearly defined social group; therefore, there was no basis for granting them civil rights as such.

Nevertheless, a small number of philosophes began to undermine the legal arguments against sodomy in piecemeal, oblique, and mostly unconscious ways. Their most radical commitments to secularism, their evolving views about nature, and their reevaluations about human history proved particularly effective in demanding reappraisal of the way the law treated this capital offence. When the implications of these arguments were made clear, the most progressive thinkers called for more humane laws with respect to sodomy, while advocating, much more sinisterly, new methods of controlling it.

Many Enlightenment thinkers, from Pierre Bayle to Cesare Beccaria, asserted that legal systems based in religious bigotry were antithetical to the pursuit of justice. Consequently, they called for the elimination of laws against blasphemy, heresy, and witchcraft as well as against inhumane judicial practices, such as the burning of Jews in the infamous autos-da-fé of the Spanish Inquisition. Because anti-sodomy laws were fundamentally anchored in Christian teaching, questions also arose about how to deal with it legally. In *Spirit of Laws*, for instance, Montesquieu reflected on the relationship between sodomy and other forms of irreligion:

> It is strange that among us three crimes—magic, heresy, and the crime against nature, of which it could be proved, in the first case, that it does not exist; in the second, that it is susceptible to a great number of distinctions, interpretations, limitations; and in the third, that it is very often hidden—have been punished, all three of them, by the penalty of burning.[23]

For Montesquieu, the law proved ineffectual at best in attempting to regulate sodomitical behavior. Unwilling to push his conclusions very far, he suggested that it would prove more efficacious if the great public created an environment antithetical to the spread of sodomy. Advocating the promotion of "domestic education," which would the allow nature to "defend her rights," Montesquieu implied that the law should generally stay clear of this matter.

Voltaire took a slightly different approach in undercutting the religious argument for criminalizing sodomy. He maintained that people had mistakenly confused sodomy for heresy, arguing that these two strands needed to be carefully differentiated. Asserting, incorrectly as it turns out, that "There was no law in France for its [sodomy's] pursuit and punishment," he maintained, "People thought they found one in the Institutes of Saint Louis ... The word bulgarie, which only means heresy, was taken for the sin against nature, and it was on this text that they based themselves in burning alive the few unfortunates convicted of this filth, more fit to be buried in the darkness of oblivion than to be lit up by the flames of stakes before the eyes of the multitude."[24] It would be better simply to ignore sodomy, according to Voltaire, than to prosecute it under the law.

In different ways, then, an argument separating out the strands of religion and criminal justice emerged, which had important implications concerning the criminal status of sodomy, as Montesquieu and Voltaire suggested. Philosophes became less inclined to recite the litany of religious proscriptions against such behavior than to discuss it in relationship to nature and society. Some thinkers made what we might anachronistically call a "social constructionist" argument; for them, the design of nature mandated generative sexual relations, and deviations from this norm were due to malignant social practices. They followed Montesquieu, who maintained that the "crime against nature" thrives when people were "led to it by some custom, as among the Greeks, where young people performed all their exercises in the nude; as among us, where domestic education is out of fashion; as among the Asians, where some individuals have a large number of wives whom they despise, while the others cannot have any."[25]

Conservative legal commentators maintained that even if sodomy did make appearances in different times and places, it was universally met with aversion and condemnation. Some of the more progressive philosophes, however, were willing to test this claim, and their commitment to intellectual honesty ended up challenging conventional wisdom. They found that different societies exhibited a wide variety of morals, customs, and beliefs when it came to sexual practices. In his posthumously published *De l'Homme* (1773), for example, Claude Adrien Helvétius said that the ancients did not find anything dishonorable in "Greek love." In fact, he maintained, "there is no act of indecency that superstition has not somewhere made an act of virtue. In Japan, Buddhist monks can love men and not women. In certain cantons of Peru, acts of Greek love are acts of piety."[26] Although Helvétius challenged the argument that sodomy had universally been condemned, he was reluctant to conclude that in a morally absolute sense, sodomy might not be indecent.

Jacques André Naigeon proved willing to push the implications of this train of thought further. Despite his personal aversion to sodomy, it was necessary to investigate it with an open mind. "If one examines this matter with a mind free of prejudices and as a philosopher," he averred, "one will see that there are a large number of actions that, remaining the same, change names from one century or one city to another and that to make the same man look alternatively guilty or innocent, chaste or lewd, good or bad, just or unjust, virtuous or depraved, it is often necessary only to relocate him."[27] When it came to sexual morality, the implications of this cultural, and indeed moral relativism, call into question the universalizing Christian-based arguments for the criminalization of sodomy.

While chipping away at the traditional rationales for anti-sodomy laws, philosophes also critiqued the harshness and utility of those laws as part of a more general call for penal reform.[28] We do not know the exact number of men executed for sodomy in early modern France, but in comparison with some of its neighbors, it was relatively few. Concerned that executions would publicize the crime and inspire imitation, magistrates seem to have primarily applied the death penalty when other crimes such as murder were involved. They preferred to mete out less severe, yet still cruel, punishments, such as imprisonment, banishment, and deportation to the colonies. That said, Parisians were reminded of the harshness of the law in 1750, when two otherwise nondescript men, having been caught on the street in flagrante delicto, were burned at the Place de Grève for this act alone.[29] One of the most straightforward condemnations of this kind of brutality came from the Marquis de Condorcet, better known for his advocacy for gender equality. "Sodomy, when there is no violence, cannot fall within the competence of the criminal laws," he wrote. "It does not violate the rights of any other man. It has only an indirect influence on the good order of society, like drunkenness [or] love of gambling. It is a vile, disgusting vice, whose true punishment is scorn. The penalty of burning is atrocious… [I]t must not be forgotten to note that it is to superstition that one owes the barbarous practice of punishment by burning."[30]

Whereas Condorcet concentrated on the penalty's cruelty, other writers, such as Joseph Elzéar Dominique Bernardi de Valernes, highlighted its counterproductivity. "These penalties will fail through their very severity," he claimed, "and they will only serve to prove that punishments cannot replace morals."[31] Jean-Paul Marat, later to become the Revolution's most famous martyr, also made clear the undesirable consequences of the persecution of sodomites by the law. In his *Plan de législation criminelle* (1780), he warned, "Fortunately, these crimes are uncommon, unless they have been favoured by certain customs. We must be careful, then, not to bring them out from the darkness that covers them. To crack down on certain very rare crimes always gives them birth."[32] Thinkers like Bernardi de Valernes and Marat did not advocate moderating these laws out of kindness; instead, they called for legal reform in order to prevent the proliferation of sodomy throughout society.

Marat and similarly minded commentators maintained that sodomy was quite rare in Paris. The police, in contrast, thought it exceedingly common and therefore worried even more about its potential to spread, especially through prostitution. The assumption that sodomitical relations, ipso facto defined as depraved, would also lead adolescent boys into the sexual trade may lie at the heart of an important transition in terminology used in police reports, as well as in society at large, during the 1770s and 1780s. "Sodomite," the capacious designation for anyone engaged in non-procreative sexual behaviors, came increasingly to be replaced by the term "pederast" when referring to same-sex relations. Originally referring to a man who engaged in sexual relations with an adolescent boy, by the 1780s, it designated any male who engaged in sexual relations with another male.

Despite ongoing antipathy toward sodomites and pederasts, changes in policing practices in Paris in the 1780s suggest that some of the critiques made by philosophes were finding a receptive audience. Although the police had arrested sodomites in the capital throughout the eighteenth century, they began to send out "pederasty patrols" in 1780 to apprehend suspected pederasts more systematically. To give an idea of scale, the police went out on patrol ninety-four times in 1786 and arrested more than 130 men.[33] The police detained some of these men because of their actions, such as making indecent propositions or touching another man sexually. Many men, however, were arrested simply because they were suspected of being pederasts. Patrolling was then quite suddenly curtailed. In 1787, officers were sent out only forty-five times and arrested about a dozen men. The following year, they went out on thirty-three occasions, bringing only a couple of men into custody. The commissioner, whose portfolio included the policing of pederasty during this shift, reported that when his officers were on patrol, they "saw and noticed a number of pederasts, several of whom had been recently arrested, prowling, cruising, and speaking with the greatest audacity, but none could be surprised in flagrante delicto and arrested."[34] The bar had obviously been raised over a short space of time; only when homosexual acts occurred in public were men now at risk of arrest.

As we have seen, philosophes did not draw on rights discourse to argue on behalf of sodomites. On the contrary, they advocated what they took to be a more effective way of policing sodomitical behavior, that is, through public disapproval. Jacques Pierre Brissot, later one of the leaders of the less radical Girondin faction during the Revolution, took this position in an essay entitled "Sodomy": "It harms the population; it should therefore be prohibited. But it is not by death that it should be punished, for the remedy would be worse than the problem. That is to harm the propagation of men doubly. All crimes against morals should be punished by public opinion. It is with the seal of ignominy that those who attack morals [and] public modesty should be marked."[35] Whereas it had traditionally seemed appropriate for law to regulate something seen as immoral, this focus on the harm reputedly done society by sodomy suggested that it was appropriate for society itself to thwart it.

In the eighteenth century, then, a number of philosophes undermined the rationale for the criminalization of sodomy by critiquing the harshness and efficacy of the law. But decriminalization did not result from the Enlightenment alone. After all, the writings that we have explored here were read in many other countries, but it was only in France that sodomy was effectively rendered legal. The Enlightenment was necessary, in short, but it was clearly not sufficient in and of itself. The Revolution of 1789, which replaced the Old Regime with a new representative government, was also required.

Revolutionary paradoxes

After the National Assembly committed to writing a constitution for the new regime, it decided that a national penal code was also in order, one that would replace the patchwork of laws that had hitherto governed France. To that end, it created the Committee of Criminal Legislation, tasking it to draft the code that would deal with felonies, the most serious class of crimes. It meanwhile entrusted the Constitutional Committee to write the Code of Municipal Police and Correctional Police, which would regulate misdemeanors.[36]

The first of these codes to be approved by the Constituent Assembly was the Code of Municipal Police, on July 22, 1791. Given that sodomy had traditionally been treated as a capital crime, it would have been somewhat surprising to see it included in the code regulating misdemeanors, and indeed, it was not explicitly mentioned. Several articles contained within this code, however, intimated that sodomy could be regulated, albeit indirectly: "Those accused of having committed a gross public indecency, by a public offence against the decency of women, by unseemly actions, by displaying or selling obscene images, of having encouraged debauchery, or having corrupted young people of either sex, will be immediately arrested."[37] While not explicitly criminalizing sexual relations between persons of the same sex, words like "indecency" and "corrupted" easily brought to mind images of same-sex sexual behavior, especially when paired with "young people of either sex," and one could well imagine that such laws might be applied more forcefully against male sodomites. When presented to the Assembly, some discussion of these new provisions ensued, but no significant impediments emerged to prevent their adoption.

Meanwhile, the Committee of Criminal Legislation was busy drafting the Penal Code. Six of the committee's seven members were either magistrates or lawyers. Generally sympathetic to the Enlightenment, they tended toward political moderation.[38] In the draft of the Penal Code to the Constituent Assembly they submitted for approval on September 25, 1791, sodomy did not make an explicit appearance, despite its status as a capital crime during the Old Regime. Although it is impossible for us to know what motivated them to exclude sodomy from this new body of law, we do have some clues about what might have been on their minds. First, as Lynn Hunt reminds us, "the revolutionaries did everything they could to push out the boundaries of personal autonomy."[39] They passed laws, for example, against primogeniture and in favor of divorce. This more general commitment to expanding freedom, at least when it did not endanger someone else's rights, went hand in hand, at least conceptually, with the decriminalization of sodomy, and of prostitution and incest, too, which were, as mentioned above, also left out of the penal code.

Secondly, the revolutionaries wanted to secularize the law, as Michael Sibalis has pointed out.[40] In a report outlining the basic principles for the new Penal Code, committee spokesman Louis Michel Lepeletier de Saint-Fargeau underscored this commitment: "You will no longer find here those great crimes of heresy, divine treason, sorcery, and magic, whose truly sacrilegious pursuit has for so long offended the divinity, and for which so much blood has stained the soil in the name of heaven… [We seek] to focus on the real outrages which affront the nation, rather than these factitious offences, created by superstition, feudalism, the tax system, and despotism."[41] The close historical association between sodomy and other religious interdictions suggests that when the revolutionaries eliminated "crimes" like blasphemy, heresy, and magic from the legal code, they effectively undercut the justification to criminalize sodomy. It is also well worth recalling that on September 27, 1791, only two days following the adoption of the new penal code, the Assembly voted to grant full civil rights to Jews, a clearer indication of the church's weakening grasp on the new political order.

Sibalis might well be right that it was "likely that the decriminalization of sodomy was simply a fortuitous and unforeseen consequence of their secularization of criminal law."[42] But we have already seen how other factors also came into play. Some philosophes promoted using reason to evaluate, as objectively as possible, laws that had been heretofore justified by custom, and legislators were doubtless influenced by such ideas. In the very year that the new penal code was promulgated, for instance, Jacques André Naigeon seemed to provide a rationale for decriminalizing sodomy. When it came to the ancients, he maintained,

> The legislators had the wisdom and the good sense to think that, far from taking cognizance of these secret disorders that I have just spoken of and making them the specific object of a law, they should not even imagine them or decree any penalties against the various excesses to which man may abandon himself at the instigation of the most violent and most universal passion in nature, no matter what the kind of these excesses and the object toward which his passion drags and throws him.

"It seems to me," he continued, "that in the case in question here, public opinion can be directed in such a way as to give it greater and more effective coercive force than that of penal laws."[43]

Such progressive arguments still rested on the notion that sodomy should be suppressed, but by public opinion rather than law. Another philosophe, however, Anacharsis Cloots, staked out a much more radical position in *The Orator of Humankind*, which also appeared in the year that sodomy was decriminalized. Born Jean-Baptiste du Val-de-Grâce, Baron de Cloots, this Prussian noble had moved to Paris as a young man, working with Diderot and d'Alembert on the Encyclopedia, and later became an enthusiastic supporter of the Revolution. Fascinated by Greek history, he adopted the pseudonym, "Anacharsis," after a "barbarian" philosopher from the sixth century BCE who moved to Athens, where he garnered a reputation for speaking honestly and directly. Just as the original Anacharsis became the first foreigner to be granted citizenship in Athens, Cloots followed in his footsteps to become a naturalized citizen of France. And when it came to writing about the touchy subject of sodomy, at least, Cloots showed himself to be similarly sincere and forthright. "It is important to reason correctly," Cloots declared.

> So, Achilles loved Patroclus, Orestes loved Pylades, Aristogiton loved Harmodius, Socrates loved Alicibiades, etc. Were they less useful to their country for that reason? The charms of Briseis would have made the siege of Troy fail, if not for the charms of Patroclus. And the Athenians would have languished for a longer time under the tyranny of the sons of Peisistratus, if not for the intimate union of the two virtuous lovers who were declared the liberators of the country.

According to Cloots, history teaches that homoerotic relationships led time and again to some of the most heroic acts of the ancient world. But he drove his point even further. "People are surprised about the corruption of the gymnasiums," he reports, "as if electrical bodies dressed in excitable tassels could move together without experiencing frequent explosions. I would just as soon call tickling and itching crimes against nature."[44] As we have seen, even the most progressive of thinkers proved incapable up to this point of seeing homosexual behavior as morally neutral, let alone positive. When liberated from the constraints imposed by traditional cultural norms, however, Cloots demonstrates in this passage how it was finally possible to articulate a positive valuation of homosexual relations.

At the other end of the political spectrum, the anonymous author of a counterrevolutionary pamphlet published in 1790 under the title "The Children of Sodom to the National Assembly" also sheds light on attitudes about sodomy on the eve of decriminalization.[45] This royalist satire was clearly not intended to be a defense of sodomy. In fact, its purpose was to build on pejorative notions of sodomy in order to critique revolutionary politics. At the same time, the logic undergirding the political positions expressed by the sodomites within the text suggests that some of the implicit arguments made by philosophes had found resonance, even if they were here being held up to ridicule.

This over-the-top lampoon begins by mocking the constitution of political interest groups across society, from nobles to commons, tailors' assistants to servants, cuckolds to prostitutes. Late to the game, some of the most notorious sodomites decided that they needed to call a gathering of their kindred spirits in order to ensure that their political interests be represented, too. Constituting themselves as the Order of the Cuff, taken from the slang term used in eighteenth-century Paris to designate men who engaged in homosexual relations, they were immediately joined by women who engaged in anal sex with men and/or sexual relations with other women. Here, the author blends older and newer ways of thinking in very telling ways. The sodomites are defined in traditional terms; that is, they include men and women who engage in various forms of illicit sexual behavior. But the notion of constituting a defined group rests on a more recent conceptualization. Consequently, when the sodomites boldly—and publicly—announce themselves as a group in the pamphlet, they are able to make claims for fundamental human rights.

Once established as a distinct social grouping, the Order of the Cuff commemorated their forbears, that is, those sodomites who had been viciously persecuted throughout history. By defining themselves as a group through history, sodomites could now look forward to a happier future, thanks to the progress being made by the new revolutionary order. It is important to reiterate that the pamphlet's author did not intend for his words to be taken at face value; rather, he wanted to ridicule the Revolution by linking it to the lascivious buggers who comprised the Order of the Cuff. But what is interesting for our purposes here is that even when meant to invite scorn and contempt, the framing arguments set out in this satire by the sodomites are strikingly similar to those made by philosophes in favor of decriminalization. More fascinating still, the author's coupling of sodomy and individual human rights, while meant to disparage, suggests at the same time that they could now be thought of as linked, thereby opening up new conceptual possibilities for the future.

The decriminalization of sodomy in 1791

In the contemporary era, we typically challenge legal injustices against LGBTQ people on the basis of demanding our fundamental human rights as individuals. We maintain, for instance, that we should have the rights to marry the person we love or use bathrooms that correspond to our gender identity. During the Old Regime, in contrast, it was on the basis of belonging to circumscribed groups, such as being a member of a guild, living in a monastery, or enjoying noble status, that particular privileges were conferred. Leading up to the Revolution, a growing number of people began to argue that it was simply wrong to exclude individuals from basic civil rights simply on the basis of their group identities, and in the early years of the revolutionary decade, women, slaves, Jews, Protestants, property-less men, actors, executioners, and others demanded such rights, albeit with uneven degrees of success.

If we try to examine the decriminalization of sodomy through the lens of rights discourse, however, we will be sorely disappointed. We might have expected a radical thinker like Condorcet to make just that kind of argument. After all, in Condorcet's view, "so long as an activity did not violate any human rights, it should not be criminalized," as Lynn Hunt has pointed out.[46] But the legal sanctions against sodomites did not lie in their belonging to a distinct, recognizable social group; rather, they were individuals who because of their sexual behavior were regarded as indecent and corrupt. It was virtually impossible, then, for Condorcet to portray them as deserving full human rights, even while he was able to criticize their inhuman treatment at the hands of the law. Or let us take the case of Cloots, who was fervently devoted to the Declaration of the Rights of Man and Citizen, the revolutionary catechism of human rights written and adopted by the National Assembly in 1789. Consider article 4, which stipulated that "Liberty consists of doing anything which does not harm others," and article 5, which mandated that "The law has the right to forbid only actions harmful to society." To our modern eyes, it does not seem difficult to relate these principles to sodomy, but in his defense of sodomites, even the radical thinker Cloots failed to draw such a connection.

Once we separate ourselves from rights discourse, we can begin to make sense of what made decriminalization of sodomy possible. We find that decriminalization was not an accident, as the counterrevolutionary pamphlet makes clear. Nor did it mark a radical turning point. Instead, as Jeffrey Merrick has argued on many occasions, things look remarkably similar on either side of the revolutionary divide.[47] As we have seen, some of the progressive philosophes had already set out an agenda before the Revolution about what to do with sodomy. They did so not on the basis of thinking about sodomites as constituting some group of people, but rather as individuals who committed particular types of crime. Yet they ended up staking out a quite radical position, largely because of their opposition to law based on superstition, overly harsh legal punishments, and the negative consequences for society of having such a law. And as we have also seen, the police had moved decidedly in that very direction even before the outbreak of the Revolution, especially when it came to acts in private.

Although unable to make a positive case for sodomites via the principle of human rights, the more progressive philosophes made sodomy thinkable in new ways through their critiques of Old Regime law. At the same time—and this sounds counterintuitive— they strove to make it possible to forget. They did not like the idea of sodomy, and they did not want to talk about it. They considered it dangerous to bring sodomy to the public's attention, and they thought it harmful for the country. Although there was no legal right to privacy, either before or after the Revolution, they seemed to imply that it would be best to ignore such sexual behavior in the private sphere. But they were committed to preventing such activity in the public sphere, either through the application of laws regarding public indecency or prostitution, or through public scorn.

This argument carried the day, at least for about 200 years. Sodomy may have been decriminalized, but as Scott Gunther states in relation to France, "various forms of repression continued over the course of the nineteenth century and into the twentieth century, and in some respects became more severe."[48] Society generally continued to typify homosexuals as sinful, abnormal, and criminally inclined, and the findings of William Peniston show how dogged the Paris police could be in their pursuit and harassment of homosexual men.[49] The rise of the new profession of psychology, with its focus on diagnosing various forms of "perversion," provided even more ammunition that could be used against them.[50]

Of course, the situation for homosexuals would have been far worse had the antisodomy laws remained in France's penal code. To be sure, the police found ways to make life difficult for people attracted to their own sex, but as Michael Sibalis reminds us, "the Revolution opened the modern era in which, whatever social opprobrium French homosexuals might still encounter in their daily lives, they need no longer fear legal penalties" for homosexuality per se.[51] Let us not forget that just across the English Channel, more than fifty men were executed for sodomy in Great Britain between 1800 and 1835.[52]

Conclusion

Legal scholar Nan Hunter's work on the decriminalization of sodomy in the United States and historian Lynn Hunt's study of the history of human rights help us in our evaluations of the meaning of 1791. Both see such legislation as part of a larger puzzle. In the case of *Lawrence v. Texas* (2003), Hunter states, "The Supreme Court performed a double move, creating a dramatic discursive moment: it both decriminalized consensual homosexual relations between adults, and, simultaneously, authorized a new regime of heightened regulation of homosexuality." "Decriminalization is not deregulation," she continues, "[n]or is it a marker of full equality."[53] She could well have been writing about the decriminalization of sodomy during the French Revolution when she concludes, "Lawrence v. Texas marked a dramatic milestone in efforts to limit state power to control homosexuality, but the product is likely to be a different regulatory regime rather than a libertarian utopia."

Although she does not focus on sodomy per se, Lynn Hunt also helps us parse the meaning of 1791's legislation. "Human rights," she asserts, "require three interlocking qualities: rights must be natural (inherent in human beings); equal (the same for everyone); and universal (applicable everywhere)."[54] In some ways, the decriminalization of sodomy implied, at least implicitly, these three qualities, and as such, it was a sign of significant progress. "Yet even naturalness, equality, and universality are not quite enough," she warns. "Human rights only become meaningful when they gain political content."[55] Ironically, the anonymous author of "The Children of Sodom" understood the importance, and, in his eyes, danger, of activating rights through politicization. But as we know all too well, we have much more work to do in order to ensure real freedom for sexual minorities, in France and in the rest of the world.

Notes

1   A notable exception is Lynn Hunt, *The French Revolution and Human Rights: A Brief Documentary History* (Boston: Bedford/St. Martin's Press, 1996).
2   Flora Leroy-Forgeot, *Histoire juridique de l'homosexualité en Europe* (Paris: Presses Universitaires de France, 1994), 64.
3   Marc Daniel [Michel Duchein], "Histoire de la législation pénale française concernant l'homosexualité," *Arcadie*, no. 96 (December 1961): 618–627.
4   Thierry Pastorello, "L'abolition du crime de sodomie en 1791. Un long processus social, répressif et pénal," *Cahiers d'histoire: Revue d'histoire critique* 112–113 (2010): 197–208.

5   See, for example, Michael David Sibalis, "The Regulation of Male Homosexuality in Revolutionary and Napoleonic France, 1789–1815," in *Homosexuality in Modern France*, ed. Jeffrey Merrick and Bryant T. Ragan, Jr. (New York: Oxford University Press, 1996), 80–101.
6   For an excellent discussion of the complex ways that prostitution was both decriminalized and somewhat paradoxically more heavily regulated in the French Revolution and thereafter, see Clyde Plumauzille, *Prostitution et Révolution. Les femmes publiques dans la cité républicaine (1789-1804)* (Ceyzérieu: Champ Vallon, 2016).
7   James A. Brundage, *Law, Sex, and Christian Society in Medieval Europe* (Chicago: University of Chicago Press, 1987).
8   Leroy-Forgeot, *Histoire juridique*. In the present chapter, I will follow the convention of using "homosexual" occasionally as an adjective to describe same-sex sexual behavior, but this descriptive phrase should not be taken as emanating from "homosexual identity" in the modern sense.
9   David F. Greenberg, *The Construction of Homosexuality* (Chicago: University of Chicago Press, 1988).
10 Maurice Lever, *Les bûchers de Sodome* (Paris: Fayard, 1985).
11 Michael Sibalis, "Male Homosexuality in the Age of Enlightenment and Revolution, 1680-1850," in *Gay Life and Culture: A World History*, ed. Robert Aldrich (London: Thames & Hudson, 2006/New York: Rizzoli International Publishers, 2006), 102–123.
12 Jeffrey Merrick and Bryant T. Ragan, Jr., *Homosexuality in Early Modern France: A Documentary Collection* (New York: Oxford University Press, 2001).
13 The literature on this distinction is voluminous. An excellent starting place is David Halperin, *How to Do the History of Homosexuality* (Chicago: University of Chicago Press, 2002).
14 Michel Foucault, *The History of Sexuality*, trans. Robert Hurley, 3 vols. (New York: Pantheon, 1978–86), 1:101. Since the publication of Foucault's work, many studies have shown that sodomy was even more capacious, including many other sins that were not sexual in nature. See Helmut Puff, *Sodomy in Reformation Germany and Switzerland, 1400–1600* (Chicago: University of Chicago Press, 2003), 7–9.
15 Brundage, *Law*, 472–474.
16 Lever, *Bûchers*, 47; F. R. P. Akehurst, *The Etablissements de Saint Louis: Thirteenth-Century Law Texts from Tours, Orléans, and Paris* (Philadelphia: University of Pennsylvania Press, 1996), 304.
17 Lever, *Bûchers*, 48.
18 Antoine Bruneau, *Observations et maximes sur les matières criminelles* (Paris, 1715); For the English translation, see Merrick and Ragan, *Early Modern*, 17. Professor Merrick and I translated and included many of the sources used in this present chapter in that volume. In the future, I will simply cite such texts in the following form: M&R, 17.
19 Claude Lebrun de la Rochette, *Les Procès civil et criminel divisé en cinq livres*, 2 vols. [1611] (Lyons, 1618); M&R, 15.
20 Bruneau, *Observations*; M&R, 17.
21 Daniel Jousse, *Traité de la justice criminelle de France*, 4 vols. (Paris, 1771); M&R, 18.
22 Jousse, *Traité*; M&R, 20.
23 Montesquieu, *De l'Esprit des lois*, in *Oeuvres complètes*, 3 vols. [1748] (Paris, 1758); M&R, 154.
24 Voltaire, *Prix de la justice et de l'humanité*, in *Oeuvres complètes*; M&R, 160.

25 Montesquieu, *Lois*; M&R, 154.
26 Claude-Adrien Helvétius, *De l'Homme* (London, 1773), 235–236.
27 Jacques André Naigeon, *Encyclopédie méthodique: Philosophie ancienne et moderne*, 3 vols. (Paris, 1791–94); M&R, 167.
28 Marc Ancel, "The Collection of European Penal Codes and the Study of Comparative Law," *University of Pennsylvania Law Review* 106, no. 3 (1958): 329–384, esp. 343–345; Leroy-Forgeot, *Histoire juridique*, 64.
29 M&R, 77–79.
30 Marie Jean Antoine Nicolas de Caritat, marquis de Condorcet, footnote in edition of Voltaire, *Prix*; M&R, 160–161.
31 Joseph Elzéar Dominique de Bernardi de Valernes, *Bibliothèque de législation du législateur, du politique, ou de jurisconsulte*, ed. Brissot, 10 vols. (Berlin, 1782); M&R, 164.
32 Jean Paul Marat, *Plan de legislation criminelle*, third edition (Paris, 1790 [1780]), 103–104.
33 Archives Nationales, Y11727–11732.
34 Archives Nationales, Y11731.
35 Jacques Pierre Brissot, *Théorie des lois criminelles* (Berlin, 1781); M&R, 162–163.
36 Daniel, *Histoire*, 623; Sibalis, "Regulation," 82.
37 Sibalis, "Regulation," 82–83.
38 Daniel, *Histoire*, 623.
39 Lynn Hunt, *Inventing Human Rights* (New York: W. W. Norton & Co., 2007), 62.
40 Sibalis, "Regulation," 82.
41 *Oeuvres de Michel Lepeletier Saint-Fargeau* (Brussels: Arnold Lacrosse, 1826), 95–97.
42 Sibalis, "Regulation," 82.
43 Naigeon, *Encyclopédie*; M&R, 166–167.
44 Anacharsis Cloots, *L'Orateur du genre humain* (Paris, 1791); M&R, 218.
45 *Les Enfants de Sodome à l'Assemblée Nationale, ou Députation de l'ordre de la manchette aux représentants de tous les ordres pris dans les soixante districts de Paris et de Versailles y réunis* (Paris, 1790); M&R, 173–185.
46 Hunt, *French Revolution*, 10.
47 Jeffrey Merrick, "Commissioner Foucault, Inspector Noël, and the 'Pederasts' of Paris, 1780-3," *Journal of Social History* 32, no. 2 (1998): 287–307.
48 Scott Gunther, *The Elastic Closet: A History of Homosexuality in France, 1942-Present* (New York: Palgrave Macmillan, 2009), 6.
49 William A. Peniston, *Pederasts and Others: Urban Culture and Sexual Identity in Nineteenth-Century Paris* (New York: Harrington Park Press, 2004).
50 Foucault, *Sexuality*.
51 Michael Sibalis, "Homosexuality in Early Modern France," in *Queer Masculinities, 1550-1800: Siting Same-Sex Desire in the Early Modern World*, ed. Katherine O'Donnell and Michael O'Rourke (London: Palgrave Macmillan, 2006), 211–231, see 227.
52 A. D. Harvey, "Prosecutions for Sodomy in England at the Beginning of the Nineteenth Century," *The Historical Journal* 21, no. 4 (1978): 939–948, see 939.
53 Nan D. Hunter, "Sexual Orientation and the Paradox of Heightened Scrutiny," *Michigan Law Review* 102, no. 7 (2004): 1528–1554, see 1554.
54 Hunt, *Inventing Human Rights*, 20.
55 Hunt, *Human Rights*, 21.

3

Arguing against Intolerance: Louisiana and Britain in the Early Nineteenth Century

Charles Upchurch

In the winter of 1814–15, the legislature of Louisiana rejected by an immense majority, a bill "For the better observance of the Sabbath; for punishing the crime of sodomy; for preventing the defacing of Church-yards; for shutting the theaters and stores on Sunday, and for other purposes;" the chief opposer of the bill declaring, on the legislative floor, "that such *persecuting intolerance* might well suit the New-England puritans, who were descended from the bigoted fanatics of Old England, who were great readers of the Bible, and, *consequently*, ignorant, prejudiced, cold-blooded, false, and cruel; but could never be fastened on the more enlightened, liberal and philosophical inhabitants of Louisiana, the descendants of Frenchmen."[1]

The above may be the most widely circulated unequivocal denunciation of a sodomy law in English in the early nineteenth century, and while highly problematic as a source, it is nevertheless important for understanding how greater legal tolerance for acts of same-sex desire might have been achieved in the early nineteenth century. Making use of this quote requires not only taking steps to verify its authenticity, but also working to place it within the context of its time. The battle of New Orleans occurred in the middle of this particular legislative session, and the contest of wills then playing out between General Andrew Jackson and the Louisiana Legislature seems crucial to this statement being made with such force. The contest between Jackson and the legislature hinged on ideas of loyalty, and the degree to which those who were recently made American citizens could be trusted as Americans.[2] This debate placed issues of the law at its center, taking the law as the primary force that, when agreed to by free men, could bind them together in the present while still allowing for the continuation of previous affiliations and allegiances, with the logic of that debate having consequences for all subjects as well as citizens. In this context, embedding the denunciation of the sodomy law in a list of other foreign laws also rejected does not diminish the importance of this debate for the history of sexuality, but instead, draws attention to the similarities between this legislative denunciation of a sodomy law and another parliamentary move against sodomy laws, in this case the British sodomy laws, beginning in the 1820s.[3]

The common thread between these two episodes, one in London and one in New Orleans, it will be argued, points to a potential new focus for the historian of same-sex desire working before the late nineteenth century. Instead of placing the pursuit a stable subject motivated by same-sex desire at the center of the project, this new approach focuses instead on bringing into the history of sexuality the analysis of a widely embraced ideological position from which the persecution of homosexual acts, along with other acts of intolerance and injustice, could be resisted.[4] Doing this places efforts to lessen the sodomy laws in dialogue with other humanitarian movements of the late eighteenth and early nineteenth centuries, suggesting heretofore neglected connections humanitarians may have made across divisions of race, class, gender, and sexual preference.

How reliable is the source?

The most problematic aspect of the quote is the difficulty in confirming these actual words were spoken within the Louisiana Legislature. This passage was originally published in New York and London by John Bristed, in *The Resources of the United States of America, or, A View of the Agricultural, Commercial, Manufacturing, Financial, Political, Literary, Moral and Religious Capacity and Character of the American People*. The passage was reprinted in *The British Critic*, the *Quarterly Review*, and at least three other publications over the next few years.[5] The period invoked in the passage aligns with the First Session of the Second Louisiana Legislature, which ran from November 10, 1814, to February 1815.[6] The *Journal de la Chambre des Representans* for this session runs for over 100 pages but did not directly record the debate or the proposed legislation. The *Journal of the Senate* for this session did not survive, and at several points in the *Journal of the Senate* for the previous session, near the end of the summary of the day's events, was a note to "(see journals of secret proceedings)."[7] Efforts to recover these other secret journals were also unsuccessful. The surviving Louisiana newspapers for the period of this legislative session are so incomplete that little should be read into the fact that what remains has no reference to this particular incident.[8] This lack of state records and contemporary newspaper reports therefore shifts the focus back to the initial writing of John Bristed and the reliability of his published work.

John Bristed was born in England, in 1778, the son of a clergyman of the Church of England. After graduating at Winchester College, he studied medicine and law before moving to the United States in 1806. Before coming to the United States he published many works, including a two-volume book on traveling the Scottish Highlands, a volume of philosophical essays, a novel, and an examination of the Quaker faith.[9] He was successful as a Counsellor at Law in New York City, while still publishing a considerable amount. In 1807 he conducted the *Monthly Magazine*, and his publications while living in New York in the 1810s included *Hints on the National Bankruptcy of Great Britain* (New York, 1809) and the *Resources of the British Empire* (1811), in addition to the 1818 *Resources of the United States*. It was a mark of his social standing in New York that in 1820 he married Magdalen Astor (1788–1832), a daughter of John Jacob Astor, and their son, Charles Astor Bristed, went on to have a successful literary career in his own right.

Bristed's personal support of religion and bias against the French Revolution is clear. In *The Resources of the United States of America* he argues that that "many serious people doubt the permanence of the federal constitution, because in that national compact there is *no* reference to the Providence of God."[10] He also strongly criticizes revolutionary France for having "the execrable honour of having first reduced the individual and national atheism to a regular system."[11] By the end of the 1820s he had shifted careers, completing his studies in Divinity under the rector of St. Michael's, in Bristol, Rhode Island, being ordained and made the rector's assistant in 1828, and eventually serving as the rector of the parish until his death in 1855.[12] Thus, based on his personal beliefs, Bristed had a motivation for exaggerating the rhetoric in his report on the debate in Louisiana Legislature quoted above. That said, that a sodomy law might be proposed in this way at this time is consistent with what was then occurring throughout the United States, and also consistent with the specific debates and confrontations occurring between General Jackson and the Louisiana Legislature in the weeks before and after the Battle of New Orleans, making it seem at least plausible that such an incident might have occurred.

The broader context within the United States

Most of the original British North American colonies had laws against sodomy dating from the seventeenth century, but these were rarely enforced then, and all but abandoned in the eighteenth century.[13] When Louisiana became a US territory in 1805 the first Territorial Legislature passed a hurried, stop-gap general criminal statute. It provided a system of criminal law for Louisiana simply by denouncing as crimes a number of offences and then saying that such crimes should be construed according to the traditions of the common law of England, about which at that time the people of Louisiana knew practically nothing. It is significant that this method of law enactment was condemned by a provision in the 1812 Louisiana constitution.[14] Every legislature thereafter added new criminal statutes, with no systematic codification occurring before the twentieth century.

There was also a movement in the first decades of the nineteenth century across the United States to strengthen legislation regulating morality. As Clare Lyons and others have shown, these changes were evident in legal policy, in judicial decisions, in print culture, and in religious culture—redefining publicly acceptable attitudes toward sexual desire and behavior. Combining a law related to sex between men with laws against blasphemy, Sunday trading, and other moral legislation happened in other states, as part of an evangelical-led movement to roll back the greater permissiveness on matters of morality and sexuality that had characterized previous generations.[15] This evangelical movement was a reaction to the culture that had been created by what Faramerz Dabhoiwala has described for Britain as the First Sexual Revolution of the early eighteenth century, which saw more public discussion of and public displays of sexual behavior and desire, a greater emphasis on the pleasures of sexual acts, as well as a loosening of church, state, and family control over sexual behavior.[16]

In the United States, the movement to roll back these greater personal freedoms gained strength after the American War of Independence. Because the American nation-state existed to some degree as a representation of its citizens, the sexual activity and gender order of Euro-Americans became one measure of the virtuousness of the new republic. For the evangelicals within this movement, the sexual freedom and emphasis on pleasure of the first sexual revolution was emblematic of the most democratic, radical, anarchic, and fearful possibilities of the American Revolution. They attempted to restrict sexual behavior, curtail discussion, and circumscribe knowledge in the public realm. At its more benign (but still problematic) it worked to restrict sexual behavior to a norm of monogamous, heterosexual, and intra-racial marriage that rested on a redefinition of manhood and womanhood as complementary opposites.

The process of turning United States' territories into new states within the Union should be seen as related to these themes. New states, and the governments, laws, institutions, and enforcement possibilities that came with them, would produce a patriarchal and democratic society, and in the process, the greater legitimacy that inter-racial relationships had in these regions, or the greater rights and public responsibilities afforded to women or free people of color, would also be delegitimized. The establishment of states would define white Americans as distinct from their European ancestors and neighbors, and the Africans and indigenous Indians who lived among and beside them.[17] This new order recognized only a narrow band of behavior and relationships as bestowing status within society, such as the right to pass property to legally recognized spouses and children. It would also become a prime way of colonizing native peoples, controlling African Americans, and limiting the freedom of white settlers. This was a fundamental and early part of establishing the American state and identity, and crucial, in the words of Malcolm Rohrbough, to turning borderland into a bordered land.[18]

The specific context within the legislature

All of these issues were present in the new state of New Orleans in 1814 and 1815, exacerbated by the crucible of war and the question of loyalty in the final days of the War of 1812. In August 1814, the Governor of Louisiana, William Claiborne, wrote to General Jackson before his arrival in New Orleans, letting him know that there were many in the state "much devoted to the interests of Spain" and with "their partiality to the English ... not less observable than their dislike for the American Government." There was a concern as to whether the Louisiana militias would hold together, or follow previous loyalties. General Jackson was also allegedly informed that the Legislature, dominated by men of French dissent, "has been accused of lukewarmness and even want of patriotism."[19]

Governor Claiborne had served as the territorial governor from 1804 to 1812. He was born in Virginia, studied law, and served on the Tennessee Supreme Court before taking the seat in the US House of Representatives previously held by Andrew Jackson. Although appointed territorial governor by the president in 1812, he was subsequently elected the first Governor of Louisiana, defeating a Frenchman, Jacques Villeré.

The Legislature cooperated with Governor Claiborne and General Jackson, but they refused to take any steps that might abrogate their authority. The legislature refused to suspend the writ of habeas corpus, as suggested by Jackson and proposed by Claiborne, and when Governor Claiborne requested the Legislature adjourn itself for twenty-five days as the battle loomed, this also was refused. General Jackson then declared martial law on December 16, 1814, just a day after his public address to the people of New Orleans in which ended "with the ominous words: 'Those who are not for us are against us, and will be dealt with accordingly.' "[20]

The Legislature ceased to sit after the arrival of the British in the region on December 23, as all its members were engaged in the work of defense, either as soldiers in the field or in companies of veterans, or as members of relief committees. Every day, however, at noon, three or four members of the Senate and of the House met in their respective halls to effect an adjournment. On December 28, the President of the Senate, and two members, on arriving at the government house, found on the staircase a sentinel, who forbade them to enter the Senate chamber, and a similar thing happened to members of the House. When asked why he took such a step, Jackson told the representative of the Legislature that he had been advised by one of his aides "that the Assembly were about to give up the country to the enemy."[21]

The contest continued several weeks later, after the British left, with the questions of loyalty in a pluralistic society and the role of the law in cementing such bonds even more central issues than before. Not only had Jackson illegally suspended the Legislature during the battle, but he had also violated the constitutional rights of the French citizens of New Orleans after the conclusion of the fighting. At issue was that Frenchmen who had taken up arms in the militia to fight against the British wanted permission to return to their families. Jackson refused to release them, but soldiers could still get a leave by having their political representative provide a certificate of their nationality, and, after being signed by an officer of sufficient rank, this document allowed for an individual's release from the militia. But Jackson felt these were granted too easily, and Jackson ordered that all men with such discharges had to leave New Orleans, retiring at least as far north as Baton Rouge.

This incensed Louis Louallier, a member of the Legislature, who wrote to *Courrier de la Louisiane* on March 3, 1815, that these Frenchmen were also American citizens, and could not be subject to such an arbitrary order. "To remain silent ... would be an act of cowardice, which ought not to be expected from a citizen of a free country." "The French have until this moment been treated in the United States with that regard which a great people deserves and requires." "Those brave men ask no other reward but being permitted peaceably to enjoy among us the rights secured by them by treaties and the laws of America." "We do not know any law authorizing General Jackson to apply to alien friends a measure which the President of the United States, himself, has only the right to adopt against alien enemies."[22] Louallier concluded his public rebuke of Jackson by arguing that

> it is high time the laws should resume their empire; that the citizens of this State should return to the full enjoyment of their rights; that in acknowledging that we are indebted to General Jackson for the preservation of our city and the

defeat of the British, we do not feel much inclined, though gratitude, to sacrifice any of our privileges.[23]

This defiant public letter greatly incensed Jackson. Louallier, an American by naturalization and a Frenchman by birth, was arrested by Jackson to be tried by court-martial as a spy. Even after the court-martial acquitted Louallier Jackson refused to release him, and it was not until the president of the United States had directed that all military offences be pardoned that Jackson released Louallier.

This was also most likely the time, based on an examination of the *Journal de la Chambre des Representans*, and the *Journal of the Senate* for this and surrounding sessions of the Louisiana Assembly, that the vote was taken that led to the rejection of the sodomy law, and other laws related to the enforcement of evangelical codes of morality. While vehemently arguing for their loyalty to the United States, these men in the Louisiana Legislature were also arguing that the basis of that loyalty was grounded in the law—the agreement struck on accession to the union, and while that agreement imposed limits on some behaviors, it left others untouched. Those freedoms would be tenaciously and vociferously defended against "the bigoted fanatics" who might claim a religious right to impose new standards, which, according to "the more enlightened, Liberal and philosophical inhabitants of Louisiana," were in fact "ignorant, prejudiced, cold-blooded, false and cruel." Rather than shrinking from it as "unspeakable," these, the most elite and powerful men in the state of Louisiana, defended their right, as citizens of the United States, to not have a sodomy law. The principle on which that refusal was based was central to their identity as independent men, even if the specific issue of sex between men was most likely not one for almost all of them.

The broader meaning

At about this same time, in the early nineteenth century in London, there is evidence to suggest that another refutation of a sodomy law was being put together by a limited number of parliamentarians.[24] Much like the quote that began this chapter, the evidence for this group in London and their activities is both highly suggestive and ultimately, at least as of yet, impossible to confirm in key aspects. The primary evidence for the existence of this group and its goals is a 100-page document, the poem *Don Leon* and its accompanying endnotes. It is a poetic defense of same-sex desire, along with other forms of sexual desire, long known to Byron scholars, and already the subject of excellent analysis by scholars, including George Wilson Knight and Louis Crompton. From the early 1950s, however, the assumption formed that the poem was written in 1833 or later, and this has lead to a significant underestimation of the importance of the political discussion within the poem.[25] Based on specific political references imbedded in the verse, it can be shown that *Don Leon* is describing a specific parliamentary debate in 1825.[26] It was a debate where Robert Peel added a clause to the 1823 Threatening Letters Act, changing the definition of "infamous crime" within English Law. In 1822 Viscount Castlereagh had committed suicide, but not before telling Peel, King George IV, and others that he was being blackmailed for alleged homosexual acts. Peel crafted legislation that could help men in Castlereagh's situation, but the courts found the wording in the 1823 legislation was ambiguous, and an amending clause was added to the Threatening Letters Act in the spring of 1825. The summer of 1825, shortly after the passage of this amendment, saw what seems to be the largest wave of prosecutions for sex between men in London for the whole of the nineteenth century. In addition to the publicized arrests of dozens of men in London, the summer of 1825 also saw three members of Parliament, all directly connected to the *Don Leon* poem, either flee the country or commit suicide under either public or private allegations that they had had sex with men. One further MP mentioned in the text of *Don Leon* survived as a member of the House of Commons in the 1820s before his involvement in two further scandals involving sex with men forced him to flee the country in the early 1840s.[27]

If the main documentation we have recording the Louisiana denunciation of sodomy laws is a short, published, and widely reproduced report, no such public statement was made by the men in London, who quietly and privately circulated their much more extensive arguments. While the majority of the *Don Leon* poem seems to be the work of one individual, the endnotes were added by multiple hands, and updated several times over more than two decades.. The endnotes also make extensive reference to another published work, now lost, that was more of an extended legal and philosophical argument against the sodomy laws. It was titled *A Free Examination into the Penal Statutes, xxv Henr. VIII, cap. 6, and vEliz. c. 17*, and it was "addrest [sic] to Both Houses of Parliament."[28] The authors of the poem and the endnotes address the reader directly at several points, and use plural pronouns, such as when it is mentioned that quoted material was "taken from *A free Examination* ... a book which we recommend all persons to peruse, if they can get it, for it has become very scarce."[29] At other points, the authors of the poem and the endnotes demonstrate a familiarity with the seating arrangement within the House of Commons, and with personalities of its members.

The arguments contained in *Don Leon* are written from the perspective of someone who feels same-sex desires to be natural and inborn in some individuals, but the narrative is also framed in a way to convince other individuals, those who do not feel such desires, of the justice of removing the death penalty for sodomy. Much of the evidence marshaled, such as examples of the acceptability of same-sex desire in the ancient world, of the ambiguity of the Christian prohibition against such acts, of the great men in history who have felt such desires, and of the indefensibility of the death penalty for sodomy within a rational legal code, are unique only for detail with which they are elaborated and the eloquence of their presentation. More unexpected is how these rationalist arguments are coupled with a narrative of individual self-awakening, where one man's story is recounted from the innocence of childhood, to the dawning of sexual-self-awareness at university, through to the personal and sexual fulfillment he experienced during travels in the Eastern Mediterranean.[30] Justifying same-sex desire is not the exclusive focus of the text, though, as poem is more accurately characterized as an argument for the naturalness of both opposite-sex and same-sex desires, with the emphasis on the idea that it is the prohibition of the natural same-sex desires that warps and distorts individuals. Such prohibitions, the authors feel, have gotten stronger in recent decades, as "once these were epigrams to raise a laugh, [but] the world is grown too scrupulous by half. Deprived through life of fundamental joys, things can no longer find their equipoise."[31]

When the notes and the poem are taken together what is presented is not only an argument for extending rights, in this case the right to pursue desires natural to an individual, but also the model subject worthy of the rights that such a legal change would provide. This message in the poem and the notes was directed at the men in Parliament who could quietly allow the death penalty for sodomy to be dropped as part of the broader criminal law reform. Such a broad criminal law reform was long anticipated by British parliamentarians in the years before it finally came to pass in the late 1820s and 1830s.[32]

Both of these parliamentary efforts against sodomy laws—one in Louisiana and one in Britain—one voiced publicly and forcefully by an elite man in a colonial legislature who likely did not strongly identify with feelings of same-sex desire, and the other voiced quietly, privately, and anonymously by a group of British men at the metropolitan center who did strongly identify with their feelings of same-sex desire—draw on the same logic.

Both of these arguments are appeals to individuals to apply deeply held convictions over the nature of justice in general to same-sex desire specifically. In the poem *Don Leon*, a prominent supporter of animal rights is chastised for not being willing to apply the principles of justice and compassion that he was known for to this area of the law as well, with the poet faulting him for being more sensitive to the cruelties done to lower creatures than those inflicted on his fellow man.[33] Other individuals known for championing humanitarian causes were similarly chastised. Even though much of the poem is a defense of the naturalness of same-sex desire, the conclusion of *Don Leon* is framed as an appeal to those who do not feel those desires, but who could see the logic of a rationalist legal philosophy that calibrated the severity of the punishment to the severity of the crime, and which set a high bar for state intrusion into areas of private behavior.

It was the same with the debate in Louisiana, where the elite propertied men in the legislature were being called on to defend a deeply held moral, philosophical, and legal principle that had already been extended to justify many other rights and privileges. Perhaps, in addition to looking for the extremely illusive evidence of individual desires or opinions in relation to sex between men, we can tell a substantial part of the story of the genealogy of same-sex marriage by refocusing on these ideological positions from which the sodomy laws might be resisted, and greater equality before the law established. Doing so opens up a substantial body of sources going back to the early eighteenth century. Such a perspective would easily incorporate evidence from the mid-eighteenth-century tract against the sodomy laws, Burke's willingness to denounce the excessive cruelty associated with the pillorying of men for acts of same-sex desire, and Bentham's extensive private arguments against the sodomy laws in the 1780s and 1810s.[34] But it would also incorporate within its logic those arguing for expanded rights for women under the law, from Mary Astell forward, and some of those arguing against slavery, against the treatment of slaves in the colonies, or against the recognition of slavery within England.[35] The logic underpinning all of these efforts stems from the same sources, and new and unexpected connections, may be possible if we pursue such connections between race, class, gender, and sexuality from the eighteenth century forward.

This might give us another reason to look to the colonies when attempting to understand events shaping politics and the regulation of same-sex desire in London in the 1820s. As Jennifer Spear has shown, New Orleans looked different to the Americans who visited. Not just the mix of Spanish and French architecture, but the people, "white men and women, and of all hues of brown, and of all classes of faces, from round Yankees to grisly and lean Spaniards, black negros and negresses, filthy Indians half naked, mulattoes, curly and straight-haired, quarteroons of all shades, long haired and frizzled, the women dressed in the most flaring yellow and scarlet gowns, the men capped and hatted."[36] Many commented with amazement at this racial, ethnic, and linguistic diversity. But Spear also shows how, even as the laws were shifting after 1803, free people of color in New Orleans knew what their legal rights were, and resisted further reductions in their status by calling on "their intimate and patronage ties to Euro-New Orleanians when necessary."[37] Even as the laws were creating a more rigid and stark divide between the races, sympathetic whites, especially judges, could enforce and preserve the property rights of the free peoples of color, could recognize the de facto nature of interracial marriages, even if they were not recognized specifically as marriages under the law, and in this way preserving the property of people of color against more distant white relations. We therefore have evidence of not only people of color and women using the law to protect their rights, but also elite white men acting in ways driven by the logic of law to support principles of justice and greater equality rather than loyalties to their own race, or gender or rank.

Such a connection was at play in London in the 1820s too. The magistrate most central to changing the way that elite men in London were prosecuted for acts of sex between men was Henry Moreton Dyer, magistrate at Marlborough Street, the principal police court for the West End.[38] From his involvement in the 1822 Bishop of Clogher case onward, Dyer became more aggressive in setting high bails, insisting on real names, and attempting to prevent cases from being moved to a higher court where upper-class men were more likely to prevail. Dyer was central to ensuring that upper-class men faced public tribunals in the 1820s, in a way different from earlier and later periods, and while many factors certainly contributed to his individual stand in these matters, it does seem worthy of note that Dyer held judicial posts in the West Indies before his time as a London magistrate, serving as sole judge in the Court of Vice Admiralty in Nassau as early as 1805.[39] He was more of an outsider to the systems of class solidarity and upper-class masculinity than many of his peers in the London magistracy, and he too put the law and justice above the imperative to protect men of high rank. In doing so he played an instrumental way in changing how the law, politics, and sexuality intersected in the early nineteenth century.

Emphasizing how rationalist logical arguments made alliances across previous lines of division, or allowed individuals to see connections previously unmade, places these early struggles against the sodomy laws in conversation with the process that led to same-sex marriage within the United States. Writing for the majority in the 2015 *Obergefell v. Hodges* case, Justice Anthony Kennedy argued that the US Constitution "promises liberty to all within its reach, a liberty that includes certain specific rights that allow persons, within a lawful realm, to define and express their identity."[40] The idea that the right to marry was a fundamental form of such expression had been established in other Supreme Court decisions, the most famous of which was *Loving v. Virginia*, which legalized interracial marriage throughout the United States.[41] The decision in *Obergefell v. Hodges* was not based on finding a specific right to same-sex marriage in the constitution, but rather by looking at the right to marry as it applied to everyone, and finding, in light of the fact that the identification and protection of those rights has never been reduced to a formula, that there no reason to exclude those who wished to marry someone of their own sex. An argument about a specific "gay identity" is missing from the argument, although the existence of one is undoubtedly what put the issue on the agenda in the first place.

Notes

1   John Bristed, *The Resources of the United States of America, or, A View of the Agricultural, Commercial, Manufacturing, Financial, Political, Literary, Moral and Religious Capacity and Character of the American People* (New York: J. Eastburn & Co., 1818), 395. Also published in London for Henry Colburn, Public Library, Conduit Street, Hanover Square, 1818. Available on the Internet Archive: California Digital Library.
2   Alcee Fortier, *A History of Louisiana, vol. III The American Domination* (New York: Goupil & Co., of Paris, 1904).
3   Charles Upchurch, "The Consequences of Dating Don Leon," in *Queer Difficulty in Art and Poetry: Re-thinking the Sexed Body in Verse and Visual Culture*, ed. Christopher Reed and Jongwoo Kim (New York: Routledge, 2017), 24–33.
4   This effort draws on the ideas explored by Tim Hitchcock, Thomas Laqueur, Michael McKeon, Leila J. Rupp, and Randolph Trumbach in their respective articles in the summer 2012 issue of *Signs*. For an overview, see Michael McKeon, "The Seventeenth- and Eighteenth-Century Sexuality Hypothesis," *Signs* 37, no. 4, "Sex: A Thematic Issue" (Summer 2012): 791–801.
5   *The British Critic*, volume 10 (London: F. C. and J. Rivington, 1818), 500; Passage quoted in "Bristed—Statistical View of America" [attributed to William Jacob], in *Classical Economics*: vol. III January 1819 to January 1820, ed. Donald Rutherford (London: Routledge, 1999), 7; *The Quarterly Review*, vol. XXI (London: John Murray, Albemarle Street, January and April, 1819), 394; Thomas Hartwell Horne, *Deism Refuted: Or Plain reasons for Being a Christian*, sixth edition (London: T. Cadell and W. Davies, Strand, 1819), 69–70; Augustus Campbell, *The Rights of the English Clergy Asserted, and the Probable Amount of Their Incomes Estimated*, second edition (London: Liverpool, G. F. Harris's Widow and Brothers, for… John Richardson, Booksellers, 1823), 32, *Encyclopaedia Metropolitana, or Universal Dictionary of Knowledge*, ed. Edward Smedley, Hugh James Rose, and Henry John Rose, vol. XIV (London: B. Fellowes, 1845), 422.
6   Based on the published *Acts of the Legislature* for 1814–1815, the Third Session of the First Legislature ran from January 3, 1814, to approximately March 7, 1814.
7   "(See the journals of secret proceedings)" was the penultimate sentence in the entries for Monday, February 22, as well as for the preceding meeting. Louisiana, *Journal of*

the Senate During the Second Session of the First Legislature of the State of Louisiana (New Orleans: Printed by Peter K. Wagner, State printer, 1813), 38. Louisiana, *Journal de la Chambre des Representans pendant la première session de la seconde législature de l'etat de la Louisiane* (Nouvelle-Orléans [La.]: Imprimé par P.K. Wagner, imprimeur de l'etat, 1814).

8 "The Louisiana Newspaper Project: Chronological Printout, United States Newspaper Program" (Baton Rouge: Louisiana Newspaper Project, Louisiana State University Libraries, 1990). According to this source, only scattered issues of the *Louisiana Gazette and New-Orleans Advertiser* (1812–1815) and *Time Piece* (Saint Francisville, LA., 1812–1815) survive for the period from November 1814 through February 1815.

9 *A Pedestrian Tour through Part of the Highlands in Scotland in 1801* (2 vols., 1804), *The Adviser, or the Moral and Literary Tribunal* (4 vols., London, 1802), *Critical and Philosophical Essays* (1804), *The System of the Society of Friends Examined* (1805), *Edward and Anna, a novel* (1805).

10 Bristed, *The Resources of the United States*, 394.

11 Ibid., 396.

12 In the early 1820s he published *Thoughts on the Anglican and Anglo-American Churches* (New York and London: B. J. Holdsworth, 1823).

13 William N. Eskridge, Jr., *Dishonorable Passions: Sodomy Laws in America: 1861–2003* (New York: Viking, 2008), 16–23. "Louis Crompton, Homosexual and the Death Penalty in Colonial America," *Journal of Homosexuality* 1 (1976): 277–293.

14 J. Denson Smith, "The Louisiana Criminal Code: Its Background and General Plan," *Louisiana Law Review* 5, no. 1 (December 1942): 1–5; Louisiana, *The Laws of the Territory of Louisiana: Comprising All Those Which Are Now Actually in Force within the Same* (St. Louis [La.]: Printed by Joseph Charles, 1808). [at Bobst & NYPL].

15 Clare Lyons, *Sex among the Rabble: An Intimate History of Gender and Power in the Age of Revolution, Philadelphia, 1730–1830* (Chapel Hill, NC: University of North Carolina Press, 2006), Clare Lyons, "Discipline, Sex, and the Republican Self," in *The Oxford Handbook of the American Revolution*, ed. Edward G. Gray and Jane Kaminsky (Oxford: Oxford University Press, 2013), 560–577.

16 Faramerz Dabhoiwala, *The Origins of Sex: A History of the First Sexual Revolution* (New York: Oxford University Press, 2012); Richard Godbeer, *Sexual Revolution in Early America* (Baltimore, MD: Johns Hopkins University Press, 2002); John D'Emilio and Estelle Freedman, *Intimate Matters: A History of Sexuality in America*, third edition (Chicago: University of Chicago Press, 2012). Joyce Appleby, *Inheriting the Revolution: The First Generation of Americans* (Cambridge, MA: Belknap Press, 2001), Jay Fliegelman, *Prodigals and Pilgrims: The American Revolution against Patriarchal Authority, 1750–1800* (New York: Cambridge University Press, 1982).

17 Kathleen Brown, *Good Wives, Nasty Wenches, and Anxious Patriarchs* (Chapel Hill, NC: University of North Carolina Press, 1996).

18 Malcolm J. Rohrbough, *Trans-Appalachian Frontier: People, Societies, and Institutions, 1775–1850* (Bloomington, IN: Indiana University Press, 2008). David Sehat, *The Myth of American Religious Freedom* (New York: Oxford University Press, 2011), 65.

19 Fortier, *A History of Louisiana*, vol. III, 89, 104.

20 Ibid., 106.

21 Ibid., 120.

22 Ibid., 152, 154.

23 Ibid., 155.

24 Upchurch, "Consequences of Dating *Don Leon*."

25 This misdating is based on the earliest material from the endnotes and a reference to a change in the law regulating sex between men. That change was assumed to have been the one in 1828, since the 1825 change was eclipsed by it. See George Wilson Knight, "Who Wrote Don Leon?" *Twentieth Century* 156 (1954): 67–79; and Louis Crompton, "Don Leon, Byron, and Homosexual Law Reform," in *Literary Visions of Homosexuality*, ed. Stuart Kellogg (New York: Haworth Press, 1983), 68–70.
26 Upchurch, "Consequences of Dating *Don Leon*," 24–33.
27 The full description of these events is the subject of my current book in progress, *"Beyond the Law": Ending the Death Penalty for Sodomy in Nineteenth-Century Britain*.
28 *A Free Examination into the Penal Statutes, xxv Henr. VIII, cap. 6, and vEliz. c. 17*. Louis Crompton was the first recent scholar to find that "Henry Ashbee in his *Index Librorum Prohibitorum* describes a copy bearing the date 'London, 1833,' though he suggests that it was 'printed probably in Paris.' He also gives a fuller version of the title, which indicates that it was "address [sic] to Both Houses of Parliament." Crompton, "*Don Leon*, Byron, and Homosexual Law Reform," 57.
29 Emphasis added. Note 10 in "Notes to Don Leon," quoting *A Free Examination*.
30 *Don Leon, A Poem by the Late Lord Byron ... to Which Is Added Leon to Annabella: An Epistle from Lord Byron to Lady Byron* (London: Printed for the Booksellers, 1866), 7–10, 15–24.
31 Ibid., 52.
32 Leon Radzinowicz, *A History of the Criminal Law and Its Administration from 1750: The Movement for Reform 1750–1833*, vol. 1 (New York: Macmillan, 1948), 567–582.
33 *Don Leon*, 37.
34 Louis Crompton, *Homosexuality & Civilization* (Cambridge, MA: Belknap Press of Harvard University Press, 2003), 530–532, 561; F. P. Lock, *Edmund Burke*, vol. 1 (Oxford: Clarendon Press, 1998), 464.
35 William Kolbrener and Michal Michelson Mary Astell, *Reason, Gender, Faith* (Aldershot, England: Ashgate, 2007); John Salter, "Adam Smith on Slavery," *History of Economic Ideas* 4 (1996): 225–251.
36 Jennifer Spear, *Race, Sex, and Social Order in Early New Orleans* (Baltimore: Johns Hopkins University Press, 2009).
37 Spear, *Race, Sex, and Social Order*, 183.
38 Charles Upchurch, "Politics and the Reporting of Sex between Men in the 1820s," in *British Queer History: New Approaches and Perspectives*, ed. Brian Lewis (Manchester and New York: University of Manchester Press, 2013), 28, 30–31.
39 *The Times*, May 18, 1841, 6; University College London, *Legacies of British Slave Ownership Database*, www.ucl.ac.uk/lbs/person/view/1234.
40 Supreme Court of the United States, OBERGEFELL v. HODGES, 576 U. S. ____ (2015), Opinion of the Court, 2. http://www.supremecourt.gov/opinions/14pdf/14-556_3204.pdf.
41 Supreme Court of the United States, OBERGEFELL v. HODGES, Opinion of the Court, 11–13.

4

Regarding Pratt and Smith, the Last Couple of Sodomites to be Hanged in Britain

Dominic Janes

The law in Georgian England was not always effective in preventing forms of public awareness of same-sex relationships that included elements of sympathy on the part of observers. I will argue that the move during the nineteenth century away from hanging and the pillory toward penal incarceration can be understood in relation to official attitudes to the public visibility of those found guilty of "unnatural offences." Changing modes of punishment can be seen as part of an attempt to restrict popular awareness of same-sex desire as a matter of the emotions as well as of the genitals, of couples as well as coupling. Because English law has long been intent on criminalizing sodomitical acts it has been slow to address homosexual persons. One of the significant effects of this was to focus attention on the image of two individuals committing a sexual offence with each other, rather than on them as a couple. To take one example, this is what appears in a print which may be by Isaac Robert Cruikshank; "The arse bishop Josilin g [sic] a soldier-or-do as I say not as I do," which was published in London in July 1822 (see Figure 4.1).

Percy Jocelyn (1764–1843), was the third son of the First Earl of Roden and in 1820 became Bishop of Clogher in the Protestant Church of Ireland. On July 19, 1822 he was found in a sexually compromising situation with Private John Moberley of the 1st Regiment of Guards in a bedroom at the White Lion pub, St. Alban's Place in London. The two were taken off to the Watch House, and examined next day at Marlborough Street magistrate's court. Jocelyn was deprived of his position in the Church but avoided trial for sodomy by breaking the terms of his bail and fleeing to Scotland, where he worked as a butler under an assumed name.[1] The print depicts an act of casual sex between a corrupt cleric and a youthful—and rather imbecilic-looking—soldier. The two are divided by age, social position and, in this representation, by the embodiment of law and order. They are not shown as a couple, but rather as a pair of more of less culpable malefactors. This is how they are regarded by the other people viewing this scene in the background. A woman shouts, "hang the dogs I say let them not disgrace our gallant Soldiers shoot the beasts." A man says, "they must not live to disgrace the Church and the Army." And from behind come the words, "send them to Hell or Turkey; Send them to China; The Pillory the Pillory; Hang them in Chains."

Figure 4.1 *The Arse Bishop Josilin g a Soldier—or—Do as I Say Not as I Do*, published by H. Fores, July 1822, 24.8 x 33.9 cm, Courtesy of the Trustees of the British Museum, London © (1868,0808.8554).

These cries give voice to familiar strains of execration which linked sodomy to satanic and oriental practices. The expected response from the authorities is for them to be fastened in the public pillory where they would have to endure the attentions of the mob. This was not the worse that could face a convicted sodomite, since this remained a capital offence until 1861.

While this print may represent reasonably accurately what took place at the White Lion it also depicts what many people assumed would be popular attitudes toward sodomites. However, such humorless abhorrence was not universal as can be seen from another print which depicted this incident: "Confirmation, or the Bishop and the Soldier," which forms the frontispiece of *A Correct Account of the Horrible Occurrence which Took Place at a Public-House in St. James's Market, in which it was discovered that the Right Rev. the Bishop of Clogher was a principal actor with a common soldier!*, published by J. L. Marks in London, 1822 (see Figure 4.2).

In this image the bishop is shown kneeling before a slim soldier who is partly cross-dressed as—and seated in the characteristic pose of—a woman. This is, in other words, a representation which treats sodomy through humor. It does not show the bishop as a predatory aristocrat but as a deluded suitor. This work is still, of course, hostile, but the depiction evokes relations with a courtesan rather than with a common prostitute. It also visually places the two men together, thus creating a stronger association of them as having some more complex relationship than that of immediate sexual gratification.

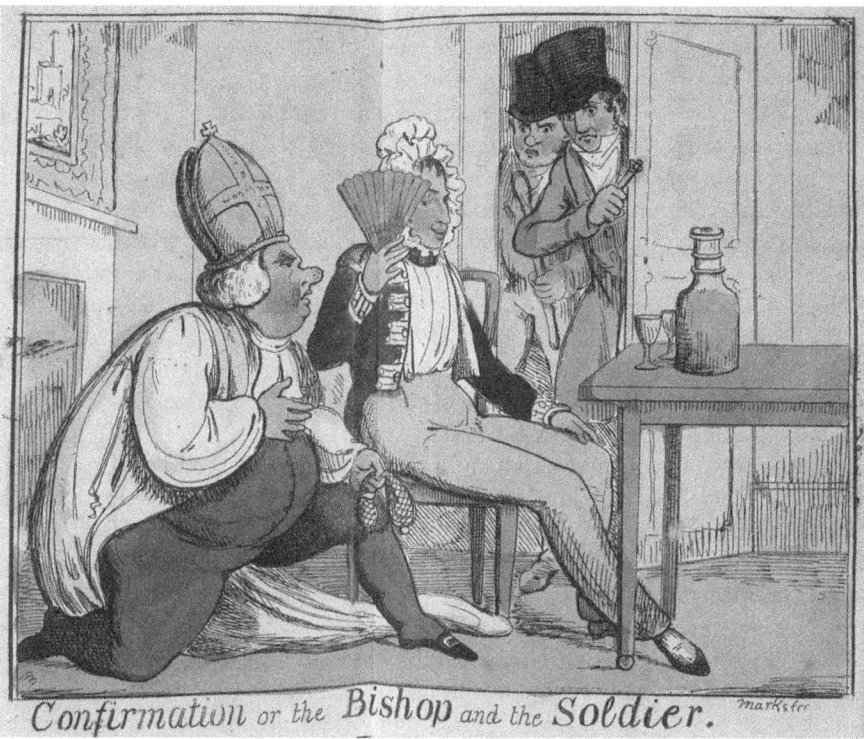

Figure 4.2 *Confirmation or the Bishop and the Soldier*, frontispiece, J. L. Marks, *A Correct Account of the Horrible Occurrence which Took Place at a Public-House in St. James's Market* (London: J. L. Marks, 1822), hand-colored etching, © The British Library Board (cup.363. gg.31, image C13670-78).

I will go on to show that sodomitical pairs could at times be viewed as couples and that one of the purposes of changing patterns of punishment for "unnatural" offences was to attempt to prevent this.

In the course of the nineteenth century the death penalty for sodomy was abolished and the horrors of the public pillory were confined to the past. That did not mean, by any means, that public attitudes toward such sexual acts had become substantially more liberal. Rather these changes need to be seen as part of a wider process of legal reform that saw the steady reduction in the number of capital offences and a vast expansion of the prison system of incarceration. One of the effects of this change was to make the body of the convicted sodomite invisible to society where once it had been put on public display. One of the reasons behind the ending of public hangings was the supposedly debasing effect of these events on the audience which, it was feared, was often composed of those who viewed such proceedings as a species of entertainment. There were, however, those who viewed the punishment of sodomites from a wide range of emotional viewpoints which ranged from delight to pity and dismay. One of the exceptional features of the offence of sodomy was that its prosecution often produced two prisoners rather than the more usual pattern of a victim and a malefactor. This meant that the spectacle of the punished sodomite was, in fact, very often a joint affair in that what the public saw or read about was the treatment of a pair of sodomites. In some cases these men came together as a result of a casual encounter but in others they would have known, or even loved, each other. This means that it was the fate of sodomitical couples that often preoccupied the media. This situation invited speculation on the emotional as well as the sexual relations between the condemned men. It will be suggested that the desire to limit affective, and perhaps even sentimental, responses was one of a series of factors that led to the replacement of the crime of sodomy with that of gross indecency. In due course this impetus to retire the sight of the homosexual couple from public view can even be understood to have underwritten the safe concealment of two men behind a locked door that was produced by the Sexual Offences Act 1967.

At the core of the offence of sodomy, which was often referred to as buggery, was an act of criminalized penetrative sex, generally anal sex, with ejaculation between two men, a man and a woman, or a man and an animal. Since ejaculation was hard to prove many prosecutions were for the lesser charge of assault with sodomitical intent. In 1828 the Offences Against the Person Act removed the need to prove emission of semen, but in practice the death penalty was rarely enforced. Indecent assault was established as an offence in common law from the eighteenth to the nineteenth centuries and was codified in the 1861 Offences Against the Person Act, which abolished the death penalty for sodomy. This presaged the appearance of gross indecency in English law in 1885 which had the effect of punishing a wide, and unspecified, set of sexual acts by the imposition of prison terms.[2] Moreover the 1861 act, unlike its predecessor, separated sodomy from rape as one of a series of violent offences against the body and re-categorized it under the separate heading of "unnatural offences."[3] Another important, associated change was that the usual punishment for same-sex crimes became a prison term, sometimes with hard labor, rather than public shaming in the pillory. The issue of the incarceration of convicted sodomites in the nineteenth century is explored by Ben Bethell in Chapter 5 of this current volume. He explains the challenge that this posed the authorities in terms of ensuring that opportunities for homosex were kept to a minimum in the all-male environment of the prison.[4] That issue notwithstanding incarceration did remove the punishment of the prisoner from a public arena in which popular reactions were far from entirely under the control of the authorities. As Peter Bartlett has commented, "the pillory was a space where, subject to minimal controls, the crowd held sway. The pillory therefore was a site for this crowd to articulate its values and norms."[5] That crowd was sometimes a representative assortment of local citizens but it might occasionally consist of friends and sympathizers, or, quite the reverse, of those who had gathered specifically in order to express their hatred.

One of the most extreme cases of this last situation took place at the pillorying of the "Vere Street coterie" who were arrested in 1810, two of whom were hanged and six pilloried. They were widely described in the press in terms of horror and detestation as in "The monsters," an article that appeared in *The Morning Post* on September 28,

1810. This describes how shops along the route shuttered their windows lest they be damaged by the mob, as "ammunition wagons" of decaying produce from the markets were wheeled into position.

> It is impossible for language to convey an adequate idea of the universal expressions of execration, which accompanied these monsters on their journey ... From the moment the cart was in motion, the fury of the mob began to display itself in showers of mud and filth of every kind. Before the cart reached Temple Bar, the wretches were so thickly covered with filth, that a vestige of the human figure was scarcely discernible ... before they reached half-way to the scene of their exposure they were not discernible as human beings.[6]

Particular fury was directed toward one man: "Dead cats and dogs, offal, potatoes, turnips, &c. rebounded from him on every side, while his apparently manly appearance drew down peculiar execrations on him; and nothing but the motion of the cart prevented him from being killed on the spot."[7] The fact was that the appearance of those convicted did not, in every case, match popular expectations of the sodomite as a womanly "molly," bearing in mind that it was commented at the time that "it is a generally received opinion, and a very natural one, that the prevalency [sic] of this passion has for its object effeminate delicate beings only."[8] Such figures among the coterie as an athletic bargeman and a coal heaver confounded popular stereotypes that conflated and confused transgressions of gender and sexual object-choice.[9] The Morning Post shared the apparent enthusiasm of the crowd for "the adoption of every means to effect the destruction of so detestable and diabolical a race" rather than have to face the reality that contemporary sodomites were often indistinguishable in appearance from ordinary men.[10] George Haggerty has argued in his article "'Dung, guts and blood': sodomy, abjection and gothic fiction in the early nineteenth century," that sodomites were made into monsters by the crowd. He argues that "these men are identified as monstrous, and the threat they pose is so serious that they must be covered with filth as a sign of their crimes."[11] But in the newspaper's account matters went even further than this: the effect of the crowd's actions was to erase the sodomites' humanity. That this was felt to be particularly pressing in the case of the more manly prisoners provides eloquent testimony to the construction of the masculine sodomite as an obscenity that must be removed from public view.

The pillory, however, was not well suited to act as a mode of visual erasure because it was intended, in its very essence, to shame the accused through making them publicly visible. A similar dynamic operated in the case of hangings which were also carried out in public. The decline of the pillory and public execution alike has often been attributed to decreasing enthusiasm on the part of the authorities for convicted criminals to be viewed in public in this way. For example, Vic Gatrell, in his book *The Hanging Tree: Execution and the English People 1770–1868* (1994), argues that changes in forms of punishment came about as a result of genteel squeamishness at such displays, rather than due to progressive thought concerning criminality.[12] Danger to public order from enraged mobs must also have been on the minds of the authorities who restricted the use of the pillory in 1816, before formally phasing it out in 1837.

It is also important to stress that although executions for sodomy were rare occurrences, they did reach a higher level during the Napoleonic Wars in association with rising concern about public order.[13] The last public executions for sodomy took place in the 1830s. The numbers were not large in that decade since they ran at two or so per year. The last such event took place on November 27, 1835, when John Smith (aged 40) and John—also known as James—Pratt (aged 30) were hanged outside Newgate Prison in London. The landlord of William Bonill, aged 68, who lived in a rented room in Blackfriars Road on the south bank of the Thames, testified that he became suspicious of his tenant who often had male visitors, many of whom arrived in pairs. On the afternoon of August 29, 1835, Pratt and Smith visited Bonill and the landlord climbed up onto a neighboring roof so that he could see what was happening within. What he glimpsed from his vantage point led him, and his wife, to peer through the keyhole of the chamber. What they said they saw was Pratt and Smith engaged in sodomy. The door was forced and the men caught in the act. At this point Bonill arrived bearing a jug of ale which, it seemed, he intended to give to the miscreants. All three were arrested.

On 29 September *The Times* reported that the death sentence had been pronounced the previous day on a series of men at the Central Criminal Court. Six men were condemned to hang for burglary and five for highway robbery. Three further men were then dealt with separately; these being Pratt, Smith, and one Robert Swan who had been found guilty of "robbing Mr. Reynolds, the Quaker, under aggravated circumstances." The Recorder addressed them, saying,

> "You have been severally convicted of offences by which your lives are justly forfeited to the outraged laws of your country. I have felt it my duty to separate and to distinguish you from the other unhappy offenders who have been called upon the receive the dreadful sentence of the law. I have felt that, great as their crimes are, they would have been contaminated by your presence ... " The learned Recorder then, in an impressive manner, called upon the prisoners to reflect upon their awful and hopeless condition, and sentenced them to death. The unhappy men wept bitterly during this address.[14]

Bonill, meanwhile, received a sentence of fourteen years for aiding the commission of the crime. The theater of punishment then moved from the court-room to Newgate Prison, where executions had taken place since the removal of the gallows from Tyburn in 1783. The condemned were kept in cells separated from Newgate Street by a thick wall and the "hanging tree" itself was constructed by a window outside. Those who could not wait for the spectacle of the execution itself could visit the prison beforehand by obtaining a permit. A contemporary broadsheet depicted the scene in a crudely done wood engraving (Figure 4.3).

This shows the two men after death, side by side, their heads lolling in an identical direction. They are shown as a pair, but can we read a degree of empathetic identification into this representation such that they might have been regarded as, in some sense, a couple?

It is notable how different the tone of *The Morning Post* was on this occasion compared with that which had taken place in 1810. The event on Saturday, November 28, was reported as follows:

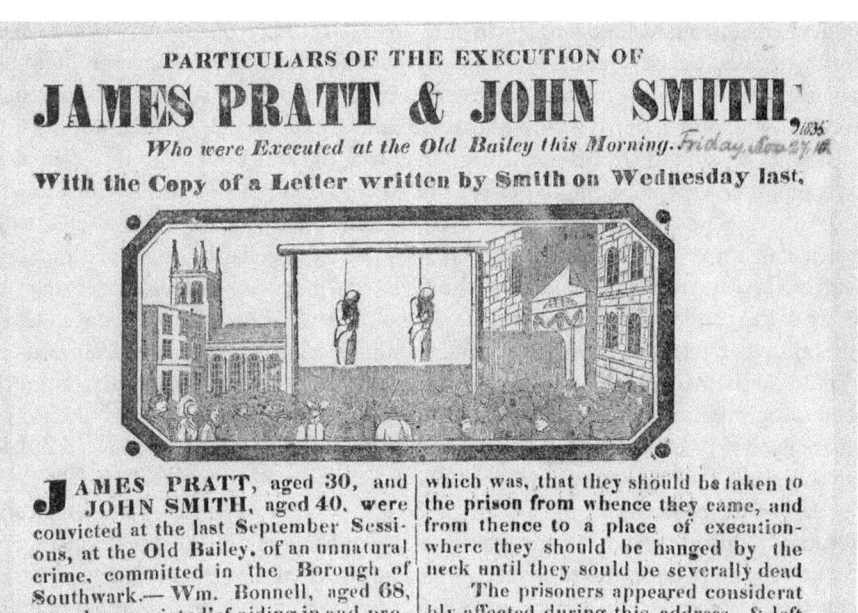

Figure 4.3 Detail, wood engraving, from *Particulars of the Execution of James Pratt and John Smith* (London: Thomas Birt, 1835), Harvard Law School Library, http://nrs.harvard.edu/urn-3:HLS.Libr:1087981.

Pratt, especially, appeared dreadful weak and dejected. While Smith was being pinioned, Pratt appeared to suffer dreadfully. His groans resounded through the prison, and while he was pinioning [sic] he repeatedly exclaimed, "Oh God, this is horrible, this is indeed horrible." He at this time was so weak that the executioner's assistants found it necessary to hold him in their arms to prevent him from falling to the ground. All the preparations having been completed the melancholy procession proceeded to the scaffold ... The moment the culprits were perceived they were received with groans and hisses, which lasted during the whole of the time the hangman was making the necessary preparations. These having been performed the bolt was drawn, and after a very short struggle the culprits ceased to exist.[15]

The crowd expressed its hatred and disgust, albeit in a much less extreme manner than had been the case with the pillorying of six members of the Vere Street Coterie. It is notable, however, that this account does not so much align the affective response of the reader with the crowd as with Pratt and Smith. And moreover, it draws attention to the fact that Pratt suffered most piteously while Smith was being pinioned.

Other press reports praised the conduct of the condemned, as was the case in one that appeared in *The Times* on August 25, 1835, which described the final moments of Richard Sheppard and John Sparshott. In this instance Sheppard was executed for aggravated burglary and Sparshott, who was aged 19, for having committed "an abominable offence." Both were described as praying fervently, and "exhibiting much fortitude and resignation." Their bodies were handed over to their friends and "the silly custom of passing the hands of the dead men over the necks of two or three females, as a supposed cure for glandular enlargements, was upon this occasion had recourse to."[16] There is no sense in this report that the offence of Sparshott was treated with particular horror or that his person was regarded as peculiarly contaminating. This suggests that there was a range of both official and popular opinion concerning the body of the condemned person whether or not they were a sodomite. It was in these circumstances that it can be argued that the scaling back of the use of the death penalty should not be read as representing a "humane moment" in British history, so much as a recognition by the authorities that the public display of turpitude could not be guaranteed to produce the desired deterrent effect of disgust. Or, otherwise, if it did, to do so in ways that did not become excessive and problematic in themselves.[17]

Part of the problem for the authorities was that there was a rising interest in the scrutiny of alleged government tyranny in a general sense on the part not only of radical papers but also their liberal counterparts, such as *The Times*. This was not, of course, tantamount to anything like a public campaign for decriminalization but it did lead to ambivalent responses to the process of justice.[18] Furthermore, there is evidence in the records of pleas for clemency that a minority of viewers did indeed think that sodomy should not be an offence at all, let alone a capital one. Pleas for clemency were of great importance to trials at this time because defendants were deprived of the right to speak in their own defense.[19] Thus the magistrate Hensleigh Wedgwood, who had committed Pratt and Smith to trial, later wrote to the Home Secretary, Lord John Russell, arguing for the commutation of the death sentences. In his view it was

> the only crime where there is no injury done to any individual and in consequence it requires a very small expense to commit it in so private a manner and to take such precautions as shall render conviction impossible. It is also the only capital crime that is committed by rich men but owing to the circumstances I have mentioned they are never convicted.[20]

This statement makes two important points. First, the official view of sodomy as injurious was disputed. Secondly, it was suggested that this was a crime in which there was, in effect, one law for the rich and another for the poor. And it might be added that not only did the poor lack access to private quarters where such acts could be committed undisturbed but the rich often had the opportunity to abscond abroad on bail, as in the case of the Bishop of Clogher. This meant that convicted felons might be seen as victims of, in effect, class oppression.

This was not an isolated incident. Similar radical sentiments were expressed in an anonymous letter to Sir Robert Peel in the case of Martin Mellett and James Farthing, both aged 19, who were found guilty of buggery on September 17, 1828. It was in the view of this writer inappropriate that the law should obstruct a man in the "free use of any parts of his own body," particularly because sodomy "pervades all classes of society"; being, for instance, common in schools, without bringing society to any obvious state of ruin.[21] The fact that the sentence was commuted to transportation to Australia after the two youths had spent three months on "death row" in Newgate may owe something to this plea to clemency, but it is perhaps more likely that it was also due to the nature of the evidence against them which, once more, was supplied via a keyhole. Or rather, it may truly be due to the nature of the person who testified against them since *The Morning Chronicle* had reported that "Mr. Adolphus (after the Court had been cleared of boys and females) stated the case for the prosecution, and expressed his regret that the only witness he could call to prove the commission of this disgusting offence was a female."[22]

It has long been known that Jeremy Bentham had developed arguments that sodomy should not be criminalized, but it is becoming clear that similar views were starting to emerge in public.[23] The prosecution of sodomy, therefore, faced a minor threat from what might be termed extreme utilitarianism, but it is possible to suggest that a bigger threat was played by a quite different phenomenon: sentimentality. It is possible to explore some of the ways in which sentiment can be seen to have become entangled with the fate of the sodomite at this time through reference to the example of Charles Dickens. On November 5, 1835, a day redolent with political melodrama, Dickens visited Newgate and he recorded his experiences as one of his *Sketches by Boz* (1836). He saw there the three—Pratt, Smith, and Swan—who had been separated from the other condemned men. Swan, the robber, was described dismissively as "lounging, at the greatest distance he could place between himself and his companions, in the window nearest to the door." Although Dickens did not say anything admiring about the couple of condemned sodomites, he did make great efforts, by contrast, to regard them carefully.

> The other two men were at the upper end of the room. One of them, who was imperfectly seen in the dim light, had his back towards us, and was stooping over the fire, with his right arm on the mantel-piece, and his head sunk upon it. The other was leaning on the sill of the farthest window. The light fell full upon him, and communicated to his pale, haggard face, and disordered hair, an appearance which, at that distance, was ghastly. His cheek rested upon his hand; and, with his face a little raised, and his eyes wildly staring before him, he seemed to be unconsciously intent on counting the chinks in the opposite wall.[24]

The emotional intensity of this ghastly, ghostly vision is thought to have had an important influence on Dickens' depiction of Fagin in the condemned cell in *Oliver Twist* (1837–1839) in his chapter "Fagin's last night alive":

> Those dreadful walls of Newgate, which have hidden so much misery and such unspeakable anguish, *not only from the eyes, but, too often, and too long, from the thoughts, of men,* [my emphasis] never held so dread a spectacle as that. The few who lingered as they passed, and wondered what the man was doing who was to be hanged to-morrow, would have slept but ill that night, if they could have seen him.[25]

The appearance of Fagin's band of boys, likewise, seems to have been influenced by seeing, on the same visit, fourteen shameless pickpockets who were "evidently quite gratified at being thought worth the trouble of looking at; their idea appeared to be, that we had come to see Newgate as a grand affair, and that they were an indispensable part of the show."[26] Ben Bethell, in the current volume, has pointed out that authorities viewed sodomites and receivers of stolen goods (such as Fagin) as similar in their capacity for moral contagion in the environment of the prison.[27] Fagin and his boys have received a range of queer readings from literary scholars. Importantly, these do not so much stress Dickens' horror at the thought of sodomy as his artfully concealed fascination. Thus Larry Wolff has argued that "Oliver's embattled innocence makes the boy into pornographic bait for readers, and precisely for that reason the possibility of his sexual exploitation within the novel must remain unrecognized."[28] It has been suggested in particular that these ambivalent feelings derive from Dickens' youthful emotional reliance on a certain Bob Fagin, a fellow worker at the blacking warehouse in which he had been forced to labor when his father was in debtors' prison.[29] The fictional Fagin was, it is thought, also based upon Isaac Solomon, an infamous receiver of stolen property, but this does not negate the fact that the character was imagined not simply as a Jew, but also as queer.[30] The cartoon by George Cruikshank of *Fagin in the Condemned Cell*, which was published in the book version of Dicken's novel shows Fagin as a hook-nosed, almost rat-like creature, caught in the act of gnawing at his own fingers in terror (see Figure 4.4). However, Cruikshank's original sketch, which is close to the version employed on the wrapper of the serial edition of this chapter, emphasized fearful isolation and does not distance the Christian viewer through the depiction of Fagin as an anti-Semitic stereotype (see Figure 4.5).

Holly Furneaux, in her book *Queer Dickens: Erotics, Families, Masculinities* (2009), has argued that Dickens was interested in exploring a range of alternative models for affective family bonds.[31] Such a stance was favorable to viewing sodomites as more than men who had committed a disgusting physical act. Dickens' own gaze moved between Pratt and Smith in their shared place of confinement and his account of this led readers to speculate on the possibilities of an emotional relationship between condemned prisoners. Similar curiosity can be seen to have seeped out from some of the newspaper coverage, such as in that which reported the execution of Pratt and Smith. It is possible to argue that what appear to be empathetic views expressed in the liberal press are nothing more than reflections of an urge to condemn autocratic use of judicial force that outweighed traditional disgust as sodomitical offences.[32] Yet it is important to pay attention to the rising cult of "sympathy" at this time which promoted the view that aggressive punishment had a tendency to brutalize not only those subjected to it, but also those who administered it and who observed it. Reform agendas that placed a premium on sympathy and sentiment "provided a program for transforming threatening encounters with other people into the reassuring discovery of a common humanity."[33] This was not intended to mean that crimes were to be condoned; nevertheless, the sodomite, in this scheme of things, was not to be seen as a monster, but as a human being who had tragically erred. If we glance again at the lolling heads in the print depicting the execution of Pratt and Smith with a "sympathetic" eye, we are looking not so much at the necessary actions of justice as at a preventable

Figure 4.4 George Cruikshank, *Fagin in the Condemned Cell*, published in Charles Dickens, *Oliver Twist, or the Parish Boy's Progress* (London: Richard Bentley, 1838), volume 3, after p. 296.

tragedy. For a sentimental writer such as Dickens sodomitical tragedies were part of the greater pattern of human drama that was characterized by the breakdown of relationships. The end of executions for sodomy removed much of the tragic drama of the script of the sodomites' downfall and can be seen, in that light, to have saved a few lives: but it also sustained support for the maltreatment of homosexuals by the state because its punishments were carried out beyond the public gaze. The physical and emotional ordinariness of most of those who were convicted of what was held by the authorities to be an extraordinary offence was thereby also concealed.[34]

The legal changes in the punishment of same-sex offences during the nineteenth century were, therefore, fully in accordance with a long-standing preference on the part of the authorities not to draw attention to sodomy.[35] It was often feared that ostentatious punishment might have the unfortunate side effect of publicizing the offence and thereby potentially contributing to its spread.[36] This can be seen as part of an otherwise mysterious reluctance on the part of the legal system to talk openly about same-sex desire. According to Peter Bartlett, the effect of such references to sodomy as the

Figure 4.5 George Cruikshank, detail of sketch for *Fagin in the Condemned Cell*, pencil, pen and ink (1830s), Courtesy of the Victoria and Albert Museum, London © (9995J).

"crime not to be named among Christians" was to ensure that sodomy itself "remains in silence, a void in which the metaphoric meanings can thrive."[37] The construction of the pilloried sodomite as a gothic monstrosity was, ultimately, far less effective than the demonizing of the homosexual who was—supposedly—hidden in society and who must be removed to prison for the safety of the public. The apparently liberalizing legal changes of the nineteenth century were partly designed, it can be argued, to ensure that such men were seen as predatory loners and not empathetically viewed as lovers and to ensure that their coupling was seen as nothing more than a nasty physical act that required these men's separation from their friends, families, and communities.

Notes

1. Rictor Norton, "The Bishop of Clogher," *The Gay Subculture in Georgian England*, April 5, 2010, http://rictornorton.co.uk/clogher1.htm (accessed January 11, 2016).
2. Charles Upchurch, *Before Wilde: Sex between Men in Britain's Age of Reform* (Berkeley: University of California Press, 2009), 89–93.
3. Leslie J. Moran, *The Homosexual(ity) of Law* (London: Routledge, 1996), 79–81.
4. Ben Bethell, "Defining 'Unnatural Crime' : Sex and the English Convict System, 1850–1900," in the current volume, 57–69.
5. Peter Bartlett, "Sodomites in the Pillory in Eighteenth-Century London," *Social and Legal Studies* 6, no. 4 (1997): 553–573, at 569.
6. "The Monsters," *Morning Post*, September 28, 1810, 3.
7. Ibid., 3.
8. Robert Holloway, *The Phoenix of Sodom, or the Vere Street Coterie* (1813), in Ian McCormick, *Sexual Outcasts: 1750–1850*, vol. 2 [of 4], *Sodomy* (London: Routledge, 2000), 183–214, at 189.
9. Holloway, *The Phoenix of Sodom*, 195.
10. "The Monsters," 3.
11. George Haggerty, "'Dung, Guts and Blood': Sodomy, Abjection and Gothic Fiction in the Early Nineteenth Century," *Gothic Studies* 8, no. 2 (2006): 35–51, at 36.
12. Vic Gatrell, *The Hanging Tree: Execution and the English People* (Oxford: Oxford University Press, 1994), 596.
13. A. D. Harvey, "Prosecutions for Sodomy in England at the Beginning of the Nineteenth Century," *Historical Journal* 21, no. 4 (1978): 945–946.
14. "Central Criminal Court, Monday, September 28," *The Times*, September 29, 1835, 4.
15. Quoted in ed. Rictor Norton, "The Last Men Executed for Sodomy in England, 1835," *Homosexuality in Nineteenth-Century England: A Sourcebook*, September 12, 2014, http://rictornorton.co.uk/eighteen/1835last.htm (accessed November 1, 2015).
16. "Executions," *The Times*, August 25, 1835, 7.
17. Gatrell, *The Hanging Tree*, 590.
18. Charles Upchurch, "Politics and the Reporting of Sex between Men in the 1820s," in *British Queer History: New Approaches and Perspectives*, ed. Brian Lewis (Manchester: Manchester University Press, 2013), 17–38.
19. H. G. Cocks, "Making The Sodomite Speak: Voices of the Accused in English Sodomy Trials, c. 1800–98," *Gender and History* 18, no. 1 (2006): 87–107, at 88.
20. H. G. Cocks, *Nameless Offences: Homosexual Desire in the Nineteenth Century* (London: I. B. Tauris, 2010), 38, discussing National Archives, London, HO 17/120, xv 13.
21. Gatrell, *The Hanging Tree*, 420, discussing National Archives PRO HO 17/88, part 2 (Qn16).
22. Quoted in ed. Rictor Norton, "Newspaper Reports, 1826," *Homosexuality in Nineteenth-Century England: A Sourcebook*, April 18, 2012, amended February 14, 2015, http://rictornorton.co.uk/eighteen/1826news.htm (accessed November 1, 2015), and Gatrell, *The Hanging Tree*, 420–421.
23. Jeremy Bentham, *Of Sexual Irregularities, and Other Writings on Sexual Morality*, ed. Philip Schofield, Catherine Pease-Watkin and Michael Quinn (Oxford: Oxford University Press, 2014) and Stephen G. Engelmann, "Queer Utilitarianism: Bentham and Malthus on the Threshold of Biopolitics," *Theory and Event* 17, no. 4 (2014),

http://muse.jhu.edu/journals/theory_and_event/v017/17.4.engelmann.html (accessed November 1, 2015).
24. Charles Dickens, "A Visit to Newgate," *Sketches by Boz*, vol. 1 [of 2], 2nd edition (London: John Macrone, 1836), 107–135, at 128–129.
25. Charles Dickens, *Oliver Twist; or the Parish Boy's Progress*, vol. 3 [of 3], (London: Richard Bentley, 1838), 299.
26. Dickens, "A Visit to Newgate," 120.
27. Bethell, "Defining 'Unnatural Crime'", 57–69.
28. Larry Wolff, "'The Boys Are Pickpockets, and the Girl Is a Prostitute': Gender and Juvenile Criminality in Early Victorian England from *Oliver Twist* to *London Labour*," *New Literary History* 27, no. 2 (1996): 227–249, at 247; see also Richard Dellamora, *Friendship's Bonds: Democracy and the Novel in Victorian England* (Philadelphia: University of Pennsylvania Press, 2004), 31, and Susan Zieger, "Dickens's Queer Children," *Literature Interpretation Theory* 20, no. 1–2 (2009): 141–157.
29. Dellamora, *Friendship's Bonds*, 40.
30. David A. H. Hirsch, "Dickens's Queer 'Jew' and Anglo-Christian Identity Politics: The Contradictions of Victorian Family Values," in *Queer Theory and the Jewish Question*, ed. Daniel Boyarin, Daniel Itzkovitz, and Ann Pellegrini (New York: Columbia University Press, 2003), 311–333, at 329.
31. Holly Furneaux, *Queer Dickens: Erotics, Families, Masculinities* (Oxford: Oxford University Press, 2009), 3.
32. Upchurch, "Politics and the Reporting of Sex," 33.
33. Randall McGowen, "A Powerful Sympathy: Terror, the Prison, and Humanitarian Reform in Early Nineteenth-Century Britain," *Journal of British Studies* 25, no. 3 (1986): 312–334, at 314.
34. H. G. Cocks, "Safeguarding Civility: Sodomy, Class and Moral Reform in Early Nineteenth-Century England," *Past and Present* 190 (February 2006): 121–146, at 123.
35. Ibid., 145.
36. Jody Greene, "Public Secrets: Sodomy and the Pillory in the Eighteenth Century and beyond," *Eighteenth Century* 44 (summer–fall 2003): 203–232, at 208.
37. Peter Bartlett, "Silence and Sodomy: The Creation of Homosexual Identity in Law," *Modern Law Review* 61, no. 1 (1998): 102–114, at 104.

5

Defining "Unnatural Crime": Sex and the English Convict System, 1850–1900

Ben Bethell

"We have reason to fear that ... unnatural crime (especially by men with lads) is practised in several Convict Prisons," warned the prison reform campaigner William Tallack, addressing England's senior prison administrator, Colonel Edmund Du Cane, in an open letter published as a pamphlet in 1878.[1] Tallack's sources, a former prison officer among them, had informed him that opportunities for "unnatural crime" occurred "when the convicts are passing along the galleries to their cells, especially in the dusk; two getting into one cell for a brief time unobserved by the warders," and that "some warders have known this to be the case, and have jocularly called certain convicts by female names as having been the objects of unnatural crime."[2]

To discuss sex between men publicly, bluntly, and in detail was highly unusual in England at the time. It was, as Sean Brady has observed, a country notable for hostility and intolerance in such matters.[3] If for some reason they could not avoid the topic, judges, doctors, clergymen, newspaper editors, and government officials would resort to terse euphemisms for what was literally unspeakable. Of these, "unnatural crime" (or "crimes") was the most common, its use long predating the 1861 Offences against the Person Act, which listed criminal acts of sex between men under the heading "unnatural offences."[4] Beyond this, as Brady shows, official legal, scientific, and medical discourse about sex between men was characterized by virtual silence. To break this *omertà* would have been to acknowledge the possibility that sex between men was as common in England as elsewhere in the world, and that Englishmen, like other men, might in daily life form and enjoy same-sex sexual relationships. This would in turn have threatened the rigid ideal of uxorious masculinity that provided British social and political order its bedrock.[5]

Tallack's remarks therefore afford a rare glimpse of sex between men in late-Victorian England, albeit taking place under somewhat atypical circumstances. If such exceptional historical insights are to be obtained anywhere, however, one would expect it to be from penal discourse. To take another example from the same period: three years before its closure in 1875, informants at the Gibraltar convict prison, the English penal system's final, decrepit overseas outpost, estimated that between fifty and sixty prisoners participated in what the prison chaplain referred to as "practices of an abominable character."[6] As one convict explained, "prisoners in a distant part of the hall make a noise for the purpose of distracting the attention of the warders [while] this act is being committed."[7] The detail provided here is again unusual and again suggests that sex was, then as now, inescapably a part of prison life.

At the same time, however, prisons were necessarily organized, as they still are today, around the imperative of surveillance. This made any form of deviance uncommonly visible, not least varieties of sexuality and sexual behavior. Hence by the early twentieth century, as Regina Kunzel argues, the prison became a "privileged site for the observation, study, and burgeoning production of knowledge about sex and sexuality."[8] Only a few decades earlier, in late-Victorian England, it would have been difficult for prison administrators to ignore sex between men or to deny that it was possible, notwithstanding the constraints against mentioning or even naming it, much less describing it. Yet given such constraints, how was the disciplinary issue of sex among prisoners addressed? Was the blind eye reported by informants typical? Or even the tacitly tolerant one? And was this attitude due to discursive paralysis at a higher level? Was sex between male prisoners ignored simply because senior prison administrators were unable to acknowledge the possibility of sex between Englishmen per se?

And what of the attempts that were made to limit opportunities for prisoners to commit what was, after all, a felony? One approach, examined in this chapter, was via the management and control of men convicted under England's sodomy laws for acts of consensual sex with other men. Such an approach, however, required grouping such prisoners into a discrete class. But this was precisely the kind of move for which English prison administrators and government officials, armed as they were only with the unwieldy category of "unnatural offences," lacked adequate medico-legal concepts and vocabulary. Incapable of classifying men sentenced for criminal acts of consensual sex, prison administrators, as we shall see, instead settled eventually for excluding all those convicted of "unnatural crime" from a new division for first offenders in convict prisons.

Introduced in 1879, this division, known as the "star class," was intended to protect novice criminals from "contamination." Employed in a penal context, "contamination" referred primarily to criminal pedagogy—the notion, that is, of prisons as "schools of crime" where novice criminals were initiated by recidivists into professional thievery. But it was an elastic term also used in relation to prisoners forming "combinations" resulting in "mutiny," or to the spiritually polluting effect upon prisoners unused to it of profane and blasphemous language. And although overlooked by penal historians, it is evident that sex among prisoners also came under the rubric of "contamination." Indeed, as discussed in the concluding section of this chapter, prison administrators treated mere conversation among prisoners about sex between men, let alone the real thing, as a grave peril. This should be understood less as prudishness than as a reflex suppression of any suggestion that sex between men might be commonplace, either within or beyond prison walls.

An expanded definition of "unnatural crime," necessitated by the exclusion of first offenders sentenced for it from the star class, sprang from a similar impulse. The 1861 Offences against the Person Act listed as "unnatural" sodomy, attempted sodomy, and assault with intent to commit sodomy. But the term "sodomy"—or "buggery," its legal synonym—referred not only to sex between men, but to sex with animals and, technically, anal penetration of a woman by a man. All were prosecutable under a 1533 statute reenacted in 1828 and again in 1861. In legal terms, however, neither sodomy nor rape (which until 1997 required vaginal penetration without consent of a female by a male) were classed as "sexual offences" as this designation, though employed by prison administrators from at least the 1890s,[9] did not exist in English law until 1956.[10]

Notwithstanding the absence of a sexual category in law, however, the wording of the recommendation excluding men sentenced for "unnatural crime" from the star class forced Home Office officials in 1879 to specify types of sexual act, as distinct from criminal offences, covered by the term. This resulted in a broadening of "unnatural crime" to include any man convicted of rape if accompanied in the act by another man or other men. Until 1897, when the rule disqualifying men convicted of "unnatural crime" from the star class was lifted, prison administrators, as part of their wider vetting of first offenders, put considerable effort into determining the category to which first offenders sentenced for rape belonged. Were they "unnatural" and thus potentially contaminating, or "natural" and therefore at risk of contamination?

This somewhat eccentric method of prisoner classification accompanied attempts to prevent star class prisoners from hearing sex between men ever being mentioned, and followed the exclusion of prisoners convicted of "unnatural crime" from England's last overseas penal colony. In detailing these measures, this chapter shows the contorted lengths to which English prison administrators were driven by the requirement that they acknowledge and respond to the quotidian reality of sexual relationships between men.

Penal servitude and the English sodomy laws

Efforts to classify prisoners sentenced for criminal acts of sex between men began in 1863, when those sentenced for "unnatural crime" were barred from transportation to England's last Australian penal settlement at Fremantle, Western Australia. Before exploring this measure in detail, it will be useful to examine a little further both the offences for which these prisoners had been sentenced, and the sentence—penal servitude—that such offences carried. As these were peculiar to English criminal law and penal practice, it may also be helpful to preface this discussion by considering briefly parallel developments and contemporary debates in two other countries: the United States and France.

In contrast to its neglect by English penal historians, prison sex has in recent years moved from the margins to the center of American penal historiography. This reassessment was led by Kunzel, who in a groundbreaking study of sex in American prisons argues that the architecture and administration of the nineteenth-century American penitentiary were driven in part by concern about sex among prisoners.[11] For some prison reformers and administrators, she observes, this bordered on an "obsessive preoccupation."[12] In a recent study of prison reform in post-revolutionary Pennsylvania, Jen Manion identifies a "sex panic" in the mid-1820s as instrumental in the establishment of Philadelphia's pioneering Eastern State Penitentiary, where prisoners were held in what amounted to permanent solitary confinement.[13] In France, similarly, according to Patricia O'Brien writing as early as 1982, "homosexual promiscuity" among prisoners was one of "two great social fears"—the other was recidivism—that in 1872 led the National Assembly to establish a special commission of inquiry into the nation's prisons.[14] Although it proved unfeasible to implement the recommendation fully, the French commission arrived at the same remedy for prison sex as had their American counterparts fifty years earlier: all prisoners should inhabit single prison cells.

Unlike France, however, where sex between men had effectively been decriminalized in 1791, or the United States, where prosecutions (under state laws rather than federal statute) were comparatively rare and sentences relatively lenient, English prison populations included men serving lengthy sentences for criminal acts of consensual sex with other men. As Dominic Janes discusses in the present volume, though the last executions in England for sodomy took place in 1835, it remained a capital crime until 1861. After that, it carried a ten-year minimum sentence and a maximum life sentence of penal servitude, the penalty introduced in 1853 to replace transportation. Attempted sodomy carried a maximum sentence of ten years' penal servitude, as did both assault with intent to commit sodomy and indecent assault, which in practice might include any sexual act between men ("indecent" functioning in English law as shorthand for criminal sexual acts that did not involve either anal or vaginal penetration).

Prosecution of these offences was, however, far from systematic. Indeed, as Brady notes, "the authorities demonstrated extreme reluctance to prosecute or pursue unnatural crime."[15] Not only was guilt in such cases difficult to prove, but frequent trials, and the publicity attending them, would have shown sex between Englishmen to be relatively common. It was therefore "not in the interests of the British state to enquire too deeply or to prosecute this crime efficiently."[16] But if members of the public took it upon themselves to report to the authorities specific incidents of sex between men, arrest, trial, and severe punishment could follow: sentences of fifteen or twenty years' penal servitude were not uncommon as late as the 1890s.

At the time of Tallack's 1878 pamphlet, the minimum term for sentences of penal servitude was five years; it had been three years until 1864 and would again be after 1891. The sentence was served in one of the convict prisons opened from the late 1840s to accommodate prisoners who would previously have been transported to Australia (or else left to languish aboard prison hulks moored along England's south coast, which was as far as many sentenced to transportation ever traveled). Convict prisons differed from England's long-established local and county gaols in one crucial respect. At the latter, prisoners serving sentences of imprisonment for up to a maximum of two years (though often far less—a week or two was common) were held in "separate confinement," sleeping, eating, and working in single cells and prevented as far as possible from having contact with one another. But as two years was believed to represent separate confinement's safe limit—any longer might risk a prisoner's sanity—prisoners in convict prisons, though they too slept in single cells, labored by day alongside one another in work gangs. Convict labor was employed in such tasks as quarrying, brickmaking, and the construction of naval and military infrastructure.

It was this arrangement that had prompted Tallack's intervention. As he explained in 1879, giving evidence to a royal commission on penal servitude, when he considered "the long hours of [the] warders, and the large parties which many of them have to overlook, and the going home of the men at dusk, and the various ins and outs of prisons," he could not "get rid of a lurking fear" that sex took place among prisoners in convict prisons.[17] Prison administrators, who, like Tallack, believed that prisoners taught one another sexual practices thus faced a dilemma with regard to men sentenced to penal servitude for consensual sex with other men. The minimum length of these prisoners' sentences prohibited permanent separate confinement, but to concentrate them in specific work gangs would be to create unconscionable ghettoes of "unnatural crime" within convict prisons. Hence there was no option but to assign such men to ordinary work gangs, despite the risk of their "contaminating" fellow prisoners.

From this perspective, it is easy to see how men convicted under the sodomy laws might become the focus of measures to curb sex among prisoners. But prisoners who engaged in sexual activity with others were not necessarily, or even very likely to be, those convicted under the sodomy laws. Nevertheless, the latter were assumed to represent the locus of sex within the male convict population. Indeed, the precise aim of the measure enacted in 1863, to which we now turn, barring men convicted of "unnatural crime" from transportation to Western Australia, was to prevent sex among prisoners by shielding them from "contamination" by sodomites.

"Schools of unnatural crime"

"[D]epravity in its worst form," explained a former convict ship surgeon consulted by the Home Office in 1858, following a near-mutiny by prisoners aboard a ship bound for Fremantle, "is known to be inseparable from ... bodies of men, deprived by the forces of circumstances [sic] to any length of time of their natural communion with the opposite sex." Such depravity, he added with rare candor, was "not of infrequent occurrence during a long voyage even in Her Majesty's Navy."[18] Five years later, giving evidence to an 1863 royal commission on penal servitude chaired by the former Whig colonial secretary Henry Grey, Third Earl Grey, Charles Measor, a former deputy governor of Chatham convict prison, described convict ships as "a source of pollution to convicts in every possible way, and of the most horrible description," claiming that he had "been informed by convicts over and over again that convict ships are nothing but schools of unnatural crime."[19]

Given an understanding that sex was likely to occur among *any* group of men separated from women, coupled with belief in the pedagogic character of "unnatural crime," it is perhaps unsurprising that the colonial authorities in Western Australia objected to the transportation there of men convicted under the sodomy laws. The colony's governor, Sir Arthur Kennedy, repeatedly accused prison administrators of reneging on a promise to transport to the colony only prisoners selected on the basis of good conduct. Indeed, this policy appeared to the colonists to have been entirely reversed and the "worst" criminals shipped instead, among them men convicted of "unnatural crime." As Western Australia's senior prison administrator, the future Metropolitan Police chief commissioner Edmund Henderson, complained in 1856 to a select committee on transportation, "the rule is merely to send out those men they do not hang."[20]

To illustrate the point, among prisoners arriving in Fremantle that year Henderson singled out two convicted of robbery with violence, one of "Rape upon his own daughter" and another of "unnatural crime."[21] Colonel Joshua Jebb, Du Cane's predecessor as convict service chairman, protested that his hands were tied: he was obliged to transport these prisoners and had received no instruction to disqualify specific types of offender.[22] Seven years later, however, in his evidence to the Grey Commission, Jebb contradicted his earlier testimony. Asked whether he was aware that prisoners convicted of "unnatural offences" had been sent to Western Australia, he replied that "it ought not to have been so if it has occurred" as "there was a special reservation that the colonists would receive all excepting those cases."[23]

James Gambier, Jebb's convict service colleague, backed him up, explaining to the commission that

> When men are ordered to be selected for embarkation … the instructions first of all are that men are to be rejected who have ever been known to have been in a lunatic asylum, or have ever shown any symptoms of insanity; secondly men who have been convicted of unnatural crimes or bestiality, those are men who are never sent.[24]

This account was, however, distinctly at odds with one given by Measor, who recalled receiving an order in 1860 "to select the men who were the most unfit for liberation in this country [England]" and sending from Chatham "as bad a set of men as I ever knew," including some convicted of "unnatural crimes."[25] For his part, Governor Kennedy cited a return made in 1858 that listed, among Fremantle's convict population of just over 1100, twenty-two men convicted of "unnatural crimes."

Asked by Grey whether he thought it "particularly objectionable to send out men who have been convicted of such offences," Kennedy replied that he thought it "objectionable to send them anywhere amongst Christian people."[26] Grey agreed: his report condemned the selection for transportation of "convicts least fit to be discharged at home" as "entirely wrong," and affirmed that any prisoner convicted of "unnatural crimes" was "manifestly unfit to be sent to a colony."[27] In August 1863, within weeks of the report's publication, the Home Office issued a standing order explicitly prohibiting the transportation to Western Australia of prisoners convicted of "unnatural crimes."[28] In excluding such prisoners from a territory covering a third of a continent and measuring almost a million square miles, this order represents the first attempt to restrict the disposal of prisoners within the English convict system on the basis of their offence. As such, it was also the first official recognition of prisoners convicted of "unnatural crime" as a discrete administrative category.

Defining "unnatural crime"

Transportation to Western Australia ended four year later in 1867, followed by the closure of Gibraltar convict prison in 1875. By 1879, when Tallack gave evidence to a royal commission on penal servitude, anyone receiving the sentence from an English court went on to serve it in a domestic convict prison. Though Tallack had not concerned himself specifically with prisoners in these establishments convicted under the sodomy laws, the commission's chairman, the Liberal politician John Wodehouse, First Earl of Kimberley, nevertheless questioned Du Cane about the risk they posed to other prisoners. Predictably enough, Du Cane dismissed concerns such as Tallack's, reassuring Kimberley that "our check upon the possibility of anything of that kind is so great that there is no fear of it."[29] Kimberley appears to have accepted this guarantee of convict chastity, though it did little to alleviate his concern about the wider problem of "contamination." This he took extremely seriously, recommending as a remedy the segregation from the general prison population of any prisoner without previous conviction sentenced to penal servitude for the first time. From 1879, these "star" prisoners were held in separate areas of convict prisons and eventually in separate prisons altogether.

A late-Victorian convict prison's star class would have comprised what were later termed "white-collar" criminals together with a heterogeneous assortment of arsonists, bigamists, abortionists, railway vandals, and other first offenders. They were joined by men convicted for the first time of violent non-property offences such as wounding and manslaughter, among them murderers whose death sentences had been commuted to penal servitude for life. As they too had often been sentenced for a first offence, it might be expected that the star class would also have included men convicted under the sodomy laws. Kimberley's recommendation, however, bore the caveat that, a first sentence notwithstanding, prisoners convicted of "certain crimes" were "obviously unfit" for assignment to the new division. It singled out two types of offender: "receiver[s] of stolen goods" and "men guilty of unnatural crimes and indecency."[30]

Bundling the "unnatural" and the "indecent" together in this way had unintended consequences. The former, as we have seen, had hitherto functioned straightforwardly as shorthand for sexual acts prosecutable under the sodomy laws, and the latter for criminal sexual acts that did not involve actual or attempted anal or vaginal penetration. Now their respective parameters grew altogether less distinct. In February 1880, Du Cane sought clarification on the recommendation's correct interpretation, which he had assumed to mean that "all men convicted of sodomy [,] bestial offences [and] rape are to be excluded from the select class." Junior Home Office minister Matthew White Ridley disagreed, contending that "the rule of exclusion from the special class should be applied *universally* to sodomites and bestiality cases"—but not, in his view, to rapists.[31]

Called upon to adjudicate, Permanent Secretary Adolphus Liddell, in a margin note to Du Cane's query, began by affirming that the rule should apply "only to sodomites, or men convicted of indecency of a sodomitical character." But he then continued:

> Bestiality with animals is usually committed by boys or very young men and is of a more usual character therefore unless the case is very gross the rule need not apply to them. It certainly ought not to apply to rape cases except when committed by two or more at a time or under conditions of great brutality. Many a man commits a rape under the excitement of the moment and there is nothing in such an offence which renders him unfit for association with *men*.[32]

In the absence, then, of any other medico-legal yardstick, Liddell appears to have fallen back on the "unnatural." Though undoubtedly "indecent," it was not "unnatural" for men to rape women—or, indeed, for adolescent males to sexually molest animals. But rape ceased to be "natural" if accompanied by excessive violence or committed with a male accomplice. Here Liddell effectively broadened the "unnatural" to include not only sex between men, but sex *involving* more than one man.

For the next sixteen years, Liddell's note would supply the classification criteria for first offenders sentenced to penal servitude for a sexual offence. Thus sixteen-year-old William Hazzard, sentenced in 1880 at Northampton Assizes to ten years' penal servitude and without a previous conviction, though precisely the kind of novice Kimberley had wished to shield from experienced criminals, was disqualified automatically from the star class as his conviction was for sodomy.[33] The same went for William Hunt, aged twenty-six, a bootmaker and former private in the Coldstream Guards, sentenced for the first time at the Old Bailey in 1883 to five years for attempted sodomy.[34] With the occasional rare exception, senior convict administrators also treated cases of bestiality as automatically ineligible.[35]

On the other hand, Charles Chown, aged thirty-six, a gasworks laborer who at the Old Bailey in 1879 received a first sentence of ten years for rape, was assigned to the star class. Greenwich constabulary confirmed that Chown acted alone and that "there was no violence used … with the exception that he effected his purpose."[36] Similarly, Hugh Frodsham, a bricklayer, aged twenty-one and "fond of pleasure & drink," who was sentenced to five years' penal servitude at Chester assizes in 1882 for raping a sixteen-year-old female servant, was placed in the star class once it was confirmed that he had committed the offence alone and not in circumstances of "special brutality."[37] Charles Williams, however, a twenty-year-old farm laborer sentenced in 1880 to five years for rape, and regarded by police in Suffolk as honest, sober, and "very hardworking," was denied star class status for having committed the offence "with others." By the same logic, the joint participation that year of farm laborers Robert Bowers, Henry Legge, and John Riches in raping a twenty-year-old woman, for which they received first sentences of eight years apiece, precluded them from being classified as star class prisoners.[38] This was despite Norfolk police describing the trio's characters as "good" and their victim as "a prostitute."

When it came to "brutality," cases such as that of John Roberts, a 21-year-old collier excluded from the star class for having battered his 65-year-old victim before raping her, were easy to appraise.[39] Elsewhere, however, interpretations varied among police forces: tearing a victim's clothing, using "very disgusting language," and committing the offence "at 9 P.M. on the Sabbath" were all variously mentioned.[40] For their part, senior convict administrators did not always (as in the latter example) concur with such assessments. In the case of William Pimblott, for instance, a seventeen-year-old farm laborer sentenced in 1881 to seven years at Chester Assizes for raping a nine-year-old girl, Macclesfield constabulary noted with regard to "circumstances of special brutality" that he had infected his victim with venereal disease. In the view of senior convict administrators, this was not strictly speaking "brutal" and Pimblott, who had acted alone and was otherwise described as honest, sober, and industrious, found himself admitted to the star class.[41]

The rule regarding joint enterprise was by contrast rigidly interpreted: men who might otherwise have been considered prime candidates for the star class were rejected solely on these grounds, while others who had acted alone and without "great brutality" were admitted regardless of the character of the offence. John Brown, for example, a forty-six-year-old seaman sentenced at Durham Assizes in 1881 to five years for raping a nine-year-old girl and indecently assaulting another, was admitted, as was George Eales, also forty-six, who raped a thirteen-year-old friend of his daughter, having first made her drunk and carried her to his lodgings.[42] Lawrence Harnett, on the other hand, a well-educated customs officer, aged twenty-five, was rejected: he had received five years at Kent Assizes for raping two women, aged sixteen and twenty-two, accompanied by another man, a surgeon, who received eighteen months for indecent assault. In a case that might today be described as "date rape," both defendants maintained that they had acted with the victim's consent and encouragement.[43]

Classing rape with a male accomplice as "unnatural" enabled a twofold discursive maneuver. First, discussion of *any* sexual act involving more than one man—including those involving both men and women—was fenced off as potentially "contaminating." This by implication included *consensual* sex between a woman and more than one man, for consent did not determine the act's "unnatural" status and rape could in other circumstances be "natural." In this way, a revised definition of "unnatural crime" served to uphold and reinforce a monogamous sexual ideal, against which any other sexual configuration was suspect. At the same time, however, again probably less by design than instinct, Liddell's expanded definition of the "unnatural" avoided acknowledging directly consensual sex between men by placing it in a category that also encompassed non-consensual sex between men and women.

Filthy talk

But why did Kimberley feel it necessary in the first place to exclude men convicted of "unnatural crime" from the star class? There was, after all, no evidence to suggest a correlation between the presence of such prisoners and the incidence of prison sex. Moreover, Kimberley appears to have been convinced by Du Cane that sex was impossible in convict prisons, later asserting that individual cells were "well calculated to prevent the possibility of such crimes as these."[44] Nevertheless, both were in agreement that "the association of such prisoners with others was obviously very undesirable."[45] Kimberley's report treated the rationale for their exclusion as self-evident, stating simply that they would "of course, not be admitted."[46]

When it came to receivers of stolen goods, the reasoning was clear: held responsible for the scale and persistence of property crime in English cities, receivers (as caricatured by Dickens in *Oliver Twist*) were the bogeymen of Victorian crime discourse. A specimen wily enough to have "escaped conviction during a long career of crime" would, Kimberley felt, "be the last man whom it would be desirable to place in contact with the younger and less hardened offenders."[47] He evidently viewed "unnatural crime" in similar terms. But given confidence in the sheer unlikelihood of sex in convict prisons, what possible danger could men convicted under the sodomy laws—or, indeed, men who had committed rape with male accomplices—have presented to other prisoners?

A clue is provided by Edward Callow, another of the commission's witnesses, convicted of fraud in 1868 and sentenced to seven years' penal servitude. Upon release, Callow had written a bestselling prison memoir, in which he described certain prisoners at Dartmoor as "creatures in human form who seem to be a different species to ordinary men." They were, he wrote, "mere brutes in mind and demons in heart."[48] Asked by Kimberley to clarify his meaning, Callow explained that he was "speaking there of men's ideas and men's language." Was this, he was then asked, something beyond the "brutal words" used "even among good men outside, of a particular class"? Callow replied that he had had in mind "something that one would hardly like to remember. While you are on that point I may say that there were prisoners there who were under sentence for unnatural crimes."[49] For Callow, then, no sexual act need take place in a prison for contamination to occur there; it was enough merely for a prisoner to overhear such an act being discussed.

The Home Rule parliamentarian and former Dartmoor prisoner Michael Davitt subscribed to a similar notion of verbal contamination. Though he acknowledged that they were "not very numerous," Davitt advocated the complete segregation from other prisoners of men convicted of "unnatural crimes," recalling in an 1885 prison memoir that "some of those perverted beings ... monopolize the surreptitious conversation of their immediate surroundings in the work-gang."[50] On this point, George Clifton, the governor of Portland convict prison, saw eye to eye with the ex-convicts. Estimating that Portland's prison population included around nineteen men convicted under the sodomy laws, amounting to roughly 2 percent of its total population, Clifton complained to Kimberley that these prisoner's language was "so contaminating even to those that come into contact with them" that they "all contaminate the others."[51] As the Gibraltar prison chaplain warned in 1872, if sex between men was "talked about ... the moral atmosphere becomes tainted. That which should be buried in the deepest silence of shamefacedness is exhumed, and breeds corruption."[52]

The exclusion from the star class of prisoners "guilty of unnatural crimes" was, then, less a matter of protecting the vulnerable from sexual predation than of shielding them from the contaminating effect of lewd conversation. This aim should not be dismissed as mere prudery. It was, rather, a reflex suppression of the suggestion that sex between men might be commonplace. As we have seen, the administration of late-Victorian convict prisons, in line with wider medico-legal discourse, was characterized by the need to avoid acknowledging the possibility of fairly widespread sex among male prisoners. To do so would have been to concede that Englishmen *beyond* convict prison walls might also engage in same-sex sex. The result was an eccentric definition of "unnatural crime" that in effect encompassed *any* sexual act involving more than one man, accompanied by a quixotic effort to protect prisoners at risk of "contamination" from even hearing in conversation that men ever had sex with each other.

The reflex was still apparent in 1897 when, as part of a wider policy shake-up, the Home Office rescinded the bar on assigning men convicted of "unnatural crime" to the star class. Explaining the rule change, Du Cane's successor, Evelyn Ruggles-Brise, wrote that whereas up to now "persons guilty of the graver forms of sexual crime had been categorically excluded from this class, whatever their antecedents may be," he had decided that "every case, without exception, should be made the subject of review, so that it may be decided on its merits." There were, he felt, insufficient grounds for excluding prisoners convicted of such offences "from a class containing, as it does, criminals guilty of all other crimes of violence, including murder."[53] As memoirs and reports dating from the interwar period confirm, first offenders convicted under the sodomy laws, as well as men sentenced for a rape committed with accomplices or under any other circumstance, were from now on eligible for the star class.[54]

When it came to the offences in question, however, Ruggles-Brise did not mention sex between men specifically (nor, indeed, sex with animals) and gave only rape as a specific example. Moreover, arguing that there was "a very clear line of demarcation between the city thief and the sexual offender," he observed that "many of the latter come from agricultural districts [and] most of them allege that they committed the offence when under the influence of drink: they break the law under the impulse of an uncontrollable passion."[55] Depicting sexual offenders simply as overheated farm-boys saved Ruggles-Brise from having to allude to the variety and complexity of human sexual behavior, some of it consensual, represented by "the graver forms of sexual crime."

Finally, what of actual sex among prisoners—as opposed, that is, to mere conversations about it? Between 1879 and the 1920s, when constraints against acknowledging sex between men finally lost some of their force, evidence for sexual activity in convict prisons is confined to one or two oblique references in prison memoirs.[56] But that does not mean it did not happen. Tallack's "lurking fear" was probably not entirely groundless. In the absence of complete cellular separation—for which, swimming against the tide of late-Victorian penal reform, he remained a stubborn advocate—opportunities for sex in convict prisons no doubt existed for those bold and determined enough to seize them.

There is, however, nothing to suggest that convict authorities considered sex among prisoners a disciplinary problem, or even something worth mentioning. Indeed, so confident was Du Cane of convict chastity, and so reluctant to acknowledge its antithesis, that he neglected to list "unnatural crime" and "acts of indecency" as punishable offences under convict prison rules.[57] As far as senior prison administrators were concerned, sex between men did not take place in English convict prisons. Perhaps everybody else simply turned a blind eye to it.

Notes

1 William Tallack, *English Convict Prisons: Some Needed Reforms (1877–78). With a Letter to the Chairman of the Directors of these Prisons* (London: The Howard Association, 1878), 16.
2 Ibid., 16–17.
3 Sean Brady, *Masculinity and Male Homosexuality in Britain, 1861–1913* (Basingstoke: Palgrave Macmillan, 2005), 218.

4 E.g., *Report from the Select Committee on Transportation; together with the Minutes of Evidence, Appendix, and Index* (1837) U.K. Parliamentary Papers [518] XIX.1, 34.
5 Brady, *Masculinity*, 154–156.
6 *Report of the Directors of Convict Prisons … for the Year 1872* (1873) U.K. Parliamentary Papers [C.850] XXXIV.1, 526 at 562.
7 *Report of the Directors of Convict Prisons … for the Year 1874* (1875) U.K. Parliamentary Papers [C.1346] XXXIX.1, 528 at 560.
8 Regina Kunzel, *Criminal Intimacy: Prison and the Uneven History of Modern American Sexuality* (Chicago: University of Chicago Press, 2008), 7.
9 E.g., *Report of the Commissioners of Prisons and Directors of Convict Prisons, with Appendices* (1897) U.K. Parliamentary Papers [C.8590] XL.105, 17.
10 Leslie J. Moran, *The Homosexual(ity) of Law* (London: Routledge, 1996), 67.
11 Kunzel, *Criminal Intimacy*, 15–23.
12 Ibid., 16.
13 Jen Manion, *Liberty's Prisoners: Carceral Culture in Early America* (Philadelphia: University of Pennsylvania Press, 2015), 169–178.
14 Patricia O'Brien, "The Prison on the Continent: Europe, 1865–1965," in *The Oxford History of the Prison: The Practice of Punishment in Western Society*, ed. Norval Morris and David J. Rothman (Oxford: Oxford University Press, 1998), 181; Patricia O'Brien, *The Promise of Punishment: Prisons in Nineteenth-Century France* (Princeton: Princeton University Press, 1982), 25–26.
15 Brady, *Masculinity*, 212.
16 Ibid., 116.
17 *Penal Servitude Acts Commission. Report of the Commissioners Appointed to Inquire into the Working of the Penal Servitude Acts…* (1878–9) U.K. Parliamentary Papers [C.2368] [C.2368-I] [C.2368-II] XXXVII.1, 67, XXXVIII.1 (referred to hereafter as *Kimberley*), 224 at 293, q.2736.
18 *Australian Colonies. Convict Discipline and Transportation. Further Correspondence…* (1859) U.K. Parliamentary Papers [2568] XXII.1, 171 at 178.
19 *Report of the Commissioners Appointed to Inquire into the Operation of the Acts… Relating to Transportation and Penal Servitude …* (1863) U.K. Parliamentary Papers [3190] [3190–I] XXI.1, 283 (referred to hereafter as *Grey*), 449 at 727, q.5553.
20 *Report from the Select Committee of the House of Lords, Appointed to Inquire into the Provisions and Operation of the … Act to Substitute, in Certain Cases, Other Punishment in lieu of Transportation…* (1856) U.K. Parliamentary Papers [404] XVII.561, 83 at 88, q.872.
21 Ibid., q.873.
22 Ibid., 111 at 116, qq.1184–90.
23 *Grey*, 68 at 346, q.759.
24 Ibid., 334 at 612, q.4009.
25 Ibid., 450 at 728, qq.5562–7.
26 Ibid., 190–191 at 468–469, qq.2382–6.
27 Ibid., 52 at 51, para 66.
28 Seán McConville, *A History of English Prison Administration: Volume I 1750–1877* (London: Routledge & Kegan Paul, 1981), 384, fn.13.
29 *Kimberley*, 34 at 103, q.406.
30 Ibid., xxix–xxx at 28–29, para 79.
31 The National Archives, HO 45/9557/70327C (emphasis original).
32 Ibid.

33 The National Archives, PCOM 3/762.
34 Ibid., PCOM 3/697.
35 E.g., ibid., PCOM 3/717 (Edward Wilson).
36 Ibid., PCOM 3/769.
37 Ibid., PCOM 3/750.
38 Ibid., PCOM 3/663; PCOM 3/738; PCOM 3/740; PCOM 3/737.
39 Ibid., PCOM 3/734.
40 Ibid., PCOM 3/743 (Albert Moors); PCOM 3/742 (Lawrence Harnett); PCOM 3/737 (William Sparke).
41 Ibid., PCOM 3/738.
42 Ibid., PCOM 3/703; PCOM 3/747.
43 Ibid., PCOM 3/742.
44 *Kimberley*, 224 at 293, q.2735.
45 Ibid., 34 at 103, q.407.
46 Ibid., xxix–xxx at 28–29, para 79.
47 Ibid.
48 Anon. (Edward Callow), *Five Years' Penal Servitude by One Who Has Endured It* (London: Richard Bentley & Son, 1877), 208.
49 *Kimberley*, 954 at 1027, qq.11985–8.
50 Michael Davitt, *Leaves from a Prison Diary; or, Lectures to a "Solitary" Audience* (London: Chapman & Hall, 1885), 230.
51 *Kimberley*, 168 at 237, q.2231.
52 *Report of the Directors ... 1872*, 525 at 562.
53 *Report of the Commissioners of Prisons*, 17.
54 E.g., Jim Phelan, *Jail Journey* (London: Secker & Warburg, 1940); The National Archives, HO 45/22661.
55 *Report of the Commissioners of Prisons*, 17.
56 E.g., Anon., *The Mark of the Broad Arrow; or the Life of a Convict by No. 77* (London: R.A. Everett, 1903), 212–213.
57 Leon Radzinowicz and Roger Hood, *A History of English Criminal Law and Its Administration from 1750: Volume 5: The Emergence of Penal Policy* (London: Stevens, 1986), 554, fn.15.

6

"It Is My Husband Who Has Such Weaknesses": A Mid-Nineteenth-Century Peruvian Divorce Case

Magally Alegre Henderson

When the Ecclesiastical Court of the Archdiocese of Lima granted Josefa Murillo her divorce in 1847, allowing her to separate after thirty years of marriage, she finally freed herself from her husband Juan Calderón and his male lover. Well before the dissolution of civil marriages was legalized in 1930, and even longer before the campaign to legalize same-sex unions in twenty-first-century Peru, under Spanish colonial rule separations like Josefa's were called "divorce," even when they did not represent full dissolution of the marital union. Although rarely granted, this type of ecclesiastical "divorce" was a relatively common request in Spanish colonial Latin America, especially during the emergence of independent Latin American nations in the first part of the nineteenth century. Josefa's unusual allegations about her husband's extramarital relationships with a man constituted the type of extreme circumstances under which an Ecclesiastical Court might approve the separation of a married couple. In a roundabout way, it also provides a unique opportunity to understand some of the dynamics of a male same-sex couple in mid-nineteenth-century Peru.[1]

The lifestyle Juan Calderón shared with his partner, the younger Martín Hurtado, was part of a dying tradition in the city of Lima. In the middle of a crowded neighborhood, Juan and Martín's daily life testified to the lack of interest of the city authorities in prosecuting same-sex sexuality. In fact, the harsh punishments against sodomy prescribed by colonial criminal legislation were seldom enforced during the first part of the nineteenth century. After Peruvian independence, when the first Republican Penal Code was written in 1862, it reduced the maximum sentence for male–male sexual acts from death to a term of up to fifteen years' imprisonment.[2] However, long-term lack of enforcement contributed to the fame of the city of Lima as rich with effeminate characters, particularly in regard to the notorious "sociability" of those known as *maricones*, and in this respect the Peruvian capital differed from comparable cities in Latin America. *Maricón* was the derogatory term given to men who partially cross-dressed and sought sexual attention from other men.

The press, pamphlets, and even paintings provide evidence of the abundance of *maricones* in the city.[3] One writer whose accounts have come down to us was the French traveler Maximilien Radiguet, who lived in Lima during the early 1840s. Radiguet was very much impressed with the vestiges of "the misconducts and licentiousness of the oft-persecuted *society of maricones*." According to one of Radiguet's articles, included in his *Souvenirs de l'Amérique Espagnole*, this ancient society of *maricones* had emerged in Lima in opposition to women and was visible enough even to have a favorite meeting place, in the Plaza Mayor, the city's main square. Radiguet defined *maricones* by their antagonism to women, highlighting in particular the spontaneous arguments that flared up between *maricones* and women in the Plaza Mayor and other public areas, where witty and malicious tirades were exchanged to defy or ridicule the opponent.[4]

A decade before Radiguet's visit to Lima, in 1827, a pamphlet entitled "The Journey to Amancaes" also represented a group of *maricones* sitting in the same plaza and poking fun at young women, sometimes even insulting or gossiping about them, as suggested by the following verse:

> [The *maricones*] They leave for the plaza
> and in the midst of it they sit;
> A little young lady then goes-by
> quite stiff with her entourage,
> and a *maricón* begins
> to insult her.
> But she, heedless
> goes about her way. Yet,
> the insolent *maricón*
> quite seriously tells the others:
> 'Look at this indecent girl,
> I saw her burying the dead,
> because she stabbed with a penknife
> Mr. Juan, the carpenter.'
> Another *maricón*, who had
> all along remained silent,
> says irritatedly: do you see, girl,
> that one rushing by?
> Well, she tried to snatch
> Don Lucas away from me ... but I don't want
> to proceed 'cos people will also say
> how insolent I am.[5]

This extract suggests that it was not only French visitors who described *maricones* using public space in the Plaza Mayor to contest loudly the public reputations of female passers-by. They were part of life in the city in the 1820s.

A plea for "divorce"

As suggested above, it was not uncommon for *maricones* to express some sort of rivalry with women over the love of a particular man.[6] The most noteworthy example of such rivalry was the lawsuit Josefa Murillo filed against her husband Juan Calderón, whereby she accused him of having an "illicit relationship" with another man, the young Martín Hurtado.[7] With the advice and support of one of her sons, Josefa Murillo presented her case against her lawful husband Juan Calderón before Lima's Ecclesiastical Court in September 1846, pleading "divorce for the mistreatment against her person, which makes the marital union unbearable, and therefore requests separation from habitation and bed."[8]

Since colonial times and until 1897, all marriages in Peru were celebrated and registered only by the Catholic Church, without civil records being kept. Civil marriage was introduced in 1897, but it was to be more than thirty years before President Luis Sánchez Cerro approved, in 1930, a Law of Absolute Divorce allowing the full dissolution of civil marriages. In Josefa's time there were three legal possibilities, mostly sought by women, for ending an ill-suited matrimonial union: annulment, separation (or temporary divorce), and permanent ecclesiastical divorce. An annulment was extremely difficult to obtain, as it was tantamount to declaring the marriage as never having existed. Separations and divorces, also rarely granted, but much more so than annulments, provided ecclesiastical and civil approval for the temporary or permanent separation from the spouse, respectively, but not for the dissolution of the marriage. Therefore, these dispensations did not grant the freedom to remarry, which was possible only in case of annulment (and, after 1930, in case of civil and absolute divorce).[9]

During an ecclesiastical divorce process, and if the request was granted, women were compelled to relocate to the residence of a reputable person, usually a relative. Another option was to take up residence in a *recogimiento*, a lay house founded with the approval of the local ecclesiastical authority, which served as a refuge for women contesting ill-suited marriages and for wayward women to repent.[10] To ensure their sustenance for the duration of the separation, the husband was obliged to pay alimony to his wife unless he could prove that he did not to have the means to do so.[11]

Josefa was not in need of being placed in a *recogimiento* thanks to the material and moral support of her son, José Jiménez, who most likely encouraged his mother to request divorce from her husband. After a failed attempt at reconciliation by the Ecclesiastical Justice of the Peace, during which Josefa claimed mistreatment due to Juan's failings as a provider for her and their children, she decided to present her case before the Ecclesiastical Court, making the following claim:

> Last year, Calderón completely neglected me and my children. He lived away from us for a year, in order to [be able to] indulge in vice and immorality, which is the main and true cause of everything. I would not like to explain further because it embarrasses me. After all, *it is my husband who has such weaknesses.*[12]

Josefa accused Juan of having abandoned her to indulge in vice and immorality, implicitly referring to his relationship with another man. Instead of simply accusing him of sodomy, since it was too shameful even to utter the word, she only indirectly referred to the same-sex relationship she believed her husband was conducting. Josefa evidently had turned to the Ecclesiastical Court in utmost despair, after nearly thirty years of marriage. Her sufferings had become unbearable and she was finally convinced that her husband was not about to change his ways:

> I have suffered much, always hoping that one day my husband would change and reform his ways; but I am already disillusioned and convinced that I am fighting against hope, and even against evidence itself.[13]

First, she requested a temporary, four-year ecclesiastical divorce (separation) "to try to convince him to change his conduct and become disposed to fulfil the obligations expected of him."[14] Rather than having any real hope, Josefa's intention was in fact to bring to a temporary end her ill-suited marriage in a discreet manner. Ecclesiastical divorce seemed to be a better solution in comparison to, for instance, denouncing her husband for sodomy.

Three decades after independence from Spain (about the time Josefa filed for divorce), Peru continued to be ruled by Spanish colonial law, and sodomy was considered a criminal offence. A vast collection of codes, from the *Fuero Juzgo* (Spanish medieval code) to the *Novísima Recopilación* (Latest Compilation in 1567, 1775, 1805), in addition to the *Leyes de Indias* (Laws of the Indies) and the *cédulas reales* (royal orders), constituted the Spanish colonial legislation that prescribed harsh punishments for the "nefarious sin," including death by burning.[15] Despite the harsh legislation, sodomy was often left unpunished, as the scant colonial and republican criminal cases prosecuting same-sex sexuality may attest. Accordingly, even if Josefa decided to overcome her shame and consider denouncing her husband for sodomy, she would have found little interest within the police and judicial system for enforcing the law against him.

Ecclesiastical divorce was not an easy solution either, since Juan Calderón was bluntly opposed to the idea of divorcing his wife. In fact, throughout the trial, he took every possible step to delay the procedure, even at the risk of exposing the real nature of his relationship with Martín. His reaction was consistent with most husbands' responses to divorce demands. According to historian Luis Bustamante, in this period there were three typical male reactions to nullity, separation, and ecclesiastical divorce processes: conciliation and regret, conflict denial, and defamation against the opposing party.[16] As such, in his first reply to Josefa's demand, her husband Juan insinuated that it was she who had abandoned their marital life by moving not to a *recogimiento* or convent—a condition for requesting the divorce provided by ecclesiastical law—but to the home of his stepson, José Jiménez.

Juan specifically denied the charges of mistreatment of his wife and provided no response to the allegations of indulging in vice and immorality which was Josefa's strategy for denouncing the illicit male friendship she believed was her husband's weakness. Moreover, Juan declared himself to be of limited means, arguing that in truth it was his poverty and not his flaws as a husband or father which had recently become an irritation to his wife and the source of her intention to divorce, particularly now that her wealthy son (and not his own) was able to provide her with more comfort.

Josefa had indeed brought to her marriage to Juan two sons, José Jiménez and Francisco Balero. Despite Juan's claims, Josefa declared that she had been responsible for the education and support of her elder children. By the time the divorce was requested, her son José had made a fortune, which allowed him to bring his mother and all her family from Guayaquil to Lima—a journey of at least 1400 km—on two occasions. José Jiménez estimated that the first trip of the family from Guayaquil and the cost of settling in Lima amounted to 3000 pesos, including clothing, accommodation, furniture, and working tools. A further 1000 pesos, plus travel costs, José claimed, had been wasted by Juan Calderón in taking his family back to Guayaquil. In addition, 600 pesos had been spent in settling the family back in Lima in 1843. Finally, several times José had lent money to Juan to start a new trade, which never prospered. Even at the beginning of the divorce proceedings, Josefa revealed the economic reasons behind her husband's opposition to the divorce, but also the motivation for her son's support during the trial:

> My good son cannot offer me sustenance apart from his own house and table, and neither can I neglect the only means left for obtaining food. My husband does not accept this because what he wants is money to spend, and a separate house that he cannot afford, or shall I say he does not want, as he does not work.[17]

In sum, in supporting his mother's divorce, José Jiménez was protecting his own finances by relieving himself of the burden of sustaining his mother's husband. However, beyond possible financial motivations, the evidence provided by Josefa also pointed to her husband's relationship with another man.

In the witnesses' words

Josefa's witnesses, neighbors, and friends all provided testimony about the illicit friendship between Juan Calderón and Martín Hurtado. One such witness was Manuel de Jesús Varas, husband of one of Josefa and Juan's daughters. Manuel declared that he had come to Lima three years before with Calderón and his family aboard a ship from Guayaquil, where he had been born. According to Manuel, Calderón brought with him a young man named Martín Hurtado, with whom he was very close. On arriving in Lima, they initially decided to stay in the same house. Manuel was given the same room where Juan Calderón and Martín Hurtado shared a bed, while Josefa and her children slept in another room.

This arrangement lasted for more than two months, until Calderón and Hurtado opened a candle shop with the means provided by Josefa's son José Jiménez, and moved out together. Juan and Martín worked together in the candle shop, and Manuel claimed he had seen them embracing and caressing each other. He also acknowledged that there were widespread rumors about the illicit relations within that family. Manuel believed the rumors because Calderón, his own father-in-law, had tried to caress him as well, but he had rejected his advances. Manuel had also heard once from the family that they had had to call a doctor to assist Josefa after Juan had beaten her.[18]

Another witness, Félix Hurtado, a 25-year-old shoemaker, also declared in favor of Josefa despite being a relative of Martín Hurtado. Félix declared that three years earlier, when he moved to Calderón's house, the neighbors had warned him that Juan and Martín were having an illicit liaison. Thus informed, Félix decided to observe them, and the result was that "he saw between them an extraordinary union and they provoked and harbor jealousy as it is commonly done among the people of different sexes." Félix also claimed to have been a direct witness of the physical relationship between Juan and Martín. Juan had once asked if he could borrow Félix's room in order to rest. Félix returned shortly afterward and spied on Juan through a window above the door. He observed Calderón and Martín on the same bed, "indecorously caressing each other," and was very disgusted and upset. Félix declared that he knew that Juan Calderón had moved to live alone with Martín for a while. Félix had then tried to separate Martín from "that life" by having Martín live with him. However, Calderón seduced Martín anew and enticed him to return.[19]

Here it is worth noting that the words "extraordinary union," "illicit relations," and "indecorous caressing" were used to refer to what up to half a century before had been known as the "abominable vice," "nefarious crime," and "sin against nature." For instance, it was acceptable for Archbishop Barroeta in the mid-eighteenth century to use the term *maricas*—a short form for *maricones*—in his edict banning cross-dressers of African descent who danced in local festivities celebrated in honor of patron saints.[20] But this was not the case in Josefa Murillo's petition, where "shame"—in the sense used by Norbert Elias—pervades all the depositions submitted in this lawsuit.[21]

Although ashamed by her husband's actions, Josefa refused to term her husband a *maricón*, his deeds notwithstanding. The witnesses Manuel and Félix also resorted to using euphemisms to refer to their claims about Juan Calderón's behavior. The *Murillo v. Calderón* case is in this regard markedly different from the criminal and Inquisition cases registered during the sixteenth and seventeenth centuries, where depositions required detailed descriptions of nakedness, terms of endearment, seduction techniques, types of caresses, and even the findings of medical examinations.

This case was different: the reserve and modesty of the ecclesiastical trial suggests the development of a "civilizing process" that prevented witnesses from accurately describing male-to-male sexual practices. Following Michel Foucault, it would be valid to ask if repression had cast a veil of censorship over sex or if the several testimonies on Josefa's defense exemplified a new regime where the multiplicity of discourses of sex contributed to expressing the "nonexistence, nonmanifestation, and silence" of male-to-male sexuality. In this ecclesiastical trial, the word *maricón* was carefully suppressed. A "civilizing process," which had begun with the development of the Enlightenment press, had begun to take root in Peruvian society, ultimately relegating *maricones* to the private domain, removing them from the public eye, and ostracizing any reference to them from the domain of what could be uttered. The "disappearance" of *maricones* may well also have gone hand in hand, as it were, with the emergence of a hegemonic bourgeois masculinity.[22]

Naming the cause

The discretion shown by Josefa Murillo and her witnesses was such that, after a few of them had made their depositions, she felt forced to amend and specify her own statements regarding the conduct of her husband. Her shame once more comes through in her deposition:

this brings me to the painful need to clarify one of my paragraphs, which I intentionally did not want to use in the first document, because it embarrassed me to give further explanations … I explained there, that the year [Calderón] abandoned [me] he [used] to indulge in vice and immorality, and it may be believed that it was with some woman. No sir, his weaknesses are sodomitic, and this is even more painful, and sadder to me, [that I have to] give his acts their proper name. The witnesses … know the person who was the accomplice of my husband in that excess, and they can point him out.[23]

Up to that moment, and out of shame, Josefa had preferred to remain silent on her main motivations for requesting a divorce: "so well-known was my intention … that I did not even dare to give them [the real causes for requesting her divorce] their proper name nor explain them with clarity."[24] She made this statement a month after initiating her claim, as part of a process by which she changed her petition from temporary separation to permanent divorce. She acknowledged that her husband did not intend to change his ways, and she also named those ways as "sodomitical" for the first and only time during the course of the trial. Revealing the true cause of her divorce plea, Josefa expressed her readiness to request a permanent separation from her husband.

Besides the discretion shown by the witnesses when testifying about the true nature of the friendship between Juan and Martín, the other significant element in the *Murillo v. Calderón* case is the role of neighbors in mediating domestic quarrels, as well as in providing information about the daily life of families and couples. As historian Christine Hunefeldt has shown, the personal physical proximities found in a Lima home or *callejón* (alley) enabled neighbors to witness all sorts of conjugal quarrels.[25] I would add that neighbors were also aware of the domestic life, occupations, and relations of sodomites and *maricones*. For instance, Manuel was aware of Josefa's and Juan's sleeping arrangements, and Félix was close enough to Juan's daily life to be able to spy on him while he was in bed with his lover.

Allowances must be made for exaggeration, which —as Delfina González del Riego has remarked—was a common aspect of many divorce processes.[26] But beyond any exaggeration, by the time Josefa's divorce proceedings were concluding, Juan Calderón had been unable to convince the Ecclesiastical Court of his innocence regarding the charges presented. He used three main arguments in his defense. First, that in almost thirty years of marriage he had fulfilled his matrimonial obligations without giving Josefa the slightest cause for grievance. Second, that he had always relied on his own work and trade to sustain himself and his family. And third, that Martín Hurtado had left his company on several occasions and expressed the intention to marry; and that at the moment he was living with doña Dominga Bedoya in her house under promise of marriage.

In spite of exposing his friendship with Martin Hurtado, and although he was accused of neglecting and abandoning his own three children, Juan called several witnesses on his behalf to attest to his great concern for the future and wellbeing of Martín Hurtado, whom he treated as a son. According to Juan, he felt obliged, as Martín's parents had entrusted him with bringing the young man to Lima, to have him learn a trade and even insisted on marrying Martín to one of his own daughters.

Juan also asked his witnesses to state that on several occasions, Martín had departed because of his intention to marry. Although the witnesses called by Juan, including Josefa Murillo herself, confirmed Juan's care for the young Martín, they all excused themselves for not knowing if Martín had indeed left his company or had given promise of marriage to anyone.[27] Thus, the testimonies given by the witnesses called on Juan's behalf and his own denial of the charges were deemed insufficient.

Hardly in his favor was the deposition of José Jiménez, who, when called by his stepfather's defense, claimed that Juan expressed his regret for having abandoned his family and his intention to amend his conduct with these words:

> [I am] convinced of the mistake I have made in abandoning my family, and how futile my work is without your [José's] aid; because in nothing have I been able to make any progress, and on the contrary I am indebted to many creditors to whom I am not able to make payment, as I have nothing left. It is because of this that I implore you, as well as your mother and my wife, to admit me and Martín again to your house, and to forgive us the faults committed until today. I hereby give my word of honour that I will not provide the slightest cause for complaint, and that from now on I will be the best father and the most faithful husband.[28]

After the statement provided by José Jiménez, who had been the main force in promoting the legal separation of the couple, Juan's fate was sealed. In November 1847, over a year after the lawsuit began, the Ecclesiastical Court ruled in favor of Josefa Murillo, granting her a permanent separation from her marriage to Juan Calderón "for the crimes of cruel treatment and sodomy."[29] The Ecclesiastical Court ruled the separation of habitation and bed, so that the couple could live separately, honestly and religiously, as they ought to do.

While ecclesiastical divorce was often requested by women, it was rarely granted. As proceedings were usually lengthy and complicated or did not produce a sentence, charges were often dropped by the petitioners.[30] The most common ground for requesting divorce was cruel treatment in the form of physical violence, but a few wives argued, like Josefa Murillo did, about the inclination of their husbands toward persons of the same sex. An earlier example is the case of doña Josefa Gallegos, wife of don Lorenzo Neira, who in 1801 asked for ecclesiastical divorce on grounds of marital cruelty. Josefa Gallegos was frequently beaten by her jealous husband. Besides, she claimed to have witnessed her husband locking himself up with a *maricón* in a room of their own house. Spying through a window, she had found her husband committing "the most atrocious crime": caressing his male lover. Furthermore, throughout the eighteenth and nineteenth centuries, several other women also accused their husbands of seeking to commit the "nefarious sin" with them, but in none of these cases was the divorce granted.[31]

Divorce was granted only when it was evident that the abuse had become unbearable for the petitioner, usually the wife, such that it prevented the couple from continuing to live under the same roof.[32] In the case of Josefa Murillo, the Court also ruled that, during the divorce, Juan should not molest, disturb, or trouble his wife, and warned him that, if he did, legal procedures would be initiated against him. Finally, although the Ecclesiastical Court stated it had proof of "the suspicious and illicit relation that said Calderón had maintained with Martín Hurtado," they only recommended to both spouses, Josefa and Juan, to behave according to their conscience.[33] No further action was taken against Juan's illicit relations, nor was Martín charged with sodomy or sanctioned in any way whatsoever.

In line with Foucault's dismissal of the "repressive hypothesis," the testimonies expressed in this lawsuit represented a multiplicity of discourses about the illicit friendship between Juan and Martín, even though there was a reluctance to name it. These omissions were nonetheless decisive evidence in demonstrating Josefa's case for divorce. Throughout the divorce proceedings, nobody had dared to call Juan or Martín *maricones*, nor were they charged with sodomy, even though some of the witnesses in the trial were themselves law enforcers. Furthermore, this discourse of the omissions regarding the illicit relations between Juan and Martín allowed what Foucault has called "an affirmation of nonexistence," granting Josefa a divorce on the grounds of sodomy, but at the same time preventing criminal prosecution because no one was arrested nor imprisoned.[34]

Conclusion

A decade after this ecclesiastical divorce case, the new Peruvian Penal Code of 1862 included sodomy as a private offence. Instead of following the Spanish legal tradition that considered it a crime against the king and the nation, the 1862 Penal Code included sodomy among the "offences against honesty" (Bk. 2, Sec. 8, *De los delitos contra la honestidad*), meaning moral outrage.[35] Article 272 equated the punishment for those who committed sodomy with that for those guilty of rape or statutory rape, with a maximum sentence of fifteen years in prison, depending on aggravating circumstances.[36] The Code transformed the consideration of sodomy as a crime concerning the nation (based on the Catholic fear of unleashing God's wrath) into a crime belonging to a more intimate sphere pertaining to a person's moral honesty.

In so doing, the 1862 Penal Code revealed a shift to making same-sex sexuality invisible, by transforming it into private offence. Just as the presence of *maricones* in the city was no longer a matter of public complaint—in contrast with the concern expressed by the press in the 1790s—so it was that sodomy became a matter of private concern. In short, once sodomy was no longer of interest for public prosecution, it became a viable cause (although in veiled terms) for requesting ecclesiastical divorce.

By the early nineteenth century, the scant official interest in prosecuting sodomites and *maricones* in Lima contrasted with the public statements in the press, pamphlets, and travel writings that showed concern about the abundance of *maricones* in the city.[37] Half a century later, the interest in prosecution had fallen even further, but the legend of a city once full of *maricones* had also almost faded away. It only survived in some diffuse references to vice and immorality as in Josefa and Juan's divorce case and in some travel accounts that described the *maricones* as characters of the past. This was the case of the French traveler Maximilien Radiguet, who described their gradual disappearance from the Plaza Mayor by the 1850s as a sign of the extinction of the "strange society of the *maricones*." Emphasizing the impression that the *maricones* were the ones who were voluntarily abandoning the public scene, Radiguet gives testimony of a process of veiling same-sex relationships starting in mid-nineteenth-century Peru in which the transformation of sodomy into a private matter instead of a public problem was the beginning of their journey into a silence that was to last until the twenty-first century.

Acknowledgments

Thanks to Carlos Pereyra Plasencia and Javier Flores Espinoza for copy-editing my text, to Dir. Laura Gutiérrez Arbulú and Melecio Tineo Morón for their invaluable help at the Archivo Arzobispal de Lima, and to my husband Norberto Barreto Velázquez, who persuaded me to present a preliminary version of this research in London in 2015. I also thank Dr. Pepi Patrón for her continuous encouragement and the Office of the Vice President of Research at the Pontificia Universidad Católica del Perú, for their generous support of my research.

Notes

1. Archivo Arzobispal de Lima, Causas de divorcio (henceforth AAL, CD), 1846, Leg. 90, Exp. 912; *Código Civil del Perú* (Lima: Imprenta del Gobierno, 1852), Lib. I, Sec. III; Decreto Ley N° 6889 (October 8, 1930); Ley N° 6890 (October 8, 1930); Código Civil del Perú—Ley N° 8305 (1936), Lib. II, Sec. III.
2. *Código Penal del Perú. Edición Oficial* (Lima: Imprenta Calle de la Rifa, 1862), 82. Available online: https://babel.hathitrust.org/cgi/pt?id=hvd.32044061588901;view=1up;seq=88 (accessed July 10, 2017).
3. Costumbrista-style paintings privileged portraying local characters and traditional festivities, including *maricones*, as shown in the Juan Carlos Verme collection at the Art Museum of Lima. For an analysis and portfolio of the various costumbrista watercolors of maricones held in this collection, see Natalia Majluf, ed., *La creación del costumbrismo. Las acuarelas de la donación Juan Carlos Verme* (Lima: Museo de Arte de Lima, Instituto Frances de Estudios Andinos, 2016).
4. Max Radiguet, *Lima y la Sociedad Peruana* (Lima: Biblioteca Nacional del Perú, 1971). Available online: http://www.cervantesvirtual.com/servlet/SirveObras/90253950982392717243457/p0000001.htm#2 (accessed November 21, 2016). (Emphasis added).
   Maximilien Radiguet (1816–1899), a French writer and illustrator, traveled to South America and Oceania as secretary to Admiral Abel du Petit-Thouars in 1841–1845. His visits to Peru and Chile (1841–1842) were described in captivating narratives and several drawings, published under the title *Souvenirs de l'Amérique Espagnole* (1856), which revealed the complexities of both postcolonial societies. Estuardo Nuñez, "Estudio preliminar," in *Lima y la Sociedad Peruana*.
5. *El Paseo de Amancaes y prisión de los maricones* (Imp. Republicana por J.M. Concha), Biblioteca Nacional del Perú, Pamphlets, 1820 box.
6. Archivo General de la Nación (Peru), Real Audiencia, Causas Criminales, 1797, Leg. 84, Cuad. 1032.

7   AAL, CD, 1846, Leg. 90, Exp. 912, f. 6r.
8   Ibid., f. 1r.
9   Ley N° 6890 (October 8, 1930); Decreto Ley N° 6889 (Oct. 8, 1930); *Código Penal del Perú* (Lima: Imp. Calle de la Rifa, 1863), Art. 268, 77. Available online: http://books. google.com.pe/books?id=27sWAAAAYAAJ&hl=en&pg=PA3#v=onepage&q&f=fal se (accessed November 30, 2016); Luis Bustamante Otero, "'El pesado yugo del santo matrimonio': divorcio y violencia conyugal en el arzobispado de Lima (1800–1805)," *Histórica* 25, no. 1 (2001): 109–160; Christine Hunefeldt, *Liberalism in the Bedroom: Quarreling Spouses in Nineteenth-century Lima* (University Park: Pennsylvania State University Press, 2000), 13; Jorge Basadre, *Historia del Derecho Peruano* (Lima: Atenea, 1984 [1937]), 333–350.

   For a history of divorce in Spanish colonial Peru, see Alberto Flores Galindo and Magdalena Chocano, "Las Cargas del Sacramento," *Revista Andina* 2, no. 2 (1984): 403–434; Delfina González del Riego, "Fragmentos de la Vida Cotidiana a través de los Procesos de Divorcio," *Histórica* 19, no. 2 (1995): 197–217; Bernard Lavallé, *Amor y Opresión en los Andes Coloniales* (Lima: IEP, IFEA, URP, 1999); Delfina González del Riego, "El divorcio en la sociedad colonial limeña," in *Mujeres y Género en la Historia del Perú*, ed. Margarita Zegarra (Lima: CENDOC-Mujer, 1999), 131–142. Also for a perspective on colonial Brazil, see María Beatriz Nizza Da Silva, "Divorce in Colonial Brazil: The Case of São Paulo," in *Sexuality & Marriage in Colonial Latin America*, ed. Asunción Lavrin (Lincoln: University of Nebraska Press, 1992), 313–340.
10 Nancy E. van Deusen, *Between the Sacred and the Worldly: The Institutional and Cultural Practice of Recogimiento in Colonial Lima* (Stanford: Stanford University Press, 2001), 144–148, 188; Nancy E. van Deusen, "Determinando los límites de la virtud: el discurso en torno al recogimiento entre las mujeres de Lima durante el siglo XVII," in *Mujeres y Género en la Historia del Perú*, ed. Margarita Zegarra (Lima: CENDOC-Mujer, 1999), 39–58. On *beaterios* also see: Christine Hunefeldt, "Los beaterios y los conflictos matrimoniales en el siglo XIX limeño," in *La familia en el mundo iberoamericano*, comp. Pilar Gonzalbo Aizpuru and Cecilia Rabell (México D.F.: Universidad Nacional Autónoma de México, Instituto de Investigaciones Sociales, 1994), 227–262.
11 The alimony petition had to be requested from the *Real Justicia* only after the Ecclesiastical Court had certified there was a petition for divorce. AAL, CD, 1801, Leg. 82, Exp. 9. For a perspective on the Peruvian history of family law, see Silvia Loli Espinoza, "Cien años de normas sobre relaciones de pareja en el Perú: 1834–1934. Una aproximación a su estudio," in *Mujeres y Género en la Historia del Perú*, ed. Margarita Zegarra (Lima: CENDOC-Mujer, 1999), 216–236; Carmen Meza Ingar, "El divorcio en el Perú," *Revista de investigación. Facultad de Derecho y Ciencia Política. Unidad de Investigación. Universidad Nacional Mayor de San Marcos* 4, no. 6 (2002): 73–79; Carlos Ramos Núñez, *Historia del derecho civil peruano. Siglos XIX y XX. I. El orden jurídico ilustrado y Manuel Lorenzo de Vidaurre* (Lima: Fondo Editorial de la Pontificia Universidad Católica del Perú, 2003). For more on ecclesiastical divorce in nineteenth-century Lima see: Otero, "'El pesado yugo'"; Luis Bustamante Otero, "Afines y consanguíneos: la parentela en el conflicto conyugal (Lima entre fines del siglo XVIII e inicios del XIX)," in *Historias paralelas. Actas del primer encuentro de historia Perú-México*, ed. Margarita Guerra Martinière and Denisse Rouillon Almeida (Lima: Fondo Editorial de la Pontificia Universidad Católica del Perú, 2005), 365–376. I thank Jimmy Martínez Céspedes for both references. Also see Luis Bustamante Otero, "'Y porque comense a irle a la mano:' la violencia conyugal en Lima durante

las postrimerías coloniales (1795–1820)" (MA diss., Pontificia Universidad Católica del Perú, 2014), 63. Available online: http://tesis.pucp.edu.pe/repositorio/handle/123456789/5518 (accessed December 10, 2016).

12 AAL, CD, 1846, Leg. 90, Exp. 912, f. 3r. Emphasis added.
13 Ibid.
14 Ibid., f. 3v, 5r–11r.
15 Basadre, *Historia del Derecho Peruano*, 325, 330–331.
16 Luis Bustamante Otero, "Notas sobre la conducta masculina en el conflicto conyugal limeño. El primer lustro del siglo XIX," in *Mujeres, familia y sociedad en la historia de América Latina, siglos XVIII-XXI*, ed. Scarlett O'Phelan Godoy and Margarita Zegarra Flórez (Lima: CENDOC-Mujer, PUCP, IRA, IFEA, 2006), 135.
17 AAL, CD, 1846, Leg. 90, Exp. 912, f. 3v.
18 Ibid., f. 3v–6v, 11r–11v.
19 Ibid., f. 7r–7v.
20 Pedro Antonio de Barroeta, "Nos el D. D. Pedro Antonio de Barroeta y Angel por la gracia de Dios, y de la Sta. Sede Apostolica, Arzobispo," in *La imprenta en Lima (1584–1824)*, ed. José Toribio Medina (Santiago de Chile: Fondo Histórico y Bibliográfico José Toribio Medina, 1966), 2: 507.
21 Norbert Elias, *The Civilizing Process: The History of Manners*, trans. Edmund Jephcott (New York: Urizen, 1978).
22 Ibid.; Michel Foucault, *Historia de la Sexualidad. Vol.1 La voluntad del saber* (México: Siglo XXI, 1999), 17, 43–45, 102–103; Michel Foucault, *The History of Sexuality, Vol. 1: An Introduction* (New York: Pantheon Books, 1978), 84.
23 AAL, CD, 1846, Leg. 90, Exp. 912, f. 10r–10v.
24 Ibid., f. 11r–11v.
25 Hunefeldt, *Liberalism in the Bedroom*, 64–65.
26 González del Riego, "El divorcio en la sociedad," 135–136.
27 AAL, CD, 1846, Leg. 90, Exp. 912, f. 32r–35r.
28 Ibid., f. 44r.
29 Ibid., f. 70r.
30 Bustamante, "'El pesado yugo,'" 121.
31 We do not know the outcome of Josefa Gallegos' demand. It was most probably left unfinished, as often divorce claims were also used for domestic bargain of a better treatment for the petitioner. Bustamante, "'El pesado yugo,'" 128, 134; AAL, CD, 1801, Leg. 82, Exp. 9; AAL, CD, 1798, Leg. 79; AAL, Litigios matrimoniales, 1796, Leg. 6, Exp. 1. Also cited in Bustamante Otero, "'Y porque comense a irle a la mano,'" 198–201.
32 Bustamante, "'El pesado yugo,'" 120.
33 AAL, CD, 1846, Leg. 90, Exp. 912, f. 70r.
34 Ibid., f. 32r–71r; Foucault, *Historia de la Sexualidad*, vol. 1, 25–64.
35 *Código Penal del Perú*, 1862.
36 Ibid., 77–78.
37 Magally Alegre Henderson, "Androginopolis: Dissident Masculinities and the Creation of Republican Peru (Lima, 1790–1850)" (PhD diss., Stony Brook University, 2012).

7

Flappers and Felons: Rethinking the Criminal Law and Homosex in Interwar Australia, 1920–1939

Yorick Smaal and Mark Finnane

In late 1930, Sydney's scurrilous *Arrow* newspaper published an extraordinary exposé on the city's sexual underworld. At an imposing, old-fashioned, and roomy house in the western suburbs, a group of sixty "male flappers" had gathered for one of the city's premier queer soirées: crowning the "Queen of the 'Kamp Kult.'" An undercover journalist had infiltrated this reportedly annual event by "devious means" and two days before Christmas his eyewitness account on "Organised Male Depravity" hit the front page.[1] And organized it was. The article described in astonishing detail the gendered rituals of contemporary Australian subcultures and the ways that men made meaning of their same-sex lives and lifestyles. Steeped in pageantry and spectacle, this queer coronation brought together "royalty" and spectators from across the nation as vows were taken and hymns sung. An officiating "Bishop" presided over the celebrations, taking his cues from a sacred book embossed with a resplendent letter "K."

This private suburban gathering was also an opportunity for guests to frock-up among friends. Men in powder, paint, and female attire strolled the event arm in arm, "examining with interest one another's beautiful frocks fitting so closely to the figure." Carmined lips puffed cigarettes held by manicured fingers and "some wore false hair, with marcel waves, others the boyish Eton crop."[2] Men addressed each other by their female names and inquired about casual sexual encounters.[3] Homosex and its potential hung in the air as couples frequently wandered off outside.[4] The *Arrow* was quick to point out the corrupting influence that this way of life had over the young. The antics of a "mother's boy," an enamored lad of no more than 16, was the saddest sight of the evening, so the paper despaired. "I have only been initiated to-night," he remarked enthusiastically to the reporter. "I am crazy about it all."[5] The absence of the authorities was equally alarming. Such depravity demanded police attention. "A clean up of Sydney's perverts is overdue," the newspaper decried. "There is plenty of work in this direction for idle policemen instead of guarding Nellie Campbell or Parliament House."[6]

This research was conducted with the support of Australian Research Council grants FL130100050 and DE140100801.

Kamp parties were all the rage in the 1920s and 1930s as queer Australia came of age.[7] These gatherings were part of a larger private and public world in which men used female gender behaviors to create meaning for themselves and those (masculine men) who desired them. The word "kamp" is a good indicator that urban subcultures had attained critical mass, even if they were smaller than in Gay New York or Queer London. The term was self-generated, and early on used interchangeably to refer to inverted and respectable identities, although it eventually lost its association with gender codes and referred simply to "male homosexuals."[8]

Whether men adorned "false hair" or "boyish crops" there was something deeply unsettling about this unconventional gendered world only a decade after Australia had lost a generation of young men to the horrors of trench warfare. The 1920s might have been a period of peace and possibility but it was also characterized as an era of social danger and sexual excess.[9] Male flappers represented the worst kind of Australian manhood: not only were they hedonistic, but also many defiantly flouted the conventions of normative masculinity in public and private. This antipathy toward queer men had the weight of the law behind it. Even as protective subcultures sprouted in large urban centers like Sydney, Brisbane, and Melbourne, criminal prosecution and the prospect of imprisonment awaited those who put a foot wrong in an otherwise morally restrained and respectable mainstream.[10] But media claims that the police were ignoring events like the coronation of the "Kamp Queen" raise important questions about the intersections of policing, prosecution, and queer identities. What do we know about the implementation of the criminal statutes and what does it tell us about social attitudes and norms? To what extent did criminal law address discursive invectives like those published in the *Arrow*? Were male flappers considered as criminal felons?

This chapter compares large-scale prosecution data across the Australian jurisdictions of New South Wales (NSW) and Queensland between 1920 and 1939 to examine the types of same-sex crimes that appeared in the superior courts, and the circumstances in which they came to notice. Crimes against male children feature prominently in the records at a time when we might rather expect significant prosecutions for gender nonconformity and its attendant sexual behaviors if the state was so concerned with queer people and places. The data reveals that indictable offences were reserved for only the most serious offences between adults—sodomy and conspicuous displays of public immorality—or the corruption of young male bodies, even at spectacular moments of community formation and sexual self-expression. We argue that the regulation of queer worlds was largely the preserve of the lower courts which summarily disposed of many homosex cases as forms of public immorality and disorder. These findings are important because they reassess the overlap between crime and sexual identities and question reliance on trial briefs and depositions to recover modern queer history.

The uses of law

Legal records have been an important source of knowledge for sexual identities and sexual behaviors in the past.[11] The prosecution process—which begins with police investigation before proceeding to the magistrates' courts where it can be dismissed, resolved, or committed for trial by jury at the higher courts—can generate large volumes of discursive material on the behaviors and attitudes of historical actors inside and outside the courts. Not only do these materials reveal official responses to homosex (in all its complexities) but they can also document the lived experiences of queer individuals and communities.

Cases that reach the apex of the criminal justice system often contain the richest evidence from which historians partly recover policing, personal, and political histories or compile statistical analyses.[12] But in doing so, historians often set aside or integrate incompletely those trials that fail to fit their narrative purpose. Crimes of buggery, indecency, and indecent assault have become proxies for queerness as historians searching for social and cultural significance conflate particular crimes with particular identities.[13] But not all acts were consensual or benign. Records of prosecution pose questions as much as provide answers to any inquiry into same-sex desire and identity.

Of course that is not to say that the association between law and lifestyles is mistaken. Queer men found pleasure and meaning in the very physical acts the law proscribed. Rich historical accounts of these lives and loves are made possible—at least in part—by the collision of private worlds and the technologies of the state.[14] The police kept certain individuals and suspect places under surveillance, under a mandate of public order and control of immorality. And so even adult men seeking privacy in public places could find themselves before the courts, no matter how discreet their intimacy.[15] One Sydney vice squad, for instance, had allegedly arrested more than 150 men over two years in the mid-1930s from a single lavatory in Hyde Park.[16]

The state also intruded into the private domain. The specter of the law could loom ominously even when homosex was cloistered within the confines of a hotel room or the home, as many histories of homosexualities attest.[17] Consider two men at the Coutts Sailors' Home in Newcastle in New South Wales in 1920. Their Friday afternoon romp in private quarters became public knowledge after the superintendent discovered them together in a compromising position.[18] But activities of men in public lavatories and hostel rooms only tell part of the story. Such examples speak strongly to the inclinations of particular witnesses—the manager of the sailors' home was probably quite familiar with conventional wisdom linking homosex with life-at-sea—or the preoccupations of particular police units with persons-of-interest or sites of vice.[19] The discriminatory state of the law, its proscription of adult consensual acts, facilitated abuse and indecision. Some police officers could be overzealous and even corrupt and violent while prosecutors made idiosyncratic and contingent decisions on what crimes to indict, when to discontinue a trial or to strike a plea.[20] Hence otherwise "victimless" crimes between consenting adults competed with other serious crimes (including same-sex offences of exploitation and coercion) for the attention and resources of the criminal justice system.[21]

These features of the law are revealed in our study of the prosecution of same-sex offences in two Australian jurisdictions between the wars (1920–1939). For New South Wales we have retrieved the details of 558 prosecutions at the Quarter Sessions; for Queensland 90 cases, all tried at the Supreme Court.[22] For the purposes of our analysis we have aggregated crimes of homosex into three groups—"assault with intent (to commit sodomy)," "buggery/sodomy," and "indecent assaults on males."[23] These categories generally correspond to levels of gravity of offence in terms of penalty, and are also associated with the status of other parties where we know whether they were a minor or not. The status of minor we have defined as under 18 years of age: in New South Wales they account for at least 56 percent of the cases where age of the complainant can be established, for Queensland no less than 77 percent.[24] In sum our data suggest that children and male youths appeared most frequently as complainants, and that serious offences committed in public rather than private were most likely to face the full force of law when the evidence was forthcoming. What are the implications of this record of prosecutions for our understanding of the role of criminal law, policing, and homosexualities in these decades?

Offences between adults

While crimes against minors made up the majority of prosecutions for this period, penetrative crimes between adults were still significantly sanctioned between the wars. These cases appeared before the courts at a moment when typical forms of masculinity were allegedly under renewed threat. Modern ways of life emerging from the shadows of the Great War brought new challenges for the sex and gender order: so-called soft city living, the free-spirited "new woman," and vibrant queer subcultures evidenced by Sydney's "Kamp Kult," undermined prewar certainties of traditional male behavior and identity.[25]

The act of buggery had been reviled since the British first colonized Australia.[26] Considered to indicate passivity, weakness, and effeminacy it challenged the dominant gender order to the extent that it was unmentionable. Queensland's Chief Justice Blair summed up contemporary thinking in 1936 when he acknowledged the convention that sodomy was "common in all the ages, and one that has been practiced by the highest and the lowest; the richest and the poorest; the most intellectual and the most ignorant; and it is an abominable crime."[27] Although no longer a capital crime, it was still subject to fourteen years' imprisonment in both jurisdictions.[28]

Prosecutors often had a compelling case when they prosecuted "abominable" offences and more often than not alternative charges were left off the indictment. And juries were likely to convict. Men charged with buggery or its attempt with other adults in New South Wales (where we have the richest sample of offences between adults) were twice as likely to be convicted (n35, 67 percent) as acquitted (n18, 33 percent) with an average sentence of 640 days. Nearly a quarter of those convicted, however, received a non-custodial sentence. Taken together, these two offence categories account for a significant proportion of charges for adult-only offences in this jurisdiction (n53, 40 percent), with similar results for Queensland. These findings raise questions about the state's continued use of buggery charges in the twentieth century when, some scholars suggest, its prevalence declined with the introduction of indecency legislation from the 1880s onward alongside the emergence of the "modern homosexual."[29] Our incongruous results suggest at least two things: first that the state did not abandon its pursuit of anal intercourse as a serious criminal offence by using "new" indecency charges to police emerging subcultures; and second, that victim status is a critical consideration in analyzing the data.

The presence of lone defendants also gestures to the specter of sexual violence between men (notwithstanding the use of *agents provocateur* or consensual partners who escaped from the scene of the crime). These offences constitute 1-in-10 prosecutions in the New South Wales' sample and indicate that the rape of adult males was reported and prosecuted, though success rarely followed. In July 1929, in regional New South Wales, for instance, a stupefied railway laborer awoke face down and partly undressed to find his drinking partner and colleague holding him down. He punched the defendant in the face and went downstairs to report the matter. The defendant fled but was identified and arrested the following evening. Eventually he was acquitted by the jury when the matter came to trial some months later.[30] The verdict in this case was not unusual. Lone offenders in New South Wales were four times more likely than co-accused men to be acquitted. The role of alcohol in this and other cases like it, along with the belief that "real" men could resist unwanted sexual advances, goes some way to explain why juries were unlikely to convict in cases of violence even if the crown prosecuted them.[31] The absence of direct observation or corroborative evidence is another factor.

Consensual or otherwise, crimes in public increased the risk of surveillance or discovery and subsequent prosecution. As Matt Houlbrook points out, policing fell unevenly on the public realm depending on where and when it occurred.[32] The young, the married, and the working classes were particularly vulnerable given that private house parties hosting male flappers catered only to certain groups at infrequent intervals. Blair's judicial remarks in 1936, for instance, concerned two young offenders (and an adolescent who was not charged), discovered in a Brisbane paddock late one Saturday evening. Their choice of location and its timing was unfortunate: the fence line where they gathered was shared with the residential block of a police officer who happened to be hosting an event in his yard that evening.[33] And in 1920 in Newcastle in New South Wales, a 40-year-old laborer and "stupidly drunk" sailor, aged 20, were observed in a compromising position in the lavatories behind the suburban Terminus Hotel. They were charged with attempting to commit buggery, although the sailor was acquitted on account of his inebriety.[34]

If some men went all the way in public, others stopped short of anal sex allowing them to button up quickly if disturbed.[35] The police (and other witnesses) nonetheless discovered men *in flagrante delicto* and the crown resorted to charges of "indecent assault" to indict the most flagrant and serious cases that fell short of penetration. Queensland prosecutors used provisions of gross indecency created by the *Criminal Code Act* 1899 and drawn from the infamous Labouchere amendment to English criminal law in 1885. The colony of New South Wales preempted those changes, amending in 1883 its definition of indecent assault to include crimes committed with consent.[36] They were well used. More than half of adult-only prosecutions in New South Wales and Queensland across the interwar years concerned indecent assaults. Conviction rates were very high: juries favored the crown in three-quarters of cases in New South Wales when crimes involved other adults (n54, 73 percent).

The high return of guilty verdicts in these cases was partly due to the element of the offence, which entailed a lower burden of proof, although the immediate presence of police or other witnesses always strengthened the crown's case. A Brisbane case in

1926 is typical. In Centenary Park in November that year two plain-clothes officers arrested a 62-year-old laborer and 43-year-old watchmaker "wriggling about on the grass" together at 9 p.m. on Thursday evening. The younger man lay propped up by his elbows with the laborer face down in his lap.[37] The depositions do not reveal how they came to be in this predicament but like many men, they probably were strangers seeking out sexual and social companionship. Others planned their outings in detail, but sometimes not carefully enough. Two Sydney men who packed the car for a nude picnic in 1937 did not count on an overly curious bicycle rider whose suspicions were aroused by the sight of their car in suburban scrubland. The witness watched them lie naked on a rug for ten minutes before sending for the police.[38]

Public order policing

The unclothed Sydney picnickers claimed that their interest in nudism, and not homosex, had motivated their outing together that sunny November afternoon. Canny readers of this case may have recognized links between nudism, physical culture, and queer ways of being circulating in other publications, but the press usually ignored cultural aspects of homosex when it reported criminal matters.[39] Explicit exposés on Sydney's male flappers and other coverage of homosex in public called for police action but failed to link this kind of immorality with serious crime.[40] Even after periods of imprisonment, members of the "Kamp Kult" were considered by the *Arrow* to be "social pests" rather than hardened felons. Its call to "clean up" such depravity was more a criticism of the failure to fulfil a public order mandate within policing, one concerned with managing the streets and public places of a large city with an eye on public decorum and the control of vice. Alternative dispositions within the criminal justice system, especially the use of police and vagrancy acts, had been in force in the colonies since the beginning of the nineteenth century.[41] The New South Wales Crimes Act (1900), for instance, provided for summary disposal for same-sex (and other) assaults and indecent behaviors, while Queensland's 1931 Vagrant's Gaming and Other Offences Act was used by the police to regulate queer sex and expressive behaviors.[42]

Magistrates could dispose of these cases through a fine, imprisonment, or other disposal. And penalties could be steep. The risk of harsh penalties combined with the reputational shame of prosecution to facilitate entrapment and corrupt prosecutions in Sydney in the late 1930s.[43] In Sydney's Central Police Court in 1925, the magistrate handed twelve months' imprisonment to a "pervert" on conviction of being an idle and disorderly person with no lawful means of support. Part of the evidence against him was "his questionable conduct with men in Hyde Park" and the "vile text" penned by a Melbourne associate who congratulated him on his new employment (presumably prostitution).[44] A case from nearby Parramatta early the following decade indicates that gender non-conformity too fell within the margins of summary offending. The police arrested two young hotel assistants in 1931 for behaving in an indecent manner after they were observed "squealing and throwing kisses to local youths" at the local park. Back at the station, the authorities searched the suspects' belongings unearthing lipstick, rouge, powder puffs, and photographs of men in drag. One defendant was wearing silk stocking under his socks.[45]

Protecting the young

Such activities were not restricted to adults. Minors also enmeshed themselves in queer subcultures, performed acts of gender inversion, and engaged in acts of homosex with contemporaries and adults. The Sydney teenager at the crowning of the kamp queen, for instance, was delighted at his initiation into the city's effeminate queer world, telling with "shining eyes" "how lovely it all is."[46] Other behaviors are harder to decipher, however. What do we make of two boys (ages unknown) who dressed in female clothing and wandered the streets of Armidale in regional New South Wales in 1935, for instance? They appeared as witnesses against an elderly man who was charged with indecent assault after the boys visited his shop in women's attire. They regularly frocked-up, but under cross-examination denied the insinuations made by a defending barrister.[47]

The state occasionally recognized the capacity of young males by prosecuting boys, although they make up only a very small proportion of indicted offenders. Boys rarely appeared with older men before the higher courts and we know of only two cases where teenagers were charged alongside their adult contemporaries. In 1928, a 15-year-old was indicted for sodomy with an elderly man in New South Wales, while in Queensland in 1920, a 16-year-old boot maker was convicted of committing gross indecency with a 28-year-old laborer. Evidence from the latter case suggests that the crown required robust and substantial evidence to proceed against younger males. Police officers had followed the two accused to a Brisbane park where they directly observed the defendants' actions and overheard their conversation at length, leaving no doubt as to the boy's complicity in the act.[48]

Of course, the absence of prosecution should not be taken to indicate the absence of collusion among some youths. Social and judicial invectives decried their behavior even when the evidence was insufficient, corroboration was missing, or in cases where juveniles turned crown's witness. The Sydney *Truth* newspaper, for instance, demanded to know why a 17-year-old youth had not been charged alongside the New South Wales' Transport Commissioner during a sensational case in the late 1930s. The boy had brazenly revealed his guilt in the witness box and the public, the paper alleged, was "puzzled at the operation of two different law enforcement methods."[49] During the trial, the defense counsel, Mr. Curtis, KC told the jury that the complainant was not "a[n] innocent boy"; the judge agreed, remarking that the boy "may be a pervert of the worst type."[50]

Such observations were not only reserved for high-profile cases. In Brisbane in 1936, Chief Justice Blair made an impassioned plea about a 15-year-old boy discovered by police as the passive party in a threesome in a New Farm paddock. He avoided prosecution but his evidence was contradictory and self-incriminating. The boy, who denied under cross-examination that he went by the name of "Mary," admitted engaging in homosex with three other males and could provide the authorities with a list of at least eight other men.[51] The judge demanded that "the authorities … strain every effort to see something is done in order to save him from this abominable thing."[52]

Despite such rhetoric, the courts were generally more concerned with protecting young males than prosecuting them. The benign disposition of the system meant that boys were more likely to appear before the bench for perpetrating sexual violence on younger contemporaries than for moments of self-discovery or pleasure. The prosecution in 1925 of a 14-year-old schoolboy in regional Queensland is a case in point. He was sentenced to two years' detention (wholly suspended) for indecently treating a 7-year-old boy.[53] Young children make up a significant proportion of complainants whether perpetrators were adolescents or adults. Where we know the ages of complainants in same-sex cases, one-quarter of New South Wales complainants and a third of those in Queensland were boys under 12 years old.

This finding is nothing new, however. Australian queer histories have recognized for many decades the prominent position that boys occupy in the criminal courts in the nineteenth and the twentieth centuries, even if they rarely acknowledge the significance of these results given their focus on sexual identities.[54] Wayne Murdoch's recent study of interwar Melbourne is an exception. Not only does he show that the largest category (42 percent) of same-sex prosecutions was for offences against boys under 14 but he concludes that queer Melbournians were not "living in a state of siege."[55] That finding is consistent with our evidence for New South Wales and Queensland.

Finally, the significance of victim status is reflected in sentencing of those convicted. In New South Wales, males convicted of crimes with minors were sentenced to an extra 275 days on average. *Modus operandi*, multiple victims, and criminal history could all be considered as aggravating features, along with the age of the complainant. At the Sydney Quarter Sessions in mid-1934, for instance, Judge Curlewis handed down a cumulative sentence of three years' imprisonment to a sea cadet troop leader for assaulting three boys aged between 9 and 11. "The accused took advantage of his position," Curlewis declared: "Nothing could be more ruinous than if offences of this nature were passed over lightly."[56]

Conclusions

The criminal law occupies a peculiar place in same-sex histories. The proscription of some same-sex practices is a measure of historical discrimination. But the statutes and their enforcement in turn provide critical evidence for the history of same-sex desire, culture, and identities. And such evidence has been widely used in the writing of queer histories. Our scrutiny of criminal prosecutions for same-sex offences in two jurisdictions in the interwar years, a time when some have argued that policing especially targeted emerging queer cultures, suggests a need for reflection on context in the use of such evidence. While all homosex was at criminal law illegal, not all homosex was prosecuted. Decisions to prosecute criminal offences appear to involve cases in which the complainant was more often a child, or where there was an element of coercion or violence. The prosecution of consenting adult males using the full penal powers of the criminal law was infrequent, although harshly treated in penetrative cases that did make it to court. Punishment following conviction on a same-sex charge appears much harsher when the complainant was a child.

This is not to suggest that criminal law was benign in this period, or that policing of homosex was never a priority. Rather we see that homosex was more actively the target of public order policing using the summary powers of the magistrate's court. One implication is that the criminal law must be read ever more critically as a source for investigating the emergence of queer identities, or for evaluating the history of homosex. In particular, the high proportion of minors among complainants in these cases suggests the ambiguity of the lessons that may be drawn from this history.

Given that homosex was outlawed regardless of age or consent, it can be difficult to distinguish young people involved in consensual but criminalized sex from those subject to coercion, maltreatment, or violence. Even pleasurable homosex motivated by inclination or desire could be inflected by consumerism, money, or security. These moments represented both danger and possibility structured by age, power, and context. If the policing of the "Kamp Kult" was not a priority for a censorious state in 1931, perhaps that is partly because higher-level prosecutions were more likely to involve judgments by prosecutors about those vulnerabilities of youth, judgments that were reflected in judicial sanctions including sentencing. Historians of sexualities or of queer identities and communities must read the records of criminal justice that document such outcomes with a great deal of mediation and reflection.

Notes

1 *Arrow* (Sydney), December 23, 1931, 1, 4.
2 Ibid., 4.
3 Ibid.
4 We use John Howard's term "homosex" to refer same-sex practices "of various sorts between two males" cutting across age, class, or ethnicity; John Howard, *Men Like That: A Southern Queer History* (Chicago and London: University of Chicago Press, 2001), xviii–xix.
5 Ibid.
6 Ibid.
7 Garry Wotherspoon, *City of the Plain: History of a Gay Subculture* (Sydney: Hale and Iremonger, 1994), 72–76; Clive Moore, *Sunshine and Rainbows: The Development of Gay and Lesbian Culture in Queensland* (St Lucia, Qld: University of Queensland, 2001), 93–94.
8 Gary Simes, "The Language of Homosexuality," in *Gay Perspectives: Essays in Australian Gay Culture*, ed. Robert Aldrich and Garry Wotherspoon (Sydney: Department of Economic History, University of Sydney, 1992), 46.
9 Lisa Featherstone, *Let's Talk about Sex: Histories of Sexuality in Australia from Federation to the Pill* (Newcastle upon Tyne: Cambridge Scholars Publishing, 2011), 121–123; Frank Bongiorno, *The Sex Lives of Australians: A History* (Melbourne: Black Inc., 2012), 175–176.
10 Wotherspoon, *City of the Plain*, 54.
11 Stephen Robertson, "What's Law Got to Do with It? Legal Records and Sexual Histories," *Journal of the History of Sexuality* 14, no. 1/2 (2005): 161–185.
12 For example, Harry Cocks, *Nameless Offences: Homosexual Desire in the Nineteenth Century* (London: I. B. Taurus, 2010); Matt Houlbrook, *Queer London: Perils and Pleasures in the Sexual Metropolis, 1918–1957* (Chicago: Chicago University Press, 2005); Clive Moore and Bryan Jamison, "Making the Modern Australian Homosexual

Male: Queensland's Criminal Justice System and Homosexual Offences, 1860–1954," *Crime, History and Societies* 11, no. 1 (2007): 27–54.

13   Rictor Norton, "F-ck Foucault: How Eighteenth Century Homosexual History Validates the Essentialist Model," Expanded Paper given at UCLA Mellon Sawyer Seminar (2010), 24–30; Kate Gleeson, "Discipline, Punishment and the Homosexual in Law," *Liverpool Law Review* 28 (2007): 337–338; Matt Cook emphasizes this methodological point in his *Queer Domesticities: Homosexuality and Home Life in Twentieth Century London* (Basingstoke: Palgrave Macmillan, 2014), 1–20.

14   Houlbrook, *Queer London*, 5.

15   George Chauncey, "Privacy Could Only Be Had in Public," in *Stud: Architectures of Masculinity*, ed. Joel Saunders (New York: Princeton University, 1996), 224–266.

16   Wotherspoon, *City of the Plain*, 69.

17   For example, Lisa Featherstone and Amanda Kaladelfos, *Sex Crime in the Fifties* (Carlton: Melbourne University Press, 2016), 163–167; Moore, *Sunshine and Rainbows*, 127–129.

18   *Newcastle Sun*, September 1, 1920, 5; *Newcastle Sun*, September 2, 1920, 5; *Newcastle Morning Herald and Miners' Advocate*, September 2, 1920, 7.

19   Houlbrook, *Queer London*, 31–36; Heather McRea, "Homosexuality and the Law: The Development of the Law Relating to Male Homosexuality in England and Australia", PhD diss., Monash University, Melbourne (1978), 168–169.

20   *Daily Examiner* (Grafton), October 31, 1931, 5; *National Advocate* (Bathurst), May 23, 1930, 1.

21   Graham Robb, *Strangers: Homosexual Love in the Nineteenth Century* (New York: Norton, 2004), 17.

22   New South Wales' data was retrieved from the NSW Police Gazette; Queensland data from the court registers, extant depositions, and newspaper sources.

23   We note that statutory offence definitions differ between jurisdictions in Australia; see Graham Carbery, "Towards Homosexual Equality in Australian Criminal Law: A Brief History," third edition (2014), Melbourne: Australian Lesbian and Gay Archives; McRea, "Homosexuality and the Law."

24   For New South Wales, age can be established for 283 of the 558 cases; for Queensland, 80 of the 90 cases.

25   Bongiorno, *The Sex Lives*, 152–185; Featherstone, *Let's Talk About Sex*, 119–141; Wayne Murdoch, "Chorus Boys and Tight-Waisted Young Men: An Exploration of Melbourne's Camp Subculture during the Interwar Period, 1919–1939," PhD diss., University of Melbourne (2015), 51–54.

26   Robert Hughes, *The Fatal Shore: A History of the Transportation of Convicts to Australia, 1787–1868* (London: Vintage Books, 2003), 264–266.

27   *Daily Standard* (Brisbane), February 27, 1936, 3.

28   s5(c), *Crime (Amendment) Act* 1924 [NSW] (which repealed life imprisonment s79, *Crimes Act* 1900); s208, *Criminal Code Act* 1899 [Qld]. On attempts, see respectively s80, Crimes Act 1900 [NSW] (5 years' penal servitude) and s209 *Criminal Code Act* 1899 (7 years' hard labor).

29   Moore and Jamison, "Making the Modern," 38; Cocks, *Nameless Offences*, 30; Walter Fogarty, "'Certain Habits': The Development of a Concept of the Male Homosexual in New South Wales Law, 1788–1900," in *Gay Perspectives*, ed. Aldrich and Wotherspoon, 59–76.

30   *Nowra Leader*, August 2, 1929, 1; *Illawarra Mercury*, July 9, 1929, 9.

31   Gary Foster, "Male Rape and the Government of Bodies: An Unusual History of the Present," PhD diss., University of Queensland (2005), 173, 182, 204.

32 Houlbrook, *Queer London*, 37.
33 Queensland State Archives (QSA), Criminal Depositions, Brisbane (1936), item 95922.
34 *Newcastle Morning Herald and Miners' Advocate*, 7.
35 Laud Humphreys, *Tearoom Trade: Impersonal Sex in Public Places* (Chicago: Aldine, 1970), 75.
36 Moore and Jamison, "Making the Modern," 5–6; Fogarty, "'Certain Habits,'" 67–68.
37 QSA, Criminal Depositions, Brisbane (1926), item 957783; *Daily Standard* (Brisbane) November 20, 1926, 9.
38 *Truth* (Sydney) December 19, 1937, 25.
39 Chris Brickell, *Mates & Lovers: A History of Gay New Zealand* (Auckland: Random House, 2008), 101–102, 202–203.
40 *Arrow* (Sydney), December 23, 1931, 1, 4; *Arrow* (Sydney) March 11, 1932, 7.
41 Andrew McLeod, "On the Origins of Consorting Laws," *Melbourne University Law Review* 37, no. 1 (2013): 114–125.
42 Yorick Smaal, "Revisiting Queensland's War-Time Sex Panics: Moral Alarm, Male Homosexuality and Policing Public Space," in *Crime over Time: Temporal Perspectives on Crime and Punishment in Australia*, ed. Robyn Lincoln and Shirleene Robinson (Newcastle upon Tyne: Cambridge Scholars Publishing, 2010), 128–130.
43 Mark Finnane, *When Police Unionise: The Politics of Law and Order in Australia* (Sydney: Institute of Criminology, 2002), 112–114.
44 *Truth* (Sydney), March 29, 1925, 9.
45 *Truth* (Sydney), September 20, 1931, 16.
46 *Arrow* (Sydney), 1, 4.
47 *Armidale Express and New England General Advertiser*, October 21, 1935, 3.
48 QSA, Criminal Depositions, Brisbane (1920), item 9025; *Truth* (Brisbane), October 24, 1920, 2.
49 *Truth* (Sydney), April 18, 1937, 1.
50 *Sydney Morning Herald*, April 10, 1937, 10 cited in Wotherspoon, *City of the Plain*, 46.
51 QSA, item 95922.
52 *Telegraph* (Brisbane) February 26, 1936, 2; *Daily Standard* (Brisbane), February 27, 1936, 3.
53 QSA, Criminal Depositions, Bundaberg (1925), item 212636.
54 For example, Bruce Baskerville, "'Agreed to without Debate': Silencing Sodomy in Colonial Western Australia, 1870–1905," in *Gay and Lesbian Perspective IV: Studies in Australian Culture*, ed. Robert Aldrich and Garry Wotherspoon (Sydney: Department of Economic History with The Australian Centre for Lesbian and Gay Research, University of Sydney, 1998), 113; Adam Carr, "Policing the 'Abominable Crime' in Nineteenth Century Victoria," in *Australia's Homosexual Histories: Gay and Lesbian Perspectives 5*, ed. David L. Philips and Graham Willet (Melbourne: Australian Centre for Lesbian and Gay Research and the Australian Lesbian and Gay Archives, 2000), 33; Moore, *Sunshine and Rainbows*, 65–66.
55 Murdoch, "Chorus Boys," 84, 97.
56 *Truth* (Sydney), July 8, 1934, 12.

8

Spain from Franco's Repressive Regime to Same-Sex Marriage

Geoffroy Huard

Spain's modern history is a turbulent one, perhaps best known to those interested in the history of same-sex relationships for General Francisco Franco's repressive dictatorship between 1939 and 1975. Key developments prior to that were the loss of the great Spanish empire by the late nineteenth century, the dictatorship of General Miguel Primo de Rivera between 1923 and 1930, and the liberal Second Spanish Republic of 1931 to 1939. The latter represented a notable democratic and progressive phase in Spain's history after the brief democratic experiment of the First Republic between 1873 and 1874. Among other measures, the leadership of the 1930s Republic offered political autonomy to the Basque Country, Galicia, and Catalonia, and gave women the right to vote. The progressiveness of the Republic prompted nationalist forces under Franco to rebel, and a civil war wracked the country between 1936 and 1939. The Spanish Civil War claimed the lives of some 500,000 people, and a similar number fled, the majority departing for South America, especially Argentina. Nationalist forces, backed by Nazi Germany and Fascist Italy, defeated the elected Republicans in 1939. General Francisco Franco proclaimed himself "Generalissimo" and head of state. Spain was supposedly neutral during the Second World War, although Franco's sympathies of course lay with the Axis powers.

There was only one legal political party during Franco's dictatorship, an alliance between his Juntas de Ofensiva Nacional-Sindicalista (JONS), and the Traditionalist Spanish Falange. This grouping, which changed its name to the National Movement in 1949, stressed Catholicism, nationalism, and anti-communism, and fiercely resisted the waves of social and cultural modernization that swept over much of western Europe in the postwar period. Spain, isolated politically and economically since the war, nevertheless experienced unprecedented economic growth in the 1960s, fueled mostly by a boom in tourism. This growth, and no doubt the exposure to tourists from different backgrounds, helped to foster Spain's eventual transition, after Franco's demise, to social, cultural, and economic modernity from the late 1970s.

After the death of General Franco in 1975, King Juan Carlos I succeeded him as head of state, overseeing reforms that moved Spain away from dictatorship. Three years later, the country approved a new constitution, which restored democracy under a constitutional monarchy. The central government began to delegate much of its authority to the regions and divided the national territory into areas known as autonomous communities. After approval by referendum, Spain joined NATO in May 1982. This was the same year that the Spanish Socialist Workers Party (PSOE) came to power, the first leftist government in forty-three years. Spain entered the European Economic Community in 1986, and in 1996, the PSOE, after having served fourteen consecutive years in office, was defeated by the conservative, Christian-democratic Popular Party (PP), in the general elections. In 2002, Spain adopted the euro, and in 2005, Spain was one of the first countries in the world to approve equal marriage between same-sex couples. This was a notable achievement given the enduring influence of the Catholic Church and the nation's political history in the nineteenth and twentieth centuries.[1]

Same-sex acts in Spain before Franco

At the legislative level, three broad stages can be distinguished with respect to the repression of homosexuals in modern Spanish history. Sodomy had been deleted from Spain's criminal code in 1822, and the code of 1870 did not make specific reference to same-sex acts in its treatment of sexual crimes. However, as elsewhere in Catholic Europe, such as France and Italy, this did not mean that homosexual acts were not occasionally prosecuted in Spain. Three main legal charges enabled the conviction of sexual acts between people of the same sex: gross indecency (which in effect meant sexual acts between adults in public); indecent assault (sexual violence); and indecency involving a minor (a sexual act between an adult and a child). During the dictatorship of Primo de Rivera (1923–1930) a revised criminal code, promulgated in 1928 and in force until 1932, referred to these three crimes but also introduced a distinction between heterosexual and homosexual versions.

The advent of the progressive Second Republic in 1931 resulted in a further revised criminal code in 1932. The three sexual offences mentioned by the previous legislations were retained, but the recently added distinction between homosexuals and heterosexuals was deleted. According to the legislation, sexual crimes were viewed in the same way regardless of whether they were committed by heterosexuals or homosexuals. This evolution was the result of the modernizing project that lay at the heart of the Republic. Less obviously but of more significance, homosexuals were not specifically mentioned in the Law of Vagrants and Miscreants (henceforth the Vagrancy Law) of 1933, which was to be widely used for surveillance and social control over the coming decades. According to the contemporary socialist jurist Jiménez de Asúa, who was one of the main proponents of the law, private life ought to be beyond the reach of criminal law. Despite the legislative novelty, the three sexual crimes were included in the Republican 1933 vagrancy law and the law remained unchanged between 1933 and 1954.[2]

At a more general level, the proclamation of the Second Republic in 1931 was followed by a series of very progressive measures in favor of greater gender equality, such as women's suffrage, a divorce law (one of the most advanced in Europe at the time), civil marriage, and a general relaxation of the social strictures of preceding decades. The same applied in sexual matters. The new criminal code introduced in 1932 ushered in a certain degree of sexual permissiveness. For example, in some publications, previously heavily censored, images portrayed women scantily clad or even naked. Advertisements for products or establishments to cure venereal diseases or combat impotence became prominent in the newspapers. Commentators widely addressed topics that were quite radical given the historical and cultural context, such as birth control, neo-Malthusianism, and eugenic improvement of the reproductive conditions of the population. There was even talk of "conscious motherhood," of abortion, of the prevention of prostitution and venereal diseases, just as there were attempts to promote sex education.[3]

Numerous publications made reference to these subjects, encouraged by the particular context of the general movement of European sexual reform of the interwar period. A new libertarian model of sexuality was not limited to reproduction alone and was not only the preserve of the well-off: it also spread to the working classes. Following the foundation of the "World League for Sexual Reform on Scientific Bases" in 1928 by sexologists Havelock Ellis and Magnus Hirschfeld, a Spanish section was created in 1932 by Hildegart Rodríguez. Its president was the great endocrinologist Gregorio Marañón, and it disseminated the new ideas widely via a magazine titled *Sexus*.

The goal of the republican authorities and the reformist movements was to establish a modern, progressive morality detached from the Catholic faith that had held sway in Spain for so long. They wanted to encourage the "healthy experience" of sexuality, and the modernization project of the Second Republic defended gender and sexual equality.[4] While it would be anachronistic to talk about equality between sexualities, it is worth mentioning a change of attitude toward homosexuality. There was no longer as much talk about moral condemnation as there had been under the aegis of Catholic morality, and the period witnessed the emergence of a more objective attitude toward homosexuals. These advances may seem very timid by today's standards, but at the time they represented an important evolution, because they moved away from Catholic moral precepts and looked more toward scientific advances with reason and culture as synonyms for progress.[5] As we know though, the very radicalism of the Second Republic provoked its own antithesis in the form of Franco's dictatorship, after the Civil War was lost to nationalist forces in April 1939.

Franco's dictatorship

The Franco regime relied on the Republic's criminal code without much modification before 1952, but the way the law was applied under the dictatorship was different. In any case, anti-republican elites and the Church, with Franco in the lead, did not delay their response until after the victory of those who had taken part in the coup d'état at the end of the civil war in 1939. Much like Hitler after Weimar, the conservative forces interpreted progressive republican legal innovations as a direct attack on national Catholic morality and the root cause of what they perceived as the moral decadence of the country. After the nationalists' victory, the Franco government abolished all rights granted during the Second Republic that represented social progress and had made Spain one of the most socially advanced nations in Europe. Also, in line with Catholic morality and displaying a zeal worthy of the Italian fascists, the Francoist authorities undertook the promotion of procreation as the sole purpose of sexual intercourse.[6]

The Francoist authorities considered homosexuals—like communists and atheists— as enemies of the homeland, since in their worldview all sexuality contrary to the procreative and virile model of life was contrary to good morals and thus endangered the nation. In their view, the decline of manhood threatened by homosexuality, because of the way it inverted established gender roles, had been at the root of national decline. According to historians Francisco Vázquez García and Richard Cleminson, the nationalists thought such crises of masculinity had also been caused, for example, by feminist demands, new models of women, "masculinism" or "mannish" women, due to the growing visibility of homosexuality in women in large cities and the alleged effeminacy of males. According to this ideology, these elements would destabilize the model of virility and would therefore endanger the integrity of the fatherland.[7]

This general cultural reaction is one of the ways the nationalist rebels legitimized the uprising of 1936 that led to civil war. They also used the metaphor of disease to describe the republican nation that they would cure. The victors would be the virile and healthy men who cured the nation of the republican disease with effeminate men at its head. In fact, Vázquez and Cleminson affirm that nationalist propaganda identified the Spanish "reds with lasciviousness and erotic debauchery, [and] being prone to sexual perversion."[8] Thus justified, the "virile" Francoists felt compelled to act against such "effeminate" republicans, to "purify" the homeland. The paradigmatic example is perhaps the execution of the poet Federico García Lorca in 1936 by Francoists at the beginning of civil war. García Lorca was and remains an emblematic figure of Spanish literature. Attacking the archaisms of society, he spoke about impossible love, beauty of Andalusian gypsies, and homosexuality. He was murdered because he represented the supposed decadence of communism and homosexuality.[9]

Revision of the Law of Vagrants and Miscreants, 1954

In this context of "purifying ambition"[10] some acts committed by homosexuals were legally repressed, principally through the gross indecency and indecent assault provisions, until the modification of the vagrancy law, with specific mention of homosexuals, in 1954, fifteen years after the establishment of the Franco's regime. As recorded in the debates kept in the archives of the Congress of Deputies, the modification of the vagrancy law to include homosexuals was justified by vague reference to "offence to the morals of our country."[11]

Accordingly, in 1954 the second and sixth articles of the original 1933 law were amended to establish not penalties but "security measures" against homosexuals. According to the legislators, the measures were designed to curb an alleged increase in homosexuality.[12] The amendments provided for the following possible measures: internment in a labor establishment or agricultural colony (homosexuals subjected to this security measure had to be admitted to special institutions, and, in all cases, with absolute separation from others); prohibition from living in a particular place or territory (usually where the detainee was convicted), and obligation to declare the home address; and submission to police surveillance. Between arrest by the police and the judge's decision, the defendant was imprisoned until the level to which he represented a "social danger" had been determined. To establish this, the suspect had to undergo a series of tests.

In general, in the files of "dangerousness" (*peligrosidad*) conserved in the archives held in Barcelona, most subjects bear witness to the same procedures. After arrest, the police prepared a report on the reasons for detention with a description of the alleged acts, the place, and the time. Then the person under arrest made a declaration at the police station before giving evidence in court. From there, the police requested a report from the general security office about the detainee's background. Also, the police carried out interviews within the local neighborhood to assess the conduct and morality of the person. The accused would then be examined by a forensic doctor who would write a detailed report about his physical and mental characteristics to help the judge in his decision. Furthermore, the police compiled another report on the detainee's employment during the five years prior to the arrest, as well as about the family relationships of the person under arrest.

The examples referred to in this chapter all come from records held in Barcelona, because it is currently one of the only cities in Spain that allows access to judicial files related to homosexuality. Moreover, Barcelona was then what we might call, using modern terminology, the "gay capital" of the nation. It was the least conservative city in Spain and over the previous years it had attracted many homosexuals who wanted to live their sexuality in a more permissive way.

The law required proof of the recurrence or "habitual" character of homosexual acts to establish the degree of threat represented by an individual. A person's criminal history, employment history, and whether he had a fixed address also influenced the official view. For example, José L., 20 years old when he was arrested in 1961, without a profession or a home address, was a homosexual with a criminal record of theft and an attempt to cross the border illegally. He was convicted because of his background, because he was a homosexual, and because "he has no justified legitimate means of living." In fact, he lived "on the income provided by such vice."[13] José L. was sentenced to a term of imprisonment of at least ninety-five days and a maximum of one year. Convictions of this type were very common.

A direct consequence of the use of these criteria to determine the social dangerousness of the individual was that the homosexuals convicted during the Franco regime in Catalonia (and the Balearic Islands that fell under the Catalonia's regional jurisdiction) all belonged to the working classes, according to the files consulted. Homosexuals from the middle classes never appear in these files. It should also be noted that the legal consequences for homosexual acts in 1950s Spain were not markedly out of step with international trends. As this volume indicates, many Western countries had similar or even more draconian laws against homosexual acts. However, in contrast to other places, Spain was to become even more repressive before things got better.

Law on Dangerousness and Social Rehabilitation, 1970

Despite its dictatorial regime, Spain, as elsewhere, underwent economic growth in the 1960s, as it transitioned from an autarchic period of economic self-sufficiency to a more outward-looking "developmental" phase. Spain's economic development was based mainly on industry and coastal tourism. This boom boosted urbanization and greatly increased the presence of foreign tourists, who in turn brought new customs from northern Europe. One such custom, according to the technocrats of the Franco regime, was "homosexualism." Although it was necessary to increase economic development and, therefore, allow the arrival of foreigners, at the same time the authorities wanted to avoid the perceived moral corruption of Spanish traditions so dear to the regime.

For this reason, from the early 1960s, some jurists argued that repression had to be increased against people classified as vagrants and miscreants: delinquents, in particular homosexuals, prostitutes, pimps and pickpockets, and so on. These sentiments were reflected in the reform of the old vagrancy law undertaken in the later 1960s. On October 4, 1967, the Ministry of Justice appointed a commission to reform this law, and the new legislation, now named the "Law on Dangerousness and Social Rehabilitation," was approved and ratified by the Head of State on August 4, 1970. It came into effect shortly thereafter.[14]

This more repressive framework was ostensibly erected to protect Spanish society from corruptive foreign visitors. It can be seen as a reactionary response to the international context, particularly the liberalization of customs that was then spreading through Europe and the United States. England and Wales decriminalized homosexual acts between adults in private in 1967 after almost ten years of campaigning. In the United States, the Stonewall riot took place in 1969, giving rise to the Gay Liberation Front. An eponymous organization emerged in London, and in France, during the events of May 1968, there were demands for an end to the repression of "erotic minorities." The Spanish authorities sought to differentiate themselves from the other European and American nations in regard to morality, and the revisions to the old vagrancy law was the Francoist response.

The fundamental difference between the Law of Dangerousness and Social Rehabilitation of 1970 and the earlier vagrancy law as far as homosexuals were concerned had to do with the type of internment and its duration. There was no longer any mention of special internment or labor establishment, but rather, of "establishments of re-education." Those convicted would be sent to such an establishment for a period of no less than six months and no more than five years.[15] Despite the slightly different treatment, in reality, this law did not imply a new interpretation of homosexuality.[16] The grounds for conviction continued to be the repetitive or habitual character of homosexual acts, criminal records, illicit livelihoods, and the absence of a permanent home, as with the previous law. Likewise, the sentences include commitment to institutions of labor for those considered "vagrant, habitual miscreants and homosexual."[17]

If the new law represented a Francoist fear of liberalization, an increase in arrests in the 1970s showed that those fears increased the commitment to repression. Police patrols and surveillance in the streets increased from the early 1970s. Efforts to monitor and oppose the threat perceived in the socially "dangerous" were all part of a conscious effort to preserve the established order. Since the vagrancy law, the authorities pointed out on numerous occasions the "scandalous" behavior or "scandals" caused by the detainees.[18] They could refer to the provision against "gross indecency" that in turn referred to an act considered contrary to the morality defended by the Franco regime. In fact, several sentences talk about "moral crime."[19] These could be, for example, "queer gestures," as was the case in 1960 with a 25-year-old male nicknamed "La Claveles" (Carnations). His gestures provoked "public scandal" in the Plaza del Teatro in Barcelona, because they infringed the cultural rules of Franco's masculinity.[20] In 1971, an 18-year-old male was arrested for "wearing a necklace."[21] A 31-year-old in 1975 was "dressed as a woman."[22] As these examples suggest, for the Francoist authorities, the problem remained above all the visibility and publicity of homosexuals and homosexual activity. These men inverted an established system, exposing to public view an alternative gender model, another model of sexuality, and a subversive model of work. For that reason, the regime persecuted them both openly and surreptitiously.[23]

Police repression, as well as higher levels of patrolling in public spaces, also included more covert monitoring. In Barcelona for example, there are innumerable cases of detention of those about whom the police merely had their suspicions.[24] No crime need have been committed—this was simply "preventive" policing. A particularly close watch was kept on Barcelona's Chinatown, which was known as a hub for criminal activity, as well as prostitution in the famous Ramblas and nearby streets (Carrer dels Escudillers and nearby for example, with alternative bars, drugs and gay bars, in today's parlance). Superficially, the efforts were aimed at curbing prostitution. When they considered it appropriate, police arrested the person considered to have a "suspicious attitude," checked his identity, criminal record, sought information about his work, his address, and whether he had a lawful means of livelihood. If not, the authorities readily judged and convicted those people. An example from 1965 was a 19-year-old male who was arrested "when he was on the Ramblas with a suspicious attitude."[25] Investigation determined that he lived "only from the money that he gets from queers."[26]

Medical persecution toward the end of the regime

Beyond the moral condemnation promoted by the Church, the authorities, and the press, recent research has drawn attention to the way the medical profession under the Franco regime also had a significant role in the repression and persecution of homosexuals and transsexuals. Even some psychiatrists recommended castration, lobotomy, and other methods to "cure" homosexuality.[27] In the Francoist prisons, doctors had opportunities to try to reform homosexuals, experimenting with different methods. According to some, doctors and biologists were powerless against these "sex offenders."[28] The sanction against homosexuality had to be, therefore, not only medical but also legal, while in the 1920s the eminent doctor Gregorio Marañón had opposed the criminalization of homosexuality.[29] This medical choice to complete the re-education of the sexually different with legal penalties was a clear step back for medicine.

At least one doctor in Spain used the aversion therapy that was made famous by Stanley Kubrick's film *A Clockwork Orange*. One subject of this treatment, in 1974, was a priest by the name of Antonio Roig Roselló.[30] Another case involved Jordi Griset, who had six months of aversion therapy in the 1970s. According to the doctor in charge, and as Kubrick's film suggests, it was a treatment that "was in fashion in the rest of Europe." The therapy consisted of projecting onto a screen the image of a naked woman, and, after several seconds, projecting the image of a man in a swimsuit, accompanied by an electric shock that lasted between five and ten seconds. The association of pain with the image of the male was supposed to convert the subject to a preference for women.[31] The patients only ever reported "negative results."[32]

Other methods could be used for homosexuals sentenced to prison terms. We know that the prison in Madrid had a special department for dealing with homosexuals, and a medical team conducted its studies there. The results of these investigations were published in 1970 by the psychologist Fernando Chamorro Gundin. The "patients" were interviewed by each member of the medical team, who wrote separate reports about the subject's intellectual capacity, personality, type of homosexuality, and the therapeutic possibilities. The doctors took into account the criminal and penitentiary report of the patient-offender, giving special importance to sexual behavior both in prison and outside; to personal interviews with the doctor; to the medical examination, in particular of some areas of the body (in Barcelona a doctor affirmed that the patient's "underarm and pubic hair [has] a clearly feminine distribution"[33]); of the "constant and attentive" observation of the officials; and of the evaluation and interpretation of the psychological techniques used. Doctors even studied the gestures of homosexual prisoners. In other cases, they came to talk about anthropological and psychic "explorations."[34]

Over a period of almost forty years, then, Spain's homosexuals and others belonging to sexually non-normative groups lived under the persistent fear of persecution, and, if sent to prison, the threat of medical intervention. In Barcelona alone, 346 such cases (344 men and two women) were prosecuted under the terms of the 1954 vagrancy law, and, between 1971 and 1977, 207 people, all men, were prosecuted under the Law of Social Dangerousness. In total for Barcelona, 553 "homosexual" persons were condemned by both laws between 1956 and 1977, and there were 673 further cases that did not reach resolution between 1956 and 1980 (i.e., this number were arrested and imprisoned, but not convicted).[35] If accurate figures for the rest of Spain could be included, the numbers would likely reach the thousands. Moreover, these figures concern working class persons to the complete exclusion of the better-off. In principle, legislation condemned all homosexuals expressly if they committed repeated acts, but the application of both laws was in practice limited to condemning working class homosexuals.

The transition from Franco to democracy

The period between the end of the dictatorship marked by Franco's death in November 1975 and the full establishment of democracy with the victory of the Socialists in the general elections of 1982 is known as the "Spanish Transition." The first legislative elections took place in 1977, after which the country was governed according to a constitution that was approved by referendum in 1978 that restored democracy to Spain. This phase constitutes the first stage of the reign of King Juan Carlos I, nominated in 1969 as successor of the dictator by Franco himself. The Francoist Law of Dangerousness continued to apply to homosexuals until 1977, after which convictions of homosexuals ceased. Why? Not only because of the enormous changes experienced in Spanish society after Franco's death, but surely also because of contemporary international demands in favor of sexual minorities. The definitive exclusion of homosexuality from the Law of Dangerousness in 1979 was a response to pressure exerted by the Gay Liberation Front of Catalonia.[36]

The Catalan movement had emerged, clandestinely, at the end of the 1960s in Barcelona. During the three years that elapsed between the appointment of a state commission and the enactment of the Law on Dangerousness and Social Rehabilitation in 1970, parliamentary debates and the pressure of an emergent Spanish homophile movement were not unanimous with respect to the type of repression of homosexuality. Faced with the danger posed by the bill for homosexuals, Francesc Francino and Armand de Fluvià, two "homophile" Catalans, decided to do everything possible to prevent the law from being enacted.[37] They failed of course, but after the law came into force in 1970, de Fluvià and others decided to launch a publishing project clandestinely. A group of four people, helped by the French homophile association Arcadie, adopted the title Homophile Group for Social Integration (AGHOIS). Shortly afterward, this was changed to the Spanish Movement of Homosexual Liberation (MELH), a group that aspired to represent the whole of Spain but that was at first limited to the city of Barcelona—for the historic reasons mentioned earlier.

As soon as Franco died in late 1975, most of the longest-serving members of the MELH created the Gay Liberation Front of Catalonia (FAGC), inspired mainly by the Homosexual Liberation Front of Argentina and the Homosexual Front of Revolutionary Action of France. The Spanish movement began a long constituent process that culminated in 1977 in the approval of its Manifesto that, according to de Fluvià, "was a model for the rest of the gay organizations which, from that date, gradually appeared in the Spanish State."[38]

Despite the great progress made in the wake of Franco's death, particularly the exclusion of homosexuality from the dangerousness law, homosexual acts were occasionally pursued by police, using the gross indecency provision.[39] For example, in Barcelona, the police charged a "homosexual" in 1979 for soliciting "clients" on the Ramblas, although the judges decided not to prosecute the case.[40] In 1980, the police arrested another "homosexual" in a club "frequented by habitual criminals," but there was no sentence here either.[41] Raids continued until at least 1981.[42] Nevertheless, the end of the Franco regime signaled a gradual decline of the repression of homosexuals. The struggle of the social movements during the 1975–1982 transition between the dictatorship and democracy was decisive for the exclusion of homosexuality from the Law of Dangerousness and Social Rehabilitation at the end of the 1970s.

From the late 1970s and early 1980s, the general countercultural phenomenon known as La Movida began, in particular in Madrid, where it was known as La Movida Madrileña. During this period, the sexually non-normative actively participated in the renewal of artistic creativity. Notable figures include the illustrator Nazario Luque, the artist Martin Ocaña, and the film director Eloy de la Iglesia, who treated themes of homosexual love and desire in his 1977 film *Los placeres ocultos*. Later, films by Pedro Almodóvar such as *Matador* (1986) and *Law of Desire* (1987) showcased Spanish notions of same-sex relationships to a wide international audience. By the 1990s, the gay neighborhoods of Chueca in Madrid and the Gaixample in Barcelona had emerged, and some of Spain's autonomous communities began to recognize same-sex de facto relationships. These constituted the first legislative steps toward national Spanish recognition of same-sex marriage and full equality, achieved in 2005.

Epilogue: Official recognition for forty years of oblivion

Although equal same-sex marriage was a significant achievement, Spain went a step further. In 2007, socialist José Luis Rodríguez Zapatero's first government (2004–2008) launched a policy to recognize the way gays, lesbians, and transsexual people were repressed by the Franco regime. The authorities estimated that there were about 5000 homosexual victims of Franco's repression. Spain's Law of Historical Memory, designed to acknowledge victims of both sides of the Spanish Civil War and the dictatorship, also made it the first country to recognize sexual minorities as victims of the state. Ten years later, other nations followed suit, notably the UK in 2016, and Germany and Canada in 2017. Such recognitions offered moral and symbolic reparation, and in some places, including Spain, the authorities also included economic reparation. Zapatero's pioneering law of 2007 provided for a minimum compensation of €4000 for those who spent between one and six months in prison. Those who were jailed for between six months and three years would receive €8000, and those imprisoned for more than three years were to receive €12,000. Since 2009, 116 of approximately 180 applications have been successful, and the government has distributed a total of €624,000, an average of about €5300 per applicant.[43]

The first person compensated in Spain was Antoni Ruiz, who was also president of the Association of Former Social Prisoners. He received €4000 in 2009 after an individual struggle that began long before the advent of the Law of Historical Memory. Everything began, according to Ruiz, when in 1995 in Valencia two police asked him for documentation. When carrying out the checks, the police officers called him a "faggot" because his background was recorded by the law of dangerousness in his police and criminal record. From there, Ruiz began a long struggle to remove that aspect of his record. His journey took him through numerous institutions to get his file back. After four years, he finally recovered his file.[44]

Thanks to the 2007 Law of Historical Memory, the process of reparation for some victims has been faster, though the reparation measures provided by the law are considered insufficient by some victims. They argue, in the first place, that the search for all the victims by the state should be generalized so all can be compensated. Antoni Ruiz, as president of the Association of Former Social Prisoners, considers that the amounts granted by the State are "ridiculous," particularly when compared to the Canadian government, which distributed the equivalent of about 6 million euros among approximately 3000 people.[45] Ruiz also claims a modest pension for those who are still alive. He considers that this would help compensate for the economic and social difficulties created in the wake of a conviction.[46] Finally, some claim that Spain should follow places like Canada in establishing sites of memory, such as museums, statues, plaques, and street names, as well as providing more education for sexual diversity, public funds to consolidate archival centers on sexual diversity, and encourage research to remember the sexual victims of the Franco repression so in the future the mistakes of the past will be not committed. The social debates are ongoing, but the rate of change since the fall of Franco is something in which many Spaniards rightly take pride.

Notes

1 A good recent introduction to Spanish history is Julián Casanova and Carlos Gil Andrés, *Twentieth-Century Spain: A History* (Cambridge: Cambridge University Press, 2014).
2 Geoffroy Huard, *Los antisociales. Historia de la homosexualidad en Barcelona y París (1945–1975)* (Madrid: Marcial Pons, 2014) and *Les gays sous le franquisme. Discours, subcultures et revendications à Barcelone, 1939–1977* (Villeurbanne: Orbis Tertius, 2016).
3 Rafael Huertas and Enric Novella, "Sexo y modernidad en la España de la Segunda República. Los discursos de la ciencia," *Arbor* 189, no. 764 (2013); Javier Navarro Navarro, "Sexualidad, reproducción y cultura obrera revolucionaria en España: la revista *Orto* (1932–1934)," *Arbor* 190, no. 769 (2014).
4 Huertas and Novella, "Sexo y modernidad en la España de la Segunda República."
5 Navarro, "Sexualidad, reproducción y cultura obrera revolucionaria en España."
6 Mary Nash, "Pronatalism and Motherhood in Franco's Spain," in *Women and the Rise ot the European Welfare States, 1880s–1950s*, ed. Gisela Bock and Pat Thane (London and New York: Routledge, 1991), 160–177.
7 Richard Cleminson and Francisco Vázquez García, *Los Invisibles: A History of Male Homosexuality in Spain, 1850–1939* (Cardiff: University of Wales Press, 2007). In particular the Chapter 5: "'In Search of Men': *Regeneracionismo* and the Crisis of Masculinity (1898–1936)," 175–215.
8 Ibid.
9 Ian Gibson, *Federico García Lorca. A Life*, Earl Company, 1989 and *Lorca y el mundo gay* (Barcelona: Planeta, 2009).
10 Cleminson and Vázquez, *Los Invisibles*.
11 Quoted by Arturo Arnalte, *Redada de violetas. La represión de los homosexuales durante el franquismo* (Madrid: La esfera de los libros, 2003), 66.
12 Jordi Terrasa Mateu, "La legislación represiva," in *Una discriminación universal. La homosexualidad bajo el franquismo y la transición*, ed. Javier Ugarte Pérez (Barcelona-Madrid: Egales, 2008), 86–104; Ricard de la Rosa Fernández, "El tractament legal de l'homosexualitat pel règim franquista," in *Homosexuals i transsexuals: els altres represaliats i discriminats del franquisme, des de la memòria històrica*, ed. José Benito Eres Rigueira and Carlos Villagrasa Alcaide (coord.) (Barcelona: Bellaterra, 2008), 115–123.

13 Case file of dangerousness n° 42, 1961, Court of vagrants and miscreants of Catalonia and Balearic Islands, Arxiu Central de la Ciutat de la Justícia de Barcelona.
14 Victoriano Domingo Loren, *Los homosexuales frente a la ley* (Barcelona: Plaza & Janes, 1978), 45, quoted by Huard, *Los antisociales*, 100.
15 Victoriano Domingo Loren, *Los homosexuales frente a la ley*, 46–47.
16 Huard, *Los antisociales*, 101.
17 Case file of dangerousness n° 842, 1972, Court of dangerousness and Social Rehabilitation fo Catalonia and Balearic Islands, Arxiu Central de la Ciutat de la Justícia de Barcelona.
18 For example, case files of dangerousness n° 59, 65, 1956, Court of Vagrants and Crooks of Catalonia and Balearic Islands, Arxiu Central de la Ciutat de la Justícia de Barcelona.
19 Case file of dangerousness n° 528, 1960, Court of Vagrants and Crooks of Catalonia and Balearic Islands, Arxiu Central de la Ciutat de la Justícia de Barcelona.
20 Case file of dangerousness n° 391, 1960, Court of Vagrants and Crooks of Catalonia and Balearic Islands, Arxiu Central de la Ciutat de la Justícia de Barcelona.
21 Case file of dangerousness n° 26, 1971, Court of Dangerousness and Social Rehabilitation of Catalonia and Balearic Islands, Arxiu Central de la Ciutat de la Justícia de Barcelona.
22 Case file of dangerousness n° 379, 1972, Court of Dangerousness and Social Rehabilitation of Catalonia and Balearic Islands, Arxiu Central de la Ciutat de la Justícia de Barcelona.
23 Case file of dangerousness n° 664, 1961, Court of Vagrants and Crooks of Catalonia and Balearic Islands, Arxiu Central de la Ciutat de la Justícia de Barcelona. For the same reason I put to my book the title *Los antisociales*.
24 Case file of dangerousness n° 45, 1964, Court of Vagrants and Crooks of Catalonia and Balearic Islands, Arxiu Central de la Ciutat de la Justícia de Barcelona. It is the first of many cases.
25 Case file of dangerousness n° 611, 1965, Court of Vagrants and Crooks of Catalonia and Balearic Islands, Arxiu Central de la Ciutat de la Justícia de Barcelona.
26 Ibid.
27 Antoni Adam Donat and Álvar Martínez Vidal, "'Infanticidas, violadores, homosexuales y pervertidos de todas las categorías': La homosexualidad en la psiquiatría del franquismo," in *Una discriminación universal. La homosexualidad bajo el franquismo y la transición*, ed. Javier Ugarte Pérez (Madrid/Barcelona: Egales, 2008), 109–138; Arnalte, *Redada de violetas*, 99–114.
28 Antonio Vallejo Nágera, quoted in Adam Donat and Martínez Vidal, "Infanticidas, violadores, homosexuales y per- vertidos de todas las categorías," 124–125.
29 Gregorio Marañón, *Los estados intersexuales en la especie humana* (Madrid: Javier Morata, 1929).
30 Arnalte, *Redada de violetas*, 114.
31 Nathan Baidez Aparicio, *Vagos, maleantes... y homosexuales* (La Garriga: Malhivern, 2007), 68.
32 Case file of dangerousness n° 532 y 583, 1974, Court of Dangerousness and Social Rehabilitation of Catalonia and Balearic Islands, Arxiu Central dels Jutjats de la Ciutat de la Justícia de Barcelona.
33 Case file of dangerousness n° 87, 1964, forensic doctor report, February 19, 1964, Court of Vagrants and Crooks of Catalonia and Balearic Islands, Arxiu dels Jutjats de la Ciutat de la Justícia de Barcelona.

34 Fernando Chamorro Gundin, *Resultados obtenidos con técnicas proyectivas en una muestra de 200 delincuentes homosexuales españoles*, Dirección general de instituciones penitenciarias, Departamento de homosexuales de la central de observación, Madrid, June 1970. For a more detailed analysis of this study, see Richard Cleminson, "Instancias de la biopolítica en España, siglos XX y XXI," in *La administración de la vida. Estudios biopolíticos*, ed. Javier Ugarte (dir.) (Barcelona: Anthropos, 2005), 139–146; Alberto García Valdés, *Historia y presente de la homosexualidad* (Madrid: Akal, 1981); Huard, *Los antisociales*, 68–73.
35 I use the word "homosexuals" though not all those prosecuted would have defined themselves as such. There were lesbians and transsexuals too. I use the word "homosexual," therefore, as a verbal facility to avoid enumerating a long list of different sexual identities. It is also the term used in general by the authorities.
36 Fernando Olmeda, *El látigo y la pluma. Homosexuales en la España de Franco* (Madrid: Oberon, 2004), 311–320.
37 Armand de Fluvià, *El moviment gay a la clandestinitat del franquisme (1970–1975)* (Barcelona: Bellaterra, 2003).
38 Ibid.
39 Fernando Olmeda, *El látigo y la pluma. Homosexuales en la España de Franco* (Madrid: Oberon, 2003), 313.
40 Case file of dangerousness nº 271, 1979, Court of Dangerousness and Social Rehabilitation of Catalonia and Balearic Islands, Arxiu Central de la Ciutat de la Justícia de Barcelona.
41 Case file of dangerousness nº 111, 1980, Court of Dangerousness and Social Rehabilitation of Catalonia and Balearic Islands, Arxiu Central de la Ciutat de la Justícia de Barcelona.
42 Arnalte, *Redada de violetas*, 243.
43 Isabel F. Lantigua, "Antoni, solo 4000 euros tras estar preso por ser homosexual," *El Mundo*, January 3, 2017.
44 Ibid.
45 Ibid.
46 Ibid.

9

Affecting Legal Change: Law and Same-Sex Feelings in West Germany since the 1950s

Benno Gammerl

While working on this chapter, I was—as sometimes happens to historians—overtaken by history. On June 30, 2017, the German parliament introduced gay marriage and put same-sex relationships on a par with those of straight couples. This legal change came somewhat unexpectedly, after Chancellor Angela Merkel had mentioned in an interview with the women's magazine *Brigitte* that she would like to leave the decision for or against same-sex marriage to the individual members of the *Bundestag*. With conservative resistance crumbling and the party whips being safely stored away, marriage equality came surprisingly quickly, in fact only four days after Merkel had indicated her change of mind. Regarding the interplay between feelings and legal change which this chapter sets out to explore, the way Merkel motivated her shift of opinion is particularly interesting. In the interview she said that children who live with gay or lesbian parents might actually grow up in very caring and loving families.[1] So it was ultimately an emotional faculty that paved the way for gay marriage when the chancellor, not without sounding some homophobic undertones, hesitantly conceded the ability to love and care to same-sex couples.

How did specific emotional patterns and practices propel developments in the legal sphere? And how did the law in turn prevent or encourage particular feelings? This chapter examines the German history of homosexualities with these questions in mind. Due to the excitement around gay marriage, another hallmark caesura in the history of legal discrimination against homosexuals in Germany went almost unnoticed. On June 22, 2017, the *Bundestag* revoked the post-1945 verdicts based on paragraph 175 that had criminalized sex between men. Because of West Germany's particular history, then, the chapter not only pinpoints the links between love and marriage, but also the connections between grief, suffering, and reparation.

After a long period of denial, legislative and judiciary institutions finally acknowledged their responsibility for the suffering gay men had to endure and admitted to their former involvement in what is today considered a violation of human rights. As in many other countries, consensual intercourse between adult men was illegal in West Germany until the penal code's infamous paragraph 175, which dated back to 1870, was reformed in 1969 and 1973. This history of criminalization is particularly troublesome for the Federal Republic's legal system as it actively enabled the uniquely harsh version of paragraph 175 established by the Nazis to persist well into the postwar era. Until 1969 the penal law facilitated fierce prosecution by making punishable a wide range of behaviors that could indicate same-sex desire.

Yet while the sentences passed according to this section until 1945 had already been revoked in 2002, the legislature and judiciary were much more hesitant to repeal the verdicts that had been issued after 1945. Their doing so in June 2017 ultimately amounted to the confession that not only the Nazis but also the early Federal Republic had unjustly and fiercely persecuted homosexual men. The legal system obviously found it difficult to adopt such a self-critical stance. Yet following an initiative by Christine Lüders, director of the Federal Anti-Discrimination Agency, later picked up by Heiko Maas, the minister of justice, the debate gained fresh momentum in 2016.[2] Since the decision of June 2017, at least some of the approximately 45,000 men who were sentenced according to paragraph 175 between 1949 and 1969 may still live long enough to see their verdicts repealed and to receive financial compensation for the unjustified prison terms they had to serve. Together with the institution of same-sex marriage this attempt at reparation shows that legal systems, legislatures, and societies are actually able to learn and to adopt new, more accepting ways of dealing with sexual diversity. And one may hope that they will—given that queer emancipatory movements maintain their pressure and their efforts at persuasion—continue to do so.

These developments demonstrate how profoundly the legal treatment of same-sex love and desire has changed during the last five decades. The compensation for men who suffered from prosecution moreover indicates that counting convictions alone does not suffice to redress the harm inflicted. The detrimental consequences of criminalization reached far beyond prison terms and ranged from relationship breakups to suicides. To trace these wider ramifications of laws regulating homosexuality, this chapter highlights their emotional implications. The focus on feelings brings shame and its interpretation as "internalized homophobia" into view.[3] It also shows how fear of exposure could engender strategies that enabled men to have sex with one another in spite (or because) of their dreading the penal consequences. Simultaneously emotions like rage or hope were sparking political activism directed against homonegative measures and were thus decisive triggers of legal change.[4] An approach to feelings that does not reduce them to "internal" phenomena, but locates them at the threshold between the individual and the social, therefore reveals how laws played out on an emotional level, and how feelings at the same time shaped legal developments.[5]

Tracing such interactions allows the chapter to explore the emotional lives of men loving men and women loving women. It reveals how decriminalization and legal recognition were propelled either by the promotion of love and mutual responsibility within partnerships or by an emphasis on the adventurous and pleasurable lives of queer singles. The analysis simultaneously shows how laws shaped the emotional styles prevalent among gays and lesbians, for example, by rendering certain modes of expressing desire and affection particularly hazardous.

Connecting legal and emotional levels widens the scope of research in three respects. Firstly, it brings into view the productive aspects of the law that are often sidelined by an exclusive focus on its prohibitive dimensions. While the analysis does not deny that legal measures at times limited actors' scope for maneuver, it simultaneously shows that laws could also promote specific modes of emotional expression. Secondly, the approach highlights the various connections that link legal arenas to other spheres, ranging from the artistic to the educational to the everyday. Thirdly, exploring the interactions between laws and feelings reveals how closely developments in the homosexual context and dynamics in the heterosexual realm were linked. This observation can help to unsettle the often implicit and therefore particularly problematic assumption that it is possible to research different-sex settings without considering same-sex constellations and vice versa. Such views rely either on the dubious supposition that homosexuality was a negligible category when one analyses, as it were, mainstream sexuality, or on the questionable opinion that same-sex phenomena were incommensurable with and completely separated from different-sex realities.

The focus on feelings is moreover particularly fruitful because it reveals the ambivalent effects that the decriminalization or the normalization of homosexualities generated on an everyday level. From a normalization point of view, homosexuals have since the 1970s not only left the pillory of shame as well as the cages of incarceration and pathologization. Rather, they have simultaneously also been caught up in new patterns and expectations as to what a normal and successful gay and lesbian life should look like. The introduction of same-sex marriage is but one example that illustrates this dynamic. Such models enhance the pressure of self-optimization and the potential for failure among those trying to live up to the newly established standards. The new patterns available for gay or lesbian relationships thus no longer appear merely as fortunate side effects of liberalization, but as at times stressful emotional models that create fear of and shame about falling short of them.[6]

Beyond narratives of liberalization

The postwar decades are usually described as a time of harsh prosecution and cautious hiding that was ended by accelerating liberalization since the 1970s. In West Germany this development led from the reforms of 1969 and 1973 to the abolition of paragraph 175 in 1994. This repeal of the unequal legal treatment of same-sex-desiring men was actually a consequence of German unification. In the German Democratic Republic penal discriminations against homosexuals had, after a decisive attenuation in 1968, finally been abolished in 1988 by reducing the age of consent for homosexual intercourse from 18 to 16. Since then the same rules applied to homo- and heterosexuals. Six years later the West German penal code was adapted to this model of equal treatment. After the 1990s liberalization continued with affirmative legal measures that promoted the recognition of sexual diversity. The *Lebenspartnerschaftsgesetz* (life-partnership law) of 2001 introduced civil partnership for same-sex couples. In 2006 the *Anti-Diskriminierungs-Gesetz* (anti-discrimination law) followed suit. It penalized the unequal treatment of sexual and other minorities.

If mentioned at all in broader historical accounts, this rapid and dramatic shift in the legal treatment of same-sex desire is mostly framed as resulting from general liberalizing trends.[7] While not completely wrong, this argument has two flaws. Firstly, like most versions of the modernization paradigm, it implies teleological assumptions that consider the spread of accepting attitudes toward sexual diversity as a quasi-natural development. Homophobic and other adverse forces are accordingly depicted as anachronistic remnants of a bygone era. Secondly, the liberalization narrative tends to overemphasize the new chances and opportunities that open up for same-sex loving people in the post-liberation period, thereby losing sight of the new problems and challenges they have to face simultaneously. The focus on liberalization thus glosses over the at times fierce struggles gays and lesbians were and are involved in. And it disregards the contributions of gay and lesbian activists to establishing wider scopes for individual freedom and agency within society at large.

Highlighting the notion of emancipation instead shifts the perspective in a fruitful way. It brings into view how gay and lesbian movements actively enhanced the acceptance of sexual diversity, thus in crucial ways enabling legal change. Yet the focus on emancipation in turn involves the danger of reproducing heroic narratives of success. Histories of emancipation often tend to lose sight of failures and ambiguities that persisted or arose along the road to freedom and self-assertion, as it were. They are therefore in need of a critical supplement afforded by the notion of normalization. A history of emotions perspective is particularly conducive to exploring ambivalences that accompanied homosexualities' increasing social and legal acceptance. Combining a focus on emancipation with one on normalization can develop more complicated and more appropriate arguments and narratives that reach beyond oversimplifying oppositions between traditional repression and modern liberality or between closeted shame and emancipated pride.[8]

To enable such multilayered perspectives, the study draws on a range of materials that allow it to consider interactions between various domains. Besides gay and lesbian publications, the analysis also draws on oral history interviews with men loving men and women loving women who in their biographical narratives frequently refer to their own as well as to others' experiences with different-sex constellations. In addition, the inquiry's source base includes advice books from the 1960s and 1970s that addressed a broad and mainstream readership. Studying diverse materials and employing a history of emotions approach that widens the analytical perspective allows this contribution to devise new and more comprehensive explanations for the changes in the legal treatment of same-sex love and desire that have occurred over the last couple of decades. In doing so, the study places the history of homosexualities within a set of broader developments. This emphasis on the ways in which legal and emotional, straight, and queer dynamics interacted with each other ultimately enhances our understanding of why and how same-sex feelings came to be decriminalized and normalized since the 1950s.

De/criminalization: Same-sex desire between bodily lust and pristine love

Paragraph 175 of the German penal code constituted the main clause regulating same-sex desire since the 1870s and can serve as a good example of how a legal measure—in this case a prohibitive one—affected the behavior of same-sex desiring men. In some regions this paragraph discontinued the Napoleonic laissez-faire policy in sexual matters, while it replaced former sodomy laws in others. Partly in an endeavor to lend these older prohibitions more legal clarity, yet partly also in an attempt to ensure that such charges could not be leveled too easily, the proof of coitus-like intercourse—that is, penetration—between men was made a condition for a sentence according to paragraph 175.[9] This specific proscription clearly impacted the sexual behaviors of men desiring men. Practices like mutual masturbation or interfemoral intercourse made accusations and convictions less likely than others and were thus in a way advantageous.

The need for proof of coitus-like intercourse was eliminated by the Nazis when they radicalized paragraph 175 in 1935. According to the rules in force since then almost all signs of same-sex desire could be interpreted as proof of a breach of the law.[10] A kiss or a flirting look sufficed to send a person to prison. To highlight the particular ferocity of this homophobic piece of legislation the Berlin memorial to the homosexuals persecuted under the national socialist regime puts the display of same-sex kisses center stage. Thus the memorial celebrates the right that gays and lesbians have since won to express their love publicly and fearlessly. Besides memorial practices, biographical narratives also document the fact that same-sex kisses were anything but a matter of course as long as the Nazi version of paragraph 175 was in force in West Germany, that is, until 1969.

Men loving men who came of age in the 1950s and 1960s were often particularly cautious about kissing other men. Mr. Melling, born in 1949 and interviewed in 2008, draws a strict distinction between his same-sex contacts, confined to the domain "below the belt," and the intimacy he experienced with his wife that also comprised kissing and touching the upper parts of the body.[11] In a similar vein, Mr. Kuhn, born in 1938, found the mere thought of kissing another man repugnant.[12] While he did not mind engaging in various same-sex practices as an adolescent and young adult—he thought that practices like mutual masturbation were "absolutely legal"—Mr. Kuhn refrained from kissing other men until the late 1960s.[13] Only then did he stop to consider the kiss as the unmistakable sign of being gay, as the moment of no return, as the ultimate step that he was not willing to take: "as I hadn't come, er, to terms with myself, ... the *kiss was the final thing* that I then did as well in order ... to ... adapt, or to, that I accepted myself."[14]

If having same-sex intercourse without kissing his partners was Mr. Kuhn's particular way of dealing with legal prohibitions, the majority of his homophile contemporaries in the 1950s and 1960s took to another strategy. They started from the observation that the criminalization of men loving men relied on stereotypes which depicted them as sexually licentious perverts and seducers who continuously sought new erotic adventures. Against this prejudice homophile magazines like *Der Weg* developed a self-image that highlighted pristine love and long-lasting relationships between men.[15] In 1961, an article argued that such "durable friendships" could not be "based on sex," but needed to rely on "spiritual aspects."[16] And another author claimed that "if we seriously aspire to win tolerance among normal people, it is high time to bring order to our intimate relationships."[17] Propagating a new emotional style that highlighted love instead of sex and faithfulness instead of promiscuity was thus seen as a means to promote legal reforms.

This project entailed a characteristic will to adjust to "normal" emotional standards which often overlooked the fact that during the 1960s this "normality" was very much contested within the heterosexual setting. An advice book from the early twentieth century, Friedrich Wilhelm Foerster's *Lebensführung* (conduct of life) that had seen several revisions and was still widely read in the postwar period requested heterosexual couples in its 1961 edition to resist the allegedly all-pervasive "dictatorship of the drives" in order to allow the delicate flower of "true love" to grow and to blossom.[18] Similar advice was given by Jochen Fischer in 1966 who opposed sex to "real love" and highlighted non-passionate relationship characteristics that "actually" ensured happiness in his eyes, namely, "security, constancy, durability."[19]

Such parallels between homo- and, as it were, heterophile discourses hint at the fact that intimacies between women and men were also subject to legal scrutiny at the time. Parents or innkeepers who sheltered unmarried couples ran the risk of a conviction for "procuration" until 1969. In light of liberal demands for a general reform of the criminal code of sexual offences, including those parts that regulated different-sex behaviors, the advice given to young people in the 1960s was most likely intended as a bulwark against what numerous parents considered as the evil consequences of sexual liberation. In other words, if one could not any longer rely exclusively on the law to enforce conservative sex morals, one had to win over young men's and women's hearts to the cause of chastity or caution in the name of "real love." From a history of homosexualities perspective one could add yet another interpretation. Maybe such calls for self-imposed restraint, whether intentionally or not, ultimately paved the way for liberal reforms of the law by suggesting that there were other, more promising ways for containing the danger of sexual licentiousness.

In the same-sex context, the homophile emphasis on pristine love and durable friendships clearly and crucially contributed to the reforms of paragraph 175 in 1969 and 1973. These were mainly advocated and propelled by liberally minded jurists like Fritz Bauer. Bauer is mainly known for his role, as Hessian district attorney, in the Frankfurt Auschwitz trials which would not have commenced in 1963 if it had not been for his insistence on prosecuting concentration camp guards and other people who administered the Holocaust. Bauer is less well known for his support of homosexual law reform. Because of this commitment he figured as one of the addressees of a petition for the decriminalization of consensual sex between adult men drafted by the humanitarian Club Elysium in 1961.[20]

For Bauer and other liberal jurists, arguments about the extent to which the state should be allowed to infringe on individuals' private lives under the rule of law were paramount. But beyond this, the impression that same-sex love was primarily about relationships that lived up to bourgeois standards also played a decisive role and garnered support for legal reforms. The same can hardly be said for the gay liberation or emancipation movement of the 1970s. Its early manifestations were relatively insignificant for the reforms of 1969 and 1973. And later on it largely failed in achieving further amendments. The gay and lesbian-feminist movements tended to trigger developments in domains other than the legal sphere. The decriminalization of homosexuality therefore furthered the emergence of emancipatory movements that subsequently changed societal attitudes toward same-sex love and desire.

Beyond hierarchies: Equal partnerships and the normalization of homosexualities

After 1969 the crucial difference between the criminal treatment of homo- and heterosexual encounters lay in the different ages of consent. At first men up to the age of 21 were under special legal "protection." The second reform of 1973 then drew the line at 18 years for gay male intercourse, while it stood at 14 years for heterosexual sex. This distinction indicates that prohibitions and prosecution no longer focused on male same-sex desire in general, but on encounters between mature men and adolescents in particular. Since the 1970s, the stereotype of the homosexual child molester and seducer of teenagers has served as the pivotal justification for the continued discrimination against same-sex desiring men. On a societal level this homophobic strategy survived well into the twenty-first century. Since 2013, the state of Baden-Württemberg in South-West Germany has witnessed sizable protests against a plan to grant sexual diversity a prominent place in the school curriculum. Parents, teachers, and others claim to fear for children's safety and argue that they must be protected from gay and other debauchers who would lure them into the realms of same-sex desire and gender variability.

Yet legally marking out relationships between adults and adolescents has since the 1970s also contributed to the delegitimization of intergenerational and hierarchical patterns within the homosexual sphere. Homophile circles had held such pairings in high esteem, often referring to ancient Greek models in the postwar decades. The gay publications of the 1970s and 1980s, though, increasingly marginalized pederasty, pedophilia, and other relationship patterns that involved large age differences. At the same time they clearly came to favor equality-based models that highlighted the need for partners to be similar to each other in terms of age, standing, and education.[21] Partners were simultaneously expected to engage in fair negotiations whenever disagreements arose.[22] This growing emphasis on equality, readily visible in the increasingly mainstream gay press of this period, corroborates the hypothesis that legal prohibitions, in this case of same-sex contact between men of different age groups, could in a decisive fashion promote and help to establish specific emotional patterns and practices.

Yet it was not only the reforms of paragraph 175 that discredited intergenerational love and furthered the emergence of parity-based patterns. These processes were also in line with much broader developments that could be described as a democratization of partnership models. Likewise, the practices of heterosexual couples also came increasingly to rely on equality and fair negotiations. Partners had to acknowledge and to respect each other's characters and wishes, trying "peacefully and democratically" to reach a compromise, for example when they happened to have different plans for the weekend, as an advice book from 1971 had it.[23] These tendencies toward an approximation between same- and different-sex partnership ideals and practices contributed to a gradual blurring of boundaries between homo- and heterosexuality within the ever broader field of sexual experimentation. Mr. Weber, born in 1943, claims, when interviewed in 2008, that the 1970s were characterized by an overarching urge to be sexually unconventional. Back then, he says, "it was embarrassing for straight people to be straight" and "everybody was a little bit gay."[24]

These convergences furthered the increasing normalization of homosexuality since the 1970s and paved the way for the legal reforms that occurred in the 1990s and 2000s. When paragraph 175 was finally removed from the criminal code in 1994, this attracted next to no public attention. One could say that the criminalization of same-sex desire had by then already far outlived the social conditions that had once allowed jurists and politicians to deem it a necessary provision. By 1994 the continuation of this legal discrimination against homosexuals was considered out of the question by representatives of all major parties. This unanimity resulted from numerous reasons, among them the fact that gay, lesbian, and straight couples had all come to live by standards that emphasized equality and fairness.

The law introducing same-sex civil partnerships in 2001 faced considerably more opposition. Demands for a legal measure recognizing the bonds between gay or lesbian spouses had been voiced intermittently since the 1980s.[25] They had gained public currency in the 1990s with the so-called *Aktion Standesamt* (action civil-registry). This campaign brought dozens of same-sex couples to file requests for marriage with registrar's offices throughout Germany and then publicized the official denials of the right to marry.

In spite of such efforts it was only after a government formed by the Social Democrats and the Greens took over from their Christian Democratic and Liberal predecessors in 1998 that the so-called *Lebenspartnerschaftsgesetz* (life-partnership law) was passed by the German parliament. Some gay and lesbian activists celebrated this piece of legislation as an emancipatory breakthrough; others criticized it as a decisive step in the normalization of homosexuality. The latter interpretation invites a revision of all too linear and optimistic narratives of liberalization. It refuses to praise the so-called sexual revolution as a catalyst for the acceptance of sexual diversity, reaching its apogee, as it were, in the institution of same-sex marriage. Highlighting normalizing tendencies rather involves critiques of the commercialization and of the neoliberal emphasis on flexibility in sexual and amorous matters that this process entailed.[26] Proponents of the normalization paradigm claim that what once was considered against the norm or "unnatural" is now integrated into a dynamic spectrum of normal behaviors.[27] This transition, it is argued, generated problematic effects on an individual level as it urged actors to aspire for ever higher levels of pleasure and success in a self-optimizing fashion.[28] From this point of view the possibility of same-sex marriage put increasing pressure on gays and lesbians to live up to the ideal of establishing and maintaining an emotionally gratifying long-term partnership.

Such criticisms of same-sex marriage have been voiced since the 1980s.[29] In most cases this institution was and is blamed for copying a heterosexual model and for stripping same-sex-desire of its transgressive qualities, fencing in its alleged unruliness. Such arguments fail to acknowledge two important aspects, though. First, heterosexual marriage has itself, not least because of the growing visibility of homosexual couples, been subject to redefinitions since the 1970s. Legal inequalities between husbands and wives have diminished and divorce has become an ever more widespread phenomenon. Simultaneously, concepts like free love or polyamory have also triggered debates about reforming the legal frames that regulated different-sex relationships.[30]

Second, the argument errs when it exclusively blames same-sex marriage for propelling the normalization of homosexualities, while ascribing anti-normalizing potentials to sex lives that involve frequently changing partners. Quite to the contrary, the appreciation of certain forms of promiscuity, especially within the gay scene, also enhanced the pressure to self-optimize in terms of attractiveness and generated normalizing effects and aspirations for the flexible lifestyle of an economically successful single or for an open relationship.[31] Normalization is thus not due to the increasing prominence of the marriage model alone, but rather to the combination of this development with a seemingly contradictory one that foregrounded brief affairs and encounters with different partners. This tandem of monogamous and promiscuous expectations and ambitions was in a way also reinforced by the debate about how gay men should react to and protect themselves against the threat of HIV infection. While some experts recommended only having sex with long-term partners, others advocated safer sex that allowed individuals to engage in intercourse with various partners in a responsible fashion.[32]

Ultimately it is exactly this twofold standard of a perfect love and sex life with one and with many persons that propelled the normalization of homosexualities and intensified the pressure for self-optimization. This somewhat contradictory juxtaposition made it difficult for individuals to successfully master all the challenges and enjoy all the pleasures a gay or lesbian life had to offer. This in turn increased the likelihood of "failure" and fostered feelings of anxiety and regret. Seen from a normalization point of view, liberalization and emancipation thus not only endowed men loving men and women loving women with new opportunities, but also burdened them with a set of new emotional problems.

Whether the emancipatory benefits outweigh the normalizing downsides of same-sex marriage remains an open question, but there can be no doubt about the favorable effects that the debate had on the public visibility of lesbians. The marriage discussion for the first time granted them a prominent place in arguments about the legal treatment of homosexuality. In West Germany and elsewhere, sex between women was rarely considered during discussions about criminalization or decriminalization. The dominant assumption was that lesbian sexuality did not involve penetration and was thus decisively less "dangerous" than sex between men. In 1957 the *Bundesverfassungsgericht* (the West German constitutional court) relied on this argument when it ruled that the different treatment of male and female homosexuality in the penal code did not violate the constitution's principle of gender equality.[33] After 1969, the law's focus on sexual encounters between male adults and adolescents or children continued to further lesbian invisibility, not least because feminists themselves explicitly denied the possibility of female pedophilia.[34]

Yet the call for same-sex marriage and the debate about queer families brought lesbian couples to the fore. For Mrs. Lehmann, one of my interviewees born in 1954, her wish to gain the right to marry was the trigger that moved her to engage politically as a lesbian in the first place. In 1994 she, her partner and other couples—gay and lesbian alike—founded an organization that demanded legal frameworks which would allow same-sex partners to share property and which would end discrimination against them when it came to inheritance tax and related matters. The *Aktion Standesamt* of

1992 likewise involved gay and lesbian couples on an equal footing, as Mr. Albrecht, born in 1960, remembers.

This shift in visibility also contributed to a decisive change in the emotional style that was publicly associated with men loving men and women loving women. In order to gain popular support for the marriage-for-everyone-claim, the campaign channeled images of gays and lesbians—having breakfast together, kissing each other good night, celebrating with their families, and so on—that highlighted tenderness and mutual responsibility. These qualities very much characterize the emotional landscape within which the debate about same-sex marriage evolved. Its proponents wanted to demonstrate that gay and lesbian couples shared the same joys and sorrows as heterosexual ones and that they therefore deserved the same degree of legal protection and privilege. Equal partners caring for each other were thus at the core of the emotional style that paved the way for the introduction of civil same-sex partnerships in 2001, and ultimately of gay marriage in 2017. And these enabling legal measures in turn shaped the emotional patterns and practices that gays and lesbians employed, either by encouraging couples to buy into the ideal of living happily ever after, or by explicitly refuting this model and stressing their independence—sexually and otherwise.

Retrospect: The ambivalent emotional ramifications of legal change

These observations once more highlight the complexity of the emotional effects that changes in the legal sphere trigger and the intricate ways in which feelings and laws interact with each other. In the history of same-sex relationships in West Germany, emotional patterns proved decisive in propelling developments in the legal sphere, while the law itself both prevented and encouraged particular feelings. Focusing on this interplay allows the analysis to trace the similarities and interdependencies between developments in the homo- and the heterosexual context that are often overlooked. It also enables the argument to detect the ambivalent effects of legal change at an everyday level, where emancipatory opportunities often emerged alongside normalizing pressures.

Ambivalences surface as well when examining the time-related feelings that are triggered by shifts in the legal sphere such as the introduction of civil partnerships and ultimately same-sex marriage. These amendments generated hope and optimism about a happy and harmonious future where sexual diversity would meet with widespread acceptance and recognition. Such positive outlooks can in fact provide fresh impetus to ongoing struggles for queer emancipation.

Retrospectively, these changes also generated regret and melancholia, though, directed toward the past. While some lament the disappearance of spaces and practices that were paramount when same-sex desire was still illegal and illicit, others sadly note that things that today are completely "normal" for young gays and lesbians were unthinkable in the time of their own youth. "I'm often a bit envious," says Mr. Meyer, born in 1943, "when I see these young people in those community centres … holding their hands and snogging …, I had nobody, when I was 14, 15, 16, 17, 18, 19, 20."[35]

This kind of regretful gaze into the past adds another layer of complexity to the history of laws regulating homosexuality. By employing a history of emotions approach this chapter has critiqued and revised the all too linear narratives of liberalization. It extended the purview of legal history by considering the wide-ranging and often ambiguous emotional implications of legal change between love and lust, rage and shame, hope and fear, pleasure and commitment. Mr. Meyer's present-day envy and retrospective grief now ultimately allow for addressing one further dimension that counters the clear-cut linearity of progress.

Queer approaches to temporality have emphasized the untimeliness of sexual alterity and same-sex desire's deviation from the generational linearity implied in heterosexual reproduction.[36] In the quoted passage, Mr. Meyer performs a queer narrative twist in exactly this sense that elicits highly confusing temporal as well as emotional patterns. The mutual love others perform in the present coincides with his envy, which is in turn linked to memories of his past isolation, thus creating multivoiced resonances that seem simultaneously to mitigate and exacerbate his current loneliness. This intricate entanglement shows that indignation at bygone injustice and hope for a better future are by no means the only feelings that inform queer history. Consolatory longing for former troubles, preemptive contempt for coming achievements, and many other such attitudes play a role as well. Taking this emotional and temporal complexity into account can only benefit past as well as future struggles for affecting legal change.

Notes

1 Bastian Brauns, "Merkel adoptiert die Ehe für alle," *Zeit online*, June 27, 2017, www.zeit.de/gesellschaft/zeitgeschehen/2017-06/angela-merkel-ehe-fuer-alle-gewissensfrage (accessed May 15, 2018).
2 Kate Connolly, "Germany to Quash Historical Convictions of Gay Men," *Guardian*, May 11, 2016, www.theguardian.com/world/2016/may/11/germany-quash-historical-convictions-gay-men-criminalised-law (accessed May 15, 2018).
3 On the intricacies of shame, see David M. Halperin and Valerie Traub, eds., *Gay Shame* (Chicago: University of Chicago Press, 2009).
4 See Deborah B. Gould, *Moving Politics: Emotion and Act Up's Fight against Aids* (Chicago: University of Chicago Press, 2009).
5 On emotions as liminal phenomena, see Benno Gammerl, "Emotional Styles – Concepts and Challenges," *Rethinking History* 16, no. 2 (2012): 161–175. On the interplay between law and emotions, see the special issue of *the Journal of Social History* 51 (2017): 219–312.
6 On these ambiguities, see Benno Gammerl and Volker Woltersdorff, "'Sie ham mir ein Gefühl geklaut...'. Queer-feministische Perspektiven auf Bewegungen zwischen Sex und Gefühl," *Freiburger Zeitschrift für Geschlechterstudien* 20, no. 2 (2014): 27–41. Jeffrey Weeks, Brian Heaphy, and Catherine Donovan, *Same-sex Intimacies: Families of Choice and other Life Experiments* (London: Routledge, 2001).
7 See, for example, Michael Kandora, "Homosexualität und Sittengesetz," in *Wandlungsprozesse in Westdeutschland. Belastung*, Integration, *Liberalisierung 1945–1980*, ed. Ulrich Herbert (Göttingen: Wallstein, 2002), 379–401.

8   See Craig Griffiths, "Sex, Shame and West German Gay Liberation," *German History* 34, no. 3 (2016): 445–467.
9   Jens Dobler, *Wie öffentliche Moral gemacht wird. Die Einführung des § 175 in das Strafgesetzbuch 1871* (Hamburg: Männerschwarm, 2014).
10 Michael Schwartz, ed., *Homosexuelle im Nationalsozialismus. Neue Forschungsperspektiven zu Lebenssituationen von lesbischen, schwulen, bi-, trans- und intersexuellen Menschen 1933 bis 1945* (München: Oldenbourg, 2014).
11 Mr. Melling, int. 1, seq. 24; see also int. 1, seq. 20. Every respondent was interviewed twice (int. 1 and 2). The sequence numbers (seq.) refer to the particular passage of the transcript. All interviewees' names are pseudonyms. See also https://www.mpib-berlin.mpg.de/en/research/history-of-emotions/project-anders-fuhlen/the-study-and-first-results-in-german (accessed May 15, 2018). All translations from German sources are by the author.
12 Mr. Kuhn, int. 1, seq. 260.
13 Mr. Kuhn, int. 1, seq. 272.
14 Mr. Kuhn, int. 1, seq. 266 (emphasis in the original).
15 See Gammerl and Woltersdorff, "Sie ham mir ein Gefühl geklaut …."
16 O.Z., "Eine Antwort auf den Beitrag der Oktobernummer," *Der Weg* 11, no. 11 (1961): 248–249, 248.
17 Foltro (pseud.), "Ist die Erotik unser tägliches Brot?," *Der Weg* 11, no. 10 (1961): 224–225, 225.
18 Friedrich Wilhelm Foerster, *Lebensführung. Ein Buch für junge Menschen*, revised edition (Mainz: Mathias-Grünewald-Verlag, 1961), 147 and 174.
19 Jochen Fischer, *Nicht Sex sondern Liebe. Eine Orientierungshilfe für junge Menschen* (Hamburg: Furche-Verlag, 1966), 12f.
20 See Anon., "Die Bremer Pfingsteingabe," *Der Weg* 11, no. 6 (1961): 133–138.
21 See for example Hans Daniel, "Eine feste Freundschaft hat viel für sich," *Don* 3, no. 6 (1972): 32–33.
22 See for example Anon., "Gedanken über die Freundschaft," *Don* 4, no. 4 (1973): 24. For a critique of hierarchical relationship models, see also Wolfgang Müller, "Radikale Emanze," *Don* 10, no. 2 (1979): 24.
23 Kurt Seelmann, *Zwischen 15 und 19. Information über sexuelle und andere Fragen des Erwachsenwerdens* (München and Basel: Ernst Reinhardt Verlag, 1971), 215–216.
24 Mr. Weber, int. 1, seq. 111.
25 For early requests for same-sex marriage see Anon., "Homo-Heirat," *Don* 10, no. 1 (1979): 13. Anon., "Sozialversicherung erkennt erstmals Lesbierinnenpaar an," *Lesbenstich* 4, no. 2 (1983): 34.
26 For such critiques see Ilona Bubeck, ed., *Unser Stück vom Kuchen? Zehn Positionen gegen die Homo-Ehe* (Berlin: Querverlag, 2000).
27 Peter-Paul Bänziger and Julia Stegmann, "Politisierungen und Normalisierungen: Sexualitätsgeschichte des zwanzigsten Jahrhunderts im deutschsprachigen Raum," in *H-Soz-u-Kult*, November 5, 2010, http://hsozkult.geschichte.hu-berlin.de/forum/2010-11-001 (accessed May 15, 2018).
28 For similar developments in a heterosexual context see Christiane Reinecke, "Statistiken der Liebe, oder: Dr. Kinsey fragt die Frauen. Umfrageforschung und ihre mediale Vermarktung in transnationaler Perspektive," *Comparativ* 21, no. 4 (2011): 29–44. Lutz Sauerteig, "'Wie soll ich es nur anstellen, ohne etwas falsch zu machen?' Der Rat der Bravo in Sachen Sex in den sechziger und siebziger Jahren," in *Fragen*

Sie Dr. Sex! Beratungskommunikation und die mediale Konstruktion des Sexuellen, ed. Peter-Paul Bänziger et al. (Frankfurt/Main: Suhrkamp, 2010), 123-158.

29 See Anon., "Ist Klappensex was Böses?," *Rosa Flieder* 23 (1981): 46-45. Anon., "Pro und Contra. Sollen Schwule heiraten?," *Du&Ich* 13, no. 12 (1981): 69. Anon., "Scene-intern," *Lesbenstich* 7, no. 4 (1986): 1.

30 Christian Klesse, "Polyamory and Its 'Others': Contesting the Terms of Non-Monogamy," *Sexualities* 9, no. 5 (2006): 565-583. Ingrid Bauer, Christa Hämmerle and Gabriella Hauch, eds., *Liebe und Widerstand. Ambivalenzen historischer Geschlechterbeziehungen* (Wien: Böhlau 2005).

31 See, for example, Anon., "Rechnen Sie Ihren Sex-Quotienten aus!," *Don* 10, no. 10 (1979): 20-21 and 52. Anon., "Was ist Klappensexualität?," *Rosa Flieder* 23 (1981): 34-36. Anon., "Risiko hat seinen Reiz – gemeinsam lieben, getrennt leben," *Don* 15, no. 3 (1984): 52-53.

32 Magdalena Beljan, "Aids-Geschichte als Emotionsgeschichte," *Aus Politik und Zeitgeschichte* 46 (2015): 25-31.

33 Christiane Leidinger, *Lesbische Existenz 1945-1969* (Berlin: Senatsverwaltung für Arbeit, Integration und Frauen, 2015), 28-29.

34 Alice Schwarzer, "Wie frei macht Pädophilie? Interview mit Günter Amendt," *Emma* 4, no. 4 (1980): 26-31, 29.

35 Mr. Meyer, int. 2, seq. 400.

36 Carolyn Dinshaw, et al., "Theorizing Queer Temporalities: A Roundtable Discussion," *GLQ* 13, no. 2-3 (2007): 177-195.

10

The Sexual (Geo)Politics of Loyalty: Homosexuality and Emotion in Cold War Security Policy

Kate Davison

It is no secret that the biggest concentration of homosexuals can be found in the diplomatic services of Western countries. [...] The Soviet Intelligence officers were amazed at the sense of mutual consideration and true loyalty among homosexuals.
Alexander Orlov, Handbook of Intelligence and Guerrilla Warfare, *1963*[1]

On September 12, 1962, British civil servant John William Vassall was arrested in London and charged under the Official Secrets Act. In 1954 while on assignment to Moscow, Vassall had become drunk at a party, was photographed in "a homosexual orgy," and subsequently blackmailed into spying for the Soviet Union.[2] On October 22, 1962 (the same day that news of the Cuban missile crisis broke), he was sentenced to eighteen years in prison, and branded a traitor. This breach of national security was an embarrassment for the conservative Macmillan government. After a decade of positive security vetting in staff recruitment, how had they failed to detect his sexual perversion? The report of the investigative tribunal, released on April 25, 1963, found that "there was nothing either in Vassall's conduct or conversation that indicated even to a sharp observer a man addicted to homosexual practices."[3] The problem of inadequate detection methods was seized upon by the *Sunday Mirror*, which published a contemptuous how-to guide for the Admiralty, Foreign Office, and MI5 under the heading "How to Spot a Possible Homo."[4] "They are everywhere," the article panicked, "and they can be anybody." Had Vassall's sexuality and his "vain and greedy" demeanor been detected, went the narrative, so would his likely betrayal have been.

Vassall was by no means the only person to have spied for the Soviet Union, but around the globe, the particular circumstance of his case—that is, his homosexuality—lent renewed fervor to hard questions about whether traitorous behavior could be predicted in sexual orientation, following earlier revelations and public profiling of the bi- and homosexual orientations of the Cambridge defectors Guy Burgess and Donald Maclean. It symbolically reflected anxious concerns in this period within both government administration and medical science around how homosexuality and homosexual behavior could be detected, determined, and handled or treated—especially among psychiatrists influenced by behaviorism—and, indeed, whether the Communists were better at it.[5]

This chapter analyzes how homosexuality as a Cold War issue extended beyond the Anglophone world and across the so-called iron curtain. Because the "homosexual" seemed to fit unnoticed into society more easily than other "deviants," invisibility and detection became direct concerns for security agencies—indeed, the entire spying apparatus was built upon disguise, deception, and the ability to assimilate unnoticed. Security and intelligence agencies sought expert advice, at first from psychiatrists and medical professionals, but later, influenced by behaviorism, firsthand observation of homosexuals' emotional behavior and motivations.

We know from the work of David K. Johnson, Patrick Higgins, and Gary Kinsman and Patrizia Gentile, among others, that the phenomenon of pursuing anti-homosexual policies in connection with national security was a trend common across Anglophone countries in the postwar decades on the basis that they constituted a "security risk," reaching a climax in the early to mid-1960s before being destabilized by the Gay Liberation Movement.[6] This process, known in the United States as the "lavender scare," came to be typified by the portrayal of homosexuality as a "character weakness" or "character defect" that seriously jeopardized its bearer's ability to exhibit loyalty to the nation or sovereign. Homosexuals, somewhat akin Communists, constituted "a select clique which extends internationally," as the Australian security chief Charles Spry put it in April 1964, loyal to one another rather than their country; that is, they could not be trusted with state secrets.[7]

Collectively, the work of these scholars gives us a broad overview of the unique domestic circumstances of such practices. Yet while interstate entanglements have been treated as axiomatic given the national security context of these homophobic policies, a more attentive transnational approach to the history of homosexuality can offer new insights into the geopolitical dynamics of the Cold War. There is a growing body of scholarship, part of the so called "transnational turn" in the history of sexuality, which seeks to transcend a seemingly still-existing Berlin Wall in narratives of the sexual past; this new work shows that there is much potential for comparative research, not least in problematizing the Western-centric explanatory framework that has characterized much sexuality scholarship to date.[8] Furthermore, there are important lessons in these new histories for how we comprehend the role of queer sexuality and gender in present-day geopolitical dynamics.[9]

It is also worth revisiting these historical developments using insights from the field of the history of emotions. As Dagmar Herzog observed in 2013, it is "not least because sexual matters evoke complicated feelings that human beings are, apparently, so politically and socially manipulable in this area"; nevertheless, historians have "too rarely reflected openly on this complicatedness when trying to explain why and how sexual cultures change."[10] While analyzing the connections made by security agencies between sexual deviance and disloyalty or untrustworthiness has been central to the work of several historians, to date this has not extended to the historicization of emotional concepts such as loyalty and trust themselves in light of changing understandings of sexuality and the body.

This chapter offers a close reading of two selected security documents: one from the files of Australian Security Intelligence Organisation (ASIO) and one allegedly created on behalf of the East German *Ministerium für Staatssicherheit* (MfS, commonly known by its abbreviation "Stasi"). By doing so, it is hoped that we can gain an insight not only into continuities and differences in how sexuality was approached by states in East and West, but also into how understandings of emotion were linked to understandings of sexuality, and seen to be relevant to a geopolitical security context. This will be preceded by a short discussion of theories of emotion and the body, and addressing the emerging historiography on concepts like loyalty and trust. Perhaps influenced by what Naoko Wake and colleagues have called the "behaviourist Zeitgeist"[11] of the mid-twentieth century, these security agencies sought advice on the identification of homosexuals by their emotional dispositions and behavior based on field observation (as distinct from psychiatric knowledge), indicating that understandings of both sexual and emotional orientations became ontologically bound up with one another. It is useful, therefore, to historicize postwar incoherence around whether homosexuality was a sign of psychosexual arrest, a physically detectable state, an emotional disposition, a genetic trait, or some other phenomenon.[12] In order to be of practical use in national security and/or espionage, to predict either their likelihood of betrayal or degree of utility, emotional and behavioral knowledge of homosexuals—knowing how they *feel*—was key.

Sexuality, the body, and emotions in international Cold War security policy

The analysis developed here has been influenced by theoretical developments within the history of emotions, particularly around the body. Monique Scheer advocates the use of a Bourdieuian approach through the concept of *habitus*, in order to overcome methodological and conceptual difficulties seen in the dissonance between biologist and cognitivist definitions of emotion.[13] According to Scheer, historians of emotion have tended toward a cognitive framework whereby emotions are defined primarily as mental processes or judgments, due to an assumption that in order to historicize emotions, they must be separated from a seemingly ahistorical or unchanging bodily organism. Bourdieu's concept of habitus, by contrast, refers to the effect of structural processes by which human agents come to *both* embody and perpetuate social relations through practices.[14] Another method suggests that historians look for patterns of "emotional styles." According to Benno Gammerl, whereas "emotional habitus" implies a unitary ontological state, the concept of "emotional styles" enables a plurality of emotional strategies by actors depending on location and context.[15] It recognizes that emotional patterns and practices develop within "spatial constellations" that "depend on historically specific economic, cultural and political conditions and are thus subject to variability."[16]

These methods can assist us to unpack transnational Cold War attempts to develop a taxonomy of the homosexual based not only on body, appearance, or psychology but emotions as well. A further method proposed by Barbara Rosenwein more closely addresses the social relations of emotion through the concept of "emotional communities," groups built around "fundamental assumptions, values, goals, feeling rules, and accepted modes of expression"; like Benedict Anderson's "imagined communities," they are "created and reinforced by ideologies, teachings and common presuppositions," yet offer a specific focus on bodies and emotions and how they manifest collectively or socially.[17]

Together, these approaches can help us to analyze and historicize notions of sexuality, body, and emotion evident in security discourse, and how they contributed to the construction of both hegemonic and subordinate emotional communities, in relation to geopolitical and nation-building processes. Was loyalty or disloyalty, for example, a feeling, style of behavior, or practice, and could it be detected in the body or in sexual orientation? Is this what enabled the construction of postwar nations as emotional communities that excluded sexual "deviance"? In applying the methods outlined here to an investigation of Cold War sexual politics, we can begin to identify how various actors (both governmental and their subjects of observation) were cognizant of the possibility and necessity of employing a variety of emotional styles, and that it may have been precisely this aspect that was so concerning to especially Western security agencies, perhaps explaining their attempt to pin down a definition of a homosexual habitus for the purposes of national security policy.

Definitions and dispositions

Like all emotions, loyalty, trust, patriotism, and other emotional concepts relevant to the geopolitical sphere are historically dynamic ideas subject to ongoing definitional debate.[18] The question of whether they properly constitute "emotions" is far from settled, yet it is arguable whether such categorization is even necessary. The philosopher John Kleinig suggests that while loyalty certainly entails "strong feelings and devotion," the absence of a verb to match the feeling one has when one feels loyalty means that "the test of loyalty is conduct," and he therefore describes it as "a practical disposition."[19] In tracing the history of trust, Ute Frevert suggests that under the conditions of modernity, due to altered class compositions and political formations, trust emerged as "an attitude, an emotion, or emotional practice" in a social sense, whereas it had previously entailed a primarily spiritual connection with God.[20] For the purposes of this paper, these concepts will be treated as practical emotional dispositions: attitudes implying a certain set of behaviors and feelings involving the body, which then interact with other concepts that fit more straightforwardly into the category of emotion.

This approach is useful when thinking about the relationship between emotions and social rules governing moral conduct. Scholars broadly agree that there is a decidedly moral element to concepts like trust and loyalty.[21] International relations scholar Torsten Michel points out that in the absence of this moral element, which can exist only between human actors (as distinct from nation-states, for example), one can no longer speak of "trust" but rather "reliance"—that is, trust is a human phenomenon.[22] Yet the moral element can also be more explicit. For example, historian Nachman Ben-Yehuda has described betrayal, which is "intimately connected to both loyalty and trust" as "a form of deviance."[23] Ute Frevert suggests that trust is commonly found to involve mutual cooperation and dependence, and is also highly contingent on matters of class, age, sexual orientation, and other markers of distinction.[24] In defining national character, such mutual cooperation might conceivably imply upholding a certain moral framework or sexual mode in practice, whereby trust would constitute a kind of covenant to maintain a certain mode of intimacy based on heterosexual reproduction. In this framework, it would be a kind of betrayal to deviate sexually, and it is precisely this idea that emerges in Western security discourse.

Methodology and context

It is difficult to overstate the importance of security documents to how the anti-homosexual atmosphere within Cold War security policy unfolded. Gary Kinsman has highlighted such texts were "mobilized" by state security regimes in ways that proved devastating to the lives of their subjects: they formed "an integral part of the construction of heterosexual hegemony."[25] Naoko Shibusawa, noting the "slim documentation" available to historians interested in the postwar anti-homosexual security panic, argues it is therefore necessary to "analyze more deeply" the few documents we do have, especially from the perspective of investigating the sexual politics of "Empire," because they often "articulate[ ] what was seldom articulated in a coherent argument": the perceived connections between homosexuality and the "decline" of the nation-state.[26] Security policy and practices thus offer a useful case study in identifying precisely what moral ideas were or were not connected to ideas of nationhood or the body politic.

Echoing Kinsman, Shibusawa reminds us that such memos are not mere administrative artefacts; rather, they are "imaginative acts" with palpable consequences for those affected.[27] While any claims about the material consequences of the two documents analyzed here can only be speculative, it is nevertheless valid to view them as *suggestive* of "coherent" views held by the organizations that commissioned them, and indicative of how dominant moral politics seeped into strategic geopolitical considerations. They also offer insights into the impact that these "imaginative acts" were able to have *within* the security and intelligence establishment.

For example, from a transnational perspective there emerges a sense that, sometime in the late 1950s and early 1960s, an interest in behaviorist approaches based on longer-term observation of homosexual networks became more prevalent than medical or psychiatric diagnoses. Documents produced in the United States between 1950 and 1955 indicate that psychiatric advice was important.[28] Likewise in Canada, Dr. Frank Wake, a professor of psychiatry, was specifically employed by the government to develop homosexual detection methods, after a 1959 Security Panel memorandum warned of the extreme security risk homosexuals posed. Common characteristics included "instability, willing self-deceit, defiance towards society, a tendency to surround oneself with persons of similar propensities … none of which inspire the confidence one would hope to have in persons required to fill positions of trust and responsibility."[29]

This memorandum remains one of the most coherent examples of the conflation of sexual deviance with an inherent or in-built emotional disposition of disloyalty and untrustworthiness in the Western intelligence establishment. It was this description that was quoted by ASIO Director Charles Spry in his submission to have "Communist sympathisers" and those with "character defects"—homosexuals—banned from the Australian public service.[30] But by the early 1960s, security agencies were seeking more practical, direct, and eyewitness knowledge of homosexual milieus.

Security-intelligence practices and emotions across the Iron Curtain

The two documents selected for analysis here include one briefing paper entitled "Some Notes on Homosexuality," created by ASIO as part of the background research for its call to ban homosexual employees from high-security positions, and one allegedly recreated from an original draft report for the MfS in East Germany on the "usability of homosexuals within an intelligence framework."[31]

ASIO's Submission 199 in 1964 was the first time in Australia that "homosexuality" was explicitly identified as a discrete category of security risk. Originally drafted in 1952 with a focus on Communists, homosexuality was later elevated to the primary threat. For Spry, the recent Vassall case was proof that the Russians "were successfully exploiting homosexuality for the purpose of espionage," a claim that was bolstered in 1963 by ex-NKVD major and defector to the United States Alexander Orlov.[32] Spry believed that not only could Communists adeptly identify the weak links in the Western services, but that they employed "a group of homosexuals for the express purpose of compromising Westerners" and could actually induce homosexuality in those already displaying other weaknesses such as drunkenness.[33] ASIO sought an "expert" opinion—but rather than consulting medical and psychiatric professionals, they commissioned "a male homosexual" to advise them, whose own homosexuality constituted the core of his expertise. Across seventeen pages of transcribed text, the author (whose identity remains redacted) offers ASIO officials a detailed overview of different kinds of homosexuals, their aspirations, feelings, motivations, behaviors, and likely allegiances—in other words their emotional habitus—within the context of their relationship to "Queen and country" and society at large.

The German document was created a bit later, with the intention to offer "an assessment of which types of homosexuals would in principle be worthy of consideration for intelligence work."[34] The title page identifies it as a "Report on a draft prepared for the MfS-Berlin during the period of 1962–3 at the request of MfS Officer WOLF," reconstructed three years later in "Bonn, October/November 1965" by the author after his "escape" to West Germany.[35] These details contain a strong implication that it was reconstructed for the *Bundesnachrichtendienst* (BND), the West German security and intelligence agency.[36] This aspect itself requires further investigation, but raises questions about as-yet under-researched contrasts and connections between the two countries in the history of sexuality.[37] In comparison with ASIO's "Notes," this report was a much longer dossier—surviving now only in truncated form. At first glance it seems to confirm Spry's assertion that the intelligence services of the Communist Bloc countries had established targeted commandos of homosexual "Romeos."[38]

Written in very different political contexts by authors with different relationships to the matter at hand, the similarity in their explicitly emotional—as distinct from psychological—descriptions of their homosexual subjects is striking. Read side by side, they serve as veritable catalogues of how the "amateur expert" authors understood homosexuality in emotional terms, but also how the state apparatus itself viewed homosexuals' emotions with respect to geopolitical and intelligence concerns. Where they differ is in considerations of national or political loyalty. While the "Report on a draft" for the MfS speaks of trying to flush out individual citizens guilty of anti-state bias, its author refrains from drawing a general conclusion that homosexuals *per se* were anti-Communist, indicating that political loyalty took priority over sexual orientation. By contrast, the ASIO document is deeply preoccupied with the connection between sexual deviance and civilization, national honor, pride, and loyalty, suggesting a more ontologically integrated belief that homosexual desire was a key indicator for eventual disloyalty.

It should be noted that such documents entail critical methodological challenges for the historian, given the scarcity of reliable information on their provenance. ASIO's "Notes on homosexuality," though contained in the ASIO file on Submission 199, is not directly referred to in any correspondence, nor is it in the Submission itself. The provenance of the German "Report on a draft" is even more elusive. According to an introductory note by historian Florian Mildenberger, it was handed to him by the widow of a personal acquaintance who had worked for the BND, yet Mildenberger himself was not in a position to conduct further research on the document's background.[39] In anticipation that further research will yield more reliable information, both documents nevertheless offer a rich discursive source for insights into the symbolic connections drawn between sexual deviance and emotions or emotional dispositions within a Cold War context.

ASIO: "Some notes on homosexuality"

All of what we know about the author of this document is by his own admission: an Oxford-educated journalist of forty, he had spent five years in the UK from 1946 to 1951, evinced an obvious interest in literary culture and, politically, was a "Tory by temperament." A willing and generous consultant, he emphasized to his ASIO interlocutors that he possessed no medical training or specialist knowledge.

Throughout the notes, emotional factors are central to his description of the homosexual habitus. The author repeatedly refers to desires, senses, and feelings in describing likely motivations for a homosexual in his or her relationship with state and nation. These include loneliness, shame, pride, trust, cynicism, suspicion, self-love, or esteem (*amour-propre*), patriotism, resentfulness, embarrassment, cowardice, courage, spitefulness, fear (of police), panic, a yearning for national belonging, and what he calls "bullyable temperament[s]." A list of behavior-based "signs which lead one to suspect a person of Prevailing Homosexuality" are emotionally evocative, such as drinking "alone in pubs" and keeping "a dog which is large or of a reputedly ferocious breed."

Several direct questions appear to have been put to him by ASIO, ranging from the general—"Is homosexuality a voluntary condition?" and "Are 'queers' physical cowards?"—to more pragmatic queries designed to aid detection—"Is there some mystic link which always enables an homosexual to know and discern another at sight," and "Can one infallibly detect a 'queer' to refuse his application for a Service or afterwards to screen him from Security-sensitive Material?" Many of these questions echoed those being asked in this period by psychiatrists debating treatment methods and conducting early behavioral research into sexual reorientation.[40] The author's primary commission, however, was to give ASIO an educated opinion on the likelihood of homosexuals to betray their country, by either committing treason or allowing themselves to be exposed to blackmail. He offered practical steps to be taken in "Breaking Down a Homosexual who is Suspected of Being Subject to Espionage Blackmail," and enumerates general "Points Apt to be Helpful to Security Officials." One final section, "Homosexuality and Patriotism," concluded that due to their sense of social exclusion, homosexuals were even more likely to feel patriotic and were no more likely to become traitors than their fellow citizens.

These questions and section headings speak volumes about the emotional focus of ASIO's inquiries. Nowhere in the Submission 199 files is there any reference to ASIO officials consulting medical or scientific personnel—their priority was to gain an amateur expert's perspective based on firsthand experience. They did not accept all of their consultant's information at face value, however, intervening at several points in the transcription to dispute his claims. Despite the author's efforts to discourage the perception of homosexuals as a homogenous and shady group, insisting that "differences of race, creed, language, class, etc. are as divisive between homosexuals … as between quite heterosexual people[; t]here is no freemasonry," ASIO was of a different view: "(NOTE by Headquarters: This is not agreed)."

Although the author in principle rejected the concept of a homosexual typology, he nevertheless offered a rudimentary outline of three basic categories. Non-covert types included "screamers"—those who "tacitly admit their condition," and were therefore probably "less dangerous … than the covert 'queer' whom you might never detect." The other two categories were covert types who were timid and less predictable, prone to desperate acts of "bumbling ineptitude." One covert type was likely to live a "peculiarly dangerous sex life … apt to bring him scandalously to the notice of the police," while the other might for medical reasons be "to all intents and purposes sexless," described euphemistically as a "confirmed bachelor," and therefore "quite safe and trustworthy." In other words, *active* homosexuality was linked to untrustworthiness—sexual deviants could be trusted only if they were medically celibate.

The main distinguishing feature between types was neither class nor cultural literacy or education, but the intensity of shame and loneliness felt by the individual, and their desire to restore dignity and pride. The author thus advocated that the ASIO interrogator should at least pass as a homosexual, because "one homosexual is far more likely to confide in another." Furthermore, "most people snared up in treason […] are likely to feel a strong need to confide in somebody": to secure cooperation, it was best "to save his pride and to win his confidence."

But shame and pride only came into play once the homosexual was already within the purview of ASIO—in terms of *motivations* for treason or patriotism, loneliness played a far greater role. Loneliness, the author cautioned, "can scarcely be over-emphasized," especially in "covert" homosexuals. "It is far easier to be celibate," he opined profoundly, "than to be lonely in the desolate sense known to the 'queer'". It was therefore a crucial emotion for security officers to exploit, yet it could just as well be a point of extreme vulnerability. Homosexuals could be very trusting of those who might have ulterior motives, and although generally "open-eyed" when it came to blackmail, "security blackmail" might be different, because it was more "artful": "it studies the subject more and knows better the kinds of disclosure—to family, to normal friends, to his service, etc.—the 'queer' is least willing to face." In other words, a long process of study, assessment, and groundwork was necessary if a strong enough feeling of trust was to be successfully induced in the "queer," but the same was true if he was to be induced to breach his loyalty to his country.

Contrary to ASIO assumptions, it was precisely this loneliness, this feeling of social exclusion and a sense of "deracination," that could lead a homosexual to feel patriotic, loyal, and to want to fulfil a "duty" to the nation. "Far from making them traitors," the author implored, this lack of belonging "usually makes them eager to belong to a Service, armed or otherwise, which will give them a clear and honourable place in the order of things where they were born." Candidly, he described his own act of providing these notes to ASIO as an attempt to find one such honorable place, as an antidote to his own loneliness.

It is thus perhaps unsurprising that the document was not referred to in the Submission. The author's responses contradicted Director Spry's belief in an international homosexual clique standing in opposition to national loyalty, and rejected the pathologizing idea that sexual deviance would, by default, lead to national betrayal. On the question of a transnational network of homosexuals, there was some truth in the idea—though not in the way ASIO feared. Themes of betrayal, blackmail, and patriotism were already being critically discussed in well-established homophile publications in both Europe and the United States, several of which had international subscriber lists.[41] These magazines and newsletters occasionally published one another's material proving the idea of information sharing; not out of national disloyalty, but solidarity and a belief in the right to sexual self-expression. Whether or not the American *ONE* magazine and the trilingual Swiss periodical *Der Kreis* (The Circle) reached audiences in the Eastern Bloc remains unclear and the likelihood negligible. The important point for ASIO's consultant was that immediate determinations of whether an individual was loyal or patriotic based on sexual practice or visual cues alone were impossible and would anyway be of little use. Far more important was a method of long-term observation of the subject's emotional habitus.

It is this kind of long view that was both recounted and further advocated by the German author of the "Report on a draft for the MfS-Berlin." This shared feature, as noted earlier, compels a comparative analysis that extends transnationally, particularly into the increased focus on field observations of behaviors and emotions. Importantly, it compels an analysis that avoids the trap of perpetuating the polarization that was so central to the Cold War ideological framework.[42] The influence of behaviorism in the study of sexuality appears to have enjoyed a significant transnational growth in the mid-twentieth-century human sciences, not least in the wake of Kinsey's reports on *Sexual Behavior in the Human Male* (1948) and *Female* (1953; German translations 1955 and 1954 respectively), extending to the development not only of technologies of detection and surveillance, but also of behavior modification techniques on both sides of the Berlin Wall.[43] As the following comparative discussion of the East German MfS document shows, the behaviorist framework dovetailed neatly with the empirical imperatives of Cold War security concerns in relation to the uses or dangers of homosexuality, albeit with very different policy implications.

"Report on a draft prepared for the MfS-Berlin"

Although the context of its creation is more ambiguous, this twenty-page report indicates a more sustained period of observation than that undertaken by the ASIO consultant, labelled "Assignment D." Following his move from Dresden to Berlin in 1958, the author himself recommended the investigation to the MfS (this was the same year in which Walter Ulbricht, in his speech to the 5th congress of the ruling Socialist Unity Party, had exhorted East German citizens to "live cleanly and decently"[44]). Written up in 1965 but based on an earlier text from 1962–3, the report thus represents four to five years of fieldwork, for which it was necessary to start from scratch, with the help of the East Berlin vice squad. The author's brief did not rule out sexual contact as part of his field research, if beneficial and/or necessary.

The only known extant copy of the "Report on a draft" is incomplete, but the heading of the second section where the text breaks off indicates that it was originally much longer and more comprehensive, with sections organized according to homosexual "type." There is little indication of what specific circumstances motivated the author to recommend the survey; however, Jens Gieseke has noted how, starting in 1957, the MfS expanded its remit from security concerns to a "breadth and variety" of issues and tasks that "extended well beyond its classic secret-police and intelligence-gathering functions of the initial years."[45]

The author held that there were "certain psychological idiosyncrasies" and "behaviours typical to such persons," but most crucially, the instincts, feelings, and emotions he believed were common to homosexuals meant that they often already behaved in a way that is akin to intelligence workers. The homosexual's "natural aptitude for covert conduct ... the gift of imagination, a general ability to fit in or blend in, and an instinct for the emotional impulses of [his] contacts" made him a worthy potential recruit. Sexual perversion would be advantageous in compromise-operations, given that "such types are only very rarely able to fall in love ... meaning the risk of exposure is limited." Widespread social condemnation "coerces" homosexuals "into a way of behaving that, by its very nature, is similar to that practiced within the intelligence service," a similarity that even extended to his "covert conduct in choosing a partner, in the carrying out of sexual activity, in the formation of social networks, and so forth." In other words, homosexual men and spies had both developed a kind of habitus that encompassed not only professional behavior but emotional decisions and interaction as well.

Not every type of homosexual was equipped with the emotional skill-set required for intelligence work, however. Setting aside the minority of men whose homosexuality was "genetically determined," men exhibiting "acquired" homosexuality were of the greatest interest, because the traits required for this line of work were "traits acquired through assimilation," and could easily be reoriented for intelligence purposes. Fear of public attention, anxiety to fit in or assimilate, shame arising from failed efforts to suppress or displace desire that could possibly lead to suicidal feelings, and a yearning for close friendship were all key aspects for the intelligence establishment to comprehend in their subject of observation, as well as the fact that when the subject did find an "ideal candidate" for intimate partnership, he would be eager for his partner to "share in his private and occupational or professional experiences."

The homosexual's ability to induce trust meant that he could be strategically deployed in operations targeting women, given that the contact often "unconsciously feels like she is understood" by homosexuals. Likewise, men with acquired homosexuality would often "trust women with their most intimate secrets" and for this reason female intelligence workers could be deployed to make contact with homosexual men.

While the word "loneliness" [*Einsamkeit*] does not appear, the author asserts that the homosexual constantly seeks society within homosexual circles that serve "the individual's need for social contact." It also served his need "for information relevant to his orientations," which was why the homosexual was in possession of so much valuable information (to the MfS) about those in his milieu and beyond. It was thus crucial for intelligence officials to properly grasp the almost "seismographic sensitivity" of the homosexual along with their "need to share."

The substantive section of the surviving copy focuses on what the author calls the "transvestite homosexual"—not to be confused with the "true transvestite." This type—due to his "obsession with personal hygiene, the craving for admiration, vanity, and so on"—was well represented in fashion, theater, and retail, often rising through the ranks to "higher" social networks. His "tremendous" need for information meant that he knew "everything about everyone, down to the most intimate details [… and] his knowledge about homosexuals and their private lives [was] not confined by any state or national border." Yet while this homosexual type could be used well as an unknowing source of information, his "need to share" meant that he was rarely appropriate for recruitment.

Here, it was emotional, sexual, and material needs, rather than any moral, legal, or political considerations, that motivated him. Even "absolute opponents" of the GDR were more likely to be apolitical than actively sympathetic to the West. It was of utmost importance, argued the author, for the MfS agent to understand the homosexual's "emotional world," which was intensely felt and often polarized. While his spectrum of emotional expression was narrow, "the depth-effect [was] all the more intensive." Establishing trust and gathering information were relatively easy, provided the MfS agent "possesses precise knowledge about the mentality and modes of behaviour of homosexuals."

From the document itself, it is impossible to ascertain the extent of the author's knowledge of psychiatric and medical literature, aside from a brief reference to Freud. Was he, for example, familiar with the work of East German physician, sexologist, and neurologist Rudolf Klimmer, West German sociologist Helmut Schelsky, and physician and sexologist Hans Giese?[46] Was he familiar even with the work of Czechoslovakian psychiatrist Kurt Freund, whose research on diagnostics and treatment of homosexuality was first published in German by the GDR, and who had played such a pivotal role in the decriminalization of homosexuality in Czechoslovakia in 1961?[47] The absence of citations to medical literature is likewise conspicuous in ASIO's commissioned briefing paper, and although the Australian author made repeated cultural references, there is no indication that he or his commissioners sought information from available medical, psychological, and psychiatric publications.[48]

These questions notwithstanding, the German author's overall recommendation for the MfS was for long-term observation of the homosexual's emotional motivations, in order to ultimately put them to use for state interests. Importantly, he drew similar conclusions to ASIO's amateur expert: his assertion that "the homosexual possesses a kind of special receptor for the psychological impulses of men" echoes the "mystic" sixth sense mentioned in the ASIO "Notes." He further concluded that homosexuals had better skills in terms of emotional manipulation, but were simultaneously more emotionally vulnerable in terms of needing close companionship and friendship, and, due to their conditions of social isolation and loneliness, had already developed an emotional habitus that closely resembled that of the spy.

Conclusions

Despite the widely divergent contexts in which these two documents were produced, their major agreement, based on firsthand observation rather than medical or psychiatric knowledge, was that there was a particular affinity between the emotional disposition of the homosexual and the requirements and dangers of the national security environment. In the East, it was thought that the homosexual's abilities to hide true emotion and to be particularly attuned to (especially) other men's emotional needs—skills borne of and necessitated by his social isolation—meant these people were especially suited to intelligence work or, at the very least, exploitation by intelligence agencies as a source of information both domestically and abroad. For ASIO, it was feared that the homosexual's emotional disposition—his unpredictability in terms of national loyalty and general untrustworthiness—was precisely the thing that was feared within a security framework, yet their expert consultant emphasized loneliness, rather than perversion, as a key motivating factor for homosexuals to want to seek society and fulfil a service to his country of birth.

Yet a major divergence between the two documents is over the question of loyalty. The "Report on a draft" for the East German MfS barely touches upon the question of national loyalty. The only mention of the homosexual's emotional relationship with the state (as distinct from his emotional habitus or his emotional relations with peers) is in the author's assertion that the "transvestite homosexual" is "indifferent" to politics, and that "genuine civic attitudes are not within [his] purview." It was not political motivations that led numerous homosexual men to flee the GDR, but pragmatic considerations of the possibilities of emotional and sexual fulfilment; and yet "anti-Socialist" views were not thought to constitute a characteristic peculiar to the homosexual.

This striking difference calls into question the motivations of the Western security and intelligence establishment in their construction of the homosexual subject as virtually incapable of feeling loyalty to the nation, or at least adhering to its requirements in action or practice. In the Anglophone countries, the assumed emotional dispositions of homosexuals were not deduced from particular external behaviors such as gestures, weeping, laughing, facial expressions, other forms of body language indicating anger, devotion, or love, but rather the homosexual himself was considered to be constitutionally—that is, internally—emotionally unsuited to national service. Certainly this tone was set by developments in the early 1950s in the United States: one succinct representation of this theory was that of Rosie Goldschmidt Waldeck, published in 1952 and read into the US *Congressional Record*. Waldeck argued that in fact blackmail was not the key issue, but rather that homosexuals, "by the very nature of their vice ... belong to a sinister, mysterious, and efficient International" and, "[w]elded together by the identity of their forbidden desires, of their strange, sad needs, habits, danger, not to mention their outrageously fatuous vocabulary," constituted "a world-wide conspiracy against society."[49] Given the US role in setting the tone for Western allies in the Cold War in general, it is not surprising that this ideological position trickled down to other countries, especially in the wake of the Vassall scandal.

Despite this major difference, security agencies on both sides of the Iron Curtain in the early 1960s actively sought out expert descriptions of the emotional habitus of the homosexual. One of the key concerns on both sides was determining how homosexuality could be detected—both sides were keen to establish whether there were visual markers on the body, or whether longer, more emotional observation required to establish just what relevance or use the homosexual subject could have for intelligence purposes. The expert opinions consulted on both sides closely echoed one another in rejecting a pathologized or medical-diagnostic view of homosexuality as "perversion," instead creating a detailed and complex emotional typology of varying degrees and manifestations of subjects with homosexual orientations.

Notes

1 Alexander Orlov, *Handbook of Intelligence and Guerrilla Warfare* (Ann Arbor: University of Michigan Press, 1963).
2 NAA A4940/1 Item C643, "Communists and Communist Sympathisers in the Employ of the Commonwealth—Policy."
3 Cmnd 2009, "Report of the Tribunal Appointed to Inquire into the Vassall Case and Related Matters," *H.M.S.O.* (1963); "Vassall Case (Tribunal's Report)," House of Commons Debate, May 7, 1963, *Hansard*, vol. 677, cc240–372.
4 "How to Spot a Possible Homo," *Sunday Mirror*, April 28, 1963.
5 On medical debates, see, for example, Desmond Curran and Denis Parr, "Homosexuality: An Analysis of 100 Male Cases Seen in Private Practice," *British Medical Journal* 1, no. 5022 (April 6, 1957): 797–801; Kurt Freund, "Some Problems in

the Treatment of Homosexuality," in *Behaviour Therapy and the Neuroses: Readings in Modern Methods of Treatment Derived from Learning Theory*, ed. Hans Jurgen Eysenck (London: Pergamon Press, 1960), 312–326; Irving Bieber et al., *Homosexuality: A Psychoanalytic Study* (New York: Basic Books, 1962).

6   The case of continental Europe bears some contrast to this; cf. Dan Healey, "Sex and Socialism," *Contemporary European History* 22, no. 2 (May 2013): 289–293, and Dagmar Herzog, *Sexuality in Europe: A Twentieth-Century History* (Cambridge: Cambridge University Press, 2011). On the US, David K. Johnson, *The Lavender Scare: The Cold War Persecution of Gays and Lesbians in the Federal Government* (Chicago: University of Chicago Press, 2004); Miriam G. Reumann, *American Sexual Character: Sex, Gender, and National Identity in the Kinsey Reports* (Berkeley: University of California Press, 2005); Douglas M. Charles, *Hoover's War on Gays: Exposing the FBI's "Sex Deviates" Program* (Lawrence: University Press of Kansas, 2015). On the UK, Leslie J. Moran, "The Uses of Homosexuality: Homosexuality and National Security," *International Journal of the Sociology of Law* 19 (1991): 149–170; Patrick Higgins, *Heterosexual Dictatorship: Male Homosexuality in Post-War Britain* (London: Fourth Estate, 1996). On Canada, John Sawatsky, *For Services Rendered: Leslie James Bennett and the RCMP Security Service* (Harmondsworth: Penguin, 1983), chapter 13; David Kimmel and Daniel Robinson "The Queer Career of Homosexual Security Vetting in Cold-War Canada," *Canadian Historical Review* 75, no. 3 (1994): 319–345; Gary Kinsman and Patrizia Gentile, *The Canadian War on Queers: National Security as Sexual Regulation* (Vancouver: University of British Columbia Press, 2010). On Australia, Kate Davison, "Pinks Under the Bed? Homosexuality, Communism and Nationalist Sentiment in Cold War Australia," Honours thesis, University of Melbourne, 2005; Graham Willett, *Living Out Loud* (St Leonards: Allen & Unwin, 2000); Dino Hodge, "Homosexuality: The Makings of a Cold War Threat to State Security," unpublished paper, Australian Homosexual Histories Conference, University of Melbourne, November 2013; Robert French, "'Persons With Serious Character Defects': Homosexuals in the Commonwealth Public Service, 1953–1974," in *Intimacy, Violence and Activism: Gay and Lesbian Perspectives on Australasian History and Society*, ed. Graham Willett and Yorick Smaal (Clayton: Monash University Press, 2013).

7   NAA, A6122/26, Item 1194, "Policy or directives about the employment of homosexuals," correspondence dated April 15, 1964, Melbourne.

8   Robert Kulpa and Joanna Mizielińska, eds., *De-Centring Western Sexualities: Central and Eastern European Perspectives* (Farnham: Ashgate, 2011); Elizabeth A. Povinelli and George Chauncey, "Thinking Sexuality Transnationally: An Introduction," *GLQ* 5, no. 4 (1999): 439–449; Heike Bauer and Churnjeet Mahn, "Introduction: Transnational Lesbian Cultures," *Journal of Lesbian Studies* 18, no. 3 (2014): 203–208; Anjali Arondekar and Geeta Patel, "Area Impossible: Notes toward an Introduction," *GLQ*, Special Issue: "Area Impossible: The Geopolitics of Queer Studies" 22, no. 2 (2016): 151–171; Rasa Navickaitė, "Under the Western Gaze: Sexuality and Postsocialist 'Transition' in East Europe," in *Postcolonial Transitions in Europe: Contexts, Practices and Politics*, ed. Sandra Ponzanesi and Gianmaria Colpani (London: Rowman and Littlefield, 2016), 119–132 (see also the editorial introduction to that volume); Catherine Baker, ed., *Gender in Twentieth-Century Eastern Europe and the USSR* (Basingstoke: Palgrave, 2016).

9   Charles E. Morris III and Thomas K. Nakayama, "Leaking Chelsea Manning," *QED: A Journal in GLBTQ Worldmaking* 1, no. 1 (Spring 2014): vii–viii; Cynthia Weber, *Queer*

International Relations: Sovereignty, Sexuality and the Will to Knowledge (Oxford: Oxford University Press, 2016).

10 Dagmar Herzog, "What Incredible Yearnings Human Beings Have," *Contemporary European History* 22, no. 2 (2013): 303–317. The title is a quote from Kurt Starke, the leading empirical sexuality researcher in the former German Democratic Republic, in a post-unification interview with Uta Kolano, "Ein Romantisches Ideal," in *Nackter Osten*, ed. Uta Kolano (Frankfurt/Oder: Frankfurter Oder Editionen, 1995), 103–104.

11 Naoko Wake, James H. Capshew et al., "Kinsey's Biographers: A Historiographical Reconnaissance," *Journal of the History of Sexuality* 12, no. 3 (July 2003).

12 See, for example, the range of theories gathered in Hendrik Ruitenbeek, ed., *The Problem of Homosexuality in Modern Society: An Anthology* (New York: Dutton, 1963). On Pavlovian or pathophysiological understandings of mental illness, see Mark Savelli and Sarah Marks, eds., *Psychiatry in Communist Europe* (Basingstoke: Palgrave Macmillan, 2015) and Dan Healey, "Russian and Soviet Forensic Psychiatry: Troubled and Troubling," *International Journal of Law and Psychiatry* 37 (2014): 71–81. See also Nathan Ha, "Detecting and Teaching Desire: Phallometry, Freund, and Behaviorist Sexology," *Osiris* 30 (2015): 205–227.

13 Monique Scheer, "Are Emotions a Kind of Practice (and is that what makes them have a history)? A Bourdieuian Approach to Understanding Emotion," *History and Theory* 51 (May 2012): 193–220.

14 Pierre Bourdieu, *Outline of a Theory of a Practice* (Cambridge: Cambridge University Press, 1977), 93–94.

15 Benno Gammerl, "Emotional Styles: Concepts and Challenges," *Rethinking History* 16, no. 2 (June 2012): 161–175, here 162–164.

16 Ibid., 164.

17 Barbara Rosenwein, *Emotional Communities in the Early Middle Ages* (Ithaca: Cornell, 2006), 24–25.

18 Cf. Morton Grodzins, *The Loyal and the Disloyal: Social Boundaries of Patriotism and Treason* (Chicago: University of Chicago Press, 1956); John Schaar, *Loyalty in America* (Berkeley: University of California Press, 1957).

19 John Kleinig, "Loyalty," in *Stanford Encyclopedia of Philosophy*, ed. Edward N. Zalta (Fall 2013), http://plato.stanford.edu/archives/fall2013/entries/loyalty/ (accessed July 10, 2017).

20 Ute Frevert, "Does Trust Have a History?" European University Institute Max Weber Program Lecture Series (2009), http://cadmus.eui.eu/handle/1814/11258 (accessed July 10, 2017). Cf. Ute Frevert, ed., *Vertrauen: historische Annäherungen* (Göttingen: Vandenhoeck & Ruprecht, 2003).

21 Geoffrey Hosking, *Trust: A History* (Oxford: Oxford University Press, 2014); Torsten Michel, "Time to Get Emotional: Phronetic Reflections on the Concept of Trust in International Relations," *European Journal of International Relations* 19, no. 4 (2012): 869–890; George P. Fletcher, *Loyalty: An Essay on the Morality of Relationships* (New York: Oxford, 1993); Nachman Ben-Yehuda, *Betrayal and Treason: Violations of Trust and Loyalty* (Boulder: Westview Press, 2001), 310.

22 Michel, "Time to Get Emotional," 873.

23 Ben-Yehuda, *Betrayal and Treason*, 311.

24 Frevert, *Vertrauen: historische Annäherungen*, 7–9.

25 Gary Kinsman, "'Character Weaknesses' and 'Fruit Machines': Towards an Analysis of the Anti-Homosexual Security Campaign in the Canadian Civil Service," *Labour/Le Travail* 35 (Spring 1995): 133–161, here 134.

26 Naoko Shibusawa, "The Lavender Scare and Empire: Rethinking Cold War Antigay Politics," *Diplomatic History* 36, no. 4 (September 2012): 723–752.
27 Shibusawa, "The Lavender Scare and Empire," 742.
28 For example, "Employment of Homosexuals and Other Sex Perverts in Government: Interim Report Submitted to the Committee on Expenditures in the Executive Departments," 81st Congress, 2nd session, doc. 241, December 15, 1950; "Report on Homosexuality with Particular Emphasis on This Problem in Governmental Agencies," Committee on Cooperation with Governmental (Federal) Agencies of the Group for the Advancement of Psychiatry, Report no. 30, January 1955; "Infiltration of subversives and moral perverts into the executive branch of the United States Government," March 1950, discussed in Johnson, *Lavender Scare*, 80; Gary Kinsman and Patrizia Gentile, *The Canadian War on Queers: National Security as Sexual Regulation* (Vancouver: University of British Columbia Press, 2012).
29 D. F. Wall, Memorandum to the Security Panel, "Security Cases Involving Character Weaknesses, with Special Reference to the Problem of Homosexuality," May 12, 1959, 12; quoted in Kinsman (1995), 133–134. Many thanks to Gary Kinsman for providing me with a copy of the entire memorandum.
30 NAA, A4940/1, C643, "Communists and Communist Sympathisers." This goal was pursued by Spry for twelve years from 1952 to 1964.
31 NAA, A6122/26, 1856, "Security Personnel," document "Some notes on homosexuality"; "Die Stasi und die Homosexuellen: Ein Überläufer berichtet (1965)" with introduction by Florian Mildenberger, in Wolfram Setz, ed., *Homosexualität in der DDR: Materialien und Meinungen*, second edition (Hamburg: Männerschwarm, 2006), 203–236. All English translations from this document are my own.
32 NAA, A6122/26, 1194. Cf. Orlov (1963). NKVD stands for *Naródnyi komissariát vnútrennikh dél*, the Soviet secret police from 1934 to 1946. According to former Soviet intelligence officer Boris Volodarsky, Orlov had been a co-handler of Guy Burgess in Moscow in the 1930s; Boris Volodarsky, *Stalin's Agent: The Life and Death of Alexander Orlov* (Oxford: Oxford University Press, 2015), cited in Stewart Purvis and Jeff Hulbert, *Guy Burgess: The Spy Who Knew Everyone* (London: Biteback Publishing, 2016), Kindle edition, location 1008–1017.
33 NAA A4940/1 Item C643, "Communists and Communist Sympathisers."
34 "Die Stasi und die Homosexuellen," 205.
35 Probably Markus Wolf. Cf. "Markus Wolf," in *DDR Lexikon*, http://www.ddr-wissen.de/wiki/ddr.pl?Markus_Wolf (accessed July 10, 2017). See also Jens Gieseke, *The History of the Stasi: East Germany's Secret Police, 1945–1990* (Oxford: Berghahn Books, 2014).
36 My background research suggests that it was typed up in its existing form at the explicit request of the BND, yet this remains to be confirmed by independent sources.
37 There is a growing body of historical research in this area. On West Germany, Andreas Pretzel and Volker Weiß, eds., *Ohnmacht und Aufbegehren: Homosexuelle Männer in der frühen Bundesrepublik* (Hamburg: Männerschwarm Verlag, 2010); Jennifer Evans, *Life among the Ruins: Cityscape and Sexuality in Cold War Berlin* (Basingstoke: Palgrave Macmillan, 2011); Clayton J. Whisnant, *Male Homosexuality in West Germany: Between Persecution and Freedom, 1945–69* (Basingstoke: Palgrave Macmillan, 2012) and *Queer Identities and Politics in Germany* (New York: Harrington Park Press, 2016). On the GDR, Gudrun von Kowalski, *Homosexualität in der DDR: Ein historischer Abriss* (Marburg: Verlag Arbeiterbewegung und Gesellschaftswissenschaft, 1987); Jennifer Evans, "Decriminalization, Seduction,

and 'Unnatural Desire' in the German Democratic Republic," *Feminist Studies* 36, no. 3 (October 2010): 553–577; Josie McLellan, *Love in the Time of Communism* (Cambridge: Cambridge University Press, 2011). See also Dagmar Herzog, *Sex after Fascism: Memory and Morality in Twentieth-Century Germany* (Princeton: Princeton University Press, 2005) and Alison Lewis, "En-Gendering Remembrance: Memory, Gender and Informers for the Stasi," *New German Critique* 86 (Spring/Summer 2002): 103–134.

38 On heterosexual "Romeos," see Elizabeth Pfister, *Unternehmen Romeo: Die Liebeskommandos der Stasi* (Aufbau-Verlag, 1999).

39 Personal communication with the author, Berlin, October 20, 2014. See also Mildenberger's introduction to "Die Stasi und die Homosexuellen."

40 Freund, "Some Problems in the Treatment of Homosexuality"; see also Freund's earlier publications in Czech, for example Kurt Freund and Jan Srnec, 'K otázce mužské homosexuality; analýsa změn sexuální apetence během pokusné léčby podmiňováním' [On the issue of male homosexuality; analysis of changes in sexual appetence in experimental treatment by conditioning], *Sborník lékařský* (Archives bohèmes de médecine), 55/5–6 (May 1953), 125–182; Curran and Parr, "Homosexuality: An Analysis of 100 Male Cases Seen in Private Practice"; Norman Reider, "Problems of Homosexuality," *California Medicine* 86, no. 6 (1957): 381; Ian Stevenson and Joseph Wolpe, "Recovery from Sexual Deviations through Overcoming Non-Sexual Neurotic Responses," *American Journal of Psychiatry* 116, no. 8 (1960): 737–742 [this research was based in South Africa]; Stanley Rachman, "Sexual Disorders and Behavior Therapy," *American Journal of Psychiatry* 118, no. 3 (September 1961): 235–240. See also Brian Lewis, *Wolfenden's Witnesses: Homosexuality in Postwar Britain* (Basingstoke: Palgrave Macmillan, 2016) and Tommy Dickinson, *Curing Queers: Mental Nurses and Their Patients, 1935–74* (Manchester: Manchester University Press, 2014).

41 See, for example, "Are You Now or Have You Ever Been a Homosexual?" *ONE* 1, no. 4 (April 1953): 5–13; Harry Johnson, "And a Red Too...," *ONE* 1, no. 9 (September 1953): 2–3; David L. Freeman, "How Much Do We Know about the Homosexual Male?" *ONE* 3, no. 11 (November 1955): 4–6; "Erpresser sofort anzeigen!" [Press charges against blackmailers immediately!], *Der Kreis* 28, no. 8 (September 1960). On early transnational homophile networks, see also Leila J. Rupp, "The Persistence of Transnational Organizing: The Case of the Homophile Movement," *American Historical Review* 116, no. 4 (October 2011): 1014–1039; David Minto, "Mr Grey Goes to Washington: The Homophile Internationalism of Britain's Homosexual Law Reform Society," in *British Queer History: New Approaches and Perspectives*, ed. Brian Lewis (Manchester: Manchester University Press, 2013), 219–242; Marc Stein, "Introduction: U.S. Homophile Internationalism," *Journal of Homosexuality* 64, no. 7 (2017): 843–849 (and other contributions in that special issue).

42 The prevalence of these pitfalls has been usefully critiqued in Kristen Ghodsee and Kateřina Lišková, "Bumbling Idiots or Evil Masterminds? Challenging Cold War Stereotypes about Women, Sexuality and State Socialism," *Filozofija i Društvo* 27, no. 3 (2016): 489–503. See also Hadley Z. Renkin and Agnieszka Kościańska, "The Science of Sex in a Space of Uncertainty: Naturalizing and Modernizing Europe's East, Past and Present," *Sexualities* 19, no. 1–2 (2016): 159–167.

43 This chapter is part of a PhD research project into transnational developments in the application of "Pavlovian" behavior modification techniques in the treatment of homosexuality from the 1950s to the 1970s.

44 Jennifer Evans, "The Moral State: Men, Mining, and Masculinity in the Early GDR," *German History* 23, no. 3 (2005): 355–369, here 355–356.
45 Gieseke, *History of the Stasi*, 8.
46 Rudolf Klimmer's book *Die Homosexualität als biologisch-soziologische Zeitfrage* was published in Hamburg in 1958 after failing to secure permission to publish from East German censors. Cf. Schelsky: *Soziologie der Sexualität* (1955), Giese & Gebsattel: *Psychopathologie der Sexualität* (1962), and Giese: *Der Homosexuelle Mann in der Welt* (1964). For a discussion of these, see Robert G. Moeller, "'The Homosexual Man Is a 'Man', the Homosexual Woman Is a 'Woman'": Sex, Society, and the Law in Postwar West Germany," *Journal of the History of Sexuality* 4, no. 3, Special Issue, Part 2: Lesbian and Gay Histories (January 1994), 395–429. See also Dagmar Herzog, "The Reception of the Kinsey Reports in Europe," *Sexuality & Culture* 10, no. 1 (Winter 2006): 39–48.
47 Kurt Freund, *Die Homosexualität beim Mann* (Leipzig: S. Hirzel Verlag, 1963 [Czech original 1962]). Cf. Jan Seidl, "Decriminalization of Homosexual Acts in Czechoslovakia in 1961," in *Queer Stories of Europe*, ed. Kārlis Vērdiņš and Jānis Ozoliņš (Newcastle, UK: Cambridge Scholars Publishing, 2016), 174–194. See also Ha, "Detecting and Teaching Desire."
48 Published medical discourse on homosexuality in Australia was sparse, yet British and American literature was readily available, including papers by psychiatrists and others who had made submissions to the Wolfenden Committee from 1954 to 1957. Behavior-modification and bodily detection methods were not introduced until 1962, when Sydney-based psychiatrist Neil McConaghy learned of Freund's work.
49 Quoted in Shibusawa, "The Lavender Scare and Empire," 731–732: R. G. Waldeck, "Homosexual International," *Human Events* 9, no. 16 (April 16, 1952).

11

Homosexual Politics in the British World: Toward a Transnational Understanding

Graham Willett

It is a distressing fact that today, some seventy-eight countries, containing a third of the world's population, still have laws prohibiting people of the same sex (men, mostly) from having sex with each other.[1] In the rest of the world, however, the trend is toward decriminalization, the eradication of discrimination, and the enfolding of homosexually inclined citizens within a broad regime of social tolerance. And yet, as late as the 1950s, many societies that proclaimed their democratic natures, their liberality, their respect for individual and civil rights and for privacy, and congratulated themselves on their rich and vibrant civic life had laws that prohibited any and all sex between men, and punished it severely. Bringing an historical perspective to the question of anti-homosexual laws and attitudes, then, it is not their persistence that is surprising and in need of explanation, but their remarkably rapid and thorough overturn, and their replacement with an ever-widening and deepening commitment to legal and social equality.

One of the milestones in this process was the publication in 1957 of the *Report on Homosexuality and Prostitution*, prepared for the British government by a committee under the chairmanship of John Wolfenden. The committee's recommendation that consenting adult males should be allowed to engage in sexual behavior in private came as a bolt from the blue for many, proposing as it did a radical change to centuries-old laws and challenging apparently well-established religious, legal, and professional opinions, not to mention common sense. Parliament declined to enact its recommendations. But far from putting paid to the issue, this only ensured that it remained topical, and continued to be debated long after the Committee's less contentious recommendations on prostitution were put into law.[2]

The Wolfenden Report's impact was by no means confined to Britain. In the countries of what I am calling the British World (see below) the Report attracted considerable attention. Newspapers and political magazines responded initially with only slight attention, but with greater frequency over time until the Report's defining slogan—the consenting adult in private—became a topic of regular discussion. It is not hard to see why this international interest might have been the case: many countries had laws directly based on British law. In this chapter, I want to examine the origins and diffusion of *homosexual politics* in Britain and the settler states (or *British World*)—terms that need careful definition. In doing so, I offer a broad outline of the way in which transnational methodologies can enhance our understanding of this process.

The Committee and its report

The *Report of the Committee on Homosexual Offences and Prostitution* was the work of a British government committee, chaired by John Wolfenden, which reported after more than three years' work in September 1957.[3] Its central recommendation was: "that homosexual behaviour between consenting adults in private should no longer be a criminal offence."[4] The "consenting adult in private" was a crisp summary of what was being recommended. In a few sharp words, the Committee had proposed a way of legalizing homosexual acts that addressed the deepest anxieties and objections of the public: "consent" stood against the ever-present fear of homosexual assault and harassment of heterosexual men; "adult" against the fear of the homosexual child-molester; "In private" against flaunting public displays, outrages against public decency, loitering in public conveniences. It rested in turn on an equally briskly stated foundation: "It is not, in our view, the function of the law to intervene in the private lives of citizens, or to seek to enforce any particular pattern of behaviour further than is necessary to … preserve public decency, to protect the citizen from what is offensive or injurious, and to provide sufficient safeguards against exploitation and corruption of others."[5]

The most surprising recommendation of the Committee was surely that homosexual acts should be legalized. The Committee's courage here is often overlooked by contemporary scholars whose views, shaped by the world created by gay politics after 1969, have led them to see it as rather timid.[6] These objections certainly carry weight in relation to the Committee's definition of "adult": it opted for an age of consent of twenty-one. But even this could not save the Report from condemnation by elite and popular opinion. The Cabinet was appalled, and the House of Commons refused at its first opportunity in late 1958, and repeatedly for a decade after, to enact any such reform. The popular press and public opinion were strongly opposed (although the middle-class press tended to be supportive).[7] Galvanized rather than deterred by all this, supporters of decriminalization established the Homosexual Law Reform Society, which toiled for a decade to bring the Committee's work to legislative fruition.[8]

Homosexual politics

It will be obvious from this description of the Wolfenden Report that it was by no means an expression of the gay politics that erupted in the late 1960s.[9] Rather, what we have here is a statement of, and a basis for, activity around what I want to call *homosexual politics*—which is a very different thing. "Homosexual politics" was concerned almost entirely with the decriminalization of sex acts between men. It was conducted by citizens whose sexual identity was formally irrelevant to their work; it was reforming rather than transforming; and it involved working within the structures of normal political life to persuade politicians and opinion-makers of the need to legislate. This politics can be traced back to the work of Karl-Heinrich Ulrichs in Germany in the 1860s and 1870s.[10] It was a significant force through the first third of the twentieth century in those parts of western and central Europe in which homosexual acts were illegal.[11] But it is a politics that is a very long way from that which emerged in the 1970s with the lesbian and gay movement, where identity, defiance, and pride were central; and demands were made for radical changes in laws, attitudes, and social institutions that were very wide and deep in scope—encompassing anti-discrimination laws, the recognition of same-sex relationships and families headed by same-sex couples, challenging anti-homosexual prejudice and discrimination, addressing the specific health and welfare needs of these populations, and so on.

Nor should homosexual politics be confused with "homophile politics," as practiced in Western Europe by organizations established and reestablished in the late 1940s and into the 1950s in the Netherlands, Denmark, Sweden, and France,[12] and in the United States between 1948 and 1969 by organizations such as Mattachine, Daughters of Bilitis, and One.[13] Homophile politics was undertaken by homosexuals (or "homophiles," as they often called themselves) speaking openly from and about their own experience, even if they often felt compelled to use pseudonyms to ward off the threat of social prejudice. Homophiles showed no great interest in the law, preferring to engage with professionals of various kinds, to educate them about the realities of homophile lives and to bring about a change in views. Thus enlightened, it was assumed, these opinion leaders would contribute to wider attitudinal change in society that would eventually bring an end to discrimination and unjust laws.

Decriminalization was not unimportant to homophile politics, but it was not the immediate goal, nor was it usually tackled directly or head-on. There were reasons for this—in much of Western Europe, laws against sex between men had been eliminated in the nineteenth century. Homosexual politics, therefore, had little relevance there. Where there were laws against homosexuality, there were, to be sure, efforts at decriminalization, but the structures in place were not those of the British World. In the United States, for example, although laws against homosexuality existed in all fifty states, this meant that no plausible strategy for challenging those laws could be imagined given the tiny resources of the activists. The sole example of decriminalization in the United States during the period before 1969 was in Illinois in 1961, where the American Law Institute's Model Penal Code was adopted. The Code and its implementation can indeed be explained as an isolated American example of homosexual politics in action.[14]

The British World

For the most part homosexual politics was fought out at the national or subnational level. This was inevitable. In the British World, buggery and gross indecency laws were enacted by national parliaments in Canada, New Zealand, South Africa, and the Republic of Ireland, and by subnational jurisdictions ("states") in Australia. The UK has a remarkably complex legal structure, and the national parliament could and did legislate differently for the kingdom's component parts (England and Wales, Scotland, Northern Ireland, the Crown Dependencies). Histories of these laws and the efforts to overturn them tend, therefore, to focus upon these levels of analysis. But if we step back, it is clear that there is a transnational element to this history too. The challenge to sodomy laws in the postwar period was not confined to any one country; nor were the campaigners unaware of, or indifferent to, efforts taking place elsewhere. The content of the struggles—the arguments, the strategies, and the tactics—was remarkably similar. It is the contention of this chapter that our understanding of the postwar challenge to sodomy laws is greatly enhanced if we bring our attention to this transnational level.

Scott de Groot has made the observation that transnational history is more often talked about than done, though his own work on gay liberation as a transnational movement in the Anglo-American world is itself an important exception to this.[15] But even in relation to the pre-gay period (i.e., the period prior to 1969), a number of studies have been produced. David Minto has emerged from close work in the archives with a study that highlights the "importance of the international affiliations to postwar homophiles, reformers and their allies," putting relations between Antony Grey of the London-based Homosexual Law Reform Society (HLRS) and European and US activists at the center of his story.[16] David Churchill examines the ways in which connections between United States and European homophiles were established and maintained by publications, correspondence, and trans-Atlantic visits.[17] Leila Rupp focuses on the international work of the Dutch homophile organization *Cultuur- en Ontspannings Centrum* and the International Committee for Sexual Equality that it established.[18] It is striking how rarely, with the exception of Minto's work, Britain appears in these studies; and the British World appears not at all. For the most part this speaks to the isolationist attitudes of the British HLRS and the literal isolation of Australia, New Zealand, and Canada in a world where communication flows, especially among marginalized peoples, were patchy.

This "British World" to which I am referring is not the same thing as the British Empire,[19] nor is it intended to draw upon the politicized (usually conservative) approaches characterized by labels like "Anglosphere." Rather, it is a reference to those societies created by the mass migrations beginning in the eighteenth century, during which millions of Britons uprooted themselves and settled in North America, Australasia, and southern Africa, creating the "settler states" as they are usually known.[20] Indigenous cultures were overwhelmed and marginalized by this swarming and swamping, and the British culture, institutions, and laws that came with these populations created nations that were, and for the most part felt themselves to be, part of an international community of British peoples and states—"the Empire," later "the Commonwealth." By the mid-twentieth century, these settler states were—allowing for some constitutional nuances—independent countries. But they were, at the same time, profoundly British in nature. Characteristics of this Britishness, which marked it off from other colonial-imperial worlds (e.g., French, Spanish, Portuguese), include society-shaping institutions and structures such as the dominance of the English language, the Church of England as the largest religious denomination, the persistence of the common law and British precedent in legal reasoning, parliamentary (or Westminster) forms of government. But it included, too, more easily overlooked elements of day-to-day culture, such as dominant literary forms and canons, preferred foods, public holidays and celebrations, and national histories embedded in imperial narratives. And until the 1950s, Britain's wars were always the British World's wars.[21] As these cultural forms suggest, as well as the institutional and structural legacies, in all these societies there was a powerful sense of attachment toward Britain and things British that animated populations, drawing their attention and affection to what many referred to as "Home" or "the Old Country."

My research project includes South Africa, Ireland, and Scotland, but in this chapter I want to focus on what we might think of as the purest forms of the British settler states—Australia, New Zealand, and Canada. One thing that the countries of this British World had in common (and which most other states and worlds within the West did not) was sodomy laws. These had their origin during the reign of Henry VIII of England, specifically in a 1533 law that provided a more "condign punishment," as the Act said, than had hitherto been the case.[22] The "abominable crime of buggery" was punishable by death in Britain and the British World until the nineteenth century. But even when the penalties for homosexual offences were reduced, the range of activities caught up in the net of the law expanded markedly. In 1828, faced with the difficulty of proving "emission of seed" (ejaculation) in buggery cases, the UK Parliament amended the law to ensure that evidence of penetration alone would be sufficient to convict. In 1861, the death penalty for acts of buggery was replaced with a maximum punishment of life imprisonment, but the statute included a reference to attempted buggery, which, in Patrick Higgins words, "covered every homosexual act ... from fellatio to a kiss (to) invitations to a sexual act."[23] In 1885, the Labouchere amendment created offences of "gross indecency" with a penalty of two years hard labor. In 1898, the Vagrancy Act added homosexual "importuning or soliciting" for immoral purposes to the catalogue of offences.[24]

The settler colonies had inherited the British laws at the time of their foundation and, even after they had achieved self-government, they invariably followed the British lead. In the Australian states, New Zealand, and Canada, parliaments legislated as Britain did (albeit in their own good time) for the abolition of the death penalty, penetration laws, gross indecency, and the Vagrancy Act. The laws, then, that governed sexual behavior between men in the British settler states were of a kind, because they had a common origin and a common history. And so, when the idea of decriminalization started to surface in the 1950s, the arguments put forward in Britain were immediately applicable to the different jurisdictions.

This situation is an example of what social movement scholar Marco G Giugni refers to as "structural affinity": "the existence of similar structures in different countries that may lead to convergent patterns in movement activity." The deep structures of the British World—an effect of the settler-colonization process—were expressed in almost identical sodomy laws, in a common legal system based on that of Britain, as well as the values and assumptions that underpinned all of these. The result was a homogenous transnational field of political activism that encompassed the different countries of the British World. This is directly relevant to the homosexual politics with which this chapter is concerned.

Giugni identifies two other ways in which similarities between social movements can be explained: *globalization* and *diffusion*.[25] Each of these contributes significantly to our understanding of homosexual politics in the British World in the 1950s and after. Structures generally change only slowly. Yet one of the remarkable features of homosexual law reform is how rapidly it emerged onto the political agenda at a particular point in time, and how rapidly it was implemented. Here I think Giugni's other two models can contribute to our understanding. The globalization model injects an element of dynamism into the analysis. It identifies the way in which "the *increasing* interconnectedness of the world stimulates transnational structures and processes."[26] The British World existed within a global world that in the postwar period was changing deeply and rapidly, and it was precisely this dynamic transformation of all of the structures of the post-1945 world (economic, political, social, and cultural) that allowed for the emergence of new kinds of politics (modernization and liberalization, and a new radicalism). Homosexual politics, although its ideas can be traced back centuries, (re-)emerged in the 1950s and 1960s as an element of this broader modernization/liberalization politics.

But if the transformation of the globe's various societies in this period created the conditions for a new politics, and the particular structures of the British World shaped how these unfolded therein, it is not the case that there was anything inevitable about this course of events. It is, after all, people who make history. And here Giugni's attention to diffusion becomes important. The *diffusion model* explains similarities among movements "through direct (networks) or indirect (mass media) cross-national flows of information"[27] and brings our attention to the way in which those who took up homosexual politics in the postwar period drew heavily upon and contributed to each other's work. Networks and media were indeed powerfully important in transmitting ideas and activities.

In the following sections I want to sketch the ways in which the globalization and the diffusion models help us to understand more thoroughly the emergence and spread of homosexual politics in the British World during the post–Second World War period.

Modernization and its liberalism

The Marxist historian Eric Hobsbawm has examined and written about these processes of change in his *Age of Extremes*.[28] In this work, he identifies the period from 1945 to 1974 as constituting a period of "extraordinary, unprecedented, fundamental changes [in] the world economy, and consequently human societies."[29] One element of this transformation is the process by which "Personal liberation and social liberation ... went hand in hand."[30] Hobsbawm is not alone in connecting the great economic, social, political upheavals of the post-1945 period to cultural transformation in quite fundamental ways. Ronald Inglehart, in a number of studies in the 1990s, embedded what he called "post-materialist values" within the emergence of technological advance, its need for an educated workforce, and the creation of human beings whose primary drives were around "belonging, self-expression and the quality of life."[31]

Hobsbawm and Inglehart both comment on the impact of this transformation on homosexual people, seeing structural transformation as providing the conditions for the emergence of homosexual subcultures, politics, and visibility.[32] There are differences, both of content and emphasis in their accounts, but the broad outlines of the analysis are already reasonably clear. The new middle class generated by the new economy was much more educated and open-minded than the old and was open to the arguments put forward by a new modernizing liberalism. While this liberalism did not take state power until the 1960s (Kennedy and Johnson in the United States, Wilson in the UK, Trudeau in Canada, Whitlam in Australia, Kirk in New Zealand), its progress through the culture and society was unmistakable for a decade before. In the professions (law, religion, medicine) the new middle-class values were shaking up the dominant paradigms, generating new, liberally inflected, thinking on social problems, including the problem of homosexuality. In the 1960s, alongside the idea that homosexuality was a sin, a crime, a mental disorder, the idea that it was mostly harmless to society increasingly came to be heard. In the context of the sexual revolution in the West—where sex roles and gender expectations came to be doubted, ignored, challenged, overturned; where abortion, promiscuity, pornography, and sexual experimentation captured imaginations, spreading out from small and marginal communities of people to ever-wider social circles—homosexuality began to be less shocking, and the laws and attitudes that discriminated against it, more so.

The liberalizers' discussion of homosexuality relied upon Wolfenden's slogan, the consenting adult in private, and its underpinning assumption that behavior should be criminalized only to the extent that it was socially damaging. More and more frequently it was asserted that there was no social harm attendant upon the existence of homosexuality, nor was any likely to develop as a result of its legalization. References to those parts of Europe that had long since decriminalized were commonly made, noting the absence of social disruption there.[33] The unfairness of criminalizing some sexual behaviors and not others (lesbianism, fornication, adultery) further highlighted the problems in the law as it stood. The severity of the law also came to be a reason for rejecting it. The Vancouver-based Association for Social Knowledge pointed out that the penalties for rape, murder, domestic violence all attracted penalties of three to fifteen years. Homosexuality could get a man a life sentence.[34]

Diffusion

To the extent that supporters of Wolfenden's recommendations might have expected a quick implementation, they were to be sorely disappointed. The Cabinet and the Parliament both said no.[35] In the British World, the report went largely unnoticed except in the press. Only one parliament even came close to considering it at the time. In New Zealand in 1959, the Minister of Justice, moved, it was said, by the suicide of a homosexual friend, turned his mind to the possibility of law reform. The reaction was swift and universally hostile, and his party leader was quick to disavow any suggestion that his colleague had intended to "adopt the recommendations of the Wolfenden report." When New Zealand produced a consolidation of its Crimes Act in 1961, homosexuality remained an offence.[36]

Given all this, it was clear that reform would not just happen—it was going to have to be *made* to happen. The Wolfenden Report had provided the case for decriminalization, and the sociocultural transformation of the postwar period provided the environment in which that case could be heard and acted upon. But the bringing of the report and its recommendations to fruition was the work of many years and many people. And so, homosexual politics emerged onto the public stage—initially in London with the foundation of the HLRS.[37] For a decade the HLRS educated and lobbied, raised funds, and, through its counselling arm, The Albany Trust, offered support to homosexual men and women. It held a public meeting in May 1960, produced a magazine called *Man and Society* (which dealt with a range of social issues) and a quarterly journal called *Spectrum* and met quietly with opinion-leaders inside and outside parliament, as well as addressing universities, Rotary Club meetings, political organizations. Its first pamphlet, *Homosexuality: Some Questions and Answers*, was a calm and balanced argument for reform—and it sold 6000 copies in a very short time.[38] Its correspondence with individuals and organizations overseas was very active.[39]

The most detailed study to date of the connections between homosexual activists and organizations in the British World is Scott de Groot's deeply researched examination of the gay liberation movement in what he calls the "Anglo-American World" (Australia, English Canada, New Zealand, the UK, and the United States), covering the period from the late 1960s to the early 1980s. Among his important discoveries is that this movement was genuinely, and not merely rhetorically, transnational, using its publications to bring "otherwise disconnected activists, ideas, analyses, news, material resources, and so forth into association."[40] The gay liberation movement consciously and actively drew upon international experience via frequent, dense, and multidirectional intercommunication across national borders, whereas homosexual politics as well as having more modest goals communicated almost entirely along a single axis, between center and periphery; specifically, between the HLRS in London and the organizations that were established in the early 1960s.

The earliest organizations established outside Britain—apart from a failed attempt in Melbourne in 1958—were the Dorian Society in Wellington, New Zealand, in 1962 and the Association for Social Knowledge in Vancouver, Canada, in 1964. The Dorian Society was a social club for homosexual men that within a year had set up a Legal Subcommittee, to "(a) to educate the public on all aspects of homosexuality; (b) work with others for a removal of legal restrictions on consenting adult males; (c) advise and assist club members on legal and social matters." Its job, among other things, was to contact sympathetic people within the legal and medical professions and churches, and respond to opportunities to educate and inform public opinion. The subcommittee lapsed fairly quickly but was revived, with almost the same membership, as the Homosexual Law Reform Society in 1967.

The Association for Social Knowledge (ASK) was set up to "to promote a better knowledge of the homophile and his definite existence in society," coincidentally at the very time when steps to organize around homosexual law reform were being taken in Ottawa, the federal capital. In April 1964, New Democratic Party (NDP) members of the national parliament were proposing a series of private members' bills addressing many of the issues raised by the modernizing liberal agenda—including a bill to reform the laws on homosexuality "along the lines ... similar to those suggested in the Wolfenden Report in Great Britain."[41] A (somewhat shadowy) Committee on Homophile Reform was already at work in Ontario. ASK's Board of Directors wrote to the NDP, advising of the existence of their organization and asking for a copy of the draft Bill. They intended to launch a letter-writing campaign to support passage of such a law. Nothing came of this request or of the proposed reform, and ASK turned its attention in a homophile direction, working to create a viable gearing place ("clubrooms") and an educational program directed at its members and sympathetic professionals. It was not until 1968 that the group's focus changed, when, in response to an intensified level of public discussion of the buggery laws, ASK declared: "our main aim is to work toward the changing of the Canadian Laws with regard to Homosexuality."[42]

Both the HLRS and ASK were in close communication with, and modelled themselves on, the HLRS in London. The leaders of the UK organization were very clear that theirs was not a society for homosexuals, but rather one dedicated to the cause of decriminalization. Any suggestion that it might be motivated by self-interest was to be firmly deflected, in part by the very kind of organization that it was—respectable, businesslike, polite, detached, and rational, headed up by men who could be assumed to be heterosexual (though, of course, they often weren't). And the HLRS was not at all backward in making it clear to Wellington and Vancouver that they ought to follow this model.[43] Within the limits of their resources and competing demands upon them, the local organizations adopted this advice. In Wellington, the Dorian Society operated with a membership and social gatherings, but established a separate organization to lobby for law reform. The leadership of ASK responded to the early opportunity to push for decriminalization but soon retreated from this, without denying individual members the right to deal with police and professional associations, a path actively pursued by Doug Sanders, its longtime leader.[44]

In the archives of these organizations we find clear evidence of the communications flow—folders containing a variety of materials produced by the HLRS: newsletters and copies of its journal *Man and Society*, pamphlets, roneoed material, texts of speeches, and extracts from UK parliamentary debates. There are clippings from British and local newspapers and magazines, as well as local ones, reporting on the progress of law reform in the UK. From correspondence we know that HLRS sent copies of its pamphlets to the NZ HLRS and ASK for distribution to academics, church leaders, and legal and medical professionals who it was thought might be prepared to "advise or support such an organisation."[45]

In strategy, too, London's hegemony was strong: "keep hammering a rational line of thought in public discussions," the secretary of the HLRS in London wrote to Doug Sanders.[46] But ultimately, it was assumed, that the countries of the British World would need to wait for the British breakthrough: "I would hope that the achievement of the reform here within the next year or two, and the various developments which are taking place in the United States, should make the reform possible in Canada within the next five years or so."[47] And indeed, the transformation of the British World (a part of the broader transformation of the West) was enabling law reform societies to emerge and flourish.

The arguments for decriminalization were circulating ever more widely over the course of the 1960s, moving beyond the activist groups and into the wider fields of public debate and discussion. We see evidence of this in the various realms of society: in politics (MPs, the executive, public servants, political parties), in professional associations (medical, legal, trade unions), in lobby groups, the courts and police forces, in churches, at universities among academics and students. In journals and symposiums, at synods and conferences, in private and public discussions, the consenting adult in private was more and more frequently heard about. Initially, the most liberal elements of the press were the smaller current affairs magazines that usually had audiences that were open to the emerging modernizing liberalism of the 1950s and 1960s. In the UK, the *New Statesman*; in Australia, *Nation Review* and the *Bulletin*; in Canada *Maclean's* and *Saturday Night*; in New Zealand, the *Listener*, carried news and opinion on homosexual legal issues. But in the 1960s, the rise of the new, liberal middle class led many newspapers to tack toward this territory.[48]

Breakthrough

For most of the 1950s and 1960s, homosexual politics is visible mostly in the archives and, occasionally, in newspapers and magazines. In 1967, however, after a decade of debate and discussion, the British parliament legislated to legalize homosexual acts between consenting adults in private.[49] Two years later Canada followed suit. In 1972 South Australia acted as well (though in such a rushed and messy way that they needed to revisit the issue in 1975, thus becoming both first and second Australian state to decriminalize). In the space of a few short years, laws that had been on the books since 1533 were being swept away. Other jurisdictions would follow over the coming years.

Historians have generally researched and written on these developments from national perspectives. And yet it is clear that the ideas surrounding the decriminalization of homosexual acts had been advancing in a number of countries simultaneously, as a result of the deeper and wider forces at work. By a close attention to the ideas, organizations, and communications between different groups of reformers in different counties, we are drawn to see that this simultaneity was not an accident, but was rather a transnational process, rooted in, and made possible by, a deep sociocultural transformation. The slogan of the "consenting adult in private" spelled out in the Wolfenden report of 1957 spread widely. The common adoption of a cautious, respectable, reasoned approach to lobbying, with all suggestion of self-interest carefully eschewed, was, we can see, the result of insistent advice from the British reformers and a general agreement as to what was possible at the time. Differences certainly existed between the advocates of homosexual politics but it is necessary to revisit those national histories in order to write in their transnational roots.

Notes

1   Aengus Carroll and Lucas Paoli Itaborahy, *State Sponsored Homophobia 2015: A World Survey of Laws: Criminalisation, Protection and Recognition of Same-Sex Love* (Geneva: ILGA, May 2015).

2   On Wolfenden and Prostitution, Helen J. Self, *Prostitution, Women and Misuse of the Law: The Fallen Daughters of Eve* (London: Frank Cass, 2003). On homosexuality, Antony Grey, *Quest for Justice: Towards Homosexual Emancipation* (London: Sinclair Stevenson, 1992) and Stephen Jeffery-Poulter, *Peers, Queers and Commons: The Struggle for Gay Law Reform from 1950 to the Present* (London: Routledge, 1991).
3   Patrick Higgins, *Heterosexual Dictatorship: Male Homosexuality in Postwar Britain* (London: Fourth Estate, 1996), 9–10.
4   Committee on Homosexual Offences and Prostitution, 1957. Report of the Committee on Homosexual Offences and Prostitution (London: Her Majesty's Stationery Office 1957). [Hereinafter Wolfenden Report].
5   Wolfenden Report, paras 14, 13.
6   See, for example, Matt Houlbrook, *Queer London: Perils and Pleasures in the Sexual Metropolis, 1918–1957* (Chicago and London: University of Chicago Press, 2005), 254–263.
7   Higgins, *Heterosexual Dictatorship*, 116–122.
8   Grey, *Quest for Justice*; Jeffery-Poulter, *Peers, Queers and Commons*.
9   Equally, my research project has little connection to the queer world and queer lives of the 1950s and 1960s, which existed alongside the world of homosexual politics, but which rarely interacted with it and is, anyway, conceptually a quite distinct phenomenon. On the "new queer British history," see Chris Waters, "Distance and Desire in the New British Queer History," *GLQ* 14, no. 1 (2007): 139–155. Recent contributions to the history of queer lives during the postwar period include Brian Lewis, ed., *British Queer History: New Approaches and Perspectives* (Manchester and New York: Manchester University Press, 2013) and Heike Bauer and Matt Cook, eds., *Queer 1950s: Rethinking Sexuality in the Postwar Years* (Basingstoke: Palgrave Macmillan, 2012).
10 Hubert Kennedy, *Ulrichs: The Life and Works of Karl Heinrich Ulrichs. Pioneer of the Modern Gay Movement* (Boston: Alyson, 1988).
11 Ralf Dose, "The World League for Sexual Reform: Some Possible Approaches," in *Sexual Cultures in Europe: National Histories*, ed. Franz X.. Eder, Lesley A Hall, and Gert Hekma (Manchester and New York: Manchester University Press, 1999), 242–259; Ralf Dose, *Magnus Hirschfeld: The Origins of the Gay Liberation Movement*, trans. Edward H Willis (New York: Monthly Review Press, 2014).
12 Nicholas C. Edsall, *Toward Stonewall: Homosexuality and Society in the Modern Western World* (Charlottesville and London: University of Virginia Press, 2003), 284–291.
13 John D'Emilio, *Sexual Politics, Sexual Communities: The Making of a Homosexual Minority in the United States, 1940–1970* (Chicago: University of Chicago Press, 1983).
14 William N. Eskridge, Jr., *Dishonorable Passions: Sodomy Laws in America, 1861–2003* (New York: Viking, 2008), 118–127.
15 Scott Frederick de Groot, "Out of the Closet and into Print: Gay Liberation across the Anglo-American World" (PhD thesis, Queen's University, 2015), iii. For a recent example of the "writing about" mode, see Leigh Boucher and Robert Reynolds, "Thinking Transnationally about Sexuality: Homosexuality in Australia or Australian Homosexualities?" in *Transnationalism, Nationalism and Australian History*, ed. Anna Clark, Anne Rees, and Alecia Simmonds (Singapore: Palgrave Macmillan, 2017), 149–165.
16 David Minto, "Mr Grey Goes to Washington: The Homophile Internationalism of Britain's Homosexual Law Reform Society," in *British Queer History: New Approaches*

and *Perspectives*, ed. Brian Lewis (Manchester and New York: Manchester University Press, 2013), 219–243 at 220.
17 David S. Churchill, "Transnationalism and Homophile Political Culture in the Postwar Decades," *GLQ* 15, no. 1 (2008): 31–66.
18 Leila J. Rupp, "The Persistence of Transnational Organizing: The Case of the Homophile Movement," *American Historical Review* 116, no. 4 (2011): 1014–1039.
19 On the British Empire's sodomy laws, imposed in the African and Asia colonies, see *This Alien Legacy: The Origins of "Sodomy" Laws in British Colonialism*, Human Rights Watch, 2008, www.hrw.org/sitesearch/alien%20legacy (accessed October 5, 2017). As this report makes clear, the flow of anti-sodomy laws was not all one way. It describes the Queensland Penal Code of 1901 that was deployed in British Africa in particular as "the second most influential penal code" after the Indian Penal Code of 1860.
20 James Belich, *Replenishing the Earth: The Settler Revolution and the Rise of the Anglo-World, 1783–1939* (Oxford and New York: Oxford University Press, 2009).
21 Carl Bridge and Kent Federowich, "Mapping the British World," in *The British World: Diaspora, Culture and Identity*, ed. Carl Bridge and Kent Federowich (London: Frank Cass, 2003), 1–15.
22 *An Acte [sic] for the Punishment of the Vice of Buggerie* (25 Hen. 8 c. 6).
23 Higgins, *Heterosexual Dictatorship*, 155.
24 The above paragraph, H. G. Cocks, "Secrets, Crimes and Diseases, 1800–1914," in *A Gay History of Britain: Love and Sex between Men since the Middle Ages*, ed. Matt Cook (Oxford, Westport Connecticut: Greenwood World Publishing, 2007), 109–112.
25 Marco G. Giugni, "The Other Side of the Coin: Explaining Crossnational Similarities between Social Movements," *Mobilization: An International Journal* 3, no. 1 (1998): 89–105.
26 Ibid., 91 [emphasis added].
27 Ibid.
28 Eric Hobsbawm, *The Age of Extremes: The Short Twentieth Century, 1914–1991* (London: Michael Joseph, 1994).
29 Ibid., 256.
30 Ibid., 333.
31 Ronald Inglehart, *Culture Shift in Advanced Industrial Society* (Princeton NJ: Princeton University Press, 1990).
32 The major work on how these social forces and the associated political and social struggles have redefined sex, gender, and sexuality is Jeffrey Weeks' remarkable *The World We Have Won: The Remaking of Erotic and Intimate Life* (London and New York: Routledge, 2007).
33 In fact, the experience of Western Europe was a little more complicated than the liberalizers assumed. Even those countries that had adopted (or been forced to adopt) Enlightenment law reform during the Napoleonic years, or after, did not offer the sort of unfettered freedom that some imagined. During the war years, fascist authorities had (re)imposed criminal sanctions (France, the Netherlands) or adopted administrative measures (Italy) to penalize homosexual acts. While these were generally repealed after 1945, unequal age of consent laws often remained in place and social and political hostility often made life for homosexuals rather uncomfortable.
34 "Quick Canadian Facts," *ASK Newsletter*, December 1967.
35 Grey, *Quest for Justice*, 24–25, 34–36; Jeffery-Poulter, *Peers, Queers and Commons*, 34–35.

36 Laurie Guy, *Worlds in Collision: The Gay Debate in New Zealand, 1960–1986* (Wellington: Victoria University Press, 2002), 46–47.
37 Grey, *Quest for Justice*; Jeffery-Poulter, *Peers, Queers and Commons*; Papers of Antony Grey, Hall-Carpenter Archives, LSE, HCA/GREY.
38 Homosexual Law Reform Society, Minutes of Executive Committee, March 21, 1960, Antony Grey Papers, HCA/LSE, 1/2(a).
39 Albany Trust papers, HCA/LSE, file 7/44 Australia; Albany Trust papers, HCA/LSE, file 14/112 Correspondence with New Zealand; HLRS; James Egan to Antony Grey, 22 February 1964; Albany Trust papers, HCA/LSE, file 14/17 Correspondence with Canada.
40 De Groot, Out of the Closet 3.
41 Wayne MacDonald, "New Democrats Push 'Hot' Bills" [clipping from *Vancouver Sun*, April 11], 1964 reprinted ASK Newsletter, 1:1, April 1, 1964, 2.
42 *ASK Newsletter*, January 1968, np.
43 For example, New Zealand: Letter Antony Grey to JGW, June 27, 1963, Jack W Goodwin, Personal Correspondence 1963–1969, Lesbian and Gay Archives of New Zealand (LAGANZ), MS 0493.
44 The Sanders papers in the CLGA contain materials relating to his liaison with the Morality Squad and interventions directed at the British Columbia Bar Association, Sanders Papers, CLGA, ref 2003–025/01.
45 Letter Jack W. Goodwin to M. Holcroft, May 20, 1963, Jack W. Goodwin, Personal Correspondence 1963–1969, LAGANZ, MS 0493.
46 Antony Grey, to Douglas Sanders, Sanders Papers, CLGA, ref 2003–025/01 (03).
47 Grey to Sanders, Sanders Papers, CLGA, ref 2003–025/01 (03).
48 See the clippings files of the Canadian Lesbian and Gay Archives, the Australian Lesbian and Gay Archives, and the Lesbian and Gay Newsmedia Archive (originally part of the Hall-Carpenter Archives).
49 Partially, anyway. The Sexual Offences Act applied only to England and Wales; it defined "in private" to mean in the presence of no more than two people; it excluded the merchant marine and the armed services, and provided for an age of consent of twenty-one. On the startling exclusion of Scotland from this process, see Jeffrey Meek, *Queer Voices in Post-War Scotland, Male Homosexuality, Religion and Society* (Basingstoke: Palgrave Macmillan, 2015), especially chapter 3.

12

Gender and the Politics of Marriage in Postwar Australia and Britain

Rebecca Jennings

Much of the contemporary debate around same-sex marriage has been framed in legal terms. Campaigners and lobbying groups for same-sex marriage have inevitably focused on the issue of legal equality, arguing that the inability of same-sex couples to marry represents a form of legal discrimination, while the success of such campaigns has been hailed as an indicator of equality before the law. Some academic commentators and historians have located these recent changes in the context of a more gradual progression from legal oppression to equality over the course of the nineteenth and twentieth centuries. In his 2001 work on same-sex marriage in the Netherlands, Kees Waaldijk argued that the attainment of marriage equality legislation in that country was the result of an inevitable progression toward legal equality that resulted from the gradual liberalization of attitudes toward homosexuality over the preceding century.[1] Marriage equality from this perspective is therefore framed as the ultimate and final signifier of a successful battle against legal discrimination and for social acceptance of homosexuality.

Amid this optimistic rhetoric, a less vocal, but equally powerful, critique has been articulated by queer scholars in recent decades, questioning the representation of marriage as an ideal or universal model for same-sex relationships. In 2002, Lisa Duggan coined the phrase "homonormativity" to describe a neoliberal vision of limited equality on depoliticized, "private" terms. Arguing that neoliberal policies in the United States and Britain have forged "a politics that offers a dramatically shrunken public sphere and a narrow zone of 'responsible' domestic privacy," Duggan describes marriage equality as "public recognition of a domesticated, depoliticized privacy" and claims that the quest for lesbian and gay marriage "does not contest dominant heteronormative assumptions and institutions but upholds and sustains them."[2] For Duggan and other queer critics of the marriage rights movement, the concentration on this issue risks removing the radically transformative potential of queer sexuality from lesbian and gay activism and further outlawing those queer subjects whose sexual practices cannot be encompassed within the framework of the new homonormativity.[3] Similarly, Judith Butler has argued that the debate around marriage equality has created a distinction between those recognized lesbian and gay subjects, in a stable relationship, who could potentially be legitimized by marriage and those illegitimate subjects whose sexual agency functions outside these parameters and thus could never be absorbed into the sphere of legitimacy. She notes:

> The petition for marriage rights seeks to solicit state recognition for non-heterosexual unions, and so configures the state as withholding an entitlement that it really should distribute in a nondiscriminatory way, regardless of sexual orientation. That the state's offer might result in the intensification of normalization is not widely recognised as a problem within the mainstream lesbian and gay movement.

However, she suggests normalization should be regarded with considerable concern as: "Variations on kinship that depart from normative, dyadic, heterosexually-based family forms secured through the marriage vow are figured not only as dangerous for the child, but perilous to the putative natural and cultural laws said to sustain human intelligibility."[4]

While these two broad arguments have dominated liberal academic debate about same-sex marriage, both I would suggest have, in different ways, tended to obscure questions of gender. In focusing on marriage equality as a final stage in a teleology of homosexual law reform, campaigners and commentators have drawn on a broadly masculine framework that moves from nineteenth-century legislation against sodomy to mid-twentieth-century male homosexual law reform and culminates in gay marriage. Given the relative infrequency with which Western legal frameworks explicitly prohibited lesbian sexuality, this model is less helpful in considering same-sex marriage between women, and tends to obscure the different social and cultural forms of oppression faced by lesbians.[5] Similarly, the focus by queer critics on the dangers of "normalization" posed by marriage equality invites us—quite rightly—to consider how marriage excludes those whose relationship models do not fit the pattern of a monogamous, long-term commitment between two people established by marriage. However, less attention is paid to the internal power dynamics within such a relationship and the ways in which gendered inequalities existing in wider society can be reproduced and maintained through the institution of marriage.

It is this inequality that has been at the heart of feminist critiques of the institution of marriage since the late eighteenth century. From Mary Wollstonecraft's 1792 refusal of marriage as a surrendering of rights over her property, body, and children, to the Radicalesbians' 1970s critique of marriage and all monogamous relationships as oppressive of women and destructive of individual agency, feminists have drawn attention to the ways in which marriage is particularly disempowering for women.[6] Nineteenth-century feminist debates about marriage drew on liberal ideals of freedom and bodily autonomy to attack the legal principle of coverture, which subsumed a married woman's legal existence into that of her husband. Campaigns sought to give married women the right to hold property and capital and retain their own wages, to be entitled to custody of their own children, to reform divorce law, and to enhance women's rights over their own bodies. As Lucy Bland has argued, marriage campaigns were centered on the theme "of a married woman's right over her own person—her personal autonomy—and a transformed, purified and moral relationship between the sexes."[7] Thus many feminists promoted ideal marriage as an emotional and spiritual union between two equals, rather than an institution designed solely to legitimate sexual relations and the procreation of children. Feminists were successful in achieving a number of legislative reforms in the late nineteenth and early twentieth centuries, and the ideal of companionate marriage had gained widespread acceptance by the mid-twentieth century. However, many of the structural inequalities in the marital relationship remained and critiques of the institution emerged with new vigor in the 1950s and 1960s, with the work of Simone de Beauvoir, Betty Friedan, Viola Klein, and Germaine Greer.[8] Drawing on social science research and philosophical perspectives, feminists highlighted the disparity between social norms that represented marriage and motherhood as the ultimate goals for women and the persistent unhappiness of many housewives in the postwar West. Much of this unhappiness was located in the institution of marriage itself and the gendered inequalities that it perpetuated. As Rosemary Auchmuty reflected in her summary of feminist critiques of marriage: "Marriage has been shown to endow men with a better lifestyle, greater freedom and more power, while it has the opposite effect on women, limiting, impoverishing, and rendering them vulnerable to abuses of power by their husbands."[9]

However, while feminist critiques of marriage have been voiced consistently throughout the same-sex marriage debate in recent decades, their impact has been limited. The very different experience that women have historically undergone in marriage is rarely acknowledged, and contemporary debates about marriage equality continue to elide gender differences between lesbians and gay men. This chapter is an attempt to open up this debate and explore some of the questions that arise when we begin to consider the impact of gender, rather than sexuality, in shaping the experience of marriage for lesbians. What, for example, can individual women's experiences of both heterosexual and lesbian marriage-like relationships tell us about gendered roles in marriage and the social meanings given to marriage for women? Has women's experience of heterosexual marriage in the postwar period reflected feminist critiques of the institution? Have women found marriage to a man to be "limiting, impoverishing, and rendering them vulnerable to abuses of power by their husbands"? Finally, if this is women's experience of marriage, does same-sex marriage have anything different to offer women, or is it unavoidably a restrictive institution that oppresses women?

In her 2007 book *Between Women: Friendship, Desire and Marriage in Victorian England*, Sharon Marcus argues that middle- and upper-class Victorian women were able to form female marriages that were both accepted and acknowledged by their respectable, legally married peers and yet that, in their avoidance of coverture and other gendered inequalities, also represented a model of an ideal companionate marriage that inspired feminist campaigns for marriage reform. She claims:

> Although women in a female marriage did not have the benefit of a legally recognised union, they already enjoyed two of the privileges that women married to men fought for over the course of the century: independent rights to their income and property, and the freedom to dissolve their relationships and form new ones. They also created unions that did not depend on sexual difference, gender

hierarchy, or biological reproduction for their underpinnings, as most Victorian marriages between men and women did in legal theory if not in social fact.[10]

Female marriages, instead, combined romantic notions of marriage as based on love and fidelity, with an understanding of marriage as a contract between equals. Marcus' work therefore highlights the flexibility of marriage as an institution and points to the potential for same-sex marriage to rework the institution itself.

In exploring these questions, I will draw on oral history interviews, conducted by myself for a project on lesbian relationship models in postwar Australia and Britain, as well as interviews with British lesbians contained within the Hall Carpenter Archive at the British Library, to consider whether and how women's imagined and lived relationships with other women have differed from those with men. Both sets of interviews were conducted with women who identified as lesbian at the time of the interview and explore, among other themes, women's experiences and understandings of relationships. In the context of postwar social pressures on women to marry in both Britain and Australia, many of the women interviewed had experience of both heterosexual marriage and long-term same-sex partnerships, and their accounts therefore afford a rare opportunity to compare women's expectations and experience of opposite-sex and same-sex relationships. While these women's accounts of their heterosexual marriages were inevitably framed through the prism of their subsequent identification as lesbians, rendering them potentially less positive about heterosexual marriage than many of their contemporaries, their accounts are valuable as evidence of the flexibility of marriage as an institution. Many women who had experienced heterosexual marriage as a limiting and unequal relationship nevertheless went on to forge marriage-like relationships with other women, which they described in more positive, equal terms. Any attempt to explore the potential for same-sex couples to rework the institution of marriage is necessarily rendered problematic by the different legal and social contexts in which opposite-sex and same-sex marriages have been understood in the past. Same-sex marriage was not legally recognized in Britain prior to the Marriage (Same Sex Couples) Act 2013 and has only very recently been recognized in Australia in 2017. There is therefore no shared legal or social framework for comparing opposite-sex and same-sex marriages in the postwar period. While opposite-sex marriage brought with it legal protections and structures as well as social approbation, same-sex marriage in this period was typically a private relationship with few or no legal protections that, unlike its Victorian counterpart, was as likely to draw familial and social disapproval as commendation. While the legal and social context in which a marriage exists is undeniably important in shaping individual women's experiences of the married state, it is, however, the private, interpersonal aspects of the married relationship that are the primary concern of this chapter.

In the immediate postwar decades, social attitudes toward marriage and motherhood as the ideal social role for women framed women's experience in Australia and Britain and prompted many women to marry, sometimes despite an awareness of their attraction to other women. Historians have stressed the social importance of marriage in this period, and Lisa Featherstone has argued that in 1950s Australia, "For all men and women, marital heterosexuality was clearly constructed as both the ideal and the norm."[11] Marriage rates remained high in the 1960s, reaching a peak in Britain in 1972, when fewer than 5 percent of women remained unmarried. However, from the early 1970s, a growing acceptance of premarital sexuality and unmarried motherhood fostered increased rates of cohabitation before marriage, and the importance of marriage as an indicator of respectability declined in the 1980s and 1990s.[12] This shift in attitudes toward marriage is reflected in women's personal accounts of their experience of marriage in the postwar period. The desire for social approval or the need to have children within a socially acceptable framework dominated women's accounts of their motivations for marrying between the 1950s and 1970s. Sharley, who came to Britain as a refugee from Germany on the Kindertransport in the 1930s, said that she married a British conscientious objector in the 1940s in response to a psychological need to be a British citizen. A matron at the hospital where she worked had treated her badly for being German and she hoped that marriage to a British man would offer some protection from such attitudes. She recalled that she "quite liked" Alan, her husband, and "probably thought she was in love" but "hated being touched" by him. In addition to the security of British citizenship, marriage allowed her to find an outlet for her "strong maternal drive" and, after having children, she ceased sexual activities with her husband and subsequently came out as a lesbian.[13] A decade later, college student Cynnie confided in a friend about her passionate physical relationship with another woman. Her friend told her that she was "clearly the most obvious lesbian I've ever seen." Confronted with this new word and concept, Cynnie tried to make sense of her lesbianism in the context of the only socially acceptable intimate relationship she was aware of: marriage. She recalled:

> And I think the male-female married relationship was, to me, the only possibility, and if I fell in love with a woman, who was clearly a fairly feminine sort of woman, and I was clearly a tomboy, then I must be the one who was in some way wrong, and the way to put things right would be to have operations to change my sex and then we could get married and then perhaps we could have children.

Unable to imagine herself married to a man, but equally unable to conceive of a relationship between two women as acceptable, Cynnie at first believed that it was only by becoming a man herself that it would be possible for her to achieve both the loving relationship and social respectability she desired. After several years of indecision, the relationship ended when Cynnie's lover sought the respectability of legal marriage and Cynnie herself began to explore the possibility of a non-marital relationship between two women.[14] In late 1970s Australia, after a period of relationships with and attractions to other girls in her adolescence, Jenny also considered heterosexual marriage as providing the only route into social acceptance. She had experienced bullying and social ostracism at school when her peers discovered her same-sex attractions and explained her decision to marry as a response to this:

> I had this weird thing that I wanted to be very normal, and that involved getting married and having kids, and being successful and doing all those things that, I suppose, those people that taunted me when I was younger, it was a case of, you

know, I'll show you, this is how I am. I did that for a very long time. I did, I had a very successful relationship, very successful children.

Jenny described her marriage as motivated entirely by a desire to conform to her understanding of what was regarded as "normal" and "successful" in society at large. Asked to reflect on her own role within the family she created, she replied:

> Both within the family and externally, we were this wonderful family that people used to think, oh, they're great ... but at the time, it was important to me that people knew that we were happy and doing things that families should do—you know, eating at the table every night and all those sorts of textbook things you read about. We were the textbook family. We did all those textbook things.[15]

Many women emphasized the importance of marriage as the primary site for motherhood in both countries for much of the postwar period. Both for women who wanted to have children, and for those who found themselves unexpectedly pregnant, marriage was understood as the only acceptable option in the 1950s and 1960s. Margaret, who met her long-term lover, Vera, in Coventry in 1950, described how Vera left her after fifteen years in order to marry and have children. Recalling their relationship, she explained:

> While I was [in Coventry] I met the love of my life then. Vera. We were together about 15 years. But Vera wanted to have a little family. At the beginning of our relationship after about three or four years she wanted these children. She didn't like it that we weren't married and we couldn't be married. I'd read in the national paper, *News of the World* I think, about this woman who'd had a sex change. So I thought that's the answer ... I had to see my doctor and told him I wanted to have a sex change ... [but] he said ... he couldn't do anything ... sometimes when we'd been very close, making love, and she'd cry sometimes afterwards because she wanted a baby and she knew there was nothing that could come of it.[16]

Margaret's experience was echoed by many women in Britain and Australia whose same-sex relationships came to an end when one partner decided to marry in order to have children. Others found themselves drawn into marriage through either the fear or reality of extramarital pregnancy. Australian Jan recalled that marriage offered the only protection against the disgrace of becoming pregnant out of wedlock. Jan married a fellow student at university in the 1950s and reflected:

> See back in those days the other issue was, if you were sexually active that the possibility of a shotgun wedding was massively important ... you could lose your scholarship, you couldn't finish your course, I mean it was really dramatically bad for you career-wise and I wasn't all that careerist, but I was quite keen to finish my course. So the only way out really was to get married because we'd all realised by then that contraception such as it was, was pretty unsafe. Yeah, so you got married.[17]

In the early 1970s, Sally was also at university in Melbourne training to be a doctor when she fell pregnant and married the father of her child.

Conventional attitudes toward roles within marriage meant that many women described their experience of heterosexual marriage as having limited their opportunities and constrained their ability to express themselves as individuals. In accounting for these inequalities, women emphasized the significance of gendered roles in shaping the internal power dynamics of relationships, rather than the institution of marriage itself. Sally recalled:

> I continued doing my course when I had the baby which was my son Adam. We were both living in Carlton and trying to study with a young child. They didn't have crèches in those days ... But I struggled on for another year or so and then just gave up. My ex-husband continued to study and he finished his course. It's not an unusual pattern.[18]

Similarly Jacinta, who fell pregnant to a boyfriend she met while fruit-picking in Queensland in the 1980s, described the experience of marriage and motherhood as a closing down of possibilities. She explained:

> When we first come back from picking, I was going to—I'd signed up for Kangaroo Point TAFE, because they did art courses down there [and I was going to do commercial art]. I'd actually looked at a house to rent. It was like a share house or whatever, and it was probably about two weeks later, I found out I was pregnant. So I suppose everything just stopped then.

Jacinta took the decision that if she was going to keep the child, she should stay with the child's father, Robert, and went on to have a twenty-year relationship and two further children with him. She described their relationship as "very up and down" and said, "he was just abusive and stuff and progressively got worse." They adopted conventional roles, with Robert working and Jacinta taking responsibility for childcare and housework (with assistance from her mother, who lived nearby) and it was the power imbalance and gendered constraints of this relationship that Jacinta emphasized as her reasons for ultimately leaving.[19]

These accounts of heterosexual marriage suggested that marriage was understood by women within a broader social context as an approved form of intimate relations and a legitimate framework within which to raise children. However, for many women, the gendered roles that were widely accepted as the norm within marriage meant that this social approval came at the cost of limiting their opportunities in the workforce and locating them in a subordinate position within an unequal relationship. In the late 1960s and 1970s, women's liberation and lesbian and gay activists began to articulate a powerful critique of marriage and the nuclear family as oppressive institutions. Feminist and gay literature, magazines, and newsletters were filled with passionate accounts of the nuclear family as a heteropatriarchal institution that crippled its individual members, oppressed women, and promoted compulsory heterosexuality. A special issue of British feminist journal *Shrew* in 1971, on the family, began with the observation: "the institution of the family is responsible for many (all?) of our hang-ups."[20] Col Eglington elaborated on this point in her submission, on behalf of lesbian and gay campaigning group CAMP NSW, to the Australian Royal Commission on Human Relationships. She argued:

> The nuclear family is a power structure, a sexist power structure in that the assigning of male and female roles to the children of the family necessarily assigns power in that women take the lesser power position and men in our society hold the power, they hold the self-determining power and also the sort of more obvious powers, money, position, careers, these sorts of things.[21]

The marriage relationship at the heart of the nuclear family, feminists argued, was oppressive and divisive for women. Reflecting on the different experiences of marriage for British men and women, *Spare Rib* argued: "The power is in his hands. He may choose to treat you well. If not—if he doesn't give you enough for the housekeeping, or if he starts to beat you up—then nobody will intervene unless you admit that your marriage has irretrievably broken down and institute divorce or separation proceedings."[22] Marriage was therefore an unequal institution in which women were placed in a subservient role, forced into unpaid drudgery, and isolated from the support of other women. In the social revolution that was to come, it was hoped new relational models would emerge to challenge and replace the nuclear family. Same-sex relationships seemed to offer an opportunity for women to explore these new, more equal, forms of relationship. As Australian, Jan Smith put it, in 1977: "The essential point of Lesbianism, and that which is usually overlooked, is that it involves not just sex, but love between women: love between equals—a potentially far healthier and more egalitarian proposition than the typical heterosexual equivalent."[23]

Women's accounts of their own relationships strongly reflect this perspective, and many women who moved from heterosexual marriages to lesbian relationships, throughout the postwar period, regarded their relationship with another woman as an opportunity to liberate themselves from the oppressive structures of marriage and forge new ways of relating. Sharley, who began a twenty-five-year relationship with Georgina in the early 1950s after a decade of marriage to husband Alan, recalled:

> Georgina would say to me, "What shall we do?" And I'd say, "What do you want to do?" … And I said, we must both take responsibility. I don't want to pressurise you into doing things and I don't want to be pressurised by you. I think we should be equal. Now she loved cooking, and I certainly didn't object to her cooking and she was more domesticated than I, but it didn't mean to say that she was into a domestic scene rather than I. She was certainly tidier … But you see, again, Georgina was political. Maybe not quite as far committed as I was, but her politics also taught her that as a woman she has got to be a responsible person.[24]

Sharley saw her and Georgina's political consciousness as having been important in shaping their ideas about their relationship and, from the 1970s onward, an increasing number of women were influenced by feminist ideas about equality and collectivity in constructing roles in their relationship. Sally left her husband for her partner, Anneke, in the mid-1980s and reflected on the shifting dynamics in their relationship:

> We've had lots of spirited discussions. We often disagree on nearly everything. We go back and forth, back and forth, back and forth for days if not weeks. So it's very tiring at times but we get there in the end. With the housework I think I probably did a bit more. I don't know—certainly we did close on even. At that stage I think I used to do more of the cooking. But that's changed now and Anneke does most of the cooking now … it evolved over time … our roles changed. We were aware that it was really hard to create roles for a lesbian relationship, and that's what we thought we had to do.[25]

While Sharley and Sally imagined their same-sex relationships as offering an opportunity to escape the gendered inequalities that they saw as inherent in heterosexual marriage, both their accounts also demonstrate that equality did not necessarily come easily in relationships between women either. Both described a process of conscious consideration and ongoing negotiation in order to achieve equal roles. Other women's accounts of their same-sex relationships suggested that gendered inequalities might be replaced by other forms of structural inequality. Angela, describing her seven-year relationship with Jean in 1960s London, referred to the power struggles caused by the age difference in the relationship. Jean was thirteen years older than twenty-year-old Angela when they met, with a young child and a career as a schoolteacher; Angela recalled that Jean "used to try to put her foot down" and "treated [her] like a pupil sometimes" during their "up and down" relationship.[26]

While many women envisaged their same-sex relationships as offering a potential freedom and equality in contrast to the gendered constraints of heterosexual marriage, attitudes toward female marriage were mixed. For Sally, the carefully considered balance and understanding that has structured her relationship with Anneke was developed in the context of a political framework that rejected marriage. However, considering the possibility of legal same-sex marriage after twenty-five years of partnership with Anneke, Sally observed:

> I basically have spent decades believing that marriage is a patriarchal institution, designed for inheritance rules. However … if Anneke were wanting to get married then yes, I think I would. But I'd feel really strange … I cannot get away from my previous beliefs of it being an institution which was bad for women. So I'll just have to update myself and get with the times. But it has so many bad connotations for me; it's really hard to get past them.[27]

Sally's grudging comment that, if her partner wanted to marry, she might have to reconsider her strong objections to marriage as an institution and "update myself and get with the times" points to a growing sense that marriage might be a more flexible institution than the rhetoric of women's and gay liberation suggested. After building an equal partnership over twenty-five years with Anneke, Sally was ready to consider the possibility that the relationship between the two of them could be sustained even in the context of the institution of marriage and that it might, therefore, be possible to move away from the historic inequalities that have shaped women's experiences of marriage in the past, toward a more personal, egalitarian model of marriage. This is a view that is supported by the accounts of a number of other women who have conceived lesbian marriage in very different terms from the oppressive institution critiqued by feminism.

Reflecting on the female marriages of Victorian actress Charlotte Cushman, Sharon Marcus observed that "The language of marriage described the quality of her commitment to a sexual partner rather than a gendered division of roles."[28] Describing what attracted them to the possibility of formal marriage with their female partners, British and Australian women in the late twentieth century similarly tended to construct marriage as an expression of private commitment. Jenny, who described her heterosexual marriage as a demonstration of success to others, framed lesbian marriage in different terms. Discussing her intention to ask her partner of seven years to marry her, she explained:

> I think it shows an even deeper level of commitment that yes, in the eyes of the law, we're a couple ... It's not just that you've shacked up together and share the expenses, and it doesn't mean that you love each other less or more, but it's showing your partner, even in the act of asking them to marry you, that you consider the relationship a very deep and meaningful relationship ... I don't know that I think too much about the public acknowledgement of the relationship ... It's about us, it's about my commitment to her, so that she knows how committed I am. It's like a formal commitment.[29]

Similarly, Jacinta, who had recently become engaged to her partner, Vicki, imagined their planned wedding as a commitment to each other. Reflecting on the fact that their Australian marriage would not be officially recognized, she said: "It doesn't bother me, because I just think if you're going to be with someone, you can stand there and make a commitment to them without signing a piece of paper and all the rest of it anyway." Jacinta, like many of the women who described their same-sex relationships throughout the postwar period, represented hers as a partnership based on equality and communication. Consciously reacting against her previous unhappy marriage to a man, Jacinta explained that her current same-sex relationship was structured on very different terms. She said:

> Because my last relationship was so nasty, he was a dictator and stuff, I've just gone these are my rules. I'm not going to let someone wipe their feet on me. It works both ways, I think, in a relationship too. There's give and take, and if there's no give and take, then obviously, there's no relationship. It's just totally different.

In practical terms, this meant that Jacinta and Vicki shared the cooking and housework on an informal basis. As Jacinta put it: "it just goes with the flow. One will do it or the other one will get up and do it. We don't have a list or anything like that." For Jacinta and Vicki, their anticipated marriage would not simply maintain the structural equality they had built in their relationship to date, but reinforce it through an expression of personal commitment to each other.[30]

In conclusion, I have drawn on long-standing feminist critiques of marriage to urge that we pay greater attention to gender difference in our discussion of same-sex marriage. While the concerns of scholars such as Lisa Duggan and Judith Butler that lesbian and gay marriage represents a potentially dangerous "normalization" of same-sex relationships have been widely acknowledged, much less consideration has been given to feminist critiques of marriage as an unequal and oppressive institution. As same-sex marriage has become a reality in Britain and in Australia, we need to reflect much more carefully on the ways in which gender has shaped women's experience of marriage differently than men's. Examining a few personal accounts of British and Australian women's relationships, I have tried to suggest that same-sex marriage need not necessarily replicate the power inequalities inherent in heterosexual marriage and that, for those women, at least, who seek to consciously reject older models of marriage, it might be possible to rework the institution into a more private and considered commitment between equal partners.

Notes

1 Kees Waaldijk, "Small Change: How the Road to Same-Sex Marriage Got Paved in the Netherlands," in *Legal Recognition of Same-Sex Partnership. A Study of National, European and International Law*, ed. Robert Wintemute and Mads Andenas (Oxford: Hart Publishing, 2001), 437–464.

2 Lisa Duggan, "The New Homonormativity: The Sexual Politics of Neoliberalism," in *Materializing Democracy: Toward a Revitalized Cultural Politics*, ed. Russ Castronovo and Dana D. Nelson (Duke University Press, 2002), 182, 190, 179. See also Michael Warner, *The Trouble with Normal: Sex, Politics and the Ethics of Queer Life* (New York: The Free Press, 1999), 82, 109–116. Writing from a feminist perspective, Barbara Baird has similarly framed the same-sex marriage debate in the context of the neoliberal politics of the family; see Barbara Baird, "'Kerryn and Jackie' Thinking Historically about Lesbian Marriages," *Historical Studies* 36, no. 126 (2005): 257.

3 Judith Butler, "Is Kinship Always Already Heterosexual?" *Differences* 13, no. 1 (2002): 20; Wendy Brown, *States of Injury: Power and Freedom in Late Modernity* (Princeton: Princeton University Press, 1995), 126.

4 Butler, "Is Kinship," 16.

5 On legal approaches to lesbianism in the UK see, for example, Laura Doan, "'Gross Indecency between Women': Policing Lesbians or Policing Lesbian Police?" *Social & Legal Studies* 6, no. 4 (1997): 533–551; and Laura Doan, "'Acts of Female Indecency': Sexology's Intervention in Legislating Lesbianism," in *Sexology in Culture: Labelling Bodies and Desires*, ed. Lucy Bland and Laura Doan (Cambridge: Polity Press, 1998), 199–213. On the Australian context, see Ruth Ford, "Lady Friends' and 'Sexual Deviationists': Lesbians and Law in Australia 1920s–1950s,'" in *Sex, Power and Justice: Historical Perspectives on the Law in Australia, 1788–1990*, ed. D. E. Kirkby (Melbourne: Oxford University Press, 1995), 33–49; Rebecca Jennings, "Sandra Willson: A Case Study in Lesbian Identities in 1950s and 1970s Australia," *History*

  Australia 10, no. 1 (April 2013): 99–124; Rebecca Jennings, *Unnamed Desires: A Sydney Lesbian History* (Melbourne: Monash University Publishing, 2015).
6. On the Melbourne Radicalesbians, see Robert Reynolds, *From Camp to Queer: Remaking the Australian Homosexual* (Melbourne: Melbourne University Press, 2002); Rebecca Jennings, "Womin Loving Womin: Lesbian Feminist Theories of Intimacy," in *Intimacy, Violence and Activism: Gay and Lesbian Perspectives on Australasian History and Society*, ed. Graham Willett and Yorick Smaal (Melbourne: Monash University Publishing, 2013), 133–146.
7. Lucy Bland, *Banishing the Beast: Feminist, Sex and Morality* (London: Tauris Parke Paperbacks, 2001), 125.
8. Simone de Beauvoir, *The Second Sex* (London: Jonathan Cape, 1953); Betty Friedan, *The Feminine Mystique* (London: Victor Gollancz, 1963); Germaine Greer, *The Female Eunuch* (London: Paladin, 1972).
9. Rosemary Auchmuty, "Same-Sex Marriage Revived: Feminist Critique and Legal Strategy," *Feminism & Psychology* 14, no. 1 (2004): 105.
10. Sharon Marcus, *Between Women: Friendship, Desire and Marriage in Victorian England* (Oxford: Princeton University Press, 2007), 205.
11. Lisa Featherstone, *Let's Talk About Sex: Histories of Sexuality in Australia from Federation to the Pill* (Newcastle: Cambridge Scholars Publishing, 2011), 242.
12. Jane Lewis, "Marriage," in *Women in Twentieth-Century Britain*, ed. Ina Zweiniger-Bargielowska (Harlow: Pearson Education Ltd., 2001), 69–85.
13. National Sound Archive (NSA), Hall Carpenter Collection (HCC) (C456), F2158-F2163, Sharley McLean.
14. NSA, HCC (C456), F2109, Cynthia Reid.
15. Interview by author with Jenny (pseudonym) on May 31, 2012.
16. Interview by author with Margaret (pseudonym) on April 15, 2015.
17. Interview by author with Jan Aitkin, June 5, 2012.
18. Interview by author with Sally (pseudonym), October 6, 2012.
19. Interview by author with Jacinta.
20. "Editorial," *Shrew*, May 1971 (Vol. 3, No. 4), p. 5.
21. C. Eglington, PP?H/lb. Human p. 3198 12/2/1976.
22. "Happily Ever After?," *Spare Rib*, March 1976.
23. Jan Smith, "Lesbianism and Mental Health," *Broadsheet*, no. 53 (October 1977): 19, contained in "Women and Madness Kit," National Library of Australia.
24. NSA, HCC (C456), F2158-F2163, Sharley McLean.
25. Interview by author with Sally (pseudonym), October 6, 2012.
26. NSA, HCC (C456), F1622-F1624, Angela Chilton.
27. Interview by author with Sally (pseudonym), October 6, 2012.
28. Marcus, *Between Women*, 200.
29. Interview by author with Jenny (pseudonym), May 31, 2012.
30. Interview by author with Jacinta.

13

From Giarre to Civil Unions: The "Long March" for Same-Sex Relationships in Italy

Yuri Guaiana and Mark Seymour

Tracing the "long march" of same-sex-attracted Italians from official invisibility to legal recognition, this chapter begins with a glance back over Italy's curious specificities since the 1860s. It makes brief mention of the significant fascist period and lays out the origins of the current republic, but the main focus is on the period since 1980. That year witnessed a notorious double-suicide by two same-sex lovers, and the event can be seen as having catalyzed persistent and concerted Italian claims for acceptance of such relationships. The suicide took place in Giarre, Sicily, less than 40 km from the legendary destination of Taormina, made famous by Wilhelm von Gloeden's idyllic and often homoerotic late nineteenth-century photographs. The two young men who died so needlessly in 1980 were unwittingly to launch a long march for same-sex relationships that finally achieved at least some of its historic aims by May 2016. This was the moment a civil-union law was finally approved by the Italian parliament, granting official recognition to same-sex relationships in Italy for the first time. The march continues, of course, but now, after an extended lag, Italian same-sex couples have at least come within sight of their western European neighbors in terms of rights and recognition.

Historical background

A unified nation since 1861, Italy presents an ambiguous historical backdrop for same-sex relationships. Characterized by relative legal freedom from the late nineteenth century, negative social and cultural attitudes nevertheless endured well into the twenty-first.[1] Reflecting Catholic doctrine, most of the various pre-unification legal codes of the peninsula criminalized sexual acts "against nature." On the other hand, prosecutions were relatively uncommon, and usually only concerned cases involving the abuse of minors.[2] The major new criminal code devised in the wake of Italian unification, which took effect from 1890, did away with reference to same-sex sexual acts entirely, and sections on violation of minors no longer referred to the gender of those involved.[3] By not mentioning same-sex acts at all, the Italian code effectively "decriminalized" them relatively early compared with many other legislations. But this also ushered the question of homosexuality out of official and public discourse, just at a time when the concept of homosexuality had begun to be applied to a particular type of person elsewhere. A curious result was that the notion of same-sex attraction became more or less invisible in Italy, except perhaps in highly specialized medical works. This official "disappearance" has made the subject difficult to trace in broad historical and cultural terms.[4]

The absence of criminal provisions and the emergence of a long-term "don't ask, don't tell" culture meant that before the rise of Mussolini's fascism in 1922 and particularly for foreigners, Italy developed a reputation for tolerance of same-sex sexuality. In the second half of the nineteenth century, certain alluring sites such as Venice, Capri, and Taormina became legendary precursors of modern gay tourism. Such places attracted well-to-do, homosexually inclined foreigners from the harsher legal climates of Northern Europe, particularly Britain and Germany. As Robert Aldrich showed in a pioneering 1993 study, these visitors were seduced by Italy's artistic riches, classical heritage, and sexual opportunities unshadowed by fear of legal reprisal.[5] From certain perspectives then—generally northern European—Italy appears as the quintessential gay paradise of the *belle époque*.

On the other hand, the lack of a law against homosexual acts did not necessarily make Italy a congenial place for same-sex-attracted Italians, nor did the march of time bring steady improvement. Lorenzo Benadusi's exhaustive study of the fascist regime's persecution of homosexuals between 1922 and 1943 showed that even without reintroducing anti-homosexual laws, a hostile regime still had many tools at its disposal to persecute homosexual men.[6] The fact that the fascist government did just that with a degree of determination suggests that the tolerance for which Italy had become known prior to the First World War was superficial, and that the 1890 criminal code's mere silence on homosexual acts had done nothing to alter fundamental public attitudes. These attitudes continued to be influenced by Catholic doctrine, and, except in some small pockets, probably remained as negative as they were anywhere else in Europe.

Fascism's demise in 1943, the revival of democracy in 1946, and the foundation of Italy as a republic in 1948 relegated state persecution of homosexuals to an era of dictatorship that most Italians wished to put behind them. But, despite Italian women receiving the vote in 1946 and other promising indications of political freedoms and post-fascist social renewal, the postwar period was no gay springtime. Neither the ruling Christian Democrats (DC) nor their main opposition, the Italian Communist Party (PCI), evinced any particular sympathy for, or even awareness of, same-sex sexuality. In fact, on the rare occasions when awareness did emerge, attitudes were severe, as demonstrated by the PCI's expulsion of Pier Paolo Pasolini—destined to become one of Italy's most prominent literary figures—on "moral grounds" in 1949, after he was denounced by a priest for sexual involvement with under-age men.[7]

Even if Pasolini's partners had been older, it would be anachronistic to look back and expect more clement attitudes. Postwar social values, including those relating to sexuality, were heavily influenced by a Church that enjoyed more cultural prestige in the 1940s and 1950s than at any time since Italian unification. The Italian republic experienced rapid modernization during its postwar economic miracle, which increased wealth and raised living standards, but also brought demographic dislocation and social disorientation. Perhaps in reaction, moral values in relation to matters of sexuality remained markedly conservative even beyond the 1960s, when they had clearly begun to relax elsewhere. The contradictions of the period in Italy were dazzlingly captured in Federico Fellini's 1960 cinematic masterpiece, *La dolce vita*. Except in certain restricted, albeit high-profile, milieux such as the elite nightclubs of Rome's Via Veneto, throughout the 1960s Catholic modesty and family values held strong sway, as demonstrated by the decade's notorious resistance to the introduction of a divorce law. Such a law was granted in Italy only in 1970, and even then, it was the subject of bitter contestation.[8]

Despite the economic, cultural, and social forces that in much of the postwar West had given rise to movements, particularly feminism, whose broad aims were to politicize "the personal," in the 1970s Italy's governments remained resistant to progressive reforms even in the heterosexual arena. For example, fascist laws regulating birth control were repealed only in 1971, and abortion was the subject of ongoing feminist struggles until it was legalized, on a very restricted basis, in 1978.[9] Italy's 1970s were thus hardly a propitious context for early attempts to claim acceptance of same-sex relationships. As the story of Pasolini's murder in 1975 suggests, finding sex with other men may have been easy, but living in an openly homosexual relationship would have been extremely difficult, even in the largest cities.[10] Ultimately, Italians had to wait significantly longer for "gay liberation" than did their counterparts in other Western countries. While in places like the United States, Britain, France, the Netherlands, and Germany the march for liberation was under way by the late 1960s, it was only in the 1980s that analogous developments began to register consistently in Italy's public sphere.

The suicide in Giarre, 1980

On November 1, 1980, the newspaper *La Sicilia* ran the headline "Homosexual Kills Partner and Immediately Suicides beside Him," followed by an article revealing the horrific conclusion to the love story between Giorgio Agatino, twenty-six, and Antonino Galatola, fifteen, in the small, but not remote, Sicilian town of Giarre.[11] The apparent involvement of Galatola's twelve-year-old nephew, Francesco Messina, to shoot the older member of the couple only added to the way a local tragedy became a national scandal that resounded loudly through the mainstream media. The press seized upon the age difference between the lovers and the involvement of a minor in the suicide, with some journalists framing the events not as a *Liebestod*, but as a necessary sacrifice against a pestilence that could corrupt modernizing societies. Beyond such generalizations, the sexual relationship at the heart of the story was a taboo that the newspapers found difficult to confront directly. In their accounts and analyses of the crime, journalists revealed their own and others' brutal ignorance about same-sex relationships, even among the educated. Such reports fanned the flames of a public reaction that, to the fledgling Italian gay liberation groups of the period, revealed prejudice and fear worthy of the Middle Ages.

The broad historical context was a nation mired in a traumatic period of political upheaval that had ensued from the violent social protests of 1968–69, and continued until the early 1980s. In Italian history the epoch became known as the *anni di piombo* (years of lead), because of the frequency of gunfire and acts of terrorism, perpetrated by extremist groups on both left and right. The best known example is the Red Brigades' 1978 kidnapping and murder of Aldo Moro, former prime minister and leader of the Christian Democrats. Moro had been the key architect of an "historic compromise," through which the DC's 1976 and 1978 governments were lent external support by the Communist Party. The "compromise" was hailed in some quarters as a progressive arrangement, but in others as unprincipled and cynical political pragmatism. On the left, many felt betrayed by what they saw as the neutralization of the Communist Party's revolutionary aspirations.

It was from this fraught political humus that notable seeds of Italian homosexual political activism began to grow in earnest, and, from the outset, the issue was more overtly politicized than in most other Western nations. The double-suicide in Giarre prompted leftist and liberal-progressive parties to reflect on a "problem" the nation's nineteenth-century legislators had sought to remove from public debate, but that had evidently not gone away. The Communist Party had on its conscience the 1949 expulsion of Pasolini, and the Giarre suicide occurred one day before the fifth anniversary of the famous writer's murder. The party had also hemorrhaged votes in the 1979 general elections, partly a reaction to the "historic compromise," but also a result of other developments, such as the rise of feminism, which drew many women's votes away from the communists. All of this prompted new levels of political soul-searching. It seems no coincidence that the left-wing daily *Paese Sera* was one of the first to confront directly the "relazione omosessuale" at the heart of the Giarre suicide.[12]

The Giarre tragedy was also seen as a "cause" from a different part of the political spectrum: the Italian Radical Party. An anti-establishment grouping that never participated in Italy's complex governing coalitions, the Radicals' main political concerns were civil liberties. The party had been a key driving force behind the divorce law of 1970, and even more so the referendum of 1974 that ultimately preserved the law. In November 1980, at the Radical Party's twenty-fourth annual conference, its leader, Marco Pannella, announced the news of Giorgio and Toni's suicide in Giarre, proclaiming that the pair were guilty of nothing more than to have "hoped to honour love, themselves, and their town, simply by walking hand in hand."[13] Later, the Radicals were the only political party to mobilize at a national level over the suicide, sending their young party secretary, Francesco Rutelli, to a press conference in the Sicilian town. He declared that if the default position was intolerance, "it would lead to a blank refusal in relation to homosexuality," and he strongly advocated the development of tolerance through discussion.[14]

Italy's liberation movements

If the events at Giarre sparked the beginning of discussion about homosexuality among the progressive and anti-clerical political parties, at the grassroots level they were also to prompt more concerted and visible activism among Italy's emergent homosexual liberation groups. By 1980 such groups had been quietly active in Italy for about a decade. One of the earliest, founded in 1971, was the Fronte Unitario Omosessuale Rivoluzionario Italiano, better known by its acronym, FUORI! (meaning OUT!), a title that aligned the movement with the United States' Gay Liberation Front (GLF, founded in 1969) and France's Front Homosexuel d'Action Revolutionnaire (FHAR, founded in March 1971). Based in Turin, FUORI! was also represented in Milan, Padua, and Rome.[15]

The group's aspirations reflected an extreme-left ideological position that, despite a prescient article in its own magazine in 1979 claiming same-sex marriage as a suitable legislative goal,[16] by 1980 had mutated into an attitude that dismissed "gay marriage" as a bourgeois institutionalization of homosexuality. Instead, FUORI! set civil unions as a worthier aspiration.[17] Nevertheless, the group's main purpose was to put discussion of homosexuality on the public agenda, and accordingly, members arrived in Sicily on November 5, 1980, with the express intention of transforming the Giarre tragedy into a productive public debate, beginning with a demonstration in the town's main piazza.[18] FUORI!'s interpretation was captured in one of the association's archival documents, which states that Giorgio and Toni died "for the simple fact of having accepted and acted upon their love for each other ... the guilty are those who consider them ill, deviants, depraved."[19]

Just over a month later, on December 9, 1980, Sicilian activists associated with the left-wing cultural association ARCI (Associazione Ricreative e Culturale Italiana—the Italian Recreational and Cultural Association), motivated by the Giarre suicide, formed a new group of gay activism. The idea was launched by a defrocked priest, Marco Bisceglia, from Potenza, in the southern region of Basilicata. In 1975 Bisceglia had been approached by two journalists from the right-wing newspaper *Il Borghese*, who posed as a gay Catholic couple asking him to bless their union—a trick for which Bisceglia fell. The journalists then wrote an article on the "blessing," which led to Bisceglia's immediate suspension from the Church. After that he "changed sides," moved to Sicily, and began to work with ARCI in Palermo. The group Bisceglia founded in the wake of the Giarre suicide was formally constituted as an association in its own right in May 1981. Known as Arcigay, it was destined to become Italy's most significant gay-rights organisation.[20]

As well as concerted endeavors by activist groups, the early 1980s also saw the cautious emergence of a more commercialized and popular gay culture in Italy. A useful indicator is the monthly magazine *Babilonia*, aimed primarily at gay men. Founded in Milan in 1983 and published until 2009, *Babilonia* described itself as the first Italian gay periodical with a national focus, and it was distributed nationally through newsagents. Copies from the early years reveal an intriguing range of content, from serious articles on "Faith and sexuality," Milan's venereal disease clinic, poetry, and film reviews (an early cover featured Brad Davis in *Querelle*), to advertisements for mail-order American pornographic videos, personals (including a small minority of women seeking women), and each month a gay guide to one of Italy's regions.[21] Photographs of male nudes also abound, many taken by the pioneering openly gay Milanese photographer Tony Patrioli.[22]

Yet it is clear from the offerings in the gay guide to Liguria in *Babilonia*'s first issue of 1983 that the main meeting places for same-sex-attracted men in Italy had not developed much since an earlier stage of gay history: public gardens, beaches, railway station restrooms, sex-shops, and cinemas. Only in the larger cities was there mention of the occasional bar (sometimes hesitantly described as "mixed?"). Symbols for rating "beats," such as a triangle for "dangerous," $ for commercial sex, and * for "recommended" are also poignant signs of those times. A report on gay life in Paris indicates a comparatively more dynamic commercial scene, with weekly publication of the guide *Gai Pied*, a twenty-four-hour radio station called "Fréquence gay," many bars, and three overtly gay saunas.[23] By contrast, *Babilonia*'s second annual pocket guide to Italy, *Italia Gay 1983*, in a listing of cosmopolitan Milan's gay venues, announces cryptically that "There are saunas frequented by gays but the managements have not authorised us to provide details."[24]

While the gay scene in Italy gradually commercialized, certain pioneering individuals mounted court cases designed to test Italian law and force the state to grant recognition to same-sex couples. The best known early example was provided by Doriano Galli, who took his case to court in 1981, arguing that neither Italy's civil law nor its constitution required marriage partners to be of the opposite sex. Galli's case was supported by his lawyer, Simonetta Massaroni, the Radical Party MP Adele Faccio, and Rome's communist mayor, Ugo Vetere. The court was forced to acknowledge that Galli had a point, but its ruling limited the ramifications by prioritizing the "intention of the legislator," resting its case upon the civil code's specific reference to "offspring" as an outcome of marriage. Nevertheless, Galli's plea did result in his same-sex relationship being granted rudimentary local-council recognition as a "family," with some legal rights.[25]

This interesting minor triumph did not provoke an avalanche of imitators, but it was not too long before political pressure by homosexual advocacy groups such as Arcigay resulted in avant-garde MPs proposing parliamentary bills for recognition of de facto families, including same-sex relationships, through civil unions. Such attempts were perceived by conservatives not as attempts to widen the institution of marriage's net, but as radical efforts to subvert traditional notions of marriage. The first proposal was drafted in 1986 by PCI Senator Ersilia Salvato and MPs Romana Bianchi and Angela Bottari (both PCI), but it did not proceed beyond the draft stage. Two years later, in early 1988, a draft bill by Socialist Party MP Alma Agata Cappiello was proposed to parliament, and, despite never being diarized for discussion, provoked widespread press commentary.[26]

In any case throughout the 1980s Italian homosexuals, particularly men, had other challenges on their minds, above all HIV/AIDS.[27] Although on the one hand the crisis helped break down political barriers and increase a sense of broad solidarity among homosexuals, at least in the early years it also tended to shift the movement's collective priorities away from finite political goals and toward social, cultural, and health matters. The issue also firmly placed homosexuality on the press and public agenda, though not necessarily in the best possible light. Ultimately though, the HIV/AIDS question did force the state to recognize and grapple with the fact of homosexuality as an integral aspect of Italian society. Symbolically, the first ever official meeting of a president of the Italian republic and gay political activists took place in this context: on the third iteration of World AIDS Day, December 1, 1990, President Francesco Cossiga met with representatives of Arcigay.

The 1990s

AIDS might initially have toned down strident political calls for state recognition and protection of same-sex relationships, but it also underlined the importance of social and legal protection. Italian gay political activism from the early 1990s returned to such goals. Some of the tactics were rather lighthearted and symbolic, and others were deadly serious. Inspired by Dutch activism of the 1980s, and taking advantage of Italy's local councils' role in officiating marriages, in June 1992 Paolo Hutter, a member of Milan's city council, "married" ten same-sex couples in the prominent piazza of La Scala.[28] Amusing as this antic might have been to some, 1992 also witnessed the foundation of an oppositional movement, in the guise of the Forum of Family Associations, a network of Catholic groups brought together to "protect families based on traditional marriage."[29]

The fact that Catholic activism mobilized to defend the traditional family at this point was a token of the success of gay associations and brave individuals in raising the visibility of alternative notions of the couple and the family. Milan's 1992 "mass marriage" was followed by various regional attempts to establish council registers for civil unions, as part of a longer-term strategy aiming toward a national law. The first city to establish such a register, in October 1993, was Empoli, a town in Tuscany about 20 km from Florence. The national authority with oversight of local-council activity abolished the register less than a month after it was established, but other councils followed suit sporadically, such that nineteen of them established same-sex civil-union registers over the course of the 1990s. These registers had no legal standing, but they embodied a need and a desire, and were highly symbolic. Italians are well known, rightly or wrongly, for their tendency to "campanilismo"—localism—but in this case, the local began to exert pressure on the national, rather than the other way around.

Through the 1990s, a few notable individuals and couples waged their own campaigns. Several same-sex couples tested their local councils' attitudes by applying to be married, or in some cases asking a sympathetic town councilor to stage a ceremony. For example, Massimo Milani and Gino Campanella staged a full marriage ceremony in a Palermo piazza, presided over by a local councilor, on Pride Day (28 June) 1993.[30] In March 1994, two men, accompanied by friends and family, trooped in to their local registry office in Viterbo (about 80 km north of Rome), asking to be married. The event featured in the national daily *La Repubblica*, which reported that the councilor, despite a touch of embarrassment, informed them that while the mayor was sympathetic, the law had no provision for such a thing.[31] A very different and disturbing act was the self-immolation of Catholic homosexual Alfredo Ormando in St Peter's Square on January 13, 1998, in protest against Vatican attitudes toward homosexuality.[32] Collectively such events—some amusing, some horrifying—always attracted media attention, and they showed that the issue was not likely to disappear. They built pressure, influenced public opinion, and, ultimately, paved the way for national legislation recognizing same-sex relationships—even though it was to be a long time in coming.[33]

Among Italy's gay communities, as elsewhere, there remained a tension between the sense that same-sex couples should aim only for civil unions, and the conviction that full equality would be achieved only if marriage itself were opened to same-sex couples.

Peculiarly, among gay activists those who desired the more socially conservative option of full marriage represented the more radical end of the activist spectrum, because they were demanding a reform that struck at the heart of one of Catholicism's most sacred symbols. By contrast the mainstream activist position in the 1990s held that it was simply unrealistic to aim for full marriage equality in Catholic Italy.[34] The situation was to change, however, in June 2005, after marriage in Spain was made available to same-sex couples, underlining that even in Catholic countries, the matter was not out of the question.

The year 1994, when those two men had marched into the local registry office in Viterbo, also witnessed an important large-scale event of homosexual visibility in Italy: the nation's first ever Pride march, held in Rome. After that, a Pride event was held somewhere in Italy every year. The most significant of these took place in 2000, when Rome hosted World Pride, and became the center of global attention. It happened also to be a papal jubilee year, and the Vatican's Secretary of State, Cardinal Ruini, fought hard to have Rome's World Pride banned.[35] The open clash between the Church and a colorfully bespangled manifestation of Italy's renegade anti-clerical subculture made for lively reportage in all the Italian dailies and on television for days. Finally, the then premier, Giuliano Amato, responded to Cardinal Ruini that "unfortunately," the constitution did not give him the power to do anything in relation to the parade.[36]

Spirits buoyed by the symbolic victory, World Pride in Rome went ahead more proudly than ever, drawing unprecedented international media attention to Italy's gay communities, and revealing the nation's less well-known irreverent and antiestablishment subcultures to local, national, and international audiences. In Rome itself the event attracted huge crowds, probably largely heterosexual judging by the sheer numbers of people, in addition to myriad representatives of the normally invisible LGBT communities who generally had little or nothing to do with political activism. It was a demonstration of peace and solidarity that transcended sexuality. According to historian Giovanni Dall'Orto, many felt indignant about condescending exchanges between the likes of cardinals, premiers, and other representatives of the powerful, and were inspired to mobilize *en masse* for the first time.[37] Among them were priceless examples such as Edda and Ada, women who said they had been together since 1943. Now in their seventies, they poignantly found themselves able to "hold hands in public for the first time ever, protected by the crowd."[38]

The twenty-first century

World Pride in Rome was certainly the most visible turning point so far in the long march for recognition of Italy's sexual minorities. The year 2000 seemed pregnant with possibilities everywhere, but perhaps even more so in a nation whose capital city's history is proudly measured in millennia rather than centuries, and to which the new millennium brought particularly high levels of hope and determination. The year 2000's aspirations were also encouraged by tangible initiatives such as the first in a long series of resolutions by the European Parliament exhorting member states to recognize same-sex relationships.[39] After that, and Rome's World Pride, Italy's progressive political parties had little choice but to make more room for representatives of the LGBT movement. In 2001 the first openly gay MPs were elected to the Italian parliament: Franco Grillini, who had been president of Arcigay from 1987 to 1998, and Titti De Simone, former president of Arcilesbica. Symbolic parades like World Pride were thus soon followed by more tangible political developments.

The presence of openly gay MPs in Italy's parliament was a significant step forward, and a direct result was the first parliamentary bill to extend civil marriage to same-sex couples.[40] But as before, the broader campaign continued to involve gestures and initiatives at both institutional and individual levels. Couples and singles alike sought to pull whatever levers history provided, some of them offered by events outside Italy. For example, in April 2002, Italian couple Mario Ottocento and Antonio Grullo, taking advantage of the Netherlands' historic 2001 same-sex marriage law (the world's first), were married in the very chamber in which Queen Juliana had married her husband in 1937. Availing themselves of a strategy similar to one that had been used during the 1960s campaign for a divorce law, the Italian couple then sought transcription of their foreign marriage into the Italian register. Among other things, it was a clever way of drawing attention to legal anomalies within the European Union.

Theirs was only the first of many examples to follow. A similar case that had particular resonance in the press took place in the heart of Rome. In 2002, Alessio De Giorgi and Christian Pierre Panicucci (the latter holding dual Italian and French citizenship) solemnized their union at the French Consulate, using the 1999 French civil-union law known as PACS (*pacte civil de solidarité*).

For a time Italy's LGBT movement saw PACS as the way of the future, and on Valentine's Day 2004, a rally was held in Rome under the banner "Kiss2Pacs," demanding Italian adoption of a law modeled on the French example. This was followed by an even more imposing rally in January 2006, ahead of the national elections scheduled for April that year. Titled "Tutti in PACS," the rally took place in Rome's Piazza Farnese, site of the French embassy, but also a stone's throw from a memorial to Giordano Bruno, who had been burnt at the stake for heresy in 1600. Underlining history's dark links even more pointedly, the date of the rally was January 13, the anniversary of Alfredo Ormando's self-immolation in front of St Peter's Basilica in 1998.

In the early years of the twenty-first century, the question of same-sex couples started to mutate into a broader concern about alternative families. Indicative was the 2004 publication, by Einaudi, one of Italy's most venerable publishers, of a book compiled by Piergiorgio Paterlini, a gay journalist and author, entitled simply *Matrimoni* (Marriages). In it, ten gay and lesbian couples discussed their daily lives and above all the families they had created around themselves—in some cases consisting of three generations. Collectively their stories made a strong case for the normality of same-sex-couple-centered families.[41] The following year, in March 2005, the association Famiglie Arcobaleno (Rainbow Families) was established, consisting of "couples or single homosexuals who aspire to or have become parents."[42] In Italy the campaign for recognition of same-sex relationships was no longer only about couples, but also their children, who had until this point been all but invisible.

Some of the aspirations expressed by individuals, couples, crowds, and publications in the early 2000s—reinforced by Spain's same-sex marriage law of 2005—were cautiously incorporated for the first time into the official program of the center-left coalition government formed by Romano Prodi after the 2006 elections. The coalition had its structural tensions, and it should be stressed that the resultant program in relation to civil unions was far from radical. To satisfy the sceptics, cautious wording was adopted that recognized the rights of "persons" who made up de facto unions, rather than the union itself.[43] This avoided putting de facto coupledom—whether hetero- or homosexual—on an equal footing with traditional marriage. The resultant bill on the "rights and responsibilities of persons in stable cohabitation" was presented to parliament on February 8, 2008. In fact the "rights" were framed as a reward for good conduct, applicable only after a certain number of years (ranging from three to nine) of stable cohabitation.

The timorousness of this first step by an Italian government toward recognizing de facto relationships underlines how wary many Italian politicians were about "meddling with marriage," whether due to their own consciences, or fears about Catholic reaction, or both. Indeed, the government initiative prompted the Catholic Forum of Family Associations that had been founded in 1992, to organize its own first mass rally, held in the Piazza of Saint John Lateran in Rome, on May 12, 2007. But the much more vitriolic response, published in *La Repubblica*, came directly from the mouth of Cardinal Angelo Bagnasco, Bishop of Genoa:

> Why say no to these various forms of stable cohabitation ... recognising and thus creating alternatives to the family? Why say no? Why say no to incest as in England where a brother and sister have children, live together, and love each other? Why say no to the party of pedophiles in Holland who say it doesn't matter if two people meet and consent? Because we must keep in mind that these aberrations of common sense are already germinating[44]

In any case, after having been diluted even further, the bill's progress stalled with the collapse of the Prodi government itself in 2008. Indignation and disappointment over the entire affair prompted the birth of two new associations. The first, founded in 2007, was the Avvocatura per i diritti LGBTI– Rete Lenford (Advocacy for the Rights of LGBTI—Lenford Network).[45] The second, founded in 2008, was the Associazione Radicale Certi Diritti (Radical Association for Certain Rights), a member organization of the Radical Party. Both these groups were convinced of the improbability of legal reform if left solely to parliamentary initiative, and took decisions to concentrate on the legal-judicial paths that had begun to bear fruit overseas, notably in the United States.[46] In 2008 the two associations jointly launched the campaign "Affermazione Civile." The title drew inspiration from a Radical Party campaign of the 1980s for the "affirmation of conscience," supporting conscientious objection to the period's obligatory military service. "Affermazione Civile" provided an unprecedentedly concerted politico-juridical strategy for the rights of all individuals, couples, and families who sheltered under the LGBTI umbrella.[47]

Building on previous one-off initiatives, the "Affermazione Civile" campaign utilized the Radical Party's Radio Radicale broadcasting network to invite same-sex couples all over Italy to lobby local civil offices to register their unions.[48] Coordinated by the *pro bono* assistance of lawyers contributing to the Lenford Network, notably Francesco Bilotta, the campaign resulted in the first degree Courts of Venice and Trent and the Court of Appeal of Florence referring matters to Italy's Constitutional Court, which held a public hearing on March 23, 2010. One of the plaintiffs, Matteo Pegoraro, recounted the intense emotions he felt in the grandeur of Rome's Palazzo della Consulta, waiting for fifteen severe-looking judges in their black robes to discuss whether he and the others might finally obtain some official recognition of their relationships.[49]

The court's decision, handed down on April 14, 2010, was a clear turning point. While it did not accept the request for marriage rights, it recognized the constitutional relevance of same-sex unions, "understood as the stable cohabitation of two persons of the same sex, who have the fundamental right to live freely as a couple ... with juridical recognition and the associated rights and responsibilities."[50] Effectively, the "Affermazione Civile" campaign had achieved as much in two short years as had two decades of mass demonstrations and individual stunts—though, of course, those twenty years of activism had prepared the ground for the legal campaign.

The result, though not a total victory, underlined the effectiveness of the legal approach, and, building on its gains, the campaign eventually sponsored three couples to take the Constitutional Court's decision to the European Court of Human Rights in Strasbourg. Meanwhile, other couples in Italy continued to stage symbolic ceremonies and present personal legal challenges to the courts, slowly building a body of jurisprudence that increased internal pressure on the Italian parliament. Nevertheless, by 2013 the government had still failed to give effect to the Constitutional Court's ruling of 2010 by framing legislation on the rights of same-sex couples, such that its president publicly admonished parliament for ignoring the Court's advice.[51]

A number of international events in these years also added significantly to the pressure on the Italian government. In February 2013 the European Court of Human Rights ruled that Austria's civil code discriminated against same-sex couples by barring adoption of the biological child of one partner by the other, while permitting second-parent adoptions for unmarried heterosexual couples.[52] In May 2013, France introduced a same-sex marriage law, producing a strong emotional impact on Italy, just as its 1999 PACS law had done. On June 26, 2015, the US Supreme Court handed down its decision on "equal marriage," making it legal across all fifty states. And in July 2015, the European Court of Human Rights delivered its judgment on applications by three Italian couples that had been coordinated in response to the Italian Constitutional Court's decision of 2010. The European court pronounced Italian law in relation to same-sex couples as failing to provide key protections and even "unreliable," recommending that Italy establish legal recognition of same-sex partnerships.[53] *La Repubblica* described the decision as "Strasbourg's condemnation of Italy."[54]

It was a condemnation Parliament could not ignore, and not only because, under the auspices of the "Affermazione Civile" campaign, plans were already afoot for a fresh series of approaches to the European court.[55] A new bill, proposed by Democratic Party senator Monica Cirinnà, had in fact already begun to make its way through Italy's labyrinthine parliamentary process in March 2015. It was strongly resisted by the Nuovo Centrodestra (New Centre-right), a minority member of Matteo Renzi's coalition government. Public opposition in the form of social media campaigns and major rallies organized by the Forum of Family Associations in Rome on June 20, 2015 and again on January 30, 2016 failed to halt the bill's progress. However, recognizing that the status of children within same-sex partnerships remained the proposed law's most contentious aspect, its proponents removed the original second-parent adoption provisions in order to guarantee approval of the law in the Senate. This dilution was a major blow to the Rainbow Families association, which had by that stage become the public face of the entire debate on same-sex relationships.

The Senate approved the bill on February 25, 2016, by which point full parliamentary approval was more or less a foregone conclusion. The lower house, the Chamber of Deputies, voted their approval on May 11, and the Italian civil-union bill was finally signed into law by the President of the Republic on May 20, 2016. Compromised victory though it may have been, the granting of civil-union recognition to same-sex couples in Italy provided an emotional resting point, at last, in a long march that had steadily gathered pace since the death of Giorgio Agatino and Antonino Galatola in Giarre, Sicily, in November 1980. As in many other nations, the degree of legal and social acceptance of same-sex relationships achieved in Italy by 2016 would have been almost unthinkable for Giorgio and Antonino in 1980.

Conclusion

Italy's path to "gay liberation" was a distinctive one, embarked on late compared with many other Western countries. Free from the menace of a law that punished same-sex sexual acts, it may well be the case, as Giovanni Dall'Orto has suggested, that the absence of a punitive law was a strangely mixed blessing. Elsewhere, anti-homosexual laws encouraged the emergence of a collective identity that led to the birth of determined liberation movements, in some cases many decades before a similar phenomenon emerged in Italy.[56] Once that march had begun in Italy, it both resembled and was distinctive from others, perhaps above all because of the determined resistance of the Catholic Church and the particular influence of the Church in Italian society and politics. If Italy's march toward liberation began differently, by the twenty-first century, ground similar to that traversed by others began to be covered. By 2016, Italian same-sex couples found themselves in a legal position that at least had a clear family resemblance to those of some of the world's most progressive legislations.

Notes

1. ILGA (International Lesbian, Gay, Bisexual, Trans and Intersex Association) Europe's 2017 Annual Report shows that Italy, despite the 2016 law on civil unions, still rates comparatively poorly against other western European nations in sociological and legal measures of acceptance: https://www.ilga-europe.org/resources/rainbow-europe/rainbow-europe-2017 (accessed January 16, 2018).
2. For example, inventories of prosecution records held by the Archivio di Stato di Roma indicate a total of ninety-seven prosecutions in the area covered by Rome's courts for

"atti di libidine contro natura" between 1870 and 1890 (on average fewer than five per year): "Inventori, Corte di Assise di Roma. Elenco Alfabetico degli imputati. Fascicoli processuali, 1871–1898," Archivio di Stato di Roma. The vast majority of cases concerned violations of minors.
3. Giovanni Dall'Orto, *Tutta un'altra storia. L'omosessualità dall'antichità al secondo dopoguerra* (Milan: il Saggiatore, 2015), 460–461.
4. See, for example, Chiara Beccalossi, *Female Sexual Inversion: Same-Sex Desires in Italian and British Sexology c. 1870–1920* (London: Routledge, 2011); and Charlotte Ross, *Eccentricity and Sameness: Discourses on Lesbianism and Desire between Women in Italy, 1860s–1930s* (Oxford: Peter Lang, 2015).
5. Robert Aldrich, *The Seduction of the Mediterranean: Writing, Art, and Homosexual Fantasy* (London: Routledge, 1993).
6. Lorenzo Benadusi, *Enemy of the New Man: Homosexuality in Fascist Italy*, trans. Suzanne Dingey and Jennifer Pudney (Madison WI: University of Wisconsin Press, 2012 [2005]).
7. Mark Seymour, "Pier Paolo Pasolini," in *Who's Who in Gay and Lesbian History: From World War II to the Present Day*, ed. Robert Aldrich and Garry Wotherspoon (London: Routledge, 2001), 314–316.
8. Mark Seymour, *Debating Divorce in Italy: Marriage and the Making of Modern Italians* (Basingstoke: Palgrave Macmillan, 2006).
9. Perry Willson, *Women in Twentieth-Century Italy* (Basingstoke: Palgrave Macmillan, 2010), 158–163.
10. Seymour, "Pier Paolo Pasolini."
11. "Omosessuale sopprime il partner e subito si uccide accanto a lui," *La Sicilia*, November 1, 1980. All references to newspapers in this chapter are to un-page-numbered clippings held in the Archivio FUORI!, Fondazione Sandro Penna, Milan. All translations from the Italian are our own.
12. Salvatore La Rocca, "Si fanno uccidere dal cugino," *Paese Sera*, November 2, 1980.
13. Marco Pannella, "Intervento al XXIV Congresso del Partito Radicale," *Radio Radicale*, November 2, 1980. Available online: http://www.radioradicale.it/scheda/6727/6744-xxiv-congresso-del-partito-radicale (accessed January 19, 2018).
14. N. Fiorito, "Hanno criminalizzato anche gli omosessuali," *Giornale del Sud*, November 7, 1980.
15. Issue "zero" of the group's monthly publication *FUORI!* came out in February 1972 but was backdated to December 1971. See Fabio Croce, ed., *Bandiera gay. Il movimento gay in Italia dalle origini al 2000 attraverso l'Archivio di Massimo Consoli* (Rome: Edizioni Croce, 1999), 22–23.
16. Maurizio Tedeschi, "Proposta: Matrimonio omosessuale," *FUORI!*, September/October 1979, 11.
17. Reported by Enzo Cucco, a contemporary FUORI! activist in Torino, in an interview with Yuri Guaiana on January 17, 2017.
18. "La gente di Giarre ha ascoltato anche il dramma di altri," *Il Messaggero*, 7 November.
19. Documento del FUORI!, *L'Ora*, November 4, 1980.
20. Giovanni Dall'Orto, "Marco Bisceglia," *WikiPink*. Available online: http://www.wikipink.org/index.php/Marco_Bisceglia#cite_ref-1 (accessed January 16, 2018).
21. *Babilonia. Mensile di cultura e informazione gay* (1, 1983).
22. Giovanni Dall'Orto, "Tony Patrioli," in *Who's Who in Gay and Lesbian History: From World War II to the Present Day*, ed. Robert Aldrich and Garry Wotherspoon (London: Routledge, 2001), 319–320.

23 Francsco Gnerre, "Paris o cara!," *Babilonia* (2, 1983): 12–13.
24 *Italia gay 1983. Guida tascabile a cura di BABILONIA* (second edition, Milan, 1983), 50.
25 Stefano Bolognini and Giovanni Dall'Orto, "Storia del matrimonio fra persone dello stesso sesso," *WikiPink*. Available online: http://www.wikipink.org/index.php/Storia_del_matrimonio_fra_persone_dello_stesso_sesso (accessed January 16, 2018).
26 Michele Angelo Lupoi et al., "Introduzione," to *Unioni civili e convivenze. Guida commentata alla Legge n. 76/2016* (Santarcangelo di Romagna: Maggioli Editore, 2016), 18.
27 Asher Colombo, *Gay e aids in Italia* (Bologna: Il Mulino, 2000).
28 Gianni Rossi Barilli, *Storia del movimento gay in Italia* (Milan: Feltrinelli, 1999), 211.
29 "Statuto del Forum delle associazioni familiari," article 2.1, a. Available online: http://www.forumfamiglie.org/chi-siamo/statuto/ (accessed January 18, 2018).
30 Claudia Brunetto, "Massimo e Gino, pionieri delle nozze «La nostra battaglia lunga vent'anni»," *La Repubblica* (Palermo ed.), February 12, 2013, 5.
31 "Matrimonio gay: il Comune dice no," *La Repubblica*, March 22, 1994.
32 Delia Vaccarello, "Io torcia umana lanciata contro il Vaticano," *L'Unità*, January 13, 2004.
33 Marzio Barbagli and Asher Colombo, in *Omosessuali moderni. Gay e lesbiche in Italia* (Bologna: Il Mulino, 2001), provide a detailed sociological analysis of life for same-sex-attracted Italians in the late twentieth century.
34 Bolognini and Dall'Orto, "Storia del matrimonio fra persone dello stesso sesso."
35 Marco Politi, "La guerra dei cardinali per impedire il Pride," *La Repubblica*, July 2, 2000.
36 "DS: Spini ad Amato, niente equivoci sulla Costituzione," Agenzia Asca, May 25, 2000. Available online: http://web.tiscali.it/rassegnales/maggio-2000/asca25maggio2000.htm (accessed January 17, 2018).
37 Giovanni Dall'Orto, "World Pride Roma 2000," *WikiPink*. Available online: *http://www.wikipink.org/index.php/World_Pride_Roma_2000#cite_note-4* (accessed January 17, 2018).
38 Saverio Aversa, "Piergiorgio Paterlini racconta dieci unioni di omosessuali e lesbiche. Matrimoni gay, la cosa più normale del mondo," *Liberazione*, February 6, 2005.
39 "Risoluzione del Parlamento europeo sul rispetto dei diritti umani nell'Unione europea (1998–1999) (11350/1999 - C5-0265/1999–1999/2201(INI))," March 16, 2000. Available online: *http://www.europarl.europa.eu/sides/getDoc.do?pubRef=-//EP//TEXT±TA±P5-TA-2000-0113±0±DOC±XML±V0//IT* (accessed January 17, 2018).
40 Franco Grillini, *Istituzione del Registro delle unioni civili di coppie dello stesso sesso o di sesso diverso e possibilità per le persone dello stesso sesso di accedere all'istituto del matrimonio*, Pdl n. 2982, tabled July 8, 2002. Available online: *http://legxiv.camera.it/_dati/leg14/lavori/stampati/pdf/14PDL0032500.pdf* (accessed January 21, 2018).
41 Piergiorgio Paterlini, *Matrimoni* (Turin: Einaudi Editore, 2004).
42 "Famiglie Arcobaleno: Chi siamo," http://www.famigliearcobaleno.org/it/associazione/chi-siamo/ (accessed January 17, 2018).
43 "Per il bene dell'Italia. Programma del governo 2006–2011," 72. Document available at http://download.repubblica.it/pdf/prog_unione.pdf (accessed January 17, 2018).
44 "Bagnasco: «No ai Dico come alla pedofilia»," *La Repubblica*, March 31, 2007.
45 "Avvocatura per i diritti LGBTI—Rete Lenford" was founded by members of the Italian legal profession and named in honor of the murdered Jamaican AIDS activist Harvey Lenford: http://www.retelenford.it/chi-siamo.html (accessed January 18, 2018).

46 On the role of courts in the US campaign, see, for example, Michael J. Klarman, *From the Closet to the Altar: Courts, Backlash, and the Struggle for Same-Sex Marriage* (Oxford: Oxford University Press, 2012).
47 Sergio Rovasio, "La battaglia finale?" in *Dal cuore delle coppie al cuore del diritto*, ed. Yuri Guaiana (Viterbo: Stampa Alternativa, 2011), 9.
48 Ibid., 11.
49 Matteo Pegoraro, "Le coppie," in *Dal cuore delle coppie al cuore del diritto*, ed. Yuri Guaiana (Viterbo: Stampa Alternativa, 2001), 16.
50 Constitutional Court ruling 138/2010, April 14, 2010.
51 "La Consulta: 'Il Parlamento ci ignora.' J'accuse ai partiti del presidente Gallo," *La Stampa*, April 12, 2013. Available online: http://www.lastampa.it/2013/04/12/italia/politica/la-consulta-il-parlamento-ci-ignora-j-accuse-del-presidente-gallo-SnCry1LjmW0sWNn38pktzN/pagina.html (accessed January 19, 2018).
52 Council of Europe, European Court of Human Rights, https://www.coe.int/en/web/portal/news-2013/-/asset_publisher/TEHtOeUO1Ozc/content/cour-europeenne-des-droits-de-l-homme-arret-contre-l-autriche (accessed January 19, 2018).
53 Council of Europe, European Court of Human Rights, https://www.coe.int/en/web/portal/news-2015/-/asset_publisher/9k8wkRrYhB8C/content/chamber-judgment-case-of-oliari-and-others-v-italy (accessed January 19, 2018).
54 "Unioni gay, arriva la condanna di Strasburgo all'Italia: «Riconosca i loro diritti»," *La Repubblica*, July 21, 2015. http://www.repubblica.it/politica/2015/07/21/news/unioni_gay_arriva_la_condanna_di_strasburgo_all_italia_riconosca_i_loro_diritti_-119511643/ (accessed January 19, 2018).
55 "Certi Diritti/Unioni omosessuali: nuova serie di ricorsi a Strasburgo," December 23, 2015. Available online: http://www.certidiritti.org/2015/12/23/certi-dirittiunioni-omosessuali-nuova-serie-di-ricorsi-a-strasburgo/ (accessed January 19, 2018).
56 Dall'Orto, *Tutta un'altra storia*, 460.

14

"It's Poppycock to Say Homosexuals Can Be Excused": Rethinking the Gay and Lesbian Movement in the Republic of Ireland, 1970s–1990s

Patrick McDonagh

On May 22, 2015, in what has been described as a "social revolution" within Irish society, forty-one of Ireland's forty-two constituencies, representing 1,202,198 people passed a referendum legalizing same-sex marriage, making Ireland the first country in the world to do so by popular vote. Three years later, on June 14, 2017, Leo Varadkar, an openly gay man, was elected Ireland's fourteenth *Taoiseach* (Prime Minister).[1] That Ireland, a country which since the foundation of the state up to decriminalization in 1993 had viewed sexual acts between males as criminal activity and homosexuals as sick, perverted, and sinful, passed such a referendum and now has its first openly gay *Taoiseach* makes both events all the more extraordinary. How could a country once renowned for its so-called strict adherence to Catholic social teaching now be considered a beacon for LGBT Civil Rights?[2]

The answer appeared relatively straightforward to those who sought to explain it. This transformation was the direct result of David Norris and his legal victory at the European Court of Human Rights in 1988. For example, in *Seanad Éireann* (Upper House of the Irish parliament), Senators congratulated David Norris on getting "the ball rolling many decades ago when it was neither popular nor profitable."[3] *Fianna Fáil's* Denis O'Donovan argued that "at that stage Senator Norris was ploughing a lone furrow, not alone in this House, but in this country and he was often scoffed at by members of my party and other parties."[4] Similarly, Senator Eamonn Coghlan described Norris as "the pathfinder on this human rights issue […] leading us to a more modern Ireland."[5] In newspapers such as *The Guardian, The Wall Street Journal,* and the *Irish Mirror,* Norris was credited with singlehandedly leading this transformation, with *The Guardian* declaring him the "driving force behind Ireland's historic decision."[6]

While recognizing the significance of Norris' legal victory, the current narrative is oversimplistic and fails to adequately account for the transformation that has taken place for gay and lesbian individuals in Irish society today. For if we are to sustain the argument that Norris' legal victory alone led to the present situation in Irish society, it would naturally follow that Northern Ireland, which decriminalized sexual activity between males in 1982, would also conceivably have same sex-marriage, which it does not. In fact, both judgments achieved only the basic move of partial decriminalization of sex between males in private. The type of law reform to be introduced was not stipulated in both European Convention of Human Rights (ECHR) judgments.

Moreover, violation of Article 8 of the ECHR has been seen as the main (if not only) argument put forward by gay activists in the campaign for gay liberation in Ireland.[7] In turn, the Irish courtroom has been viewed as the only site where gay rights were propagated. This presents a picture of a uniquely Irish experience, whereby an individual, rather than a broad movement, was responsible for the transformation of the lives of gay and lesbian individuals. By simply exploring Norris' legal battle the current narrative has overlooked the other arguments, other sites of activism, and, crucially, the role of activists in both urban and provincial areas, particularly lesbian women as agents of their own liberation and agents of social change in Irish society.

This chapter focuses on the first wave of gay/lesbian activism in Ireland between the 1970s and early 1990s. It would be misleading to view the legal campaign as the only form of resistance carried out by Irish lesbians and gay individuals during this period. I argue that the untold stories of gay and lesbian activists throughout Irish society in this period were also significant factors in the sea change in public attitudes that characterizes Irish history in the early decades of the twenty-first century. Earlier resistance was highly diverse. It fought to create lesbian and gay spaces throughout Ireland; it promoted a greater understanding of homosexuality through the media, sought to forge alliances with other groups to improve the lives of gay/lesbian individuals, and attempted to claim a full place in Irish society through public demonstrations. Irish gay and lesbian activists in the latter half of the twentieth century began a dialogue around homosexuality, which helped win over a vast proportion of Irish society and renegotiated Ireland's sexual mores.

Forging a space for Irish gay and lesbian citizens

> From infancy, we are taught and conditioned to believe that any expression of sexuality which does not conform to the rigid, procrustean heterosexual norm is perversion. We are, in fact programmed to regard all feelings of sexual or sensual attraction for a person of our own sex as a sign of moral degeneracy and decadence.[8]

The cultural climate Irish homosexuals found themselves in during the decades preceding the emergence of a gay/lesbian movement was not receptive to any individual (heterosexual or homosexual) who deviated from the accepted social mores.[9] While the Roman Catholic Church's dominance was gradually beginning to be challenged in the 1970s, church attendance was still extraordinarily high for a Western, developed country, with an average weekly attendance of between 88 and 95 percent.[10] Contraception, along with divorce and abortion, was prohibited, while laws existed (and were enforced) criminalizing sexual activity between males.[11] Coupled with these were the strict censorship laws introduced in 1929.[12] Unsurprisingly, books and films dealing with homosexuality frequently fell foul of the censorship board.[13]

This stifled any ability to better understand homosexuality and for homosexuals themselves to develop a positive understanding of what they were. This helped sustain the negative image of homosexuals who were commonly associated with prostitutes, drug addicts, alcoholics, and the mentally ill. In one letter to the *Sunday Independent* on April 13, 1969, a reader asked, "would you please write all about homosexuality in your column next week? What is the cause of it? Lack of Love? Or is it caused by T.B. or Cancer?"[14] This is hardly surprising, considering those who one might turn to for expert advice on this topic, such as Dr. Austin Darragh, director of the UCD Psycho Endocrine Centre, called in 1973 for new homosexuality laws, whereby convicted homosexuals would be sent for medical treatment, instead of jail.[15] With no organized opposition to these views, let alone any individual publicly declaring their sexuality, negative images of homosexuals were the norm, rather than the exception, in the Ireland of this time.

June 1974, however, marked a turning point with the establishment of Ireland's first gay/lesbian organization, the Irish Gay Rights Movement (IGRM), a non-party political, non-sectarian homophile grouping.[16] The non-sectarian aspect reflected the reality that the Irish gay/lesbian movement grew out of cooperation between activists both North and South of the border. Soon after, other groups began to emerge throughout Ireland, such as the Cork Irish Gay Rights Movement (1975), Liberation for Irish Lesbians (1978), the National Gay Federation (NGF, 1979), the Galway Gay Collective and Galway (IGRM, 1980/1981), and the Cork Gay & Lesbian Collectives (1981/1983).

The IGRM was responsible for the establishment of the first publicly recognized gay and lesbian center in the Republic of Ireland, the Phoenix Club, at 46 Parnell Square, Dublin, in 1976. In Cork, the Cork IGRM and Cork Gay Collective also succeeded in acquiring premises, known as the Phoenix Club on MacCurtain Street and the Quay Co-Op on Sullivan's Quay respectively. In 1979, the NGF opened the Hirschfeld Centre, on Fownes Street, which became the focal point of gay social life in Dublin for much of the 1980s. In her analysis of queer life in San Francisco, Nan Alamilla Boyd argues that "the politics of everyday life became an important venue for resisting dominant social structures."[17] These centers facilitated Irish homosexuals to resist Irish social norms, helping them to develop a positive gay/lesbian identity. Crucially, they helped challenge the dominance of heteronormativity as the only accepted form of sexuality in Ireland.

Rather than attempting to disguise the true nature of these premises, those involved actively sought to promote and advertise the venues as locations specifically geared toward or welcoming of homosexuals. The Hirschfeld Centre, not the first to be named after Magnus Hirschfeld, a pioneering German gay rights activist, even placed a pink triangle outside its entrance, while the Quay Co-Op hung a banner outside the center supporting gay pride week in 1984. While advertising these premises was tricky, primarily because mainstream newspapers refused to advertise them, activists did succeed in placing ads in more liberal local publications, such as the *Cork Review, Hot Press*, and *In Dublin*. The advertisements publicly stated the title of the organization, their location, contact details, and activities. Throughout the 1980s, advertisements for both Phoenix Clubs and the Hirschfeld Centre were a common feature of the aforementioned publications, so much so that in October 1983, *In Dublin* introduced a "Gay" section in their events guide.[18] In fact, the success of the Hirschfeld Centre was used by Maurice Haugh to partially explain the revival of Temple Bar area. In an article titled "Life Revives in a Dying Part of Dublin," Haugh noted the contribution of the Hirschfeld Centre, which he argued made that part of Temple Bar the "Gay Paree" of Dublin.[19]

In both Phoenix Clubs and the Hirschfeld Centre activities ranged from discos, discussions, a telephone befriending service, and an in-house cinema. Discos, in particular, proved to be the most popular activity and were a clear sign of the willingness, intended or otherwise, of many Irish homosexuals to resist Ireland's social mores. When the Phoenix Club first opened in 1976, the discos attracted roughly 180 individuals each Friday and Saturday.[20] By the early 1980s the Hirschfeld Centre was catering to over 1000 individuals, four nights a week.[21]

Within the Quay Co-Op in Cork, one of the most successful and enduring events organized by the Cork Lesbian Collective was the "Cork Women's Fun Weekend," which began in April 1984 and still takes place today. While this was essentially a mixed event, comprising lesbian and heterosexual women, there was an overwhelmingly strong lesbian influence, with activities such as discos, cabaret performances, women's films, discussions, and lesbian workshops.[22] The Cork Women's Fun Weekend was an event where lesbian women were firstly able to meet others like them, but secondly were able to express their sexuality in a relaxed and an enjoyable setting. This was particularly important at a time when lesbian women struggled to obtain a space within the male-dominated gay organizations.[23] Rather than remaining the "invisible phantoms of Irish society," as one Cork lesbian described them, it helped foster the creation of a lesbian identity in Cork and Ireland.[24] Remembering her time at the Women's Fun Weekend Louise Walsh stated

> It was a huge event for the Cork women to organise, but they pulled it off. Women travelled from all parts of the country. Like a lot of women in Cork, I found the idea of going to a cabaret of all women performers, having days of women's films, discussions, workshops and card games totally mind blowing. I identified as heterosexual at the time, but as I watched all these women dancing together, celebrating and flirting in this wonderful atmosphere I knew something quite important and powerful had happened. A strong open lesbian community had rooted itself in Cork.[25]

Even in areas without a gay center, such as Galway and Tipperary, activists succeeded in arranging venues to host social events for gay and lesbian individuals and played their own part in the shaping of a gay and lesbian identity. Events in these regions took on a different character from those in Dublin and Cork, reflecting the much more challenging terrain for activists in these regions. Symbols and code words were essential in enabling individuals to participate. For example, James Quinn, who attended meetings organized by Gay Clonmel at Hearn's Hotel in Tipperary in the 1980s, remembers that "the meeting was called APEX, which was completely anonymous. So, if you arrived into reception, you'd simply say, to the people, Oh, I'm here for an APEX meeting, and they would say oh that's the group over there."[26]

At these social events, besides being able to meet other homosexuals, copies of gay magazines, which otherwise could not have been freely obtained in these regions, such as *Out,* published by NGF, or *Gay News* were handed out. Discos, while not a regular phenomenon in Galway, did take place. In October 1981, the Galway Gay Collective organized the first gay/lesbian disco in the West of Ireland at the Lenaboy Hotel, where thirty people turned up. Not long after, the Galway IGRM began discos in Rockland's Hotel, also in Salthill, which attracted up to eighty people from areas as far away as Cork and Waterford.[27]

Although activities in provincial Ireland were more secretive and not as regular in comparison with events in Dublin and Cork, they nevertheless were crucial in facilitating gay and lesbian individuals to become part of a gay community. The very existence of these events, and participation by many was a strong force of personal resistance. Not only did they facilitate individuals to live a gay and lesbian lifestyle, they also provided individuals with the opportunity to foster friendships, and, in many cases, homosexual relationships. These actions should be recognized as a form of everyday resistance, for as James Scott has rightly noted:

> Everyday forms of resistance rarely make headlines. But just as millions of anthozoan polyps create willy-nilly a coral reef, thousands upon thousands of petty acts of insubordination and evasion create a political and economic barrier reef of their own.[28]

At these centers and events there can be no doubt that acts of insubordination were taking place. Irish homosexuals were evading heteronormativity and embracing homosexuality. One such individual who attended the APEX meetings in Clonmel in the 1980s, Joe O'Mara, stated in a 2013 that it was through attending the APEX meetings that he met his future partner.[29]

Coming out to Irish society

> Those of us who have shaken off the shackles imposed by lack of education and fear of social stigma can find better sources of reference for genuine research than dusty textbooks. We can no longer allow ourselves to be categorised by non-gay people, no matter how well intentioned.[30]

The creation of these venues helped foster a greater sense of community and facilitated the challenging of negative stereotypes surrounding homosexuality in Ireland. Meeting others like them and developing a greater understanding of homosexuality provided many with the confidence to publicly speak out against their oppression. Speaking on the first broadcast of RTÉ (*Radió Teilifís Éireann*) in 1961, former president of Ireland Éamon de Valera, speaking about radio itself, forewarned that "never before was there in the hands of men an instrument so powerful to influence the thoughts and actions of the multitude."[31] It was precisely this power that activists sought to harness with their appearances in the media.

In the period from 1977 to 1980, in spite of the cultural climate, Irish homosexuals cleverly utilized the media by appearing on three television programs to discuss homosexuality. The first of these was *Tuesday Report,* with Cathal O'Shannon in February 1977. In February 1980 Laurie Steele and Arthur Leahy, a gay couple, appeared on *Week End*, and Joni Sheerin of Liberation for Irish Lesbians (LIL) spoke on the *Late Late Show*. Throughout these programs homosexuals, some supported by their parents, a politician, and even a Catholic priest, confidently explained homosexuality in a positive and sympathetic manner. In his contribution on *Tuesday Report,* Sean Connolly of the IGRM explained that "I discovered that my orientation was towards members of my own sex, for the same reasons as anybody else, for companionship, emotional stimulation and the usual things one forms a relationship for."[32] Senator Noel Browne, a supporter of gay rights, maintained that homosexuality was as normal as heterosexuality; it was just a different side of human sexuality.[33] In one of the most provocative scenes of the documentary, footage of lesbian women and gay men dancing unashamedly together in the Phoenix Club was shown.[34]

While *Tuesday Report* had educated by helping to dispel many of the myths surrounding homosexuality, *Week End* with Arthur Leahy and Laurie Steele was a much more personal and poignant account of the turmoil and difficulties two individuals faced trying to maintain a gay relationship in Ireland. The interview was set in the home of Arthur and Laurie who disclosed that they had been in a relationship for five years. At the same time, they highlighted the demoralizing impact of society's attitudes on them and their families.[35] For Laurie the oppression had led to self-oppression and a sense of alienation, while also noting that "society does not accommodate gay couples, you don't see other gay couples."[36]

One of the shortcomings of the aforementioned programs was the predominance of gay male voices, at the expense of lesbian women. In an attempt to promote a greater awareness and understanding of lesbianism in Irish society, Joni Sheerin of LIL appeared on the *Late Late Show,* in 1980. The extent of the task that lay ahead for Joni was evident in one audience member's comment, who, on seeing Joni, remarked that "she doesn't look like a lesbian."[37] Like her male counterparts, Sheerin confidently discussed the challenges she encountered as a lesbian in Ireland. Despite this oppression, however, she maintained "I am a gay normal everyday person. I hold a very responsible job, I've a family, I've friends. I'm socially active. I am very happy. It's [her sexuality] not a problem."[38] She went on to explain how there were thousands of gay women in Ireland and she wanted to be a positive reference and dispel the ignorance surrounding lesbianism.

Some common themes recurred throughout these programs that activists were keen to reinforce. One such example was that homosexuals were normal everyday individuals, much the same as heterosexuals. While they may have been different because they were attracted to members of the same sex, homosexuals, as Sean Connolly noted, looked for the same qualities heterosexuals looked for in a partner. They were not sex-starved individuals or sick, and being homosexual was not just about sex. Laurie and Arthur's appearance as a gay couple sent a clear message that gay couples existed in Ireland, who were not unlike other couples, something the *Irish Times* noted:

> This programme examines the lifestyle of what appears to be a normal couple in a stable relationship, except that they both belong to the same sex. This provides the jumping off point for a serious discussion of the failure of Irish people to realise that there is a homosexual community living in our midst and the futility of pretending otherwise.[39]

By using the word "stable" the author helped reinforce the belief that homosexuality was natural, rather than deviant. In disclosing their relationship was five years old, Laurie and Arthur challenged the assertion that homosexuals were typically promiscuous. Other themes included the activists' self-presentation as both happy and proud of their sexuality, rather than expressing guilt or shame. This was something that seemed to take Gay Byrne by surprise when Joni Sheerin said she was proud. Responding, Byrne asked, "when you say you are proud, are you really Joni? Proud of it?"[40] In both the 1977 documentary and interview with Joni, individuals were asked whether they would they change their sexual orientation if it were possible, to which each individual happily replied, NO.

There can be no doubt that these programs elicited strong reactions, both positive and negative. Perhaps most surprising is the fact that the positive appear to have outnumbered the negatives. Of the forty or so calls RTÉ received following *Tuesday Report*, only four expressed anger, with twenty-six congratulating RTÉ and the remainder requesting further information on the show.[41] One of the most positive reactions came from Patrick Galvin in *Hibernia* who argued:

> If the *Tuesday Report* did nothing else for the homosexual it did, at least attempt to explode this particular myth (homosexuals are sick, weak and depraved human beings). Here was a group of normal, decent and intelligent people who just happened to be sexually orientated towards members of their own sex. They did not choose to be what they are — who does? And all they were demanding was the right to live their own lives in their own way without interference from the State, or anyone else. This is the same right that any heterosexual would demand — and get. So where's the problem? You may well ask.[42]

Similarly, while Joni's appearance elicited some negative comments, there was also praise for her, with viewers stating that "if every heterosexual was as sincere and honest as that lady, the world would be a much happier place" and "she came across as a very nice person and will surely help many people of both sexes."[43]

These media performances were important in providing a more positive representation of homosexuality to Irish society and helped instigate a dialogue around homosexuality, which was not confined to urban areas. The extent to which these lesbian and gay individuals were successful in igniting a debate was reflected in one viewer's comment that "while I realised the lesbian on this show was a genuine person, I am really tired of the topic."[44]

The greater willingness of Irish gay and lesbian individuals to resist their subjugation was further demonstrated in March 1983 with the Fairview Protest March. The march resulted from the suspended sentence handed down to five youths for the killing of Declan Flynn in September 1982, who had defended their actions on the basis that the victim was homosexual.[45] The immediate impact of the case led to the mobilization of gay and lesbian individuals on the streets of Dublin in the first large-scale public demonstration over gay rights in Ireland. The holding of this protest is hard to envisage had it not been for the creation of the aforementioned groups and centers where homosexuals came together and fostered bonds as a community.

On March 19 1983, gay and lesbian individuals, with the support of the Union of Students in Ireland (USI), Irish Congress of Trade Unions, *Sinn Féin*, Democratic Socialists, and the Rape Crisis Centre, marched from Liberty Hall to Fairview Park with banners declaring "Gays Are Human," "Gays Have the Right to Life," and "Stop Violence against Gays and Women."[46] The number of individuals who took part was reported by the media to have been 400, while the different gay/lesbian organizations claimed close to 1000 marched. Even if the 400 figure is to be accepted, this still represents a significant turnout for the first mass demonstration on gay rights in Ireland.[47] In comparison, the first Gay Pride march in London in 1972 attracted an estimated 1000 individuals, despite the so-called more tolerant climate there and the far greater population in Britain.[48]

Much like the Stonewall Riots in 1969, the Declan Flynn case and the subsequent protest march became the catalyst to fight back in the streets. The march itself led to the organization of the first gay pride parade in Ireland later that summer. Since then, gay and lesbian individuals continued to take to the streets in an increasing number of locations throughout the country, most notably in Cork, Galway, and Limerick. In one of the most blatant public acts of defiance, gay and lesbian individuals, in front of 100 onlookers, staged a kiss-in outside government buildings in 1988.[49] This was followed in 1989 by the organization of the first gay pride parade in Galway city, and in 1992 the participation of a gay and lesbian group in the Cork St. Patrick's Day parade, despite such groups being banned from doing so in the New York St. Patrick's Day Parade.[50]

Forcing change

Activists were keen to forge alliances with other groups to improve the lives of gay and lesbian individuals and to instigate institutional change. By broadening the support base outside the movement, their call for civil rights carried much greater weight. As demonstrated at the Fairview Protest March, many organizations were willing to support gay groups. The USI, for example, as early as 1974 had called for the decriminalization of sexual activity between males, bringing them into close alliance with the gay movement.[51] With this support gay activists took the issue of gay rights to college campuses through speeches, debates, and student publications throughout the 1980s. In one such example, *USI News* asked readers, "if you believe homosexual individuals should have human rights such as the right to dignity, the right to privacy, the right to control over their body […] then you believe in the same rights gay people are demanding. Gay rights are not extravagant demands, they are human rights."⁵² It was his belief that gay rights are human rights that led Hubert Mannion of the University College Dublin Students Union to write to the *Irish Press* condemning two previous articles by Reverend Denis O'Callaghan on homosexuality. In his letter Mannion argued:

> Gay people are the last minority which can be attacked and victimised with impunity. It says a great deal about the Catholic Church which received its emancipation in 1828 that in 1982 it is doing all in its power to prevent a minority in the community from being granted even the most basic of human rights, i.e. the right to love.⁵³

One organization in particular that lesbian and gay activists sought support from was the Irish Congress of Trade Unions (ICTU), which represented over half a million workers in the 1980s. The ICTU was an influential organization, in terms of the numbers of workers it represented, but also the fact that Irish governments often sought their opinion on employment law. While much has been made of the laws criminalizing sexual activity between males, the fear of losing one's job because of their sexuality was also uppermost in the minds of many individuals. This was highlighted by Ian Dunn of the Scottish Minorities Group in a speech to NGF members in 1980. In his address Dunn spoke about John Sanders, who had lost his job after information provided to the Scottish National Camps Association in August 1979 indicated that Sanders "indulged in homosexuality," actions considered unsuitable by the Camps Association.⁵⁴ Citing the support Sanders had received from the Scottish Trade Union Movement, Dunn encouraged Irish activists to recognize that "the step forward in our liberation movement was not merely to see oneself in isolation, but understanding the nature of our oppression, through organised political action."⁵⁵

Following Dunn's address the NGF encouraged gay and lesbian individuals who were part of a union to bring a motion at their union's AGM calling on them to support gay rights, which could then be proposed at an ICTU AGM.⁵⁶ Activists also brought the issue of gay rights to the unions by organizing leaflet campaigns and workshops at these gatherings.⁵⁷ One individual who was heavily involved in such activity was Kieran Rose of the Cork Gay Collective. Speaking on his motion calling on the Local Government and Public Services Union to support the inclusion of sexual orientation in the Unfair Dismissals Act, Rose argued that:

> Living as a gay person in Ireland is in many ways like being black in Alabama. [...] But employment is the most critical area where discrimination and prejudice affect gay people. In many cases gay people do not get jobs, are fired or lose promotion solely because they are gay. The right to work and to a fair deal at work are basic worker's rights which everyone is entitled to whether black or white, male or female, gay or heterosexual.⁵⁸

Rather than presenting their demands as something unique, Rose and other gay/lesbians activists situated the rights of gay/lesbian workers within the realm of basic workers' rights, rights that the trade union movement admittedly strived to uphold.

Moreover, he sought to link the suppression of homosexuals with the oppression of other minority groups, such as the disabled and unmarried mothers. Appealing to the long tradition of worker solidarity within the trade union movement Rose noted that:

> solidarity among workers is the basis of our strength and of the considerable social progress that has been achieved since the movement was founded. I trust that this meeting will support the rights of its fellow workers who are gay by giving its overwhelming support to this motion.[59]

Rose's speech had the desired effect. According to the *Cork Examiner,* of the 360 delegates at this AGM, only six voted against it.[60] At the subsequent ICTU AGM in July 1982, motion 106, supporting decriminalization of sexual activity between males and the outlawing of discrimination on the basis of sexual orientation, was overwhelmingly supported by ICTU delegates.[61] This was highly significant, particularly considering that the ICTU's British counterpart the TUC (Trade Union Congress) did not pass a motion in support of gay rights until 1985.[62]

Having the support of the ICTU was not just symbolic; it also led to material benefits for gay/lesbian individuals. One year after its passage, the Electricity Supply Board Officers Association (ESBOA) contacted the NGF asking for their assistance in promoting a greater understanding among their members on the issues affecting gay/lesbian workers.[63] Significantly, in 1986, Patricia O'Donovan of the ICTU encouraged the Minister for Labour, Ruairi Quinn, to amend the Employment Equality Act, maintaining that:

> The ICTU recognises and demands the right of everyone, irrespective of race, ethnic origin, creed, political opinion, age, sex, marital status, or sexual orientation, to have the means to pursue their economic independence and to full participation in the social, cultural and political life of the community in conditions of freedom, dignity, and equal opportunity.[64]

While the law was not amended in 1986, in 1987 the ICTU published *Lesbian and Gay Rights in the Workplace: Guidelines for Negotiators.* This document called for unions under the ICTU to ensure that future contracts drawn up with employers would include protections for gay and lesbian workers. In 1988, unions such as the Union of Professional and Technical Civil Servants, Federated Workers Union of Ireland, and the Local Government and Public Services Union affirmed their support for the ICTU guidelines.[65] That same year the Civil Service introduced a ban against discrimination on grounds of sexual orientation, while in 1989, the government included sexual orientation in the prohibition to incitement to hatred bill.[66] With cross-party support sexual orientation was finally included in the Unfair Dismissals Act in July 1993.[67] While its passage into law has been overshadowed by the Sexual Offence's Bill that legally affected only gay males, this new law affected both male and female homosexuals. Significantly, it was brought about solely on the basis of lobbying by gay and lesbian activists, and not because of a European court ruling.

Decriminalization

We're here, we're queer, we're legal.[68]

While Norris' legal victory in October 1988 was welcomed by many within Irish society, with the *Irish Times* declaring it a "sound judgement," the result itself was not all that surprising.[69] In fact, since Jeffrey Dudgeon's victory in 1981 against the same laws in Northern Ireland, there was a sense of inevitability, even recognized by advisors to the Irish government, that the laws in the Republic would sooner or later have to be reformed.[70] What was not inevitable, however, was the type of law reform that would be introduced. Beginning on June 24, 1980 at the Irish High Court, Norris argued that the state had no business in the field of private morality and therefore no right to legislate in relation to the private sexual conduct of consenting adults.[71] Despite the array of accomplished domestic and international witnesses produced by Norris, neither the High Court nor the Supreme Court in 1983 was convinced to rule in Norris' favor, with Chief Justice O'Higgins maintaining:

> On the ground of the Christian nature of our State and on the grounds that the deliberate practice of homosexuality is morally wrong, that it is damaging to the health both of individuals and the public, and finally, that it is potentially harmful to the institution of marriage, I can find no inconsistency with the Constitution in the laws which make such conduct criminal.[72]

Like Dudgeon, Norris took his case to the ECHR and successfully argued that the laws criminalizing sexual activity between males in the Republic were in breach of Article 8 of the European Convention of Human Rights.[73] On October 26, 1988, by eight votes to six, the Irish government was found to have breached Article 8. Following the ECHR decision, the gay/lesbian movement had two major objectives. Firstly, they needed to maintain pressure on the Irish government to follow through on the ECHR judgment, and secondly to ensure that legalization similar to that introduced in England in 1967 would not be introduced in Ireland.[74]

Much of the fear surrounding the 1967 law came from meetings Irish activists had with their English counterparts who stressed the limits of that legislation. For example, in one document sent from the Campaign for Homosexual Equality the weaknesses of the legalization were highlighted, such as an unequal age of consent, gay male sex still referred to in law as gross indecency, and all homosexual acts remaining a crime for members of the armed forces and merchant navy.[75] To prevent such a law in the Republic of Ireland members of the National Gay Federation, Cork Gay Collective, and Lesbian Discussion Group, with the support of the Irish Council for Civil Liberties (ICCL), came together to form Unite for Change in 1988, later becoming the Gay & Lesbian Equality Network (GLEN). Other groups such as the USI, ICTU, and the *Oireachtas* Committee on Women's Rights, among others, lent their backing to the campaign.[76]

At the heart of GLEN's message was the principle of *equality*. Irish society, they argued, had a history of justice and fair play and should embrace diversity, not enforce uniformity.[77] In a document published in 1990 by the ICCL, *Equality Now for Lesbians*

& Gay Men, it sought to ease the concerns expressed by opponents of law reform. In comprehensive fashion, *Equality Now* laid out the justifications for law reform, while strongly dismissing the assertions that homosexuals were a threat to children, were mentally disordered, or in any way harmful to society. Instead they maintained that "discrimination against lesbians and gay men, indeed against all powerless minorities, slows our progress to maturity as a free democracy founded on ideals of equality."[78]

International allies also played their role in heaping pressure on the Irish government. Since the early 1970s European gay rights organizations had written to the Irish government condemning the maintenance of the laws, describing them as out of step with European ideals. In one letter Belgium's *Federatie Werkgroepen Homofilie/ Homoseksualiteit* maintained that:

> from our own daily experience in Belgium in the field of homosexuality we cannot understand such a condemnation in a European nation. At a time when in so many countries homosexual men and women can live openly their preference we are taken aback on the out of date philosophy hidden behind this recent sentence.[79]

In the early 1990s members of the International Lesbian and Gay Association stepped up these efforts through a letter-writing campaign to government members.[80] One such letter to *Taoiseach* Charles Haughey from the *Verein zur Förderung lesbisch-schwuler Emanzipation und Integrationsarbeit* noted:

> It is very sad that a people who fought for 800 years or more for their human rights as a nation because they were born Irish should deny these human rights to people who were born with an orientation to love people of their own sex. Roger Casement, who fought so hard for the rights of the oppressed in the Congo and elsewhere must be shedding tears that a Government of his nation stands against human rights.[81]

Ireland's place within Europe was a consistent theme adopted by activists to demonstrate the damage the laws were having on Ireland's international reputation.[82] The NGF argued that their attempts to amend the law were simply "their patriotic duty to prevent the further humiliation of our country in the light of European public opinion."[83] In another letter to the Minister for Justice in 1992, the Committee on the Administration of Justice in Northern Ireland noted that "gay groups and individuals have experienced the current law [the UK's 1967 Sexual Offences Act] as creating a considerable degree of misery and there is a growing consensus that it is both unacceptable and requires amendment."[84]

The rhetoric adopted by those opposed to law reform, which was primarily the hierarchy of the Roman Catholic Church and the organization Family Solidarity, remarkably failed to win many allies. Unlike the hierarchy of the main churches in Northern Ireland that succeeded in mobilizing support against law reform in the late 1970s, no such mass opposition appeared in the Republic. In fact, the Archbishop of Armagh, Rev Dr Eames, offered his backing to law reform in the Republic.[85] Following the ECHR judgment, Family Solidarity published *The Homosexual*

Challenge in 1990, which was sent to every public representative. Throughout the sixty-four pages the threat of legalizing homosexual behavior was laid bare, with homosexuality continually referred to as a condition which, if legalized, would be detrimental to Irish society, maintaining that "the homosexual movement's demands do not merely involve private morality; if granted, they would have grave public consequences for education, health and the general good of society."[86] Reacting to the document, Gary O'Halloran, the *Fine Gael* councilor for Waterford, described the booklet as fascist in nature and one of the most provocative documents he had read in his life, insisting he was sending a copy to the Garda Commissioner to investigate it.[87] Family Solidarity's arguments were also not helped by the government-established Law Reform Commission declaring in 1989 that they were unable to "discover any compelling argument for fixing the age at which homosexual consensual conduct should be permitted at, for example 18, or 21, while maintaining the age in respect of heterosexual activity at 17."[88]

The momentum appeared to be with those advocating for greater tolerance and equality for gay and lesbian individuals. In the same year as the ECHR judgment the Galway Gay and Lesbian Collective had been presented with the Peader O'Donnell Achievement Award by Deputy Mayor of Galway Bridie O'Flaherty.[89] Not alone as we have seen were gay and lesbians permitted to march in the 1992 St. Patrick's Day Parade, but their float also received the prize for "best new entrant."[90] Later that year President Mary Robinson welcomed gay and lesbian individuals to a reception at *Áras an Uachtarain*.[91] All were an acknowledgment that one could be both Irish and gay or lesbian.

On June 24, 1993, five months after the new government committed itself to law reform, Minister for Justice Maire Geoghegan-Quinn introduced the Sexual Offences Bill, which not only decriminalized sexual activity between males, but also introduced an equal age of consent for hetero- and homosexuals.[92] In introducing the bill Quinn demonstrated the extent to which the government had adopted the rhetoric of the gay movement, announcing it as a "necessary development of human rights."[93] Perhaps most encouraging for gay and lesbian individuals was the strong cross-party support for the bill, ensuring its passage without a vote. The passage of the Sexual Offences Bill, particularly an equal age of consent, contrasted sharply with Great Britain, where attempts by MP Edwina Currie in 1994 to amend the 1967 law to allow for an equal age of consent was defeated by twenty-seven votes.[94]

Conclusion

Writing in 2015 Maire Geoghegan-Quinn stated that:

> I decided to decriminalise homosexuality, I did so because I met people, rather than statistics. Women with tears unwiped. Mothers of gay sons, terrified that their children fall foul of a law that characterised their sexuality as against the interests of the State. The women I met changed my understanding of what it meant to be gay in Ireland at the time.[95]

While these personal encounters no doubt deeply influenced Quinn, there can also be no doubt that the other actions discussed here also helped convince a broader cohort of politicians and society that gay and lesbian individuals should be treated with greater tolerance and not be subjected to discrimination. This is not to say that gay and lesbian citizens had achieved a full place in Irish society in 1993, rather that Irish society began to acknowledge the many restrictions placed on the citizenship rights of gay/lesbian individuals as unjust.

This chapter has highlighted some of the many forms of resistance carried out by lesbian and gay activists throughout Ireland between the 1970s and 1990s, a period that has been ignored by historians in the achievement of lesbian and gay rights in Ireland. Irish homosexuals did not hide behind David Norris' court case and did not suddenly appear in Irish society in 1993 with the introduction of the Sexual Offences Bill. Instead, throughout Ireland gay and lesbian individuals had actively resisted their own subjugation, either by choosing to act out a gay/lesbian lifestyle, organizing lesbian and gay social life, publicly challenging the misunderstandings around homosexuality, or by forging alliances with other groups in the promotion of their civil rights. These earlier actions were crucial to begin a public dialogue around homosexuality. Rather than viewing other groups, such as the Women's Movement, or individual politicians, as the sole agents behind the renegotiation of Ireland's social mores, it was Irish gay and lesbian individuals themselves, who by challenging the dominant social mores with which they had been raised became active agents in their own liberation. The sites of their ongoing activism could be found in some shape or form throughout all Ireland. Their resistance and ability to win over support outside the gay/lesbian movement laid the firm foundations for the subsequent changes that have taken place in recent years for gay and lesbian citizens.

Notes

1. "Finance and Public Expenditure Combined as Cabinet Is Named," https://www.rte.ie/news/2017/0614/882589-new_taoiseach/ (accessed June 14, 2017).
2. "Ban Ki-moon Praises Ireland on Marriage Equality Vote," *Irish Examiner*, May 24, 2015, http://www.irishexaminer.com/breakingnews/ireland/ban-ki-moon-praises-ireland-on-marriage-equality-vote-678570.html (accessed May 25, 2015).
3. "Some puffing out of the Norrisonian chest," *Irish Times*, May 27, 2015, http://www.irishtimes.com/news/politics/oireachtas/miriam-lord-some-puffing-out-of-the-norrisonian-chest-1.2227038 (accessed May 27, 2015).
4. Ibid.
5. Ibid.
6. "David Norris, Hero of Gay Marriage Vote," *The Guardian*, May 30, 2015, https://www.theguardian.com/world/2015/may/30/david-norris-gay-marriage-interview (accessed October 20, 2016).
7. Diarmaid Ferriter, *Occasions of Sin: Sex and Society in Modern Ireland* (London: Profile Books Ltd., 2009), 487–509.
8. National Library of Ireland, Irish Queer Archive (henceforth NLI, IQA), MS 45, 966/5—"Fairview Park."

9   Lindsey Earner Byrne, "Reinforcing the Family: The Role of Gender, Morality and Sexuality in Irish Welfare Policy, 1922–1944," *The History of the Family* 13, no. 4 (2008).
10 Irish Catholic Bishops Conference, *Religious Practise and Values in Ireland*, http://www.catholicbishops.ie/wp-content/uploads/images/stories/cco_publications/researchanddevelopment/evs_4th_wave_report.pdf (accessed October 26, 2016).
11 1861 Offences Against the Persons Act and the 1885 Criminal Law Amendment Act.
12 Censorship of Publications Act, 1929, http://www.irishstatutebook.ie/eli/1929/act/21/enacted/en/print.html (accessed June 15, 2017).
13 Examples of books censored included, *East of Eden*, by John Steinbeck, *The African Queen*, by C. S. Forester, *The Heart of Matter*, by Graham Greene and, in 1976, the Irish Family Planning Association's booklet, *Family Planning—A Guide for Parents and Prospective Parents*. In 1968, Kenneth Marlowe's *The Male Homosexual* was censored, while in 1971 *Boys in the Band* was banned. In 1977 Rita Mae Brown's, *Rubyfruit Jungle* also fell foul of the censorship board.
14 *Sunday Independent,* April 13, 1969.
15 "Don't Jail them, pleads doctor," *Irish Independent*, November 6, 1973.
16 NLI, IQA, MS 45, 951/2—IGRM Constitution, adopted September 28, 1975.
17 Nan Alamilla Boyd, *Wide-Open Town: A History of Queer San Francisco to 1965* (Berkeley: University of California Press, 2003), 71.
18 NLI, IR 94133 I 2, *In Dublin,* October 6–20, 1983.
19 "Life Revives in a Dying Part of Dublin," *Irish Times*, July 30, 1984.
20 Public Record Office of Northern Ireland, D3762/1/10/1, Dublin Toast, *Gay News*.
21 NLI, IQA, MS 45, 946/1–1981 Weekly Disco attendances.
22 *Women's Space Newsletter*, Issue 2, May/June 1988, http://corklgbtarchive.com/items/show/60 (accessed October 21, 2016).
23 NLI, IQA, MS 45, 949/6—Report of National Gay Conference, May 15th–17th, Cork, Ireland.
24 *Munster Women's Newsletter*, c. 1985, "A Lesbian in Cork," http://corklgbtarchive.com/items/show/81 (accessed October 21, 2016).
25 Louise Walsh, "Artist-Activist," in *Lesbian and Gay Visions of Ireland: Towards the Twenty-First Century*, ed. Íde O'Carroll and Eoin Collins (London: Cassell, 1995), 172.
26 James Quinn, September 28, 2013, *Edmund Lynch, Irish LGBT History Project 2013*.
27 NLI, IQA, MS 45, 948/6—John Porter to Bernard Keogh, January 19, 1982.
28 James Scott, *Weapons of the Weak: Everyday Forms of Peasant Resistance* (New Haven: Yale University Press, 1989), p. xvii.
29 Joe O'Mara, August 4, 2015, *Edmund Lynch, Irish LGBT History Project 2013*.
30 "Right to Reply—A word to Brenda from Gay," *Sunday Independent*, August 3, 1975.
31 RTÉ TV history, http://www.rte.ie/tv50/history/1960s.html Accessed on May 12, 2015.
32 Cathal O'Shannon, "Homosexuality in Ireland," *Tuesday Report*, February 22, 1977.
33 Ibid.
34 Ibid.
35 https://www.youtube.com/watch?v=HlEZxqa3TQc Arthur Leahy & Laurie Steele interview on *Week End* (accessed October 21, 2016).
36 Ibid.
37 NLI, IR 369 I 23, *In Touch: Journal of the National Gay Federation,* Vol. 2, No. 3 March 1980.
38 Joni Sheerin interview with Gay Byrne, *Late Late Show*, February 9, 1980. Personal copy of interview acquired from Edmund Lynch.
39 "Television Today," *Irish Times*, February 11, 1980.

40 Joni Sheerin interview with Gay Byrne, *Late Late Show*, February 1980. Personal copy of interview acquired from Edmund Lynch.
41 NLI, IQA, MS 45, 943/2, *Tuesday Report*.
42 Patrick Galvin, "A Gay Dog," *Hibernia*, March 4, 1977.
43 NLI, IQA, MS 45, 940/4—Summary of Telephone Reaction received on Friday February 9, 1980.
44 NLI, IQA, MS 45, 940/4—"Summary of Telephone Reaction received on Friday February 9th, 1980."
45 "Hundreds March for Gay Rights," *Sunday Independent*, March 20, 1983.
46 "Demo over Attacks on 'Gays,'" *Evening Herald*, March 19, 1983.
47 NLI, IR 369 I 25, *Identity*, Issue No. 5, April-June 1983, "Fairview Park."
48 Sebastian Buckle, *The Way Out: A History of Homosexuality in Modern Britain* (London: I. B. Taurus, 2015), 29.
49 "The Kissing Has to Stop," *Munster Nationalist*, June 25, 1988.
50 NLI, ILB 305 G 2, *Gay Community News*, "History Victory," April 1992.
51 NLI, IQA, MS, 45, 948/1—Liam Whitelaw, Deputy President of the Union of Students in Ireland, March 27, 1981.
52 NLI, IQA, MS 45, 948/1—*USI News*, Vol. 10, No. 2, November 1980—Gay Rights Case for Europe?
53 Hubert Mannion, "Rights of Homosexuals," *Irish Press*, July 12, 1982.
54 NLI, IQA, MS 45, 948/9—John Sanders Case, Bulletin No. 1.
55 NLI, IR 369 I 23, *In Touch*, Vol. 2, No. 6 June/July 1980.
56 NLI, IQA, MS 45, 936/9—Report on trade union activity presented to the 2nd AGM of the National Gay Federation on June 27, 1981.
57 NLI, IQA, MS 45, 949/6—Kieran Rose to Secretary of ICTU, March 26, 1981.
58 NLI, IQA, MS 45, 949/6—"Kieran Rose Speech on Gay Rights Motion to Cork Branch of L.G.P.S.U, 30 March 1982."
59 NLI, IQA, MS 45, 949/6—Text of speech on gay rights motion no. 35 to Cork branch of LGPSU by Kieran Rose, March 30, 1982.
60 "Union Supports Change in Law on Homosexuality," *Cork Examiner*, May 14, 1982.
61 NLI, IQA MS 45, 949/6—Press Release July 9, 1982.
62 Buckle, *The Way Out*, 99.
63 NLI, IQA MS 45, 948/3—Bernard Keogh of Social Justice Committee of ESBOA to Tonie Walsh, general secretary of NGF, re: Trade Unions & Gay Rights, September 5, 1983.
64 National Archives of Ireland, 2014/107/76, Letter from Patricia O'Donovan, Legislation & Equality Officer, ICTU, November 26, 1986.
65 NLI, ILB 306 G 2, *Gay Community News*, "Continuing Progress for Lesbian and Gay Workers," Issues 3–4, April/May 1988.
66 http://circulars.gov.ie/pdf/circular/finance/1988/12.pdf - Irish Government Circular 12/88, Civil Service Policy on AIDS. Accessed on 7 July 7 2017. NLI, ILB 306 G 2, "Historic Decision," *Gay Community News*, Issue 14, December/January 1989.
67 Unfair Dismissals (Amendment) Act, 1993, http://www.irishstatutebook.ie/eli/1993/act/22/enacted/en/print.html (accessed June 15, 2017).
68 Kieran Rose, *Diverse Communities: The Evolution of Lesbian & Gay Politics in Ireland* (Cork, 1994), 59.
69 "Sound Judgement," *Irish Times*, October 27, 1988.
70 National Archives, 2015/51/1574—Norris v. Ireland: Draft Memorandum to government from J. Liddy, October 1984.

71 'It's Unconstitutional Gay Rights Leader Says', *Irish Independent*, June 25, 1980.
72 NLI, IQA, MS 45, 952/4, Judgement of the Supreme Court on David Norris V. Attorney General, April 22, 1983.
73 Article 8 of the European Convention on Human Rights recognized the right to respect for private and family life, http://www.echr.coe.int/Documents/Convention_ENG.pdf (accessed October 26, 2016).
74 http://www.legislation.gov.uk/ukpga/1967/60/pdfs/ukpga_19670060_en.pdf (accessed October 26, 2016). The 1967 Sexual Offences Act removed the penalty for sexual activity between males in private aged twenty-one and over.
75 NLI, IQA MS 45, 976/3—Lesbian & Gay Campaigning in England and Wales by the Campaign for Homosexual Equality.
76 NLI, IQA MS 45, 979/7.
77 NLI, IQA MS 45, 976/2—Unite for Change: Report of General Meeting, April 1st, 1989.
78 NLI, IR 340 I 18, Irish Council for Civil Liberties, *Equality Now for Lesbian and Gay Men* (Dublin, 1990), 52.
79 National Archives of Ireland, 2015/51/1575.
80 NLI, IQA MS 45, 977/1.
81 NLI, IQA MS 45, 977/1—*Verein zur Förderung lesbisch-schwuler Emanzipation und Integrationsarbeit* to Department of the *Taoiseach,* January 19, 1993.
82 National Archives of Ireland, 2012/21/582—Letter received from INFOR—Homosexuality C.C.L. in Brussels sent to Irish ambassador in Brussels, April 25, 1975.
83 NLI, IQA MS 45, 948/9—NGF Press Release, July 24, 1980.
84 NLI, IQA MS 45, 976/14—Committee on the Administration of Justice to Minister for Justice, April 30, 1992.
85 NLI, ILB 305 G 2, *Gay Community News,* "Archbishop Comes Out," Issue 35, November 1991.
86 NLI, IR 300 P 150, Family Solidarity, *The Homosexual Challenge: Analysis and Response* (Dublin, 1990), 62.
87 NLI, ILB 305 G 2, *Gay Community News,* "FS Book Fascist Says Cllr.," Issue 22, September 1990.
88 NLI, ILB 305 G 2, *Gay Community News,* "No to Anti-Gay Laws," no. 12 (October 1989).
89 *Galway Advertiser,* "Community Workers Cheered," June 2, 1988.
90 NLI, ILB 305 G 2, *Gay Community News,* "History Victory" (April 1992).
91 "A Birthday to have pride in," *Irish Times,* February 14, 2009, http://www.irishtimes.com/news/a-birthday-to-have-pride-in-1.700270 (accessed October 25, 2016).
92 Criminal Law (Sexual Offences) Bill, 1993: Committee and Final Stages, Dáil Éireann Debate, *Vol. 432 No. 8,* June 24, 1993. NLI, 1B 1258, *Fianna Fail and Labour Programme for a Partnership Government 1993-1997.*
93 Criminal Law (Sexual Offences) Bill, 1993, Private Members' Business, Second Stage, Dáil Éireann Debate, Vol. 432, No. 7, June 23, 1993.
94 Buckle, *The Way Out,* 171.
95 Marie Geoghegan-Quinn, "Decriminalisation of Homosexuality Was Just the Beginning," *Irish Times,* May 14, 2015, http://www.irishtimes.com/opinion/decriminalisation-of-homosexuality-was-just-the-beginning-1.2211452 (accessed October 25, 2016).

15

" ... Do You Want More?": A Brief History of Same-Sex Partnerships, Family Formations, and Marriage in Twentieth-Century United States

Marcia M. Gallo

" ... Do you want more?"

In 2013, American activist and attorney Urvashi Vaid published an analysis of the United States' Supreme Court's 2012 ruling in *Hollingsworth v. Perry. Perry* mounted a significant challenge to lower-court decisions regarding the State of California's same-sex marriage provisions. It paved the way for the US Supreme Court's 2015 decision in *Obergefell v. Hodges,* and three related cases, which affirmed the constitutional right to same-sex marriage in America. To frame her assessment, Vaid used the words of the legendary international reggae artist and activist Bob Marley[1] as she argued that the marriage equality movement in the United States had been both positive but, mostly, negative: "On the one hand, the movement has enlisted a large circle of non-gay allies. On the other hand, the movement has narrowed its aspirations." She went on to detail the ways that the marriage movement succeeded in part because it "removes us from the realm of sexual outlaws and makes queer sexuality more recognizable to straight society."[2]

This chapter traces some of the discussions and debates about same-sex marriage among activists in the mid- to late twentieth-century United States. It will touch on the arguments on all sides of the issues, from the earliest proponents of lesbian and gay couples creating celebrations of their relationships to the relative success of those seeking marriage equality for gay and lesbian peoples. Throughout, the chapter focuses on the ways in which the debates have been contained within an American rights-based framework, a model that has received a great deal of national and international publicity and significant legal successes in the second half of the twentieth century for racial, ethnic, and sexual minorities. What Vaid and many others argue, however, is that reliance on such a model does not provide for a radical reconfiguration of social norms.

To begin, it is necessary to examine what it means to rely on an American rights-based framework. In the United States, individuals and groups who have identified and advocated as sexual minorities in the latter decades of the twentieth century followed the same route as other peoples who are defined according to their racial, ethnic, gender, ability, religious, or other personal identity statuses. Those who are in the minority seek protection under the law from discrimination by the majority. By asserting minority status, exploited or disfavored groups can argue that they should be able to access the same constitutionally guaranteed civil rights as other Americans. Yet such access requires an adherence to liberal social constructs and institutions.

It has been only since the 1950s that lesbians and gay men have recognized and advanced their status as sexual minorities and begun to organize themselves into social and political advocacy groups. The removal of laws prohibiting homosexual speech and conduct in the United States has required sustained local activism as well as US Supreme Court challenges. For example, it was only in the first few years of the twenty-first century that homosexual conduct between consenting adults has been legal nationwide, due to a US Supreme Court decision striking down sodomy statutes (*Lawrence v. Texas*, 2003). As of 2018, fewer than half of the states in the United States — twenty-one states and the District of Columbia — explicitly prohibited discrimination based on sexual orientation and gender identity. Yet as of 2015, due to the historic US Supreme Court ruling in the case of *Obergefell v. Hodges*, all fifty states must license and recognize marriages between same-sex couples.

While forming partnerships is intrinsic to lesbian and gay life, so too is the ability to work, find housing, purchase goods and services, and generally enjoy life without being denied access simply because of one's sexuality or gender identification. Yet these contradictions—between federal versus local jurisdictions, between rights granted and those denied—are at the heart of American democratic processes. They also fuel debates over the direction of social change movements.

In addition, despite the success of the marriage equality movement, not all lesbians and gay men have wanted to imitate heterosexual pairings. In fact, one of the hallmarks of American queer history in the mid- to late twentieth century are the sometimes vociferous debates about how such partnerships should be formed. This chapter will reveal some of the salient aspects of such debates. At different times and from varying perspectives, some people have argued that gay committed relationships should be sanctioned by the government in order to enjoy the benefits and privileges that flow to married couples; other people have insisted instead that the opportunity for lesbians and gay men to reconfigure their relationships could liberate both straight and gay marriages from the confines of conformity.

"Taking a chance on love"[3]: Homophile marriage in America

The debates over same-sex marriage have gone on since the American lesbian and gay movement was in its infancy. As historian Timothy Stewart-Winter has written, "There is nothing new about gays and lesbians dreaming of marriage equality."[4] Nearly sixty-five years ago, in August 1953, the groundbreaking homophile magazine *ONE* put the question of "Homosexual Marriage?" on the cover of its monthly magazine. This bold act came in tandem with a letter from reader "E. B. Saunders." Inside, on page 10 under the large headline "REFORMER'S CHOICE: Marriage License or Just License?" "Saunders" wrote:

> Imagine that the year were 2053 and homosexuality were accepted to the point of being of no importance. Now, is the deviate allowed to continue his pursuit of physical happiness without restraint as he attempts to do today? Or is he, in this Utopia, subject to marriage laws? It is a pertinent question. For why should he be permitted permiscuity [sic] when those heterosexuals who people the earth must be married to enjoy sexual intercourse? The answer does not lie in the fact that the deviate cannot reproduce; this is irrelevant to the effect upon society of his acceptance as a valuable citizen. This effect would be one of immense consternation for it would be a legalizing of promiscuity for a special section of the population—which, incidentally, now begs for its rights on the very grounds that it desires the respectability and dignity of all other citizens ... Heterosexual marriage must be protected. The acceptance of homosexuality without homosexual marriage ties would be an attack upon it.[5]

The debate continued. In October 1953, two letters from readers responding to "Saunders" were printed. One, from Berkeley, California, asked:

> What is marriage? It is an heterosexual concept buttressed and blessed by the Church and State since man emerged out of the miasma of pre-history. It is based on protection of the young and the mate; it is based on the necessities of property inheritance; and it is founded in a mass of taboo which no one fully understands. Additional concepts of home, family, and mother support it.

The other letter blasted "Saunders" for further complicating an already difficult situation: "In the year 2053, he asks, are we to be allowed to continue our pursuit of physical happiness without restraint as we attempt to do today? Well, why the hell not? What is this tendency on the part of some people to seek more and more restrictions?"[6]

Ten years later, the editors of *ONE* went even further. They again put the issue of what would come to be called gay marriage on display on the magazine's cover but this time called for action: the June 1963 issue provocatively stated "LET'S PUSH HOMOPHILE MARRIAGE." Inside, beginning on page 5 and extending another five pages, "Randy Lloyd" presented an impassioned argument for marriage while reminding readers of the homophile movement's international roots. "Lloyd" wrote, "The concept of homophile marriage is new, a modern concept, a product of our great current homophile movement that commenced in Germany in the 1800s. I suspect that if anyone could be tagged as the first to intellectually push homophile marriage (though cautiously and embryonically), it would be the Englishman, Edward Carpenter." "Lloyd" emphasized the current barriers to the formation of lasting same-sex unions: "To find The Right One, a person whether heterosexual or homosexual has got to meet a lot of prospects. The wonder is not why under their circumstances so many homosexuals are promiscuous. It is how so many homophile marriages manage to occur. With the handicap we are under, perhaps luck has most to do with it."[7]

"Lloyd" also offered advice to those considering entering into marriage while cautioning that it might not work for everyone:

> Now, while I claim the right to rant and rave in favor of marriage and the right to rant and rave against the trouble-causing promiscuous single set, I sure am not claiming that all homophiles should be married. Not everybody is suited for marriage, including plenty of heterosexuals. I think the two viewpoints are put well and wittily by Shaw's saying that 'Marriage is the most promiscuous institution ever invented—that is the secret of its success', and Wilde's saying that 'Marriage affords the maximum opportunities for sex—but with the minimum of temptation.'[8]

Predictably, both the use of gay male caricatures on the magazine's cover and "Lloyd's" embrace of homophile marriage brought a variety of responses from *ONE*'s readers. From Atlanta, Georgia "Mr. F." wrote, "Your June issue is the best yet. Mark Haldane's cover is a masterpiece," but from "Marc Daniel, ARCADIE, Paris, France" came a very negative assessment.

> Speaking as a reader, I must tell that the cover of the June issue is more than I think admissible in bad taste. The appalling caricatures of homosexuals (which the chances of publication made appear together with the title 'Homophile Marriage,' alas!) should have been drawn by one of our worst enemies. Do really the editors of ONE think we can simply show such a publication to a non-homophile friend? And do really such drawings on the cover page contribute to giving the public a notion of homosexuals as normal healthy people?

However, the June 1963 issue also provoked personal, and sometimes painful, responses. "Mr. L." wrote to describe the loss of his own partnership. " 'Let's Push Homophile Marriage' was a fine article which I am definitely in accord with. I have tried to preach this all my life to little avail. Since I have lost my great love to the 'Grim Reaper' I have been a lonesome person, but twelve years was marvelous in its entirety. For this I am grateful." On the other hand, as "Mr. W." wrote in from California: "When someone begins to stress Homophile Marriage I sort of shudder because it is simply removing one type of regulation that fits a certain percentage and replacing it by another." "Mr. W." urged *ONE* instead to continue to "develop better understanding of the homophile's problems." Other homophile groups also weighed in. From Fullerton, California, on behalf of the "brother homophile organization" Dionysus, the group's Secretary, wrote:

> Can't you hear our enemies saying, as they read it, 'For God's sake, the queers want to marry each other?' We did not find fault with the article itself, in fact there were many good points in it, but marriage to most people is a sacred rite performed by a clergy or authorized civil authority and not something that we could be accused of making a mockery of by the heterosexual world.[9]

And what of lesbian relationships? Scholars have documented the means by which women who loved women pursued and maintained same-sex partnerships throughout history, often "passing" as men in order to work, travel, and pursue opportunities of all kinds. Further, as lesbian feminist historian Leila Rupp has noted, the popularity of so-called Boston marriages among well-educated women in the nineteenth century, such as Jeannette Marks and Mary Woolley of Mount Holyoke College in Massachusetts, further complicates historical assessments. Like many women of their era and status, Marks and Woolley never defined themselves as lesbians, yet lived in a committed relationship for nearly fifty years. In addition to their academic responsibilities and attainments, they also participated in numerous feminist and peace organizations. Although Mary Woolley died in 1947, Jeannette Marks lived on until 1964 and completed a biography of Woolley.[10]

By 1955, when the founders of the first American lesbian rights organization, the Daughters of Bilitis (DOB), met in San Francisco, the four couples who gathered were not only racially mixed and in committed relationships but also consisted of at least two women who had been married to men and had children. Thus, the issue of marriage—especially opposite-sex unions—was always on the minds of many of the early lesbian homophile activists. From its beginning in 1956, the DOB's groundbreaking newsletter *The Ladder* featured articles on marriage, but these mostly centered on whether to enter into or remain in a heterosexual marriage as a lesbian.[11]

Some of the women who had worked with *ONE* in the early 1950s gravitated to DOB and *The Ladder,* such as Stella Rush, known in homophile circles as "Sten Russell." She became the Los Angeles anchor for DOB, a founder of the local chapter, and also contributed a number of articles for the newsletter. She and another early DOB leader, Helen Sandoz, are mid-twentieth-century examples of women in a committed relationship, ardent lesbian feminists who were also devoted to one another. Rush's grief at the early death of her longtime partner was palpable decades later in interviews.[12] And, although it was not without risk in the early days of the homophile movement, their open embrace of lesbianism and lesbian feminist activism helped pave the way for the growth of both movements.

"I will survive"[13]: Rethinking marriage

As historian Peggy Pascoe reminded us, "Although the first public demands for same-sex marriage came as early as the 1950s, it was not until the 1970s that they were able to emerge from the cultural shadow" of Cold War ideology. "By the 1970s, domestic containment was under siege." Numerous challenges to personal and societal norms, including those taking aim at traditional family formations, rigid gender roles, and restrictions on employment, all helped create the conditions that would eventually lead to an expansion of social and political opportunities in the United States. "Examples were easy to find. Defiant youth of the 'counterculture' took pride in casting off their parents' suburban married stability to experiment with new 'lifestyles.'" Radical feminists argued that the family was the core institution of patriarchy. Gay liberationists ridiculed monogamy as old-fashioned, describing marriage and the family as something they had escaped, often at great personal cost.[14]

These liberatory demands included increasingly loud cries for lesbians and gay men to "come out!" after the June 1969 riots at New York's Stonewall Inn, a popular hangout for drag queens, street kids, and queers of all kinds. Self-identifying as lesbian or gay—doing so with "pride" might come a bit later—was seen as the first step in defanging enforced invisibility; it also helped further the development of queer subcultures that had begun to take shape with the early efforts of the homophile activists of the 1950s.

Given these challenges, the first lesbian and gay couples to question prohibitions on gay marriage in the early 1970s "swam both with and against this social tide," in Pascoe's assessment. She has noted that the very controversial idea of "gay marriage"—so obvious in the Letters columns of the homophile magazines like *ONE* just a few years previously—was abhorred by social conservatives and seen as "bizarre" by the public. "The sheer audacity of the demand won support from emerging gay liberation groups that considered its 'in your face' political style something of a dividing line between old and new gay politics."[15]

However, debates about the institution of marriage raged within and beyond lesbian and gay circles. Carl Whitman's brilliant "Refugees from Amerika: A Gay Manifesto," written and circulated among his friends in 1969 and published in 1970, demonized marriage as a "rotten, oppressive institution" from a radical gay man's point of view. "We are children of straight society," he wrote, "but we must stop mimicking straights."[16] This echoed claims by feminists (some of whom also were lesbians) ranging from Kate Millett and Germaine Greer to Shulamith Firestone and others.[17]

Legal scholar William Eskridge has framed the changes to the self-conceptions and aspirations of lesbians and gay men in the post-1969 period as "dramatic." "As lesbians, gay men, and bisexuals have become more open about our sexuality, and as our own subculture has grown, there have been more long-term same-sex relationships than ever before in human history." He quoted a study published in 1980 by social scientist Mary Mendola based on her survey of same-sex couples in the 1970s. "Her respondents overwhelmingly considered themselves 'married.'" Further, he noted that other "academic and empirical examinations of same-sex relationships conducted in the 1960s and 1970s found them functional in and of themselves but terminally shackled by social prejudice, legal disadvantages, and economic discrimination."[18] Some gay men and lesbians became increasingly determined to throw off the shackles.

In 1970, Jack Baker and James Michael McConnell dared to do just that. After being unsuccessful in securing a marriage license in Minnesota—which did not explicitly bar people of the same sex from marrying—they appealed to the US Supreme Court in 1971. Represented by the Minnesota affiliate of the American Civil Liberties Union, they claimed that the 1967 US Supreme Court decision in the case of *Loving v. Virginia* granted a constitutional right to marry that could not be invalidated based on the sex of the marriage partners. As the *New York Times* expert on the US Supreme Court Linda Greenhouse noted in 2013, the Court issued a one-sentence decision: "The appeal is dismissed for want of a substantial federal question." In other words, there was nothing compelling for the Court to consider. In writing about how much had changed between 1971 and 2013, she noted, "The local fame that came Jack Baker's way after the failed marriage-license application made him even more of a campus figure at the University of Minnesota than he already was as the founder of a gay student organization. He was elected and then re-elected student body president and went on to graduate from law school." However, Greenhouse also noted that his partner, James Michael McConnell, did not do as well. He was denied jobs at the University of Minnesota because of the notoriety of the case.[19] In 2016, they documented the story of their remarkable trajectory from gay liberationists to gay marriage activists and, in what must feel like a belated victory, had their story published by the University of Minnesota Press.[20]

Although much less well known than Baker and McConnell, a lesbian couple in Kentucky, Marjorie Jones and Tracy Knight, met with a similar fate when they attempted to challenge denials for a marriage license, except that they encountered even more hostility toward their relationship. "The court admitted that Kentucky laws neither offered a definition of marriage nor prohibited same-sex marriage," but the judge insisted that what the two women wanted "is not a marriage." Furthermore, according to Peggy Pascoe, the Kentucky county attorney held that the Jones–Knight relationship did not have "the requisites of a happy home, the love and affection desired by society, with the proper concern for the children involved" because it was formed for the "pure pursuit of hedonistic and sexual pleasure."[21]

Historian Elise Chenier joins other scholars and insists that in order to fully understand the underlying challenges to sexism involved in such cases we must incorporate more women into the narrative of twentieth-century gay marriage. "A handful of lesbian couples championed gay marriage, too. Women did not challenge the fundamental premise of marriage as a monogamous institution, however. Instead they challenged the popular perception of lesbian relationships as pathological, immature, and short-lived. Their efforts contributed to the public re-imagining of lesbianism as a foundation for loving relationships."[22] Chenier's work also pointedly challenges the idea that early proponents of same-sex marriage were mostly white. "In 1971, Latina Bobbi Jean Sanchez and her African-American partner Joan Kearse were married in Revered Robert Clement's Church of the Beloved Disciple, in New York. In 1974, an African-American couple, Phyllis Marshall and Grace Thornton, both of Dayton, Ohio, applied six times to the Montgomery County Domestic Relations court for a marriage certificate." They filed a $1 million lawsuit against the state but lost both it and their hopes for a marriage license.[23]

Further, the early gay and lesbian marriage cases unfortunately intersected with the push for the Equal Rights Amendment to the US Constitution that was under way in the early 1970s. Conservative opposition to the simple insertion of "sex" as a protected category against discrimination railed against the Amendment, originally written by feminists Crystal Eastman and Alice Paul and first proposed in Congress in 1923. According to Peggy Pascoe, "They turned the specter of 'homosexual marriage' into a call to arms against the feminist movement in general and the Equal Rights Amendment in particular." Such tactics also led to the passage of anti-gay laws in general as well as laws restricting marriage. "The result was the passage of a second wave of sex-specific marriage laws that, unlike the first, was specifically intended to stop same-sex couples from marrying by lodging the notion that marriages must be opposite-sex so firmly in law that it could never again be questioned."[24]

"We are family"[25]: Families we choose, domestic partnerships, and same-sex marriage

Within lesbian communities since at least the 1970s, child custody battles as well as reproductive rights organizing provided important contexts for the movement's focus on securing domestic rights. In his work on family formations among gay and lesbian parents and their children since the Second World War, Daniel Winunwe Rivers details the shift from radical reconceptions of traditional family structures to more assimilationist perspectives, emphasizing the devastating impact of AIDS and the growth of grassroots donor insemination networks. He argues that both of these developments "bridged the cultural divides" between gay and lesbian communities: "As hospitals denied access to partners of individuals with HIV/AIDS and shut them out of crucial legal and medical decisions made by families of origin, lesbian and gay rights activists became more concerned with rights previously reserved for heterosexual marriage."[26]

Given the hostility to same-sex marriage enshrined in most state laws in the 1970s and 1980s, gay and lesbian activists turned toward other means for securing some, if not all, of the benefits offered married couples. The development and pursuit of domestic partnership laws in the 1980s proved a successful strategy and helped provide practical alternatives to marriage, which were especially essential during the AIDS pandemic. Further, as legal scholar Paula Ettelbrick argued in 1989:

> The lesbian and gay community has laid the groundwork for revolutionizing society's views of family. The domestic partnership movement has been an important part of this progress insofar as it validates non-marital relationships. Because it is not limited to sexual or romantic relationships, domestic partnership provides an important opportunity for many who are not related by blood or marriage to claim certain minimal protections.[27]

Attorney and activist Nancy Polikoff wrote about the origins of the domestic partner movement in 2013, noting that such policies came about as a series of social changes in the 1960s and 1970s that "made marriage matter less." Domestic partnerships were seen as an equitable way around the marriage battles for both same- and opposite-sex couples. "In 1982, the Village Voice, a New York City newspaper, became the first employer to provide such benefits. In 1985, the city of Berkeley, California became the first public employer to do so."[28] However, by 1991, employee benefits limited to same-sex partners became more prevalent. "Such benefits were framed as an equity issue for same-sex couples who could not marry," Polikoff noted. Furthermore, "the arrival of marriage equality in Massachusetts in 2004 magnified the urgency of this issue, as many individual gay men and lesbians learned they would lose benefits if they did not marry."[29]

By the end of the 1990s, organizing for domestic partnership benefits largely were eclipsed by renewed efforts at securing same-sex marriage. One of the first court victories was in Hawaii. The *Baehr v. Lewin* decision in 1993 mobilized opponents of same-sex marriages. Much like what had happened with the advance of gay and lesbian visibility and activism in the 1970s, anti-gay marriage legislation was passed on both the state and federal levels in the mid-1990s. Laws and court decisions addressing same-sex marriage were mostly limited to the states, with one crucial exception: the federal Defense of Marriage Act, or DOMA.

In 1996, in response to the *Baehr* decision, the US Congress created and passed DOMA and President William Clinton signed it into law. The act was designed to prevent the Full Faith and Credit Clause from being applied to states' refusal to recognize same sex marriages. DOMA stated in part that:

> No state, territory or possession of the United States ... shall be required to give effect to any public act, record, or judicial proceeding of any other State, territory, possession or tribe respecting a relationship between persons of the same sex that is treated as a marriage under the laws of such other State, territory, possession, or tribe, or a right or claim arising from such a relationship.

Key provisions of DOMA were found to be unconstitutional in 2013 in the case of *United States v. Windsor*. (The lead plaintiff in the case, Edith Windsor, passed away in New York at the age of 88 on September 12, 2017.) DOMA was fully overruled on June 26, 2015 by the US Supreme Court decision in *Obergefell v. Hodges*, the landmark case in which the majority of justices affirmed that a denial of marriage rights to same-sex couples is unconstitutional.[30] As of now, same-sex marriage remains the law of the land in America.

In conclusion, a few comments about assimilation from the brilliant legal scholar and activist Ruthann Robson are a propos. In a long article from 2002, she concluded by writing,

> like other legal reform movements, the lesbian and queer movement cannot simply assume that assimilation is the answer for all of us. Unproblematized, the quest for assimilation leaves those who cannot—or will not—be assimilated outside of our community of interests. We need to envision liberation beyond the boundaries of state-sanctioned marriage; beyond the bounds of the state. To do this, we need to recognize the limits of marriage and assimilation.

Or, as Urvashi Vaid noted in 2013, paraphrasing Bob Marley, "now that you have want you want, do you want more?"

Notes

1 Bob Marley, "Now You Get What You Want, Do You Want More?" from *Rastaman Vibration* album, 1976.
2 Urvashi Vaid, "Now You Get What You Want, Do You Want More?" *N. Y. U. Review of Law & Social Change* 37 (2013): 101–111.
3 "Taking a Chance on Love," Ethel Waters, with Eddie "Rochester" Anderson, from the film *Cabin in the Sky*, 1943. https://www.youtube.com/watch?v=Ue_jOJ8GfhI.

4 Timothy Stewart-Winter, "What *Was* Same-Sex Marriage?" *The Gay and Lesbian Review / Worldwide*, January–February 2006: 33–35.
5 E. B. Saunders, "Reformer's Choice: Marriage License or Just License?" *ONE* Magazine, August 1953: 10–12.
6 Letter from "Berkeley, Calif.," *ONE* Magazine, October 1953: 11; letter from "R.H.K.," *ONE* Magazine, October 1953: 13–15.
7 "Randy Lloyd," "Let's Push Homophile Marriage," *ONE* Magazine, June 1963: 5–10.
8 Lloyd, "Let's Push," 9.
9 Letters from "Mr. F., Atlanta, Georgia," *ONE* Magazine, August 1963; "Marc Daniel, ARCADIE, Paris, France," *ONE* Magazine, September 1963: 30; "Mr. L., Philadelphia, Pennsylvania," *ONE* Magazine, September 1963: 29; "Mr. W., Alhambra, California," *ONE* Magazine, September 1963: 29; "Tony Foster, Secretary, DIONYSUS, Fullerton, California," *ONE* Magazine, September 1963: 29.
10 Leila Rupp, "'Imagine My Surprise': Women's Relationships in Historical Perspective," *Journal of Lesbian Studies* 1, no. 2 (1997): 155–176. See also Lillian Faderman, *Surpassing the Love of Men: Romantic Friendship and Love between Women from the Renaissance to the Present* (New York: HarperCollins, 1998 [1981]) and Lillian Faderman, *Odd Girls and Twilight Lovers: A History of Lesbian Life in Twentieth-Century America* (New York: Columbia University Press, 1991).
11 "Some Remarks on Marriage," *The Ladder* 1, no. 10 (July 1957): 14; Patti Brown, "Should Homosexuals Marry?" *The Ladder* 3, no. 8 (May 1959): 21.
12 Marcia M. Gallo, "Introduction to *The Ladder*: An Interpretation and Document Archive," 2010. Women and Social Movements, http://womhist.alexanderstreet.com/mgallo/intro.htm.
13 Gloria Gaynor, from *Love Tracks* album, 1978.
14 Peggy Pascoe, "Sex, Gender, and Same Sex Marriage," in *Theory in Practice*, ed. Social Justice Group (New York: New York University Press, 2000), 88–89.
15 Ibid., 88–89.
16 Carl Wittman, "A Gay Manifesto," *Liberation*, February 1970. See also OutHistory.org http://outhistory.org/exhibits/show/raisedvoicesamongprettymanners/raisedvoicescarlwittman.
17 Kate Millett, *Sexual Politics* (New York: Ballantine Books, 1969); Germaine Greer, *The Female Eunuch* (New York: McGraw-Hill, 1970); Shulamith Firestone, *The Dialectic of Sex: The Case for Feminist Revolution* (New York: Morrow, 1970). See also Vivian Gornick and Barbara K. Moran, *Woman in Sexist Society: Studies in Power and Powerlessness* (New York: Basic Books, 1971) as well as Anne Koedt, Ellen Levine, and Anita Rapone, eds., *Radical Feminism* (New York: Quadrangle Books, 1973).
18 William N. Eskridge, Jr., "A History of Same-Sex Marriage," *Virginia Law Review* 79 (1993): 1483–1484.
19 Linda Greenhouse, "Wedding Bells," The *New York Times*, March 20, 2013.
20 Michael McConnell and Jack Baker, *The Wedding Heard 'Round the World: America's First Gay Marriage* (Minneapolis: University of Minnesota Press, 2016).
21 Pascoe, "Sex, Gender, and Same Sex Marriage," 93.
22 Elise Chenier, "Gay Marriage, 1970s Style," *The Gay & Lesbian Review / Worldwide*, March 2013, http://glreview.org/article/gay-marriage-1970s-style/.
23 Ibid.
24 Pascoe, "Sex, Gender, and Same Sex Marriage," 96, 102. See also Mary C. Dunlap, "The Equal Rights Amendment and the Courts," *Pepperdine Law Review* 3, no. 1 (1976).
25 Sister Sledge, from We Are Family album, 1979.

26 Daniel Winunwe Rivers, *Radical Relations: Lesbian Mothers, Gay Fathers, and Their Children in the United States since World War II* (Chapel Hill: University of North Carolina Press, 2013), 193.
27 Paula Ettelbrick, "Since When Is Marriage a Path to Liberation?" *Out/Look National Lesbian and Gay Quarterly*, no. 6 (1989): 14–16.
28 Nancy Polikoff, "What Marriage Equality Arguments Portend for Domestic Partner Employee Benefits," *N.Y.U. Review of Law and Social Change* 37 (2013): 51–52.
29 Ibid., 53.
30 Richard Socarides, "Why Bill Clinton Signed the Defense of Marriage Act," the *New Yorker*, March 8, 2013.

16

Gay Marriage in England: After the Party

Daniel Monk

The legal recognition of same-sex conjugal relationships is, without any doubt, a hugely significant cultural and political phenomenon. But how historians of the future will explain or account for it—both nationally and internationally—must be a matter of debate. A progressive account might locate it as an almost end point in a gradual process of liberalization that began with decriminalization. Comparative perspectives will draw attention to the different legal institutions adopted across jurisdictions and to the distinct legal and constitutional methods used to achieve them.[1] Crucial here is the awareness that legal recognition is as much about "nation-making" and the refashioning of modes of legitimate citizenship as it is about providing specific benefits to couples.

In telling this broader story the arguments made for and against legal recognition are a rich source. The dominant account of these debates could easily adopt a binary perspective, with "progressives versus traditionalists" being crudely mapped onto, or reduced to, "religious versus secular" or, in a global context, "civilized versus barbaric." These accounts would miss the complexity of possible understandings and meanings of gay relationship recognition. In particular they overlook both conservative support[2] and "progressive" opposition.[3] At the heart of these alternative perspectives is a debate about the extent to which legal recognition can or should be located within or alongside "neo-liberalism" and, in Western Europe, the crisis of social democracy. These arguments have all been well rehearsed.[4] But from a historical perspective what is noteworthy is the causal dimension to the arguments for and against relationship recognition, the extent to which they are premised on predictions about the impact of legal recognition.

So, for example, within "progressive" narratives, supporters claim that recognition will "modernize" the institution of marriage (for the better), while detractors claim that it will "normalize" gays and lesbians (for the worse). These causal arguments are often crude. On both sides ideological aspirations are too often expressed as empirical predictions. Nevertheless, looking at these arguments now, when legal recognition is a familiar reality as opposed to a contested possibility, it should be possible to attempt to evaluate the predictions. And more broadly to consider where historians of the future might look to think about both how gays and lesbians have engaged with the new possibilities and the impact on the institution of marriage more widely.

What follows is a tentative attempt to explore some of these questions from a British perspective—where civil partnerships were introduced in 2004 and same-sex marriage in 2014.[5] In doing so the chapter draws on three distinct forms of data: official statistics, emerging empirical research, and three legal cases where the judiciary has been called on to adjudicate conflicts arising subsequent to the introduction of civil partnerships. While it is too early to make any bold conclusions, it suggests that while ideological investments and political opposition to legal recognition are often expressed with great certainty, lived experience tells a messier story.

Statistics

Statistics about civil partnerships and same-sex marriage are collected by the Office of National Statistics. The aim here is not to provide a comprehensive coverage of them or to contrast them with those on opposite-sex marriage, but rather, by highlighting just some of them, to demonstrate the questions that they raise, rather than the truths that they reveal. In other words, how the questions asked, and importantly those not asked, can be used both to challenge and to support established narratives.

Since the Civil Partnership Act came into force in December 2005 the total number of partnerships officialized in England and Wales is approximately 65,000. The number of same-sex marriages, available from March 2014, is approximately 15,000, and about half of the latter were conversions from civil partnerships.[6] The annual rate for civil partnerships peaked in the first quarter of 2006, as a result of many same-sex couples in long-standing relationships taking advantage of the opportunity to formalize their relations as soon as possible. But, together with same-sex marriages, civil partnerships have now steadied to approximately 1600 a quarter (ONS 2015). The take-up of civil partnerships is significantly higher than the government predicted. But because it is not possible to know with any certainty how many gay and lesbian people there are, estimates range from 1.5 to 10 percent of the population,[7] nor, within that, how many are eligible (i.e., single and of age or in an unregistered relationship), it is difficult to assess the broader statistical significance of the take-up.

That said, read alongside some very different figures, it is possible to conclude that forming a civil partnership or entering a same-sex marriage are minority pursuits. More gay people attend just two of London's gay clubs (Heaven and XXL) on a single Saturday night than get married in a year. And if every married or civilly partnered same-sex couple had taken part in London's gay pride parade in 2016, they would have represented about 10 percent of the participants. These comparisons are, of course, far from rigorous, but the idea that alongside floats and banners for "Leather Queens" or "Gays in the Military," one might also see "Married Queens" self-identifying as such is fanciful. Like the other groups proclaimed at Pride it would, of course, not be one that is exclusive from any others—you can enjoy getting tied up as much as getting hitched—but its absence reflects the fact that getting "married" is neither seen nor identified as simply a lifestyle choice but, rather, as a banner under which everybody, potentially, walks.

The statistics, however, tell us very little about the motivations for legally recognizing a relationship. Anecdotally these vary hugely. At one end of the spectrum are those for whom the legal benefits, and inheritance tax avoidance in particular, are the sole motivation and who have chosen not to have any form of celebration. At the other end are those who are totally ignorant of the legal consequences, but for whom a party or other more public event is both a form of personal commitment and an opportunity to include a partner publically in a wider familial unit. In the latter context the party or celebration can be understood as a form of family "display";[8] how creating kinship is often dependent on the actions of others, and here too provides an opportunity for family members to communicate opposition to homophobia.

In this way the political symbolic significance of relationship recognition is effective at a grounded level. The multifaceted motivations and differing degrees of legal consciousness have all been supported by empirical research.[9] What is missing from the research is an attempt to discover the effects of the legal reforms on the experiences of gay and lesbian people in relationships who have chosen *not* to have their relationship legally recognized and, more broadly, those who remain outside of "coupledom."[10] Silences are revealing and these absences from the literature paradoxically mirror the absence of a Married section at gay pride. Both, in different ways, reinforce the very distinctive and minority status of entering a legally recognized relationship. For like heterosexuality, the conventional and the normal are rarely singled out or reduced to a lifestyle choice.[11]

In addition to the rates of entering recognized relationships, statistics are also recorded about gender, age, and regions. Gendered differences are particularly significant in the context of feminist critiques of marriage. Initially the number of males forming civil partnerships was higher than females, which could have been read as confirming the perception that the institution was less attractive to women, both ideologically and on the basis of lived experiences.[12] But the numbers converged in 2009/10, and while in 2014 the majority of civil partnerships were once again male, it has been suggested that this is because more female than male couples have opted, instead, to enter same-sex marriages (ONS, 2014).[13] This is itself perhaps surprising, bearing in mind the patriarchal baggage associated with marriage; indeed this is the key reason why an opposite-sex couple is currently challenging their exclusion from civil partnerships.[14]

Two gendered differences are evident in the context of age. First, women entering civil partnerships or marriage are more likely to have been in a previous marriage and, secondly, the age gap between partners is far more likely to be more than ten years for men than it is for women.[15] It is arguably too early to be able to offer rigorous interpretations of these statistics. But they hint at possible areas for future research about gender and gay and lesbian relationships that speak to assumptions about and experiences of care and the place of inequalities in relationships premised on a contemporary norm of a companionate model premised on equality. Historically large age gaps were not unusual in heterosexual marriages, with the older party almost always being the male partner. Why this is now less likely for both heterosexual and lesbian relationships, but clearly evident in relation to gay men, is a question that warrants further research. Moreover, the statistics once again highlight silences. For example, while the higher number of women entering a second legally recognized relationship could be "used" to challenge feminist arguments about marriage, such a reading overlooks the relevance and absence of figures about the number of couples who have children, and women are far more likely to have children. Here legal recognition has additional benefits, especially for the non-biological parent.

A final statistic relating to gender relates to dissolutions of civil partnerships (the term "divorce" only relates to marriage). By the end of 2014, female partnerships were twice as likely to have ended in dissolution. The reasons for this are inevitably complex, but qualitative research by Rosemary Auchmuty suggests two possible reasons: first, that infidelity or disputes over monogamy are more "fatal" in lesbian relationships; and secondly, the different experience of mental health issues.[16] It seems that "infidelity" is not incompatible with "marriage" for gay men, which is not surprising bearing in mind the extent to which consensual non-monogamy is "the taken for granted mode of relating in much gay culture."[17] But it nevertheless challenges the predictions that marriage might somehow "normalize" gays. At the same time, it might simply confirm the fact that, for men, "the traditional" model of marriage rarely precluded extramarital sexual activity. Conversely it would be problematic to suggest that gay men were radically changing marriage: gay "fuck buddies" might simply be the new "mistresses."

The final statistic highlighted here is the unequal distribution of civil partnership formation across the country. London is by far the most popular region (with approximately a third of all registrations), followed by Brighton and Hove. While not surprising, bearing in mind the strong presence and visibility of gays and lesbians in both areas, the data, however, only indicate where the partnerships were registered and are not necessarily a good indicator of residence. That said, once again it is possible to interpret these figures to support various arguments; that, for example, the acceptance of gays and lesbians may not be as widespread as some may hope, or indeed that the dominance of London and the South East merely mirrors heightened house price values and the extent to which inheritance tax avoidance is a key motive behind legal recognition. This last interpretation is logical but simplistic. The extent to which civil partnerships and same-sex marriage are as classed as they are gendered requires further research. For while legal recognition of relationships is, unquestionably, as potentially financially detrimental for individuals on benefits as it is advantageous for those with greater wealth, these regional statistics alone are far from conclusive. Statistics that might reveal more about the relationship between legal recognition and socioeconomics are unavailable and, were they to exist, might overlook the complexities of identity and differences within relationships.[18]

Case law: Three disputes

While money is a factor that is often overlooked in celebrations of legal recognition, from the perspective of family lawyers, it is frequently a key issue. For it is at the end of relationships, on death or dissolution/divorce, as opposed to what happens at the beginning of or during a relationship, that the legal consequences are triggered. The emotional and practical negotiation of the end of a relationship is complex and, of course, intensely personal. And even where disputes arise, legal intervention rarely reaches the courts. But where it does it provides a public forum for an assessment of the impact of the legal recognition of same-sex relationships. The following three cases—all disputes about money—are revealing examples of the pleasures and perils of inviting the law into personal life.

Baynes v Hedger and others [2008] EWHC 1587 (Ch)

Mary Watson and Margot Baynes were lovers, but not in a civil partnership. On Watson's death, Baynes argued that she had not been adequately provided for and made an application to contest Watson's will. To make such a challenge, in accordance with the Inheritance (Provision for Family and Dependants) Act 1975, an unmarried partner must first satisfy the court that he or she was "living as the husband or wife of the deceased." Recent case law had established that a same-sex couple could, potentially, be considered to be living "as husband and wife."[19] But the Civil Partnership Act 2004 extended these provisions to specifically include those living "as civil partners."[20] In determining how to interpret this new statutory expression the judge, Mr. Justice Lewison, held that the following question, established by earlier case law, was one of the tests to be applied:

> Is the relationship one which has been presented to the outside world openly and unequivocally so that society considers it to be of permanent intent—the words "til death us do part" being apposite? (at para 120).

He further held that this test was an, "essential qualification"; that "it is not possible to establish that two persons have lived together as civil partners unless their relationship as a couple is an acknowledged one" (at para 150), as "both a marriage and a civil partnership are publically acknowledged relationships" (at para 125).

Applying this test to the facts of the case the judge subsequently held that Baynes and Watson were *not* "living as civil partners." And a result Baynes' challenge was unsuccessful. Whether or not she should have received more under Watson's will is debatable. But what is interesting is that the judge decided to apply a test designed for heterosexuals to a lesbian couple in exactly the same way. And despite the fact that the tests were, in his view, "statements of general principles" and, as such, "must of course be read in the light of facts of the case" as "human relationships are many and various" (at para 121). This was all the more surprising because he demonstrated a sensitive understanding of why, in this particular case, and for older gays and lesbians generally, relationships are more likely to be of a more private nature and not "presented to the outside world openly and unequivocally." In summarizing the facts of the case he noted that:

> Many of the witnesses who saw them together described them as a couple. They were seen as a couple by Margot's children. But they were of a generation for whom a same-sex relationship was not an acceptable lifestyle, and their relationship was not openly acknowledged ... They were of that age when that sort of thing was

> unacceptable and it would have upset them ... I conclude that Mary and Margot had a loving relationship which spanned 50 continuous years ... There was no falling out between them, and their relationship carried on until Mary's death. But their relationship was a private relationship ... Had any sexual element in the relationship been suggested, they would have denied it. (paras [34], [35])

There may be many reasons why a heterosexual couple might wish to keep their relationship hidden, but never because of their sexual orientation. Precisely because of this, Baroness Rendall, in the debate about civil partnerships in the House of Lords, argued for the availability of private registrations for civil partnerships, on the basis that: "In many areas of society and of the workplace, openly declaring one's sexual orientation is a risky business."[21] That parliament rejected this proposal partly legitimizes Lewison's finding. But nevertheless, the case is a classic example of indirect discrimination and substantive inequality resulting from "blind" equal treatment. Moreover, had the judge wished, he could have distinguished "civil partners" from "husband and wife" by reference to the Civil Partnership Act itself, for none of the marriage laws relating to sexual acts (adultery, non-consummation) apply to civil partnerships (and this distinction remains between same- and opposite-sex marriage). By not doing so the judgment not only renders the differences between opposite- and same-sex couples invisible, but at the same time, masks the highly gendered roots of the "openness" rule. For the requirement that marital status be public and visible has traditionally been, and still is, imposed by cultural norms far more on women than men, premised, often explicitly, on the double standards of sexual fidelity they indicate to men that a woman is "taken" and "unavailable." It is therefore at least valid to question not only whether openness is a requirement that should apply to same-sex couples at all.

The case received considerable media attention. Baynes' daughter, who also contested Watson's will, had previously been married to the film director Ken Russell and, no doubt because of this, the story appeared in the "show biz" sections of various tabloids. But the liberal broadsheet newspapers reported the case in a similar fashion. The headline in *The Independent* was, "Ken Russell's Former Wife Contests Will of Mother's Lesbian Lover" (June 26, 2008), while in *The Guardian* the headline was, "Actor Loses Court Battle over £2.3m Estate of Mother's Lesbian Lover."[22]

A tenuous link to celebrity and a story that can link death, sex, and money offer an obvious explanation for the coverage, and there is a long history of the reporting and avid public interest in wills and inheritance disputes.[23] But the reporting here also demonstrates the extent to which non-conventional sexualities are still represented as in some ways salacious.[24] The publicity that a case might attract can also be used as a strategic device against gay and lesbian beneficiaries fearful about being open about their sexuality. In *Baynes* there is a certain cruel irony to the resulting publicity as the openness of the relationship between the women was a critical factor in Baynes losing her case. Significantly, neither news story mentioned this legal point or the possible consequences for other same-sex couples. Indeed, while the creation of civil partnerships and same-sex marriage has attracted considerable attention, the failure of the media to address the impact of judicial interpretations of the legal provisions on real people is a recurring theme.

Court and others v Despallières [2009] EWHC 3340 (Ch)

The next case also concerned an inheritance dispute, but of a very different kind. Peter Ikin, a rich media executive, made a will in 2002 leaving his estate to a mixture of friends and relatives. In August 2008 he made a new will leaving everything to his lover, Alexandre Despallières. In October 2008 Ikin and Despallières entered into a civil partnership, and Ikin died in November 2008.

The case was brought by the executors and beneficiaries under the first will from 2002. Their argument was that the 2008 will was invalid as a result of a long-standing statutory rule whereby wills are revoked by subsequent marriages, a rule that was extended to include civil partnerships on identical terms.[25] The motive underlying the claim was simple: if the 2008 will was held to be invalid, Ikin would be deemed to have died intestate. And in accordance with the intestacy rules at that time, Despallières would have been entitled to a far smaller share of Ikin's very considerable wealth,[26] and a large proportion would have passed to Ikin's surviving relatives.[27]

Despallières argued that the 2008 will was valid on the basis of a statutory exemption to the revocation rule that permitted the language of the will to indicate a contrary intent. The judge, however, held against Despallières. The law relating to the interpretation of wills is complex and the point here is not that the judge was necessarily wrong, but, simply, that legitimate judicial discretion could have supported a different conclusion. The outcome of inheritance disputes is often hard to predict and judicial sympathies are often thinly veiled. The ruling here would have resulted in Despallières receiving a very considerable sum—after a very short relationship, and a civil partnership lasting just over one month—with the remainder of the estate being distributed among Ikin's relatives, with whom the 2002 will indicated he had good long-term connections. Many might consequently consider such an outcome fair. The only individuals in the case that received nothing were Ikin's friends and godchildren named in the 2002 will. Their absence from this legal resolution reflects the exclusive focus on couples and biological relatives in the law of intestacy. While this approach coheres with public opinion,[28] research focused on gays and lesbians indicates the important place of non-biological relatives and friends within constructions of their "inheritance family."[29] In other words, "equal treatment" in the intestacy laws of opposite and same-sex couples renders will-making far more significant for gays and lesbians.

As in *Baynes*, the case attracted considerable media attention, and the salaciousness here was abundant with the added ingredients of possible murder (albeit unproven). In these accounts Despallières was portrayed as a money-grabbing opportunist—little more than a high-class male prostitute. Conversely, Ikin was portrayed as a man deeply committed to his family who had fallen prey to the seductiveness of a handsome and much younger man. Ethnicity also played a part here, with the earthy wholesomeness of a family-loving Australian, pitted against an untrustworthy, but superficially charming, Frenchman. The following headlines in various newspapers give a sense of these representations: "Peter Ikin Married French Boyfriend Weeks before Death" (*The Daily Telegraph, 2008*)[30]; "Gay Frenchman Accused of Killing Friend of Elton John Freed on Bail"[31]; "The Talented M. Despallières"[32]; "A Dead Man, a Forged Will, a £10m Inheritance, and a Ruined Reputation"[33]; "Young Gay Husband Alexandre Despallières Gets Peter Ikin's Millions in Will."[34]

Whatever the truth of the stories, they demonstrate the contingency of the idealized nature of "the couple." Unlike Baynes and Watson, who despite a fifty-year loving relationship were not considered to be living "as civil partners," Ikin and Despallières *were* civil partners, but legal recognition here was qualified by other values; what was contested explicitly in the media (and arguably implicitly by the judge) was the authenticity of the relationship as one deserving the full privilege of the law. Despallières was most certainly not the "poster boy" grieving surviving partner—a figure that played a critical role in the parliamentary debates in support of the Civil Partnership Act (Monk 2011). And there is however a degree of irony that in one of the first post–Civil Partnership Act cases the surviving partner "loses out" as a *result* of having entered a civil partnership.

The judgment and media coverage provide narratives through which it is possible to trace shifting cultural and social investments in same-sex coupledom and "marriage." One way of teasing out these values is to question responses to the case had Despallières been a similar age as Ikin, or if the relationship had been of much longer duration, or if Despallières had performed a more conventional caring role. The case is also an example of one of the statistics noted above: that in male civil partners the age gap is disproportionately larger than for opposite-sex or lesbian couples. This case suggests that these relationships may be viewed with suspicion when judged against prevailing norms of equality between partners, which may have implications for other younger male partners. Another critical variation would be to imagine the same facts but opposite genders: would a woman marrying an older rich man be viewed in the same way as a man doing the same thing?

Introducing gender as a framework for thinking about the case raises questions about the applicability of the revocation rule itself. For prior to 1837 the rule applied only to women, reflecting their loss of legal identity on marriage (Law Reform Committee 1979, para 21), and its purpose was to protect not only a wife but also her property. Questioning the revocation rule is not necessarily to valorize financial independence, nor indeed to overlook the protection it provides. Rather the point here is simply to challenge the reification of inequality through *assumptions* based on marital status as opposed to an *explicit* focus on the realities of need and dependency. Some research has suggested that gay and lesbian couples are far less likely to be economically unequal than opposite-sex couples. Cases such as this question the ability of the legal rule to adapt or recognize this. As the final case indicates these questions are as acute on dissolution (and divorce) as they are on death.

Lawrence v Gallagher [2012] EWCA Civ 398

Lawrence and Gallagher had lived together—or cohabited—since February 1997. They entered into a civil partnership in December 2007, separated in September 2008, and the civil partnership was dissolved in 2009. Both men were successful in their careers; but Lawrence, an equity analyst in the City, was considerably richer than Gallagher, who was an actor. Gallagher argued that he was entitled to a larger share of their combined wealth than Lawrence was willing to agree to. The High Court held that

Gallagher was entitled to 42 percent of their combined wealth, but this was reduced by the Court of Appeal to 37 percent.

Lord Justice Thorpe opened the lead judgment in the Court of Appeal with an unequivocal statement about equality between opposite and same-sex couples: "the fact that the claim arises from the dissolution of a Civil Partnership rather than a marriage is of little moment (at para 1, 2)"

This was the only reference to the fact that he case concerned two men. As Rob George has commented, "The Court of Appeal thinks it so obvious that there can be no difference between analogously placed married couples and civil partners that it is *not even worth discussing the issue*."[35] Formal equality here consequently results in a judicial silence, one that renders gender invisible. Whether this results in a fair or appropriate decision is a matter of debate. But it is also questionable whether this commitment to equality is adhered to. In other words, it is possible to argue that had the case, with identical facts, concerned a man and woman, the court would have reached a different decision. In looking the case in this way, it is necessary to read between the lines, as Charlotte Bendall notes, "what the court does not say might be considered more interesting than what it does."[36] Challenging the judgment in this way is far from straightforward because the outcome of financial claims on divorce is always notoriously complex to predict.[37]

One explanation for the approach adopted by the Court of Appeal is to view it as part of a general shift away from the principle of "equal sharing," itself a relatively recent development, toward a more individualistic approach that emphasizes financial autonomy and a norm of independence between partners (at least or especially where no children are involved). This latter approach emphasizes gender equality as an ideal. But, as George notes, it could at the same time result in "a return to the days of valuing financial earnings above other forms of contributions to family life," an approach that overlooks deeper structural gendered economic inequalities.[38]

This concern is arguably justified. For what enabled the Court of Appeal to move away from equal sharing was the fact that in their judgment, and in contrast to the High Court, as Bendall has noted, "No mention is made as to how household labour was conducted within the relationship. Such discussion is consistently present in the context of heterosexual couples (normally with reference to the wife)." In other words, economic vulnerability resulting from care is seen as a particularly "feminine affliction."[39]

At stake here is the ongoing complex paradox that results from aspiring to be "post-gender" in what remains a highly gendered world. And this tension comes to the fore in attempts to treat opposite- and same-sex couples as identical. "Equality" as a guiding principle points in two different directions: *assuming* equality between the genders or *imposing* equal sharing to correct gendered imbalances. The former approach, of course, benefits men more than women. And in this same-sex case it benefited the man who was the higher wage earner—the banker as opposed to the actor. While the Court of Appeal did not go so far as to argue that this was a case of independent dual careers, at the same time the possibility of male economic dependency and male homemaking does not appear to have received the degree of judicial recognition that is, more often, accorded to women in heterosexual marriages. It is perhaps noteworthy that in *Lawrence*, a woman judge in the High Court—emphasizing "homemaking"—was overruled by the views of the male judges. While it is simplistic to reduce an analysis of judicial thinking to the gender of a judge, the burgeoning scholarship on diversity in the judiciary and feminist law-making highlights the value and nuanced ways of exploring this dimension.[40]

The case attracted considerable media attention and what is striking is the extent to which in this context gender roles were center stage, in marked contrast to the Court of Appeal's judgment. This was communicated—implicitly but very effectively—by the images used to illustrate the story. In a number of newspaper articles the photograph of Lawrence was that of a typical City man in a suit and tie. The photographs used for Gallagher captured him in his starring West End role as the drag queen Bernadette in the musical (based on the film) of *Priscilla Queen of the Desert*.[41] Another image of him—in a suit and tie leaving the court—was available, but the picture of him in drag was the preferred image. Accompanying these visual representations were quotations from his lawyers that emphasized that Gallagher "had played the major domestic and home making role" and that he "helped create and maintain a lovely home in the flat in various ways—soft furnishings, planting on balconies, improvement of layout and fixtures, redecoration."[42]

The headlines also served to subtly emphasize the very different gendered roles. Lawrence was described as "the millionaire banker"[43] and "City high-flier"[44]; whereas Gallagher was described as the "actor lover,"[45] "Gay actor,"[46] and "Gay 'homemaker.'"[47] There were no references to "Gay Banker" or "High Flying Actor"; and the media in these various ways consequently constructed a narrative in which the differences between the men—both economic and in terms of male roles—were constantly emphasized, rendering them more "husband and wife" than "husband and husband."

It would be overly optimistic to suggest that the media in these accounts is subtly making an argument premised on a feminist ethics of care about the inevitability and importance of interdependence and challenging gender roles. Rather, what these stories do is implicitly tease the reader with the idea that in same-sex relationships one party is the "man" and the other the "women." Consequently, while superficially very distinct, what is at stake in both the judicial and the media readings of the case is the contingency of masculinity.

Conclusion

The introduction of civil partnerships and same-sex marriage is a remarkable moment in gay and lesbian politics, and evidence, without any doubt, of a progressive shift in societal attitudes. But thinking about this moment as a beginning rather than an end point in exploring sexuality requires reflection on what exactly might be new lines of enquiry, both to explain the significance of the development and to consider its impact. The data presented here, emerging official statistics and case law, in different ways raise questions rather than answers. Two broad themes can be identified.

First, the continuing significance of gender. The new institutions are, in law, gender-neutral. Indeed, opening up marriage to gays and lesbians explicitly upholds an emerging view of that institution as one between equals. But both the statistics and the cases tell a very different story. In campaigns for equal rights for gays and lesbians the distinctiveness of gender has inevitably been marginalized. But while always present perhaps now, with formal rights achieved, scholarship can return to consider its effects. Secondly, both the statistics and the cases highlight a shifting story of "marriage." From a rights perspective, legal recognition is understandably located alongside decriminalization and gay and lesbian parenting rights. Such a narrative focuses on the importance of inclusion in the institution of marriage, but tells us little about the nature of the institution. To understand how gay marriage impacts on marriage it is more fruitful to locate it alongside legal landmarks such as the nineteenth-century Married Women's Property Acts and the Divorce Reform Act 1969. The case laws examined here are not "gay rights cases," and in none of them are the individuals pitted against explicit homophobia or discrimination. Rather, the outcomes attest to the shifting functions and understandings of marriage. And together with the statistics that tell us about the variable use gays and lesbians are making of the possibilities of legal recognition, a picture might emerge of tensions between individual expectations and aspirations and institutional restraints. In formulating questions to examine this new terrain, it may be necessary to move away from the victimhood of exclusion to a new focus on the perils and pleasures of recognition, within which sexuality, per se, is not the key determinant.

Notes

1. Jens Scherpe, "The Legal Recognition of Same-Sex Couples in Europe and the Role of the European Court of Human Rights," *The Equal Rights Review* 10 (2013): 83–96.
2. Andrew Gilbert, "From 'Pretended Family Relationship' to 'Ultimate Affirmation': British Conservatism and the Legal Recognition of Same-Sex Relationships," *Child and Family Law Quarterly* 26, no. 4 (2014): 463–487.
3. Nicola Barker, *Not the Marrying Kind: A Feminist Critique of Same-Sex Marriage* (Basingstoke: Palgrave Macmillan, 2013).
4. Jeffrey Weeks, "Liberalism by Stealth? The Civil Partnership Act and the New Equalities Agenda in Perspective," in *From Civil Partnership to Same Sex Marriage 2004–2014: Interdisciplinary Reflections*, ed. Nicola Barker and Daniel Monk (Oxford: Routledge, 2015), 29–44.
5. Nicola Barker and Daniel Monk, "From Civil Partnership to Same-Sex Marriage: A decade in British legal history," in *From Civil Partnership to Same Sex Marriage: Interdisciplinary Reflections*, ed. Barker and Monk (Oxford: Routledge, 2015), 1-25.
6. See Office of National Statistics. 2015. The coexistence of civil partnerships and same-sex marriage is under review; see Government Equalities Office 2014; and a legal challenge is currently before the courts in an attempt to open the former to opposite-sex couples *Steinfeld v Secretary of State for Education* [2016] EWHC 128.
7. *The Guardian* 2013.
8. Janet Finch, "Displaying Families," *Sociology* 41, no. 1 (2007): 65–81.
9. Brian Heaphy, Carol Smart, and A. Einarsdottir, eds., *Same-Sex Marriages: New Generations, New Relationships* (Basingstoke: Palgrave Macmillan, 2010); Rosie

Harding, *Regulating Sexuality: Legal Consciousness in Lesbian and Gay Lives* (London: Routledge, 2010).
10. Michael Cobb, *Single: Arguments for the Uncoupled* (New York: New York University Press, 2012).
11. Les Moran, "Forming Sexualities as Judicial Virtues," *Sexualities* 14, no. 3 (2011): 273–289.
12. Rosemary Auchmuty, "Same-Sex Marriage Revived: Feminist Critique and Legal Strategy," *Feminism & Psychology* 14 (2004): 101–126.
13. "Marriages in England and Wales: 2014," ONS, 2014, https://www.ons.gov.uk/peoplepopulationandcommunity/birthsdeathsandmarriages/marriagecohabitationandcivilpartnerships/bulletins/marriagesinenglandandwalesprovisional/2014.
14. See commentaries on *Steinfeld v Secretary of State for Education* [2016] EWHC 128.
15. H. Ross, K. Gask, and A. Berrington, *Civil Partnerships 5 Years On: Population Trends* (London: Office for National Statistics no. 145, 2011).
16. Rosemary Auchmuty, "Dissolution of Disillusion: The Unravelling of Civil Partnerships," in *From Civil Partnership to Same Sex Marriage*, ed. Barker and Monk (Oxford: Routledge, 2015), 1-25.
17. Meg Barker and Darren Langdridge, "Whatever Happened to Non-Monogamies? Critical Reflections on Recent Research and Theory," *Sexualities* 13, no. 6 (2010): 748–772.
18. Brian Heaphy, "Gay Identities and the Culture of Class," *Sexualities* 14 (2011): 41.
19. *Ghaidan v Mendoza* [2004] UKHL 30.
20. *Inheritance (Provision for Family and Dependants) Act 1975 s 1(1B) (as inserted by the CPA 2004 s 71, Sch 4).*
21. HL Deb 22.4.04 vol. 660 at col. 414.
22. Paul Lewis, "Actor Loses Court Battle over £2.3m Estate of Mother's Lesbian Lover," *The Guardian*, July 14, 2008.
23. Daniel Monk, "Sexuality and Succession Law: Beyond Formal Equality," *Feminist Legal Studies* 19, no. 3 (2011): 231–250.
24. For other recent examples, see *"Muriel Spark Leaves Millions to Woman Friend Rather Than Son": Evening Standard*, 14.04.07; "Why Did This Decadent Peer Leave His Millions to His Manservant?": *Daily Mail*, 20.06.2011; "Gay-lover-of-dead-flamboyant-TV-presenter-loses-legal-battle-over-property-portfolio": *Daily Telegraph*, 10.08.2011.
25. Wills Act 1837 s 18B (as inserted by the Civil Partnership Act 2004 s 71).
26. Administration of Estates Act 1925 s 46 (1) (as amended by the Civil Partnership Act 2004 s 71 Sch 4, Pt 2, para 7).
27. The law has subsequently been changed and, as Ikin had no children, under the current law Despallières would have been entitled to the whole estate: Inheritance and Trustee's Powers Act 2014 s 1.
28. G. Douglas et al., "Enduring Love? Attitudes to Family and Inheritance Law in England and Wales," *Journal of Law and Society* 38, no. 2 (2011): 245–271.
29. Daniel Monk, "Inheritance Families of Choice: Lawyers' Reflections on Gay and Lesbian Wills," *Journal of Law and Society* 43, no. 2 (2016): 167–194.
30. *The Daily Telegraph*, December 12, 2008.
31. *The Daily Mirror*, March 31, 2011.
32. B. Stone, *Bloomsbury Business Week*, June 28, 2012.
33. C. Hutchins, *London Evening Standard*, August 10, 2012.
34. J. Fife-Yeomans and C. Miranda, *The Daily Telegraph*, July 4, 2009.

35 Rob George, "Lawrence v. Gallagher [2012] EWCA Civ 394 – Playing a Straight Bat in Civil Partnership Appeals?" *Journal of Social Welfare and Family Law* 34, no. 3 (2012): 357–362.
36 Charlotte Bendall, "A Break Away from the (Hetero)norm? Lawrence v. Gallagher [2012] EWCA CIV 394," *Feminist Legal Studies* 21, no. 3 (2013): 303–310.
37 Jonathan Herring, *Family Law* (Harlow: Longman/Pearson, 2013), 227–251.
38 George, "Lawrence v. Gallagher."
39 Bendall, "A break away," 307.
40 Rosemary Hunter, Clare McGlynn and Erica Rackley, *Feminist Judgements: From Theory to Practice* (Oxford: Hart, 2010).
41 F. Gibb, "Gay 'Homemaker' and Banker Fight over £5m Divorce," The Times, Friday March 9, 2012, p. 5; Brenda Long, "Analysis: The Multi-Million Pounds 'Gay Divorce,'" Pink News, April 13, 2012. Available at: http://www.pinknews.co.uk/2012/04/13/analysis-the-multi-million-pound-gay-divorce/; Eddie Wrenn, "Millionaire Banker Wins Battle with His Actor Lover over £1.7million Landmark 'Divorce' Settlement after Their Civil Partnership Ends," Daily Mail, March 29, 2012. Available at: http://www.dailymail.co.uk/news/article-2122048/Banker-Peter-Lawrence-actor-lover-Don-Gallaghers-civil-partnership-goes-appeal-1-7m-divorce-settlement.html.
42 Gibb, "Gay 'Homemaker.'"
43 Vanessa Allen and Nazia Parveen, "The Millionaire Banker, His Actor Lover and Their Landmark £1.7m 'Divorce' Settlement," *Daily Mail*, March 8, 2012. Available at: http://www.dailymail.co.uk/news/article-2112280/Banker-Peter-Lawrence-actor-lover-Don-Gallaghers-1-7m-divorce-settlement.html; Wrenn, "Millionaire Banker Wins Battle."
44 John Bingham, "Gay Actor and City High-Flier Fight over Separation Payout," *Daily Telegraph*, March 9, 2012. Available at: https://www.telegraph.co.uk/women/mother-tongue/9131683/Gay-actor-and-City-high-flier-fight-over-separation-payout.html.
45 Allen and Parveen, "The Millionaire Banker"; Wrenn, "Millionaire Banker Wins Battle."
46 Bingham, "Gay Actor and City High-Flier."
47 Gibb, "Gay 'Homemaker.'"

17

Same-Sex Unions: In Retrospect and Prospect

Robert Aldrich

Supporters of human rights, and most gay and lesbian people, have joyously applauded recent legislation in countries of Western Europe, North and South America, and Australasia that recognizes same-sex marriages (or in some cases at least provides legal recognition for civil partnerships). For many, the possibility of being married or joined in an official union offers public recognition of their "coupledom," ensures rights previously accorded only to heterosexual couples—covering taxation, property, inheritance, and other benefits—and gives an opportunity for public celebration of love and commitment.

As the chapters in this collection show, the path that allowed gay and lesbian couples to arrive at the marriage registry has been a long one. In the British World, for instance, sodomy was made illegal, and subject to capital punishment, in the 1530s and not decriminalized (and then only with caveats) until 1967. Same-sex marriage in England, Wales, and Scotland was not allowed until 2014, and it is still prohibited in Northern Ireland. From another perspective, however, the change has been remarkably rapid. How many of those involved in the Stonewall Rebellion in New York in 1969 or the first Sydney Gay and Lesbian Mardi Gras in 1978 would have foreseen that less than fifty years later in one case, and forty in the other, same-sex marriages would be legal in the United States and Australia? How many would have guessed that what were once considered staunchly Catholic and socially conservative countries such as Spain, Portugal, and Ireland would legalize marriages between two men and between two women?

The contributors to this book explore the changes that have taken place concerning homosexuality in the last several generations, and the reasons for a transformation that may deserve that overused adjective of "revolutionary." Bryant Ragan traces the long-term metamorphosis back to the French Revolution and the decriminalization of sodomy in the new French law code adopted in 1791. Ragan provides a reminder, however, that most of the Enlightenment *philosophes* and revolutionary legislators did not condone homosexual acts or liaisons. The depenalization of sodomy more likely represented an attempt to remove from the books a host of superfluous laws that hindered the individual liberties that the new National Assembly wanted to enshrine. That decriminalization nevertheless remains of crucial significance, for it meant that in France and in countries where a French-inspired law code was adopted or imposed from the late 1700s onward, such as parts of Italy, homosex was not a crime. Such legal tolerance helped to develop an image of licentious "gay Paris" and seductive Italy.

On the other hand, while interdiction of homosexual acts did not prohibit the efflorescence of homosexual cultures in London, Berlin, and other cities, it gave them a distinctive character. London before and after Oscar Wilde had its gay culture, and homosexual acts were still illegal in the 1920s when Germany's capital seemed the epicenter of a liberated and decadent gay life.[1] The reprobate nature of homosexuality indeed brought the issue to public discussion, for instance, in the work of Dr. Magnus Hirschfeld, medical doctor, pioneering sexologist, scholar of worldwide sexuality, and homosexual emancipationist.[2]

Even in countries where sex between men, though less often between women, was not illegal, authorities deployed an arsenal of laws that made it possible to arrest and convict those with same-sex behavior or even the implication of same-sex intentions. As Geoffroy Huard's chapter on Franco's Spain shows for example, laws against offences to public morality, vagrancy and loitering, solicitation, or frequentation of "bawdy houses" were quite sufficient to allow the state to persecute large numbers of citizens. Coupling, in casual encounters or sustained relationships, presented dangers of harassment, blackmail, arrest and conviction, and the ruin of reputations. Religious beliefs, medical and psychological theories, and notions of morality and respectability mandated the enforcement of homophobic laws and attitudes.

The history of actual punishment of homosexual acts, however, was more complex than simply the record of its legal prohibition, and same-sex couples often escaped the law, found sexual pleasure, and established long-term relationships though without the benefit of official or familial blessing. Discreet behavior provided some protection, as did the benefits of wealth and high status. Heinous punishments could be imposed on sodomites in Georgian England, but Dominic Janes also suggests in this volume that authorities hesitated to draw attention to men committing "unnatural" acts by more frequent imposition of capital punishment, and, in fact, he notes a rising general current of sympathy for those accused of sodomitical crimes. On occasion, legislators elsewhere could resist implementing anti-sodomy legislation, as Charles Upchurch shows happened in Louisiana in the early years of the nineteenth century. Furthermore, judges and the public could be more tolerant than is often remembered, as Yorick Smaal and Mark Finnane show with evidence that prosecutions in Australia most commonly took place when minors were involved or when sexual activities were too blatantly brought to public attention. Nevertheless, law structured homosexual activity, just as it did heterosexual activity.

The same-sex couples and their lived experiences discussed in this volume are diverse, from a seemingly devoted and happily settled male pair implicated in a divorce case initiated by the aggrieved wife of one of the men in Peru in 1847 (explored in Magally Alegre Henderson's chapter) to a tragic story of the murder-suicide of a gay couple in Sicily in 1980 (that provides a launching pad for Yuri Guaiana and Mark Seymour's contribution). Among the couples who appear in these pages are those who lost reputations and freedom because of the law and homophobia, but there are also happier outcomes, such as two Italian women in their seventies, partners since

1943, who expressed great joy in being able to hold hands in public for the first time during Rome's World Pride event in 2000. And there are all those in Western Europe, Australasia, South Africa, North America, and parts of South America, who may now be legally married. The fact that in over twenty-five countries (and some subnational jurisdictions) two men or two women can get married is a legal, social, and cultural situation unparalleled in history.[3]

As Graham Willet suggests, the long road toward decriminalization of homosexual acts and the legislation permitting same-sex unions, as well as enactment of anti-discrimination and anti-vilification laws, was transnational. Gay and lesbian individuals and groups corresponded, ideas circulated, lobbying strategies were copied and adapted, and there has been something of a snowball effect as countries around the British World and elsewhere have moved toward greater legal rights for homosexual, transsexual, and intersexual individuals. Moreover, the globalization of new sorts of social relations in general (such as an increase in premarital sex and the parenting of children outside of marriage), and of the gay sociability of associations, clubs, and other venues, or styles of protest ranging from vociferous public militancy to quieter lobbying and negotiations, as well as the HIV-AIDS epidemic, transformed the environment in which the changes could take place. Like movements for the rights of women, indigenous people, and dissidents, "gay liberation" has been notably international.

Nevertheless, the results have varied widely, and the chapters in this volume demonstrate the importance of the particularities of national (and regional) histories. In countries such as Italy and Ireland, court rulings, in local tribunals or the European Court of Human Rights, played pivotal roles in bringing about recognition of same-sex relationships—courts could be agents to emancipation as well as subjection of sexual minorities. In the Republic of Ireland, a dynamic national campaign in 2015 convinced those casting ballots in a referendum to support same-sex marriages, clear proof of the changes in public opinion in that country. In Australia, the government insisted on a costly national postal survey of its citizens before agreeing to enact marriage equality in 2017. In the same year in Germany, as explained in Benno Gammerl's chapter, the process necessitated a personal decision by Chancellor Angela Merkel not to oppose the change despite her personal views. While some gay activists in the United States castigated same-sex marriage as a normalization of queer life, with the partners buying in to orthodox notions of matrimony, Guaiana and Seymour show that in Italy support for marriage equality became a radical stance as it attacked and undermined the primacy of the Catholic Church as arbiter of morals. In other predominantly Catholic countries as well, authorization of same-sex marriage reflects a trend of secularization and a refusal to accept wholesale the traditional precepts of the Christian religion.

Where same-sex marriage provisions have been enacted, much credit goes to activists who have championed equality, parliamentarians who have voted for legislation, media that have sympathetically publicized the cause, and courts that have ruled against prohibitions on same-sex marriage. One of the notable aspects of the campaign for marriage equality is how it brought together gay men and lesbians (as well as other sexually diverse people), providing common ground for groups that had often been at odds, or had championed different priorities, in earlier homophile and gay liberation movements. The fact that lesbian sex was less often criminalized than male "sodomy" meant that repeal of anti-sodomy laws provided a primary goal for most male activists, while many lesbians were concerned about wider issues of discrimination, abuse, and marginalization that affected both heterosexual and homosexual women. The push for same-sex marriage explicitly concerned all genders, and thus provided an opportunity for a united front.

Change in attitudes, whether concerning women, ethnic groups, or sexual minorities, often depends on the militancy of those seeking change, just as it necessitates a metamorphosis in underlying social perspectives. Provisions for marriage equality represent a dramatic legal development, but also embody profound transformations in recent decades in views about sexuality, human rights, the separation of the state from traditional religion, and community inclusiveness. Campaigns begun by "homophile" societies of the 1940s and 1950s—COC in the Netherlands, Vorbundet af 1948 in Denmark, Arcadie in France, the Mattachine Society, and the Daughters of Bilitis in the United States—pioneered efforts to promote homosexual equality and social acceptance even before the "gay liberation" movements associated with the 1960s and 1970s, and the "marriage for all" movements of the early twenty-first century.[4] In a "presentist" age, it is salutary to remember the *longue durée* of gay history, and—from the time of Hirschfeld's movement in the 1890s—more than a century of homosexual activism.

Same-sex marriage, of course, is not desired by all gay men and lesbians. Many homosexual couples will choose not to be married even if allowed to do so, as do many straight couples. Indeed, it is paradoxical that same-sex couples are now permitted to marry, just as different-sex couples are doing so less often. Living outside the bonds of holy matrimony is probably more common in Western countries, at least in the initial stages of relationships, than formalizing a union before a priest, celebrant, or civic official. Moreover, some individuals may not want or be able to find "life partners" with whom to be joined. Various types of sexual relationships (involving multiple or serial partners, for instance) are not sanctioned by marriage equality laws. Same-sex couples still face the rigmarole of paperwork and, for some, issues involving age, migrant and citizenship status, and the opprobrium of neighbors, colleagues, and families. Daniel Monk, in his contribution to this volume, introduces a topic that is an inevitable concomitant of gay marriage, that is, gay divorce and the tangled problems of separation of jointly held assets, as well as the recriminations that accompany most marriage breakups. As Monk notes, same-sex marriage is still too recent a phenomenon for scholars to be able to draw firm conclusions about its frequency, the traits of those who enter into marriage, the evolution of unions over time, the reasons for their endurance, or the causes for their ending. The findings of research on such issues, in due course, will be of great interest, both in themselves and to make comparisons with opposite-sex unions.

Where to from here? A map of countries where marriage equality now exists shows how it remains restricted to certain parts of the world. In Africa, same-sex marriage is allowed only in South Africa; no country in Asia has enacted marriage equality, though Taiwan is slated to do so, and there have been some indications that Vietnam might follow suit. (Somewhat paradoxically perhaps, there is no same-sex marriage in

Thailand, the most gay-friendly of Asian countries—a fact that suggests, of course, that having a vibrant and open gay culture does not necessarily demand or mandate gay marriage.) Same-sex marriage is very unlikely to be authorized in Arabic and Islamic countries, in several of which the death penalty can still be imposed for homosexual offences. In the Caribbean and South Pacific (where Christianity rather than Islam is the predominant creed), except for the overseas territories of Western states such as France, it is also improbable that same-sex marriages will soon be permitted.

As Willett points out, there are still seventy-eight countries in the world, encompassing a third of the world's population, where men (and sometimes women) are legally prohibited from having sex with each other, even if in some cases, the laws are rarely enforced. The difficulties in repealing those laws are not slight. In India, a 2009 lower court ruling that the prohibition of same-sex sex was illegal was overturned by the Supreme Court four years later. In 2018, however, gay men and lesbians greeted with jubilation a decision by India's highest court that reversed that judgment, the chief justice declaring that criminalizing homosexual acts is "irrational, indefensible and manifestly arbitrary."[5] Decriminalization meant that having "sodomitical" relations has become legal for more than a billion more people in the world. Yet homophobic attacks on gays remain frighteningly common—from Vladimir Putin's Russian empire (particularly Chechnya) to Egypt to Indonesia. Even in France, in 2016 SOS-Homophobie received more than 1500 reports of homophobic behavior, and that number had markedly increased since the previous year.[6]

Same-sex relationships—whether ephemeral unions or enduring partnerships—have existed throughout history and, seemingly, in every human society. Certain sorts of "homosexual" couples were heroized, even apotheosised, in ancient Greek and Roman cultures, and the gay genealogy is replete with familiar couples: Achilles and Patroclus, Harmodius and Aristogeiton, Hadrian and Antinous. Close friendships between men, often with some erotic attraction, continued in the Middle Ages and flourished in the humanistic cultures of the Renaissance.[7] The gallery of famous gay figures of later ages (not to mention unknown ones) includes many who thought themselves parts of a couple: the "Ladies of Llangollen," Edward Carpenter and George Merrill, Radclyffe Hall and Una Troubridge, among others.[8]

Same-sex relationships were not limited to Europe and colonial societies engendered by Europeans. The charge that "homosexuality" is a Western import to other regions is erroneous, though what same-sex coupling involved, how it was experienced, and how it was perceived from place to place and time to time differ greatly. A key defense of "homosexuality" made by nineteenth-century writers, such as Carpenter and Hirschfeld, was that "homogenic attachment" (in Carpenter's phrase) had been tolerated and sometimes exalted in many societies. One of the great advances in scholarship on homosexuality in recent years has been the appearance of studies of same-sex sexuality in non-Western societies.[9] They have shown that behaviors involving same-sex sexuality have existed virtually everywhere.

Western colonizers tried to combat "vice" in the areas they conquered, civil administrators and missionaries taking similar positions about sexual wickedness.[10] The law codes imposed from London account for the criminalization of homosexuality in British settler societies and in the old British colonies of Africa, Asia, the Caribbean, and Oceania. Even when colonizers did not legislate against same-sex activity, the new creeds they brought damned "unnatural" vice (as well as other sorts of "immorality"), though many of the colonizers indulged overseas in the pleasures facilitated by privileges of race, wealth, power, and opportunity. After independence some of the former colonies that had no anti-homosexual statutes criminalized homosexual acts, and many that had anti-homosexual legislation maintained the colonial-era laws.

If a brand of Western homophobia was often exported, so too a modern Western style of homosexuality was internationalized, sometimes displacing other modes of sexual behavior or coexisting with them. In Thailand, the old culture of kathoeys (ladyboys), for instance, was supplemented by a culture of Western-style bars, discothèques, and saunas, with the "boy bars" that abound in such cities as Bangkok. Western modes of sociability, identity, and aspirations have created a species of openly gay or lesbian person who thinks of himself or herself in a way that often sits awkwardly with social and cultural expectations of morality, marriage, and child-rearing in many countries. And, to complicate social patterns still further, "queer" identity questions and challenges the categories of gay and straight, while the internet has altered patterns of gay sociability in ways that could hardly have been imagined just a couple of decades ago. On chat sites and social media, men and women can connect to a seemingly infinitely number of potential partners, access erotic images, and engage in virtual sex in ways that would have gone beyond the bounds even of fantasy for earlier generations.

The surviving disjunction between (homo)sexual cultures in countries where homosexual acts are legal, homosexual rights protected, and same-sex marriages lawful and those where situations are different raises questions about cultural diffusion and perhaps cultural imperialism. In the context of issues discussed in this book, the issue of decriminalization of homosexual acts and the legalization of same-sex marriage outside "the West" is complex. Many moralizers in Africa, Asia, Oceania, and the Caribbean continue to argue that homosexuality is a sin and should remain a crime. Others feel that the legal provisions enacted in the West are inappropriate or unnecessary in their countries, or at the least that they are hardly a priority. Sex is by no means everywhere a topic for open and free discussion, and a "don't ask, don't tell" policy prevails even when there is little active and violent homophobia.

Many of those, heterosexual and otherwise, who have successfully sought the decriminalization of homosexual acts, the enactment of anti-discrimination, and anti-vilification legislation, and marriage equality would hope that such rights and protections will be enacted in countries where they do not yet exist. They argue that, like freedom of religion, freedom of assembly, democratic elections, gender equality, and protection of children, a choice of sexual behavior and identity and recognition of same-sex partnerships are questions of human rights. Jurists and specialists in human rights politics no doubt have much to say on these issues, but it is hard to disagree with the proposition that legal regimes ought to allow all people to satisfy their emotional and erotic desires, and to establish partnerships that guarantee the benefits accorded to heterosexual couples. Guaiana and Seymour quote in their chapter a 2010 ruling by an Italian court that acknowledged the constitutional relevance of same-sex unions, "understood as the stable cohabitation of two persons of the same sex, who have the fundamental right to live freely as a couple … with juridical recognition and the associated rights and responsibilities." One would not wish for couples anywhere in the world to be deprived of the personal and social benefits implied in that Italian statement.

Campaigns for same-sex marriage, as shown by the case of Italy, are the latest in a series of public debates about marriage itself, among them debates concerning connections between religious and civil recognition of marriage, the conditions in which a marriage can be terminated and divorced persons remarried, the rights of wives and children within marriage, recognition and rights for children born outside wedlock, custody of children, the status of "common law" marriages.[11] Such debates stretch back over a considerable time and have resulted in various provisions—in France, for example, divorce was legalized in 1792, disallowed in 1816, and reintroduced in 1884, although there remained different criteria for men and women to sue for divorce until much later. The structures surrounding marriage (and its dissolution) raised profound questions about the institution of marriage itself, and the basis on which it has been institutionalized. Campaigns for reform, such as contested divorce and then divorce by mutual consent, have challenged ardently held religious and social beliefs that ties were supposed to bind "until death do us part."

The move toward equality for women had to combat laws and customs that kept women as second-class partners in a marriage—in France, until the early twentieth century, having to relinquish control of their property to their husbands and not being able to work outside the home, in principle, without the permission of their husbands. Only recently have jurists recognized rape within marriage as a crime. In a landmark referendum in 2018, two-thirds of voters in the Republic of Ireland agreed to repeal a constitutional prohibition on almost all forms of abortion. Among the supporters of the campaign was the country's openly gay prime minister, Leo Varadkar. The earlier legalization of same-sex marriage was seen as leading the way for the abortion referendum, evidence both of changed social attitudes and of the possibility of campaigners successfully galvanizing public support (as Patrick McDonagh shows here for the same-sex marriage campaign) in favor of reform.

The complexities of the history of same-sex sexuality, and the road to public acceptance and recognition of homosexual relationships, are vividly illustrated by chapters in this book that reveal often convoluted attitudes in the past (and the present). Ben Bethell, for instance, shows how British law convicted sodomites, while penal reformers worried about "contamination" of fellow inmates when they were jailed; warders nevertheless often displayed little concern about the actual behavior of those incarcerated. Authorities also feared the spread of vice if convicted sodomites were transported to overseas penal colonies, but the image that sodomy was rife in Britain's Australian colonies provided one of the arguments for ending transportation.[12] In another example showing the muddle of attitudes, Kate Davison demonstrates concerns in intelligence organizations during the Cold War, in societies as dissimilar as Australia and East Germany, about the propensity of homosexuals for political subversion, yet how the perceived mental weakness of homosexuals made them seem promising recruits as spies on either side of the Iron Curtain. Issues concerning homosexuality, of course, were embedded not only in general perspectives on crime and punishment or on politics, but in gender itself, as Rebecca Jennings points out in considering the place of women in Australian society and the ways in which feminism, as theory and political engagement, was bound up with gay and lesbian life and activism. Marcia Gallo finds similar entanglements in the United States. She notes that the first pleas for "gay marriage" appeared in homophile publications there as long ago as 1953, though not until 2015 was same-sex marriage legalized; during that long period, there were continuing demands, from diverse corners of society, to "rethink marriage."

These authors, and other contributors to this collection, thus emphasize the different registers in which debates about same-sex relations played out—law, politics, religion, medicine, social mores. There are also the lived experiences of men and women. Benno Gammerl, looking at Germany, subtly focuses on the history of emotions, and how "laws and feelings" intertwine in multiple ways. He argues that while law constrained homosexuals, it promoted "specific modes of emotional expression" for men and women, both in personal relations and in education, art, and everyday life. Gammerl also provocatively asks whether legalization of same-sex marriage for some might not create new "emotional models" of socially approved behavior that induce stressful and unwanted expectations. The explicit or implicit focus on emotions in Gammerl's and other chapters provides a crucial reminder that marriage—both traditional and reinvented—is more about emotional ties than just sexual pleasures (which, in any case, have often been sought and procured outside marriage). Affect, or feelings—yes, love—are the real bonds in matrimony. Lust and its sexual expression have sometimes predominated in the study of same-sex history, but the history of emotions, and of the situations and places in which emotions are enacted, opens fresh perspectives for scholarly exploration.

The title of this volume elucidates one of the paradoxes in the history of same-sex life (and in the writing of that history). Sodomy laws criminalized a specific physical act, or a repertoire of acts subsumed under the word "sodomy," though they did not and could not outlaw feelings of erotic desire, yearnings for emotional bonding, and committed relationships between two people. Indeed, some societies that banned homosexual acts nevertheless tolerated and even lauded same-sex friendship, male (and female) bonding, and single-sex camaraderie and mateship. Legislation allowing same-sex marriage presupposes the repeal of sodomitical laws to permit the lawful satisfaction of homosexual desires, which is an integral part of marital relationships. However, in a more general sense, what the same-sex marriage legislation does is to provide recognition for emotional attachment and social commitment; in the provisions of statute books, it effectively and explicitly legalizes same-sex love.

Debates about marriage point to wider historical and political questions about private and public life, the role of the state in enforcing and regulating behavior and morals, and the very question of sexuality in human existence. Many of these issues again came to the forefront with same-sex marriage discussions. Marriage has been the legal, religious, and administrative structure around a relationship between a couple, and states determine who can enter into such a relationship and under what conditions. States continue to circumscribe marriage, no doubt legitimately, with certain regulations concerning incest, bigamy, age of consent, and the prerequisites for obtaining a marriage license. However, as defenders of "traditional" marriage were often reluctant to concede, marriage is only a subset of human coupling. The aim of same-sex marriage campaigners has been to gain legal validation for a particular type of relationship between consenting adults that over the years, at least in most Western countries, has achieved great, though not unanimous, social acceptance, as have the emotional and erotic ties embodied in such unions. Even outside the limited orbit of Westernized societies, same-sex desires are omnipresent, as are public or clandestine cultures of homosexual sociability, intercourse, and bonding.

In January 2018, the first gay couple came out, in a press interview, in the small Himalayan kingdom of Bhutan, a country renowned for its spectacular scenery and for measuring well-being not just with indices of gross domestic product but "gross domestic happiness."[13] The Bhutanese penal code (inspired by British colonial precedents) prohibits sodomy or other sexual acts "against nature," but the law has never been enforced, and Bhutan's Buddhist culture is little concerned about the particularities of sexual conduct so long as no harm is done to others. The two young men who publicly declared their relationship—their names and photographs were published—stated that they had received warm support and encouragement from their parents, and that they had also received many supportive emails. As that news report and the chapters in this book evidence, for many men and women the objective is the realization of love in situations that allow for the satisfaction of emotional, erotic, and social yearnings; the recognition of partnerships; and the right to benefits and protection enjoyed by others. This volume represents an important first step in writing the history of gay and lesbian coupling and the route toward legalization of same-sex marriage from an international perspective. Perhaps the next chapters will be written about future quests elsewhere in the world.

Notes

1 Matt Cook, *London and the Culture of Homosexuality, 1885–1914* (Cambridge: Cambridge University Press, 2009); Robert Beachy, *Gay Berlin: Birthplace of a Modern Identity* (New York: Knopf, 2014).
2 Ralf Dose, *Magnus Hirschfeld: The Origins of the Gay Liberation Movement* (New York: Monthly Review Press, 2014).
3 John Boswell's famously controversial arguments about the acceptance of same-sex "marriage," particularly by the early Eastern rite churches, in *Same-Sex Unions in Premodern Europe* (New York: Villard Books, 1994), were met with skepticism or reservations by most scholars.
4 These early "homophile" organizations, often thought of as rather timid and assimilationist by comparison with later more militant groups, have been the subject of more positive reassessment. See, for example, Julian Jackson, *Living in Arcadia: Homosexuality, Politics, and Morality in France from the Liberation to AIDS* (Chicago: University of Chicago Press, 2009).
5 *The Guardian,* September 7, 2018.
6 https://www.lemonde.fr/societe/article/2017/05/10/les-actes-homophobes-repartent-a-la-hausse_5125182_3224.html.
7 In what is now an ample scholarly literature, Louis Crompton, *Homosexuality and Civilization* (Cambridge, MA: Harvard University Press, 2003), is a good overview.

8   Jonathan Ned Katz, *Love Stories: Sex between Men before Homosexuality* (Chicago: University of Chicago Press, 2001), and Leila J. Rupp, *Sapphistries: A Global History of Love between Women* (New York: New York University Press, 2009), are among the authors who have privileged love and bonding in same-sex history.
9   Just on China, there has been, for instance, Mark Stevenson and Cuncun Wu, eds., *Homoeroticism in Imperial China: A Sourcebook* (London: Routledge, 2012), Travis S. K. Kong, *Chinese Male Homosexualities* (London: Routledge, 2012); Giovanni Vitiello, *The Libertine's Friend: Homosexuality and Masculinity in Late Imperial China* (Chicago: University of Chicago Press, 2011); D. E. Mungello, *Western Queers in China: Flight to the Land of Oz* (Lanham: Rowman & Littlefield, 2012); Cuncun Wu, *Homoerotic Sensibilities in Late Imperial China* (London: Routledge, 2004).
10 Robert Aldrich, *Colonialism and Homosexuality* (London: Routledge, 2003).
11 For reminders of how extraordinarily contested an issue such as divorce has been, see, e.g., Roderick Phillips, *Putting Asunder: A History of Divorce in Western Society* (Cambridge: Cambridge University Press, 1988) or Mark Seymour, *Debating Divorce in Italy: Marriage and the Making of Modern Italians, 1860–1974* (New York: Palgrave Macmillan, 2006).
12 Among other works on Australia, see Garry Wotherspoon, *Gay Sydney: A History* (Sydney: NewSouth Publishing, 2016).
13 https://thebhutanese.bt/bhutans-first-public-gay-couple-receive-positive-responses-after-coming-out/.

Index

Note: In this index, page references in **bold** indicate illustrations; those followed by *n* indicate endnotes.

Affermazione Civile 176–7
Africa 230
African-Americans 3, 34, 207
age of consent 115, 143, 193, 195
Aktion Standesamt 116–17
Albany Trust 148
alternative families 175
Arab countries 13
ARCI (Associazione Ricreativa e Culturale Italiana) 171
Arcigay 171
Asia 230
ASIO (Australian Security Intelligence Organisation) 128, 129–32
Association for Social Knowledge (ASK) 148–9
Associazione Radicale Certi Diritti 176
Australia
    lesbians' accounts of same-sex marriage 162–5
    national security 128, 129–32
    postal survey on marriage equality 229
    prosecution and sentencing patterns 7, 86–91
    vagrancy laws 88, 145
Austria 177
aversion therapy 102
Avvocatura per i diritti LGBTI—Rete Lenford 176

Babilonia 171–2
Baehr v. Lewin (1993) 208–9
Bagnasco, Cardinal Angelo 176
Baker, Jack 206–7
Bangkok 232
Barcelona 8, 99, 101, 103
Bauer, Fritz 114
Baynes v. Hedger and others (208) 217–18
behaviorism 127, 131–2

Belgium 194
Belize xiv
Bentham, Jeremy 38
Bermuda xiv
Bernardi de Valernes, Joseph Elzéar Dominique 22
Bhutan 235
Bisceglia, Marco 171
Bonill, William 48
Boston marriages 205
Brissot, Jacques Pierre 23
Bristed, John 32–3
"British World"
    defined 143–5
    homosexuals as national security risk in 9, 127, 129–32
    transnational homosexual politics in 9, 144, 148–50
buggery. *See* sodomy
Burke, Edmund 38
Butler, Judith 11

Calderón, Juan. *See Murillo v. Calderón* divorce case
Cambodia xii
Canada 9, 104–5, 127, 143, 145, 148–9, 150
canon law. *See* Catholic Church
capital punishment for sodomy 5–6, 18–19, 60, 74, 145, 231
Caribbean 231
cartoon depictions of sodomites 43–5, **44, 45, 53, 54**
Castlereagh, Viscount 36–7
castration 18
Catholic Church
    ecclesiastical divorce, Peru 6–7, 71, 73–4
    Ireland 194–5

Italy 167–9, 174, 178, 229
  Spain 95, 97–8
Catholic Forum of Family Associations 176
Chechnya 231
China 236 n.9
civil partnerships/unions
  France 175, 177
  Germany 111, 116
  Italy 171, 172–7
  legal aspects of dissolution and death 216–22
  "openness" about 218
  United Kingdom 214–22
Claiborne, William 34–5
clemency pleas 50
Clogher, Bishop of 43–4
Cloots, Anacharsis (Baron de Cloots) 25, 27
Cold War sexual politics 123–35
compensation for victims of sex crime imprisonment 104–5, 110
Condorcet, Marquis de 21–2, 26–7
Cook, Matt 3
Cork Women's Fun Weekend 186
Court and others v. Despallières (2009) 219–20
court cases
  Germany 117
  India xiv–xv, 231
  Ireland 11, 183, 193
  Italy 172, 176–7, 232–3
  Peru 71, 73–4
  United Kingdom 216–22
  United States 201–2, 206–7, 208–9
Czechoslovakia 134

Daughters of Bilitis (DOB) 205
decriminalization of homosexual acts. *See* homosexual law reform (post-1950); sodomy laws, decriminalization
Defense of Marriage Act (1996) 209
Dickens, Charles 51–3
divorce and dissolution
  ecclesiastical, Peru 71, 73–4
  France 233
  Italy 169, 170
  and same-sex partnerships, 222–3

sodomy as ground for 78–9
  Spain 7, 96
DOMA (Defense of Marriage Act) 209
domestic partnership movement 208
Don Leon (poem) 5, 36–8
Dorian Society 148, 149
Du Cane, Edmund 57, 63, 67
Dyer, Henry Morton 39

East Germany. *See* Ministerium für Staatssicherheit
ECHR. *See* European Court of Human Rights
Egypt 231
emotions
  emotional habitus of homosexuals 128–34
  emotional implications of normalization 10, 111–12, 116–17
  emotional typologies of homosexuals 130, 133
  law–emotions nexus 110–12
  loneliness 230–1
  love, affection and commitment 21, 25, 46, 112–14, 158, 160, 162, 204–5, 207, 217–18, 227, 231, 234–5, 236 n.8
  loyalty and patriotism 127–8, 129–31, 134–5
  melancholy and grief 118–19
  self-optimization stress 111–12, 116–17
  shame 109, 130–1
  theoretical approaches 112, 119, 124–5, 234
Enlightenment critics of sodomy laws 19–23, 27, 227
espionage
  homosexuals' aptitude for 132–4
  Vassal case 123, 128
European Court of Human Rights 10, 11, 177, 183, 193

Fagin (fictional character) 51–3, **53, 54**
Famiglie Arcobaleno (Rainbow Families) 175, 178
Family Solidarity 194–5
Farthing, James 50–1
female marriages 157–8, 164, 204–5

Fiji xiv
Flynn, Declan 190
Forum of Family Associations 173, 178
Foucault, Michel 18, 76, 79
France
   capital punishment for sodomy 18, 19, 21
   decriminalization of sodomy 4, 15–17, 23–6
   homophobic incidents 231
   nineteenth-century repression of homosexuals 27
   PACS (pacte civil de solidarité) 175
Franco regime 97–102
Freund, Kurt 134
Front Homosexuel d'Action Revolutionnaire 171
FUORI! (Fronte Unitario Omosessuale Rivoluzionario Italiano) 171

Galli, Doriano 172
gay and lesbian activism
   France 171
   Ireland 184–92, 195
   Italy 10, 169, 170–2
   queering of 2–3
   role in law reform 114
   Spain 103–4
   transnational aspects 144, 148–9
   United Kingdom 100
   United States 100, 171, 206
Gay & Lesbian Equality Network (GLEN) 193
gay liberation. *See* gay and lesbian activism
Gay Liberation Front (US) 100, 171
Gay Rights Movement (GRM) 185
German Democratic Republic. *See* Ministerium für Staatssicherheit
Germany. *See also* Paragraph 175, German Criminal Code
   acceptance of same-sex relationships 109
   recognition of homosexuals as victims 104, 110
   same-sex marriage 109, 110, 116–118
Giarre suicide 167, 169–70, 171
Gibraltar convict prison 57–8
Greek love 21, 25, 115, 231

Grey Commission 61–2
gross indecency, as crime 46, 87, 89, 96, 98, 101, 103, 143, 145, 195

hanging of sodomites 5–6, 48–50
Helvétius, Claude Adrien 21
Hirschfeld, Magnus 97, 185–6, 228
history of emotions, as concept 112, 119, 124–5, 234
HIV/AIDS 3, 172, 208
Hobsbawm, Eric 146–7
Hollingsworth v. Perry 12, 201
homonormativity. *See* normalization of homosexuality
Homophile Group for Social Integration (AGHOIS) 103
homophile movement
   advocacy of homophile marriage 202–5
   advocacy of "pristine love" 113–14
   in Europe and United States 103, 143, 185, 202–5, 230
   promotion of homosexual equality 230
   transnational aspects 144, 148–50
"homophile politics", defined 143
homosexual acts: actionable offences
   acts involving minors 96, 115
   acts offending public morality 98–101
   "gross indecency" 46, 87, 89, 96, 98, 101, 103, 143, 145, 195
   "indecent assault" 60, 85, 87, 89, 96
   sodomy (*see* sodomy laws)
homosexual acts: decriminalization. *See* homosexual law reform (post-1950); sodomy laws, decriminalization
homosexual acts: penalties
   banishment 21
   castration 18
   death 5–6, 18–19, 21, 60, 74, 145, 231
   deportation and transportation 21, 51
   fines 88
   forced relocation 99
   imprisonment 21, 46, 60, 86
   internment in labor camps 98, 100
   public pillorying 23, 27, 46–7
   re-education 100
homosexual acts: prosecution and sentencing patterns

for acts between adults in public 86–91
for acts involving minors 86, 89–90, 115
for acts involving violence 87, 90
for acts offending public morality and vagrancy laws 228
class bias 39, 50, 99, 102
leniency and non-enforcement 60, 86, 235
pleas for clemency 50
homosexuality. *See also* normalization of homosexuality
as Cold War issue 9, 124–35
construction of emotional "types" 9, 130, 133
de-legitimization of intergenerational pairings 115
in non-Western societies 231–2
as social construct v. essential nature 2–3
as "unnatural" 1–2, 7, 18, 57, 167
homosexual law reform (post-1950)
Canada 9, 148–50
Czechoslovakia 134
Germany 114, 116
impact of modernizing liberalism on 146–7
India xiv–xv, 231
Ireland 9, 150, 190–5
New Zealand 9, 147, 148
Northern Ireland 183–4
Scotland 9
South Africa 9, 230
South Australia 150
transnational aspects 144, 145–50, 172, 176–7
United Kingdom 9, 141–2, 147–9, 150
United States 143
Homosexual Law Reform Society (HLRS) 142, 148–9
homosexual political activism. *See also* gay and lesbian activism; homophile politics; homosexual politics
Italy 170
"homosexual politics", defined 142–3
homosexuals
aptitude for intelligence work 132–4
capacity for loyalty and patriotism 127–8, 129–31, 134–5
categories and types 130, 133
emotional habitus of 128–34
as national security risk 128–9
Hong Kong xiv
human rights, as argument for decriminalization 19–20, 38

Illinois 143
Indian Supreme Court xiv–xv, 231
Indonesia 231
Inglehart, Ronald 146–7
inheritance disputes 217–20
Ireland
Catholic Church 184
decriminalization of homosexual sex 11
employment equality 192
forging alliances for law reform 190–3
gay and lesbian activism 184–92
international pressure for decriminalization 194
promoting a positive understanding of homosexuality 187–90
same-sex marriage referendum 183
trade union support for decriminalization 190–2
Irish Congress of Trade Unions 191–2
Italy
Arcigay 10
campaigns for civil unions 171, 172–3
commercialized gay culture 171–2
decriminalization of homosexual acts 10, 167–8
divorce law 169–70
gay liberation movement 169, 170–2
Giarre suicide 167, 169–70, 171
influence of Catholic Church 10, 167–9, 174, 178, 229
influence of European Court of Human Rights 10
recognition of alternative families 173, 175–6
same-sex marriage 172, 177
World Pride (2000) 174–5

Jackson, Andrew 5, 31–6
Jocelyn, Percy 43–4
Jousse, Daniel 19
judicial decisions. *See* court cases

"Kamp Kult" parties 83–4
Kennedy, Sir Arthur 61–2
kissing as a crime 113

Labouchere amendment 145
La Movida 103–4
"lavender scare" 124
Lawrence v. Gallagher (2012) 220–2
Lawrence v. Texas (2003) 28, 202
lesbian and gay activism. *See* gay and lesbian activism
lesbians
    effect of same-sex marriage on 117–18
    female marriages 157–8, 164, 204–5
    gendered roles in same-sex relationships 162–4, 162–5
    in heterosexual marriages 158–62, 205
Liddell, Adolphus 63–5
Lima, presence of *maricones* 71–2, 79–80
loneliness 130–1
Lorca, Federico García 98
Louallier, Louis 35–6
Louisiana legislature 31–6
Loving v. Virginia (1967) 40, 206
loyalty and patriotism 127–8, 129–31, 134–5

Marañón, Gregorio 97
Marat, Jean-Paul 22
marches and parades 190
maricones 71–2, 79–80
marriage
    as acceptable form of intimate relations 158–60
    as acceptable option for motherhood 160–1
    anti-gay-marriage laws 207, 209
    divorce and dissolution 71, 73–4, 169–70
    female marriage 157–8
    feminist critiques 156–8
    interracial 40
    lesbians' experiences of 158–62
    power and gender imbalances in 161–2
marriage equality. *See* same-sex marriage
masculinity and male identity, threats to 84, 98, 101
McConnell, James Michael 206

Mellett, Martin 50–1
Merkel, Angela 109, 229
Ministerium für Staatssicherheit (MfS; 'Stasi') 128–9, 132–4
Montesquieu 20
Murillo v. Calderón divorce case 71, 73–9

Naigeon, Jacques André 21, 23
National Gay Federation (Ireland) 185, 187, 193
national security and homosexuals
    Australia 129–32
    German Democratic Republic 128–9, 132–4
Netherlands 155, 175
New South Wales, prosecution and sentencing patterns 7, 86–91
New Zealand 9, 147, 148
NGF (National Gay Federation) 185, 187, 193
normalization of homosexuality
    ambivalent and problematic effects 10, 111–12, 115–19
    same-sex marriage as 155–6, 216
Norris, David 183–4, 193
Northern Ireland 183

Obergefell v. Hodges (2015) 12, 39–40, 201–2, 209
Oceania 231
Order of the Cuff 26
Orlov, Alexander 128
Ormando, Alfredo 173

PACS (*pacte civil de solidarité*) 175, 177
Paragraph 175, German Criminal Code
    abolition 8, 116
    different treatment of male and female homosexuality 117
    emotional effects 110, 112–14
    reparation for imprisonment under 109–10
    specific proscriptions under 109–10, 113, 115
Pasolini, Pier Paolo 168
patriotism and homosexuality. *See* loyalty and patriotism
pederasty and pedophilia 22, 115
Peel, Sir Robert 36–7

penalties for homosexual acts. *See* homosexual acts: penalties
Peru
  ecclesiastical divorce 71, 73–4
  Lima's *maricones* 71–2, 76
  sodomy as ground for divorce 78–9
  sodomy under Spanish colonial law 74
  veiling of same-sex relationships 76, 79, 80
Philippines xiv
pillorying 46–7
pleas for clemency 50
Pratt, John 5–6, 48–50, 51
"preventive policing" 98
prison sex
  contaminating effect of lewd talk 65–7
  France 60
  Gibraltar 57–8
  late-Victorian England 57–67
  measures to limit opportunities for 62–6
  official reluctance to acknowledge 57–8, 66–7
  Tallack's warning 57, 60–1, 63, 67
  United States 59–60
prosecution for homosexual acts. *See* homosexual acts: prosecution and sentencing patterns
punishment and penalties. *See* homosexual acts: penalties
Putin, Vladimir 231

Queensland, prosecution and sentencing patterns 86–91
queer coupling and domesticity 3
queer critiques of same-sex marriage 155–6
queer theory 2–3

Radiquet, Maximilien 71–2, 79–80
Rainbow Families (Famiglie Arcobaleno) 175, 178
rape 59, 63–5
referendums and plebiscites 227, 233
Report of the Committee on Homosexual Offences and Prostitution. *See* Wolfenden Report
Rochette, Claude Lebrun de la 18
Rodriguez, Hildegart 97

Ruggles-Brise, Evelyn 67–8
Ruiz, Antoni 104–5
Russian Federation xiv

Saint-Fargeau, Michel Lepeletier 24
same-sex civil partnership. *See* civil partnerships/unions
same-sex desire
  Don Leon poems defense of 36–8
same-sex marriage
  adoption rights 10, 177–8
  ambivalent emotional effects 117–19
  anti-gay-marriage laws 207, 209
  court cases 172, 177, 183–4, 193, 201, 206–7, 208–9
  effect on lesbians 117–18
  France 177
  Germany 109, 116–18
  homophile advocacy for 202–5
  impact on emotional patterns and practices 117–19
  Italy 173–4, 229
  legal recognition 11–12
  legislation for 8
  negative aspects 12
  Netherlands 155, 175
  as normalization of homosexuality 3–4, 116–18, 155–6, 216
  queer critiques 155–6
  rights-based arguments for 40, 201–2
  Spain 104
  United Kingdom 158, 214–16
same-sex relationships, legal recognition. *See* civil partnerships/unions; same-sex marriage
Scotland 9, 227
second-parent adoption rights 10, 177–8
sex between men. *See* homosexual acts
sex in prisons. *See* prison sex
Sexual Offences Act (1967) [UK]
  deficiencies 193–4
Smith, James 5–6, 48–50, 51
sodomy
  as "abominable" and "against nature" 1, 18–21, 50, 63–4, 76, 86, 145, 235
  as distinct from homosexuality 17–18
  as ground for divorce 78–9
  pederasty and 22
sodomy laws

British parliamentarians' repudiation of 36–8
death penalty, abolition 45, 46, 60, 71, 145
decriminalization 15–17, 96, 202, 227–8
definitions of "sodomy" 18, 46, 58–9, 63–4, 109, 112–13, 145
Enlightenment critiques 19–23, 27
historical prevalence 15, 17–19, 33, 145
Louisiana Legislature's rejection of 31–6
rationales for decriminalization 23–8, 31–2, 33–4, 36–9, 51, 52, 142, 193–4
sodomy laws: penalties
banishment 21
castration 18
death 5–6, 18–19, 21, 60, 74, 145, 231
imprisonment 21, 46, 60, 86
pillory 23, 27, 46–7
transportation 21, 51, 61–2
SOGIE injustices xii–xiii
South Africa 9, 230
South Australia 9, 150
Spain
compensation for victims of sex crime imprisonment 104–5
Franco regime 97–102
gay liberation movement 103–4
medical persecution of convicted homosexuals 101–2
"preventive policing" 100–1
same-sex marriage 8, 104
sodomy law 96
sodomy under Spanish colonial law 74
vagrancy laws 96, 98–101, 103
Spanish Movement for Homosexual Liberation (MELH) 103
Sparshott, John 50
spies. *See* espionage
Spry, Charles 124, 128
"star class" prisoners 58–9, 63–7
Stasi. *See* Ministerium für Staatssicherheit
suicides 36–7, 167, 169–70
Sydney
"Kamp Kult" parties 83–4
police surveillance 85, 88

Taiwan 230
Tallack, William 57, 60–1, 63, 67
Thailand 231
transportation to Western Australia 61–2

Unite for Change (Ireland) 193
United Kingdom
abolition of death penalty for sodomy 44–6
civil partnerships 3–4, 214–16
executions for sodomy 28, 44–6
homosexual law reform 9
parliamentary debate on sodomy law (1823) 5, 36–7
recognition of homosexuals as victims 104
same-sex marriage 158, 214–16
sodomy law 44–6, 145
United Nations Human Rights Council xiv
United States
decriminalization in Illinois 143
"lavender scare" 124
legal recognition of same-sex marriage 11–12
legislation to curb sexual permissiveness 33–4
United States Supreme Court 12, 28, 39–40, 201–2, 209
United States v. Windsor (2013) 209

vagrancy laws
Australia 88, 145
"British World" 145
Spain 96, 98–101, 103
Varadkar, Leo 233
Vassal, John William 123, 128
Vere Street coterie 46–7
Vietnam 230
Voltaire 20

Waldeck, Rosie Goldschmidt 135
Weeks, Jeffrey 2
wills, disputes over 217–20
Wolfenden Report 9, 141–2, 147–8, 150
World Pride (Rome 2000) 174–5

www.ingramcontent.com/pod-product-compliance
Lightning Source LLC
Chambersburg PA
CBHW070030010526
44117CB00011B/1766